THE HISPANIC
CONNECTION

Recent Titles in
Contributions to the Study of World Literature

THE HISPANIC CONNECTION

*Spanish and Spanish-American
Literature in the Arts of the World*

Edited by Zenia Sacks DaSilva

Prepared under the auspices of Hofstra University
Contributions to the Study of World Literature, Number 122

**Westport, Connecticut
London**

Library of Congress Cataloging-in-Publication Data

The Hispanic connection: Spanish and Spanish-American literature in the arts of the world
   / edited by Zenia Sacks DaSilva.
      p.   cm. — (Contributions to the study of world literature, ISSN 0738–9345 ; no. 122)
   Includes bibliographical references and index.
   ISBN 0–275–98090–1 (alk. paper)
      1. Spanish literature—History and criticism.   2. Spanish-American literature—History and
   criticism.   3. Art and literature.   I. DaSilva, Zenia Sacks.   II. Series.
   PQ6041.H57   2004
   860.9—dc21   2003046395

British Library Cataloguing in Publication Data is available.

Library of Congress Catalog Card Number: 2003046395
ISBN: 0–275–98090–1
ISSN: 0738–9345

First published in 2004

Praeger Publishers, 88 Post Road West, Westport, CT 06881
An imprint of Greenwood Publishing Group, Inc.
www.praeger.com

Printed in the United States of America

The paper used in this book complies with the
Permanent Paper Standard issued by the National
Information Standards Organization (Z39.48–1984).

10   9   8   7   6   5   4   3   2   1

Copyright Acknowledgments

The editor and publisher gratefully acknowledge permission for use of the following material:

Excerpts from Ian Gibson, *Federico García Lorca: A Life* (New York: Pantheon Books, 1989).
Copyright 1989 by Ian Gibson. Reprinted by permission of Pantheon Books division of
Random House, Inc.

Excerpts from *Federico Garcia Lorca* by Felicia Hardison Londre © Copyright 1984 by The
Fredrick Ungar Publishing Company. Reprinted by permission of The Continuum Publishing
Company.

Excerpts from Federico García Lorca, *Deep Song and Other Prose* © Heredereos de Federico
Garcia Lorca, 1954; © 1980 by Christopher Maurer. Reprinted by permission of New
Directions Pub. Corp.

Excerpts from James Wright, "The Jewel," "The Beginning," and "Spring Images," from
Above the Water: The Complete Poems © 1990 by Anne Wright, Wesleyan Univsity Press, by
Permission University Press of New England, Hanover, NH.

Excerpts from García Lorca, "Poem of the Deep Song." English translation. Copyright © 1987
by Carlos Bauer. Reprinted by permission of City Lights Books.

Contents

Acknowledgments

We would like to recognize the incalculable contributions of the following individuals and institutions to the realization of our conference and its related activities. A mere list of their names does disservice to their generous support: President James Shuart of Hofstra University, Provost Herman A. Berliner, Dean Bernard Firestone, the Fideicomiso para la Cultura México–Estados Unidos, the Consulate General of Spain, PAMAR, Peer Music Publishers, Dr. Alexei Ugrinski, Natalie Datlof and Athelene Collins-Prince of the Hofstra Cultural Center, Dean David Christman, Director, Curator Eleanor Rait and Exhibitions Coordinator Karen Albert and Registrar Mary Wakeford of the Hofstra Museum of Art, the staff of the Axinn Library, the members of our Conference Committee, Drs. Nora de Marval McNair and James Kolb, and Barry Germond, Jeanine Schaefer, and Pina Patel of the Hofstra Computer Center. Without them our project would never have reached fulfillment.

Introduction

Zenia Sacks DaSilva

"The Hispanic Connection," a conference held at Hofstra University on October 17–19, 1997, was long a-birthing, difficult to realize because of its varied dimensions, and all the more essential because of its wealth. Literature, music, film, ballet, and the fruits of the brush—ongoing elements of the human endowment—joined across borders in mind, voice, and heart. In but three short days resonant with papers, discussions, exhibits, and performances, it celebrated some of the timeless gifts of Spanish and Spanish-American creators, whose thoughts and emotions have stirred echoes in much of the world and whose offspring have peopled its arts. Don Juan, Don Quixote, Celestina, El Cid, Don Alvaro, Don Rodrigo, Leonardo, Bernarda—We watched their reflections in the mirror of ages and their twistings and turnings in geographical frames. We saw flesh become fiction and fiction become faith, and faith become science and reason and fact. And we found there the essence of humanity's span.

The selections we offer in this volume center on ten basic themes. Let us look at them briefly before we begin.

Part I, "Icons of Early Spain," speaks of the uncontainable legend of Rodrigo, last of the Gothic kings, of the Cid in operatic versions from Handel to Debussy, of the confluence of Spain's Judaic and Islamic poetry and song and their dissemination in the diaspora, of the strange Italian reconfigurations of *Tirant Lo Blanch, Don Quijote,* and *La vida es sueño,* and of contemporary composers who have musicalized Golden Age Spanish poems.

Part II, "The Universal Don Quixote," follows the quintessential hero across the early American Western frontier, into the operas of Donizetti and Massenet, into the *Middlemarch* of George Eliot and the *Monsignor Quixote* of Graham Greene, onto the canvases of a living Bolivian painter and the stage setting of *Man of La Mancha* (in the words of its own creator), and onto the still fresh film, *The Fisher King*.

Part III, "The Peripatetic Don Juan," takes the irrepressible mocker/lover from the theater of Molière and the opera of Mozart to the satiric epic of Byron and Shaw's *Don Juan in Hell*, then across the centuries from ballad to recent film and across the breaches of the Americas to Carlos Fuentes and the Nobelist Walcott.

Part IV, "Point of Contact: New Spain," broaches three lesser-known aspects of the fusion of Spanish and Mexican cultures: the use of masks in Mexican celebrations, the legend and poetry of the Virgin of Guadalupe, and the artistic and musical interchange stimulated by Spain's exiles from the Civil War.

Part V, "Spain's Romantics et al. in Opera and Ballet," treats Verdi's fascination with Spanish romantic theater and three lesser-known works derived from the novels *El sombrero de tres picos* and *Pepita Jiménez*.

Part VI, "Modern Writers in Musical Transcription," offers a panoply of perspectives: a panorama of García Lorca in music and dance, a young American composer's own renderings of Lorca's poems, and a trilogy of essays, one by the Mexican composer Mario Lavista, who describes his own relationship with literary sources, another by a musicologist and conductor who explains Lavista's techniques in "translating" a story of Borges, and an insightful literary and philosophical interpretation of that same story.

Part VII, "From Novel to Silver Screen," probes into various film versions of Galdós, Blasco Ibáñez, and García Márquez, their virtues, and their failings.

Part VIII, "Texts Intertwined," offers a charming view of *género chico* works that parody earlier pieces, followed by three intertextual analyses of Fuentes's *Terra Nostra*, Esquivel's *Como agua para chocolate*, and Olmo's *Pablo Iglesias*.

Part IX, "Word Pictures and Stroke of Brush," presents in the words of an artist herself the interrelationship between painting and its literary sources, then delves into the shared images of the poet's pen and the brush of the painter, Hispanic, North American, and others.

Part X, "The Pointed Pen at Large," follows the variegated artistic peregrinations of such contemporaries as Márquez, Puig, Skármeta, and others.

Although we would have liked to offer you the entire proceedings of our meeting, with its many musical and dramatic presentations, book exhibits, and its displays of art, we trust that this sampling will entice you to explore for yourself the impact of Hispanic literature on the arts worldwide. Ours can yet be an exciting joint venture.

Part I

ICONS OF EARLY SPAIN

The Existential Rodrigo,
Last of the Goths

Zenia Sacks DaSilva

In my spare time I have often commiserated with those royal souls now consigned to eternity with unshakeable epithets attached to their names. Of course, some have fared quite well, if a bit pretentiously: Henry the Righteous, Alfonse the Wise, Peter the Ceremonious, Ferdinand the Saint. But think of poor Peter the Cruel, Henry the Bastard, Juana the Crazy, Charles the Bewitched, García the Tremulous, Henry the Impotent, and Ethelred the Unready—unready for what? All of which leads me to believe that history is at best an existential science made of politics, prejudice, happenstance, and faith. Merged with literature, it is the supreme existential art, a kaleidoscope of infinite perspectives and truths from which only fragments of human flesh protrude. Such is the case of Rodrigo, last of the Goths to rule over Spain. Shakespeare might have said that he bore the slings and arrows of outrageous fortune as he passed through boundless time and place. Today's bards would say it more succinctly: "Alas, poor sap. He got a bad rap." Let me take you back to the year 710.

It wasn't the best of times in the Spain of the Goths. Witiza, the king, had just died, and amid the rampant dissension of rival nobility, Rodrigo, governor of Bética (now Andalusia), ascended to the throne. In certain ways, Witiza had not been a bad ruler, though he did alienate certain of his freemen with his philandering bent. As prince, he was even said to have caused the death of the hero Pelayo's father, who had frowned on his lord's advances to his appealing young wife.[1]

Meanwhile, on the African continent that almost kisses Iberia, Moslem crusaders were sweeping toward the Atlantic shores. Among them was a chieftain named Muza who had already made forays into the region of Gibraltar, with its Christian Berbers and their leader, Count Julián (also called Olián or Olbán). For reasons yet unclear, Julián, besieged in Ceuta at the mouth of the Straits, suddenly made peace with Muza and pacted with him to invade the Goths' realm. It could have been because he was a partisan of Witiza's sons and resented Rodrigo's presence, though in fact Julián may have defected while Witiza still held the throne. It could have been that he sought a way out of his own precarious position, surrounded as he was by overwhelming hordes, or that the rumored rape, or seduction, of his daughter had some powerful bearing on his abrupt change of course. But it is known that in July 711, a large force of Muza's warriors invaded Southern Spain. Rodrigo's defense collapsed when Witiza's sons and their followers joined forces with the Arabs. Perhaps they believed their new allies would retreat once Rodrigo was ousted, but the Moslems swarmed into Sevilla, Córdoba, Mérida, Toledo. They entrenched their gains and moved onward, onward. And all that was found of the last Gothic monarch were his horse, his jewels, and his armor, wedged in a marsh near the gruesome grounds of battle.

The story does not end here. Julián prospered handsomely among the Arabs. Witiza's sons and their descendants were rewarded with copious lands and honors. Rodrigo's wife, Egilona, married Muza's son Abdeláziz, the newly named governor of the conquered regions. And the decimated forces of Rodrigo fled to Asturias, where seven years later, in a scabrous mountain pass, their leader Pelayo stopped the Moslem advance. But one great mystery remains. What became of Rodrigo? Was his corpse left to rot in the riverbed of Guadalete? Or somehow did he escape, to resume his peregrinations for twelve centuries to come in chronicle and ballad, lyric and epic, novel, theater, painting, and song? Refracted as through a prism of limitless facets, redrawn as if with the brush of a Braque, his person has evolved from nonfiction to art.

The war cries still echoed through the lands of the South when a Mozarabic chronicle of 754 recounted the saga of the Visigoths' fall (the Mozarabs were those Spanish Christians who stayed on to live under Moslem control). Among them were the aristocrats—even certain bishops, tepid Christians at most—who bound their lot with the Arabs and who blatantly throve. But there were others whose devotion to their faith and to the lost Gothic rule brought persecution and travail at the hands of their own. From these pro-Rodrigo Mozarabs came word of Witiza's corruption, of his rape of Julián's daughter, the beautiful Oliba (later called La Cava, and eventually Florinda), and the Count's sublime vengeance with the Moslem assault.[2] The story circulated in varying forms. Witiza bore the onus, Rodrigo bore the loss, but many other versions were yet to be spun.

The descendants of Witiza and their loyal supporters, adding Islamic sources to bolster their own, at last made their statement in narrative and song. For them it was Rodrigo who had stolen the throne, and who had raped Julián's daughter, or his wife, or perhaps both. It was Rodrigo who unsealed Hercules's magical tower—or cave, or coffer, or maybe his palace—only to find a portent of the disaster that was waiting to happen.[3] Eroded by time, remolded by antagonists, the heroic foil of earlier lore became Rodrigo the coward, the vainglorious, the cruel, the corrupt. Which was the real Rodrigo? Or does reality matter once the moment of truth has lapsed?

Three centuries passed, verging on four, since the Visigoth reign had come to its close. Since communication had been sparse between the regions of Spain, the legends of their peoples were not easily shared. But as the Christians of the North retook occupied lands, the Mozarabic experience slowly encroached upon theirs. In time the saga of Rodrigo, probably fragments of lost epics, plied the paths of Santiago with the itinerant minstrels, who expanded and omitted and embellished at will. One French bard among them gave it a chauvinist twist. The king wasn't the seducer; the girl seduced him![4]

By the twelfth century, Rodrigo had yielded to new epic figures: Fernán González, Bernardo del Carpio, Pelayo, El Cid. How much better to hail victories than to lament of defeat! But the enigmatic, ill-fated last of the Goths would survive in the chronicles of churchmen, kings, and Arab historians, each work born of some obscure version past, then re-formed and expanded to give birth to the next: in 1115, the *Crónica Silense*; in 1236, the history of the bishop Tudense; in 1243, the *Crónica del Toledano*, a primary source of Alfonso the Tenth's *Historia*. Enveloped in legends that refused to be stilled, the pendulum was now swinging toward Rodrigo's guilt.[5]

The year 1344 brought a new "chronicle," derived in good part from an Arabic novel. Replete with such inventions as a mythic King Acosta, it paints a love-torn Rodrigo, a despondent young maiden, and a conflicted Count Julian rent between honor and his loathing of treason. It ends with Rodrigo's disappearance in the fury of combat and with his tomb being found in a Portuguese town. But something more sinister would soon change the scenario. Swirling in a maelstrom of fanatical faith, it would be hideously reshaped by the tale of the snake.

In brief, by the late fourteenth century the story had acquired a startling new ending. Rodrigo did not die in the battle of Guadalete, but had fled to an abandoned convent in what was then Lusitania. Repentant of his errors, he sought peace as a hermit, laboring in the fields and praying for forgiveness. But his sins would require a more strenuous toll. At last, with the help of a good man of religion, the word was transmitted from Heaven above, detailing the terms of his earning God's love. He must place himself in a cave—or in a well, or his grave—accompanied only by a seven-headed snake (the more sensitive poets limit the heads to but two). He must nurture the serpent until its full length and strength, then encourage it to eat him, flesh, blood, and skin, "beginning with the part where he had most sinned." Rodrigo rejoiced to be expunging his guilt. Ecstatic in his agony, he finally surrendered his frame. The churchbells rang by themselves to honor the day, and the people were happy that the sinner was saved. A preposterous punishment? Perhaps not to one penitent usurer of thirteenth-century Cologne who, under sacred instruction, allowed himself to be devoured by ravenous toads.

By mid-fifteenth century, the snake had coiled its way into other works of prose, notably Pedro de Corral's *Crónica Sarracina*, a voluminous narrative made of fiction's whole cloth. From there it would pass into ballad and verse, and Rodrigo would be marked with the indelible words, "Ya me comen, ya me comen" [They're eating me now]. But why? Why this fascination with such a lugubrious theme? Is it the stoicism of the Roman–Spaniard Seneca, whose philosophy of nonindulgence would persist through the ages? Angel Ganivet viewed it in an opposite way. For him, stoicism was just part of being Spanish. Seneca found it already there. Be that as it may, Spain's stoic disposition offered Christianity a fertile terrain, and here is where the story of the snake comes into play.

Life was uneasy in Spain's Middle Ages. War was a constant, as were oppression and plague. High above the walls of thick-fortressed cities, only Heaven offered respite from this valley of tears. Yes, sinners still indulged in the joys of the flesh, but they knew they were flirting with the horrors of Hell. For pleasure was the shackle that bound men to earth. Denial was holiness. Punishment cleansed. Pain was the prelude to life without end. So the bells pealed in miracle and the people rejoiced as Rodrigo was absolved from the wage of his faults. I cannot dismiss an ungenerous thought. Was their jubilance solely for Rodrigo's redemption? Or lay there beneath it their own hidden sense that his sacrifice had exempted, had purified *them*? Stoicism? Perhaps in small part. But tales such as Rodrigo's were not Seneca's thrust. They were rather its fusion with the blood of the martyrs and the sufferings of Job, with the Mater Dolorosa and Christ on the Cross. Meshed with this mindset of ingenuous faith was the vigilant presence of an aligned church and state. Rebellion. Punishment. "Ya me comen."

The sixteenth century dawned to a more unified Spain; printing presses, caravelles, centers of learning, classical myths, humanists,

Italianate poetry, inquisitors, Conquistadors, wars, divine monarchs, and an empire that burgeoned to the despair of its rivals. "Una fe, una lengua, un monarca, una espada" [One faith, one tongue, one monarch, one sword]. A nation newborn, in thrall of present glory, yet seeking in the past its elusive identity. This was the time of the resurgence of heroes, as epics of old were turned into balladry, and flesh and blood deeds merged with chivalric fantasies. Actually, most of the ballads that sang of Rodrigo sprang not from the epics, but from the *Crónica Sarracina*.[6] They recounted his seduction of Julián's daughter and his prophetic vision of the loss of his reign. They echoed his lament at the Moslem invasion, and they followed him, penitent, through the tale of the snake, through his voluptuous agony and his ultimate salvation. We can still hear the voices.

Rómpase la sepultura	Break the tomb open,
porque más penes contigo	The more may thou grieve,
el mayor y sin ventura	O great and ill-starred
de España Rey Rodrigo.[7]	King of Spain Rodrigo.

As the century wore on and flowed into the next, there were other romances, learned and lyrical, that recounted the story of the last Goth, Rodrigo. There was religious theater, and there was poetry, even a mythological ode by Fray Luis de León.[8] There were legends that never tired of recomposing the tale, and "fabulous histories" that made the far-fetched seem pale. Take, for example, Luna's "True History," ostensibly composed by a fictitious Moor, Abulcácim, who took part in the invasion and found Rodrigo's own files.[9] Abysmal in content as well as in style, this strange piece would spark for the next two hundred years even the American Washington Irving, the Frenchman Deschamps, and the British romantic Sir Walter Scott.

Not to be outdone in the craft of false histories, a Portuguese named Britto gave the tale his own spin.[10] In a complex imbroglio of passions and error, he blamed neither Rodrigo nor the maiden for the destruction of Spain. The culprit this time was Julián's wife, who had fallen in love with Rodrigo and resented his attentions to her daughter, now definitively called "Florinda." The rest of the story is for you to fill in. In all, Rodrigo held small interest for Spain's Golden Age titans, though he was treated peripherally by Lope, Calderón, and Tirso.[11] Outside of Spain, however, he enjoyed a flurry of reincarnations, as in a Portuguese poem by one Silva Mascarenhas, who sent him on a journey to the gods on Olympus, then back to Spain to fight the invasion that Pluto had instigated and from which Mercury saved him![12] Undaunted past mid-century, Rodrigo landed briefly in a French moral novel, then later, more happily, in a spree of Italian operas.[13]

The German composer Handel was living in Florence in 1707 when he debuted his opera on the theme of Rodrigo. Deeply involved with the course of the plot, Handel built his score around his female protagonists: Florinda, Rodrigo's mistress and the mother of his child, and Esilona, his barren but virtuous wife. Unable to bring about Rodrigo's divorce, Florinda enlists her brother, Giuliano (Julian), to unite the king's enemies and topple his throne. Dreading the thought of war, Esilona offers Florinda both her spouse and her crown to ward off the bloodshed that would ravage their land. But the forces of battle are now fully cast. As all is about to be lost, Rodrigo is saved by Esilona, but he no longer desires his powers of old. He retires with his wife to a life of humility, leaving his kingdom in trust for his son. Though the Moslem invasion was blatantly missing and the faith of the Goths was now pagan, not Christian, Handel's opera still met its instructional goal. Its subtitle was, "To conquer oneself is the greatest victory of all."

Returning to Spain after ninety years of near absence, Rodrigo was faced with an enlightened Bourbon monarchy that brooked no depiction of royal impropriety. So the attempts of Cadalso and other pre-Romantics to capture Rodrigo were diverted to Egilona, or to Pelayo, or to a multifaced Florinda: ingenuous, passionate, indulgent, forlorn, vain, vindictive, valiant, and more. One Malagan playwright, María Rosa Gálvez, somehow avoided the censors despite her hedonistic, unsympathetic portrait of Rodrigo, but others were denied the right to perform.[14] Many would prefer exile to the tyrannical thumb.

It was a welcoming England where Spain's emigrés sought haven. Romanticism was in full blush in the early nineteenth century, and many of the young writers had become passionate Hispanists. They reveled in the courage of the simple Spanish people, who took to their arms against Napoleon's occupation. They raised their clenched fists in defiance of authority. They thundered their manifestos of conscience and liberty, and rummaged through melancholy corners of history seeking the rebels, the discredited, the heroes without portfolio. Who better than Rodrigo, Julián, and Florinda to fire the fantasy of poets like Scott, Byron, Wordsworth, Landor, and Southey?

In Scott's *The Vision of Don Roderick*, based in good part on Luna's spurious "History," a troubled Rodrigo alleges that he killed Witiza only in self-defense and that Florinda's outrage was a ploy of female jealousy. Now mortally wounded in the battle of Guadalete, he foresees Spain's glorious future: Pelayo's victory at Covadonga, the discovery of the Americas, and the rout of Napoleon from Spanish cities and villages. Southey's heroic poem, *The Last of the Goths*, like its antecedent by Britto, revisits Rodrigo's escape and repentance. But no snake is his outlet, no vile expiation. He turns instead to the cause of his people, rejoins the combat as an anonymous monk, and contributes decisively to the rout of the Moslems. Landor's *Count Julian*, linked with Corral's *Crónica sarracina*, creates a patriot Julian whose rightful rage against the usurper Rodrigo forces him to resort to the Moorish invasion. Ultimately, he spares the life of the deposed Gothic monarch, but the rewards of his magnanimity are tragically few, as his own family is slain by the Saracen intruders. Conflict, raging passions, cruel irony, rebellion. Romanticism all afire, the saga of Rodrigo stormed the British Isles.

In France, whose political perspective was different from England's, the romance with Rodrigo was more a fascination with ballads, collected and elaborated by Abel Hugo, Victor's brother, and by the poet Emile Deschamps. In Spain, on the other hand, with the return of the exiles, Rodrigo took on new guises, shuttling between Espronceda's Eastern-style cowardly potentate, replete with harem (*Pelayo*), Zorrilla's devout penitent, warrior, and patriot (*El puñal del godo*), and Rivas's despot, symbol of the hated King Fernando, with his wanton mistress (*Florinda*). From there he appeared in 1845 in *Egilona*, a play by the Cuban Gertrudis Gómez de Avellaneda, in which Rodrigo's "widow," happily married to the Moslem Abdeláziz, suddenly discovers that her first husband is still alive. As her torn heart, demolished by Rodrigo's disappearance and Abdeláziz's assassination, impels her to suicide, she declares, "Hear, you Moslems, Rodrigo still lives, and so does Pelayo!"

Stopping as well in Portugal, Argentina, Colombia, and Central America throughout much of the nineteenth and early twentieth centuries, Rodrigo put in numerous appearances in theater, musical drama, dime novels, and opera. Back in Europe after World War I, he made a sardonic reentry with the Belgian Jules Leclerq, who rewound the snake story with a cynical turn.[15] Here it is no divine revelation that seals the sinner's fate, for the holy man who delivers the message of Rodrigo's painful redemption turns out to be Julian, who imposes and then watches the self-execution in joyful revenge. But the end was not yet. Four decades later, Rodrigo would take a last daring stand in an opera by the Argentinian Alberto Ginastera.[16]

Ginastera's *Don Rodrigo*, with libretto by the Spanish dramaturg Alejandro Casona, debuted at the Teatro Colón of Buenos Aires in 1964 and again in 1966 at New York's Metropolitan Opera. An intense drama that employs unusual instrumental and vocal effects, it is an atonal neoexpressionist work of Romantic surrealism, imbued with a predilection for the supernatural and magical. Although its primary stance is derived from the Chronicle of 1344, with the now saintly Rodrigo confined to his hermitage in Vigo, it does not invoke the snake in its portrait of his noble death "amid resounding bells played by the hands of God." Its three acts, heroic, lyric, and finally tragic, portray conflicted protagonists, among them a Florinda whose rage for vengeance would see Spain burnt to ashes, but who ultimately succumbs to the power of love. Its final scene, merging with the story of Pelayo, augurs a renewal of hope: "Spain has been reborn."

So spanned more than a millenium the existential Rodrigo, plaything *par excellence* of mores and moment. Rapist or lover? Usurper or electee? A coward? A valiant? A scapegoat or a culprit? What of Witiza and his heirs: Were they victims or villains? Was Julian a traitor or a misguided patriot? Was his daughter, Florinda, a temptress or an innocent? Was Pelayo himself a hero or a sham? Incidentally, was he really Florinda's lover as well?

Don Quixote lost the distinction between history and fiction. Or perhaps he didn't lose it. He made it disappear. Amadís, who strode only the pages of chivalry, existed for him far beyond human life heroes. In truth, how much more real were El Cid and Rodrigo? Both of them were torn from their original substance, then regenerated and transposed into the life frames of others: political, religious, artistic, emotional. Only in such ways did they continue to live. I stand back and wonder was survival worth the cost of being wholly transformed? Is fact worth defending if it is bound to succumb?

Images. Perceptions. Fiction. And truth. Caught in their clutch, will the real Don Rodrigo please stand up? Look, he's turning our way. What does he see? Will the real "you and me" stand up now, please?

NOTES

1. Despite their affirmation in a number of sources, episodes such as the one about Pelayo's mother were suffused *ab initio* with legend, and time has served only to thicken the cloud. Nevertheless, it does appear that on taking the throne, Witiza exiled Pelayo, thereby creating many hostilities. At his death there was very little support among the nobles for any of his sons to assume the throne. It is said that Rodrigo, governor of the province of Bética (now Andalusia) seized the opportunity—whether by force or by election—but that opposition arose because he was not of royal blood.

2. The name "La Cava" eventually became identified with the epithet "wanton woman." Actually, the same tale of seduction and its calamitous results had been told of many European monarchs before, including Valentinian III, who was said to have caused for that very reason the invasion of Rome.

3. Moslem tradition added to the saga of Rodrigo many versions of the legend of Hercules. One of the most prevalent was the tale that when the Greeks ruled Spain they built a palace in Toledo. Divining that Spain would some day be overrun by North African peoples, they placed a magical talisman inside to protect against any such invaders. It was Rodrigo's violation of the *sanctum*

sanctorum that brought about the fall of Spain. Other legends claim that the palace (or cave or coffer) housed the four scrolls of the Evangel on which the Gothic kings took their oaths at coronation. Each subsequent king added one more lock, swearing never to open them lest disaster befall the realm.

4. The thirteenth-century French poem, *La chanson de Anséis de Cartage*, changes the names and locale of the protagonists, but its story quite clearly is the tale of Rodrigo.

5. Discrepancies continued as the legend took shape. According to the *Crónica Silense*, written around 1115, Rodrigo had exiled Witiza's sons, who went to North Africa to enlist the aid of Count Julian and the Arabs. Here entered also the seduction of Julian's daughter by Rodrigo, the battle of Covadonga, in which the traitor Archbishop Oppas was taken prisoner, and the execution of Julian and of Witiza's sons by the Moorish king for having committed treason against their monarch. Historical sources seem to contradict this, especially given evidence of the princes' thriving in Moorish occupied lands. The *Cronicón de Lucas Tudense*, completed around 1236, much like the slightly later version of the Mozarabic San Pedro Pascual, blames Witiza, not Rodrigo, for the rape of Julian's daughter. But anomalies still exist. Alleging that Witiza, in anticipation of the forthcoming onslaught, had been wrongly advised to disarm his cities and its citizens, one puts the blame on Julian, the other on Rodrigo. The *Crónica del Toledano*, completed in 1243, takes yet another turn. Here it was not Julian's daughter but his wife, supposedly the daughter of Witiza and sister of Archbishop Oppas, who was raped, and Rodrigo was then killed by Julian. Denouncing Julian's treason to his homeland, this work, linked to both Moslem and Christian sources, was of major influence on such subsequent histories as the *Primera Crónica General de España*, composed by order of Alfonso X el Sabio around 1275.

6. Pedro de Corral's *Crónica Sarracina*, was actually Spain's first historical novel, including within its 518 chapters all previous legends about Rodrigo, the *Crónica de don Pedro el Cruel*, and myriad other adventures of chivalric thrust. The themes of the hermit, the devil, and the snake prevail amid the penitence of the heroic Rodrigo and the guilt of La Cava, who flings herself into the sea. Although the work was denounced by more serious historians such as Fernán Pérez de Guzmán in his *Generaciones y semblanzas* (c. 1456), it acquired enormous popularity and credibility and gave inspiration to many subsequent poets, from the balladeers of the sixteenth century to the nineteenth-century Romantics.

7. The words of this ancient ballad are from the recording, *The Pleasures of Cervantes: Vocal and Instrumental Music of Spain of the 15th, 16th and 17th Centuries*, performed by the Polyphonic Ensemble of Barcelona, Miguel Querol Gavalda, director (translation mine).

8. Fray de Luis's *Profecía del Tajo* is a rather short poem of lyrical vein that depicts Rodrigo and the beautiful Caba lying on the shore of the Tagus when suddenly the river rises up to predict the destruction of Spain and the suffering of its people.

9. Miguel de Luna, official Arabic interpreter to King Phillip II, was a "New Christian" from among the Moors of Granada. He published the two parts of his totally apocryphal *Historia verdadera del rey don Rodrigo, compuesta por*

Abulcácim Tárif between 1592 and 1600, claiming that he had translated it from the original Arabic, including original letters penned by Rodrigo, "Florinda," and even Pelayo. Despite its flagrant deficiencies of both fact and style, this work flourished in succeeding editions for the next hundred years. Through it became established the guilt of the wanton woman known as La Cava and her perpetuation by the name of Florinda. Ironically, even though the classical scholar and historian, Padre Mariana, published a far more cogent account of the last Gothic king in his *Historia general de España* (1601), Luna's spurious effort continued to be widely accepted and quoted, while Mariana's remained almost unread.

10. Basing much of his narrative on prior chroniclers, including Luna's false Abulcácim, the Portuguese Frey Bernardo de Britto added his own chapter to the Rodrigo saga in his *Segunda parte da Monarchía Lusytana*, published in Lisbon in 1609. Among his additions are hitherto untold peregrinations and details of the ultimate penance, heaping fantasy upon fiction in disregard of any documentation.

11. The great writers of the Golden Age for the most part eschewed Rodrigo's story. Lope de Vega incorporates the plight of Florinda into his poem *Jerusalén Conquistada*. In his drama *El postrer godo*, he treats Rodrigo rather equivocally, recounting his marriage to an African princess, the suicide of Florinda, and Julián's murder by Tárif himself for having been a traitor. Derived essentially from the *Crónica general* and from Luna's false "History," this play is generally regarded as one of Lope's weakest and least well constructed. Tirso de Molina introduces the Rodrigo story into his play *La joya de las montañas*, casting the blame on old king Witiza. And Calderón de la Barca, in his *La virgen del sagrario*, includes an episode in which Tárif inculpates the venal La Cava.

12. Silva Mascarenhas's poem in nine cantos is called *A destruiçam de Espanha e restauraçam summaria da mesma* (1671). Curiously, the traditional saga of Rodrigo in Spain occupies a small part of the piece—la Cava doesn't even appear and is mentioned only peripherally—while the adventures of mythological stripe comprise the great majority of the action.

13. Rodrigo was the subject of several Italian operas between 1677 and 1696. The actual source of Handel's opera was a libretto by Francesco Silvani, *Il duello d'amore e di vendetta*, which was performed in Venice in 1699–1670. In some productions a castrato sang the role of Rodrigo and a female soprano sang that of Giuliano (Julian).

14. María Rosa Gálvez's *Florinda, tragedia en tres actos* (1806) may have escaped the censor because Rodrigo's vices are somehow redeemed by the virtue of love. Although he pursues her violently, he genuinely wishes to marry Florinda, who never really wanted to bring about Spain's destruction. In the end, Pelayo triumphs and Florinda, cursed even by her mother, is rejected by all.

15. Jules Leclerq includes this poem in his *Rimes Héroiques* (1922), in which he recreates in original French tercets several old Spanish ballads and traditional tales.

16. In fact, there were various musical versions of the story of Rodrigo in Latin America from the eighteenth century on. These include a Mexican opera, written in 1711 by Manuela de Zumaya but never produced; a successful Colombian opera by José María Ponce de León, produced in Bogota in 1880;

and a twentieth-century Chilean piece, *La muerte de don Rodrigo*, by Gustavo Becerra Schmidt.

BIBLIOGRAPHY

Ballester Escalas, Rafael. *Historia gráfica de España*. Madrid/Barcelona: Ayuntamiento, 1957.

Bergua, José, ed. *Romancero español*. Madrid: Ediciones Ibéricas, n.d.

Cheane, Anwar G. *Historia de la España musulmana*. Madrid: Ediciones Cátedra, 1974.

Dean, Winton, and Knapp, John Merrill. *Handel's Operas 1704–1726*. Oxford: Clarendon Press, 1987.

Fletcher, Richard A. *Moorish Spain*. New York: H. Holt, 1992.

Ginastera, Alberto. *Don Rodrigo*. Opera in three acts and nine scenes, with libretto by Alejandro Casona. London: Boosey & Hawkes, 1969. Sound recording from New York City Opera live performance, November 22, 1966; Julius Rudel, conductor; Plácido Domingo, tenor; Jeannine Crader, soprano.

———. *Don Rodrigo*. Symphony for soprano and orchestra. Sound recording. Indiana University Symphony Orchestra, 1964.

———. *Sinfonía de Don Rodrigo*. Pittsburgh Symphony Orchestra, William Steinberg, conductor; Jeannine Crader, soprano. American International Music Fund, Koussevitzky Music Foundation, 1968.

Historia de España. Barcelona: Ramón Sopena, n.d.

Livermore, Harold. *A History of Spain*. London: George Allen and Unwin, 1958.

Greenberg, Noah, and Maynard, Paul, eds. *An Anthology of Early Renaissance Music*. New York: W. W. Norton, 1935.

Menéndez Pidal, Ramón. *Floresta de leyendas heroicas españolas*. 3 vols. Madrid: Espasa Calpe, 1958.

Scott, Walter, Sir. *The Vision of Don Roderick: A Poem*. Edinburgh: John Ballantyne; London: Longman, Hurst, Rees, Orme and Brown, 1811.

Valbuena y Prat, Angel. *Historia de la literatura española*. 3 vols. Barcelona: Editorial Gustavo Gili, 1950.

2

The Cid:
Four Operatic Transformations
of a Spanish Classic

James J. Kolb

If, as W. S. Merwin has suggested, a cycle of Cid material began with the *Poem of the Cid* and ended "in the great age of Spanish drama" with "Guillén de Castro's two-part play *Las Mocedades del Cid*," then one might argue that a second cycle was inaugurated with Pierre Corneille's adaptation of Guillén de Castro's work in his French neoclassical tragicomedy, *Le Cid*, and continued with the adaptations of that story into opera libretti in many different languages over the next four centuries.[1] The numerous variations evident in operatic versions of *The Cid*, however, frequently show debts not merely to Corneille, but also to Castro, and perhaps to the ballads and chronicles upon which *Las Mocedades del Cid* was constructed.

William Wilson captures the essence of the story of the Cid as being "devoted to dramatizing events in Rodrigo's youth: his knighting, his victories over the Moors, his defense of Castilian territory against the claims of Aragon, and, above all, his troubled romance with Jimena, whose father he killed to restore his family's honor. Castro centers his play on the opposing demands of love and duty, but he is also concerned with portraying Rodrigo as the perfect Christian knight."[2] This chapter will examine four very different treatments of this essential story in operas by George Frideric Handel, Peter Cornelius, Jules Massenet, and Claude Debussy.

HANDEL AND HAYM'S
FLAVIO, RE DE' LONGOBARDI (1723)

George Frideric Handel, born in Halle, Germany, in 1685, settled in London in 1710 and spent virtually all of the rest of his life composing Italian-language operas and English-language oratorios. Best known for his oratorio, *Messiah* (1741), Handel composed forty-two operas, most of them before embarking on the later composition of nineteen oratorios.[3] Among them was *Flavio, Re de' Longabardi*, with a text by Nicola Francesco Haym. Following other early adaptations, Handel's opera, based on *Flavio Cuniberto* by Matteo Noris, made use of the legend of the Cid without actually dramatizing the story itself. As Haym described the text, it was "form'd of two Actions: One is taken partly from the History of the Kings of Lombardy; the other from the famous Tragi-Comedy call'd Cid, by P. Corneille."[4]

Like a Dickens novel, *Flavio* employs the device of parallel development, alternating between a story of two lovers and their quarrelsome fathers and another about clandestine lovers threatened by the amorous advances of their king. In fact, the opera begins with this second pair of lovers, Teodata and Vitige, parting at daybreak after having spent the night together. Only in the next scene do we meet Emilia (Ximena) and Guido (Rodrigo), who are in love and about to wed.[5] Flavio, King of Lombardy, invited to attend their wedding, is also preoccupied with the need to appoint a new governor for Britain. Flavio intends to appoint Lotario (Count Lozano), Emilia/Ximena's father, but changes his mind, appointing the elderly Ugone (Diego Laínez), father of Guido/Rodrigo and of Teodata instead. Flavio has fallen in love with Teodata, and his decision to appoint Ugone to Britain will get her father out of his way. Lotario, left alone on stage, reveals a rather silly anger at having been passed over in favor of Ugone. ("O, quel m'agita il cor furia di sdegno"/"O, what fury, what rage shakes my heart.")[6]

Subsequently we learn that Lotario has struck Ugone (offstage) in anger at the loss of his appointment as governor, and Ugone pleads with his son, Guido, to avenge him.[7] Challenged by his father to defend the family honor, Guido struggles, "torn between love for Emilia and anger at her father's slight" to his own father.[8] Guido seeks out Emilia, suggests vaguely that his destiny may separate them, but hopes that she will still love him. Emilia swears she will, Guido leaves, and she is left to marvel at his strange behavior (pp. 64–65).

Act 2 begins with Teodata and the king, Flavio, who is much taken with her beauty. But before Flavio is able to become more amorous, Ugone enters, still smarting from the insult visited upon him by Lotario. Ugone refuses to tell Flavio what is wrong and Flavio leaves. Teodata, of course, misreads Ugone's concern. She thinks that he has learned of her relationship with Vitige and admits not only that she loves Vitige, but that she has slept with him (pp. 70–73). This unexpected news is too much for Ugone; a new ill has been added to what he has already endured, and it provokes another seriocomic outburst (pp. 74–75).

Meanwhile, Lotario has sought out Emilia and demands that she leave with him. There will be no wedding to Guido if he can prevent it (pp. 76–79). Lotario storms out, leaving a bewildered and confused Emilia. Immediately, Guido appears and the stakes are suddenly heightened as Emilia realizes that Guido is again insisting ambiguously that she love him in spite of whatever happens. Emilia responds with a moving, emotional exit aria in which she expresses concern about their future and what destiny may have in store. She will leave as he requests, but who knows in what state she will return? Alone, Guido explodes in an aria in which he seeks to invigorate his desire for revenge (pp. 80–83).

Guido finds Lotario and their angry exchange follows that of Corneille quite closely, except that here they fight onstage and Guido fatally wounds Lotario. Emilia enters to find her dying father, and in their duet and her subsequent aria the drama is once again deepened. To the question of who injured Lotario, the answer is "Guido, Ugone's son" (p. 95).

As Act 3 begins, Ugone and Emilia both seek audience with King Flavio to plead their cases: Ugone in defense of his son's action against Lotario, and Teodata seeking Guido's punishment for the murder of her father. Flavio dismisses them impatiently. He will decide later. At the moment he is anxious to pursue his love for Teodata. Departing from the comic tribulations of Flavio, Vitige, and Teodata, the opera shifts back to the far more substantive dilemma of the Cid story. Guido approaches Emilia, offering her his sword—still red with her father's blood—and his life if she wishes to take it. Emilia takes the sword, but is unable to kill him: "O Heavens, I can't," she sings as she exits (pp. 114–115). Guido asks the king for death since he is still hated by Emilia, and Flavio realizes that "royal wisdom" is required to resolve this problem. Having ordered him to hide, Flavio informs Emilia that Guido is dead. This stuns Emilia, who demands death also. Flavio insists that she look at Guido's head before she dies, and when Emilia finally turns she discovers that Guido still lives.[9] Guido asks Emilia's pardon and Emilia answers, "I forgive you, my darling, if your fault was Honour" (pp. 124–125).

In this early adaptation of *Le Cid*, love seems more important than politics. What heroism exists is devoid of any geopolitical or national context and serves principally as a springboard to issues of the heart. It also seems clear that Handel and Haym wished to approach the material in a seriocomic vein—satire was in vogue in Handel's England—and the final sense of the piece is that honor may be important, but perhaps not important enough to die for, nor to pursue incessantly.

PETER CORNELIUS AND *DER CID* (1865)

By contrast to the prolific Handel, Peter Cornelius (1824–1874) was an opera composer of very modest dimensions. Born in Mainz, Germany, in 1824, he died there fifty years later. In 1860 Cornelius wrote his own libretto for *Der Cid*, using the plays by Corneille and Castro as well as Victor Huber's history of the Cid. *Der Cid* follows the story quite faithfully, though Cornelius gives it a somewhat Germanic spin. One might describe *Der Cid* as the "poor person's *Lohengrin*," for both musically and dramatically its sensibility has been shaped by that work.[10]

Der Cid opens at a very late stage in the story. Chimene's father, the Count of Lozan, has already been slain by Ruy Diaz. It is a time of strife and peril, and Ruy Diaz is already a warrior and hero.[11] Much like the opening of *Lohengrin* at the River Scheldt, this work begins with a public assembly in Burgos at which the king, Fernando, will sit in judgment. Chimene enters dressed in mourning, accuses Ruy Diaz of murder, and seeks revenge from the king (pp. 44–45).

Ruy Diaz arrives and is hailed as "hero," "victor," "chosen champion of Castile," and "Campeador" (pp. 46–49). The chorus seems to lack sympathy for Chimene, since they also hail Ruy Diaz for defending family honor "bloodily at Lozan," slaying the Count of Lozan "with the sword that Mudarra bore!" (p. 47), a reference to Tizona, one of the legendary swords associated with the Cid and referred to in Castro's play. As Ruy Diaz enters, a musical ensemble develops in which we learn that honor obliged Ruy Diaz to kill the count, and that a "cry from the heart" had to be crushed in the struggle, an oblique allusion to his feelings for Chimene (pp. 48–53).

In a remarkable reversal of what is conventionally done in the Cid story, Chimene kneels before Ruy Diaz, curses him, and invites him to kill her with his sword. Ruy Diaz, though shaken, turns to the king and justifies his actions, since with a "mad blow" the Count of Lozan struck his father (p. 55). Ruy Diaz offers his gauntlet in challenge to anyone who wishes to fight for Chimene. Alvar Fanez seizes it, but before combat ensues, Luyn Calvo, a bishop and uncle of Ruy Diaz, intervenes. Calvo chastises Ruy Diaz for having given in to anger, insists on humility, and demands his sword. Ruy Diaz yields it to the bishop, who gives it to Chimene, inviting her to take revenge. Chimene approaches Ruy Diaz, raises the sword, and falters. She decides she will keep Tizona, and condemns Ruy Diaz to wander swordless, helpless, and in disgrace (pp. 56–63).

Knights appear, announcing an imminent Moorish assault, as Ruy Diaz stands brooding over Chimene's curse (p. 67). The king appeals to Chimene to return Tizona to Ruy Diaz in this time of need. Chimene lays the sword at the feet of the king, for the needs of Castile are greater than her own. Ruy Diaz accepts the return of his sword, vowing to seek death in the coming battle. Amid trumpet fanfares the Spanish forces prepare for battle, because "the fatherland is in peril" (pp. 72–73).

Act 2 moves inward, both physically and emotionally. Alone in her chamber, Chimene struggles. Though she never confesses to love explicitly, it is evident from her assertion that "loneliness is death" (p. 77). Chimene prays but finds that she "cannot forgive murder, the call to vengeance rings out" (p. 79). Alvar Fanez appears and reasserts his intention to challenge Ruy Diaz after the impending battle (pp. 78–83). Luyn Calvo enters and chastises Chimene for her continuing desire for revenge: "Endure," "live," "forgive," the bishop urges. Chimene replies that what she really wishes is death, a kind of *liebestod*. Her heart yearns for "eternity!" (pp. 84–85).

A luminous scene between Chimene and Ruy Diaz follows. Chimene again invites Ruy Diaz to plunge his sword into her breast to relieve her agony, but the breeze "full of tears" and the "holy night" attired in mourning begin to have an effect. Diaz pleads for a word, a gesture. Together they envision a "fearful voyage on dark waves" (pp. 92–93), and seek "a wonderland, carpeted with flowers in the heat of the sun" (pp. 94–95). As the sun rises the army is heard preparing to march. Ruy Diaz begs Chimene for some words of hope, and she is able to say, "Depart! May you be forgiven!" and "Ruy Diaz! Triumph!" (p. 97). He leaves, awed by "Chimene's blessing!" while she falls to her knees and prays for his safety (p. 99).

Act 3 opens with a prayer for victory, immediately answered by trumpet calls. The king announces the defeat of the Moors, and the army returns in a stirring victory march. Several Moorish kings appear and present themselves to the king of Castile, having been sent by him whom they call "the Cid," "Lord" in Arabic. The king declares that all shall call him by that name, but then learns that after the battle Alvar Fanez, as Chimene's champion, has challenged the Cid to a duel. Almost immediately Chimene sees Alvar Fanez enter and expects the worst; her "seed of vengeance" has grown "bloodily into a poisonous blossom" (p. 107). Alvar Fanez places his sword at Chimene's feet and tries to apologize for failing to defeat Ruy Diaz, but Chimene misunderstands: "Be silent! Keep secret what I cannot endure! . . . I loved him, I have always loved him!" (p. 109).

Ruy Diaz now enters. Before Chimene can speak, the king grants him lordship over various cities, and offers a "higher reward, . . . the reward of love" (p. 111), inviting him to ask for Chimene's hand. The

Cid asks for death before the "dream" the king has offered disappears. Chimene replies that it is not a dream, that her love overcomes death (p. 111). Just as they longed for a wonderland in Act 2, Chimene and the Cid now accept the reality of their "dream" and pray that it will last. The Cid swears by Tizona always to be true to Chimene, and asks the bishop for his blessing. In a kind of *liebestod* and resurrection, Chimene describes her own dream in which she saw the Cid dead amidst the Moorish army, how a light streamed from the sky, how she ordered his corpse to be tied to his horse, and how she led it against the enemy. She promises to continue leading the Cid to "victory [even] in death!" (pp. 114–117).

This ending is faithful to the tradition of Spanish legend. Wilson tells us that the first General Chronicle of the Cid "ends with the fanciful statement that St. Peter appeared to the Cid in a vision, telling him that he would die within thirty days, but assuring him that he would be victorious over King Bucár even after death."[12] Elsewhere he notes that one ballad tells the story of Chimene and how the dead Cid, "his corpse, clad in armor and mounted on his horse, Babieca, is led into battle fighting the troops of King Búcar to such an extent that they flee in panic."[13]

Unlike Handel and Haym, Cornelius depicts Spain as a warrior culture, besieged and surrounded by Moorish enemies. The claims of Chimene for revenge must be balanced with the needs of the state. The ceremonial aspects of monarchy, the king's public hearing in the first act, and the various royal processions and military marches also convey a sense of place. In contrast to Corneille's Rodrigue, Cornelius's knight includes a religious dimension, though the Cid's legendary piety will be explored more fully by later librettists. In other ways, *Der Cid* says as much about mid-nineteenth-century Germany and German perceptions as it does about medieval Spain. The many "*Heils*" and references to the "*Vaterland*" have a resonance that one suspects is more Germanic than Spanish, and the mystical aspects of the relationship between Chimene and the Cid not only reflect the influence of *Lohengrin* but also anticipate some aspects of Wagner's *Tristan und Isolde*, particularly Chimene's preoccupation with love and death.[14]

JULES MASSENET, ADOLPHE PHILIPPE D'ENNERY, LOUIS GALLET, ÉDOUARD BLAU, AND *LE CID* (1885)

Jules Massenet, born in Montaud, France, in 1842, spent his working career as a composer in Paris and died there in 1912. His opera *Le Cid* (1885) is the sixth he composed out of a total of twenty-five. One of his best-known works, *Manon*, was composed immediately before *Le Cid* in 1884, and *Werther* came three operas and seven years later in 1892.[15]

Massenet and his librettists borrowed freely from both Corneille and Castro. Unlike Cornelius, they begin much earlier in the story of the Cid and depict a youthful Rodrigue whose recent victory over the Moors is about to be rewarded with knighthood. In the opening scene, Chimène has hopes and her father, Le Comte de Gormas, has expectations. She learns from her father that he approves of Rodrigue as "a worthy choice" for Chimène, while Gormas expects to be appointed guardian of the king's son.[16] Alone, Chimène expresses joy that she may now "love freely before all!" (p. 35), but the Infanta, the daughter of the king, enters and reveals her own love for Rodrigue. In a duet Chimène pleads with the Infanta not to love Rodrigue, and the Infanta assures that her honor and rank do not allow her "the right to love!" (p. 37). In order to devise the duet, with its tension between the women, the librettists have conflated aspects of Corneille's Dona Urraque and Castro's Doña Urraca. If there were any question about the mixing of sources for this libretto, the next scene resolves it, a scene derived from Castro's play and not found in Corneille: the investiture of Rodrigue as a knight.

Bells ring and the chorus praises God for the recent defeat of the Moors (pp. 38–39). Rodrigue is formally knighted, and the king presents him with a sword that "has gleamed faithfully in ten battles!" (p. 43). In Castro the king bestows armor and golden spurs, as well as a sword described as having "won five field battles." Rodrigue vows not to wear it until having won five more.[17] The librettists have conflated these various bestowals and inflated the result from five to ten battles already won. Swearing to be a true knight, Rodrigue salutes his newly acquired sword, "O noble lame étincelante" [Oh, noble sword that gleams] (pp. 44–45). It is a stirring piece—martial, mystical, and erotic—and includes Rodrigue's description of a "vision" that he sees as he glances at Chimène and then looks Heavenward: "Angel or woman, my days are bound to thine" (p. 45).

As Rodrigue enters the church to complete his investiture, the king chooses Rodrigue's father, Don Diègue, as the guardian for his son. The Comte de Gormas protests, but the king leaves for his palace with the admonition: "To attack my choice is to question me!" (p. 49). Again the librettists have looked to Castro as well as Corneille, for in Castro's version not only does Count Lozano protest, but he actually slaps Diego Laínez in the king's presence.[18] In Corneille the appointment occurs offstage, and we learn about it only in the scene in which the slap occurs. Having begun the scene in the style of Castro, the actual incident of the insult and slap more closely resembles Corneille. Even closer to Corneille is Don Diègue's aria in response to the slap, "O rage, ô désespoir, ô vieillesse ennemie!" [Oh rage, oh despair, oh vile old age!] (pp. 52–53). Act 1 ends with a scene between father and son, as Don

Diègue reveals the insult to family honor and Rodrigue demands to know the name of the offender (pp. 56–57). He learns it soon enough; it is the father of Chimène, and he exclaims, "Alas! all my happiness is lost!" (pp. 56–59).

Act 2 begins with Rodrigue alone singing an aria adapted directly from Corneille ("Percé jusqu'au fond du coeur" [Pierced to the bottom of my heart] (pp. 58–59) that explores the consequences of his choice. The count enters and the exchanges between the two men are a truncated version of those in Corneille. They duel, Rodrigue strikes home, and the count dies on stage.[19] Don Diègue and others enter the stage, encountering Rodrigue and the dead count. Don Diègue thanks his son, but Rodrigue responds, "For you, I have lost all" (pp. 66–67). The body of the count is carried off as Chimène rushes in, seeking her father's killer. As a requiem begins, Chimène, singing in counterpoint, vows to strike down whoever killed her father. In a scene not found in any of the Cid sources, Chimène circles the stage confronting the various members of the crowd, asking, "Is it you?" (pp. 68–69). Finally she stands in front of Don Rodrigue and sees the truth in his pale expression: "Ah! Him! God! Rodrigo! It's him!" as the scene ends (pp. 68–69).[20]

The action of the opera is now delayed for twenty minutes by the presentation of a ballet that actually serves both theatrical and dramatic ends.[21] It contains some lovely music in the Spanish style, imitating seven forms of dance, and functions as a pleasant divertissement. But it also helps to create dramatic suspense by delaying the inevitable moment when Chimène interrupts the celebrations, seeking justice from the king.[22] Don Diègue and Rodrigue also appear, and the shape of the scene is probably derived from Corneille, though it is very similar in Castro. Massenet is able to heighten the effect of the conflict between Don Diègue/Rodrigue and Chimène by the development of a musical ensemble in which the principals, the king, Infanta, and chorus express their feelings simultaneously (pp. 76–79).

Before the king is able to resolve the dilemma, a Moorish knight arrives, interrupting the crisis at hand by provoking a new one. He informs the king that his master has "tired of his rest that you call retreat"; the Moorish army is once again on the march (pp. 80–81). No such interruption occurs in either Castro or Corneille. In both plays the king dismisses the parties and suggests that more time is needed to resolve the problem. But we noticed earlier that Cornelius made use of this device in *Der Cid*, and it is a good one. It raises the stakes for all concerned, it provides for a good melodramatic moment on stage, and it connects more powerfully and dramatically the private story of Rodrigue and Chimène with the public issues of beleaguered Spain.[23] The king tells the Moor, "We will come," but immediately realizes that Rodrigue has killed the ablest knight in the kingdom. Rodrigue requests permission to lead the army (pp. 80–83). While the king wishes Rodrigue victory and God-speed, Chimène curses him, and the curtain falls.

Act 3 begins with Chimène alone in her room. It is night, and she struggles over the "frightful combat" in her soul (p. 85). Often hailed as one of the finest moments in the opera, the aria "Pleurez, pleurez mes yeux!" [Weep, weep my eyes!] dramatically explores Chimène's grief (pp. 84–85). The obligatory scene follows in which Rodrigue appears and tells Chimène that he wishes to see her once more before he dies. He does not offer her his sword, as occurs in other versions, since it is clear that he has a higher duty to lead his army into battle. In a beautiful duet they reminisce about their "days of . . . first love" and Chimène is torn. Rodrigue urges her to hate him, but she replies, "I do not hate you! . . . I cannot! Alas! . . . I demand your life and fear I will get it!" (p. 89). Rodrigue responds: "Could I have believed it? God! . . . she will pardon me!" (p. 91). Inspired by the hope of her pardon, Rodrigue is sure of victory, but Chimène once again wavers: "I have said nothing! nothing! nothing! Ah! no forgetting and no pardon! Farewell, go! These words will make me die of shame" (p. 93).

The scene changes to the battlefield. Rodrigue's camp is in disarray as his soldiers drink and sing. It is the pious Rodrigue who enters and chastises his men for reveling rather than praying on the eve of battle. In a scene taken from Castro and not used by Corneille, Massenet further develops the pious nature of Rodrigue. In his memoirs he tells us, "I was reading the romance of Guilhem [sic] de Castro, and I came across an incident which became the tableau where the consoling apparition appears to the Cid as he is in tears—the second tableau in the third act."[24] Massenet is referring to the leper who appears in Castro's play. Rodrigo treats the leper with Christian charity, shares food with him, and gives him his blanket. Rodrigo's companions are nauseated by his kindness to the leper and leave. As Rodrigo watches over the sleeping leper, he too falls asleep and the leper appears to him as St. Lazarus, promising him, "you will be an incredible figure throughout our history, an admirable captain, an invincible conqueror; and so much so, that you alone will humans see conquer after death."[25] We have already encountered this vision of the Cid after death, tied to his horse and entering battle, both in Spanish ballads and in Chimène's dream as used by Peter Cornelius. Massenet adjusted the vision to suit his needs. This Rodrigue prays to St. James, the patron saint of Spain, for assistance in the coming battle, and St. James promises, "You will be the victor" (pp. 96–99).

As Act 4 begins, Don Diègue has learned mistakenly from soldiers who fled that the army has lost and Rodrigue is dead. As Diègue accepts his son's death and berates the cowardice of the deserters, Chimène and the Infanta enter and hear his words. Chimène weeps as trumpets are heard and the king enters. He cannot understand her tears. "Listen," he says. Chimène hears the trumpets and exclaims: "Ah! Rodrigue is alive!" "Alive and the victor," replies the king (pp. 100–105).

The opera concludes with a "triumphal march," and the chorus celebrates him whom the Moors call "the Cid." The king acknowledges Rodrigue's newly won name and offers any further prize he might wish. The Cid says that the king cannot give him what he desires, only one other person can. The king calls Chimène forward and offers to exact whatever revenge she wishes, but Chimène demurs (p. 107). The king presses her for an answer, and Rodrigue reaches for his sword, offering to kill himself, when finally Chimène sings, "Oh my father, you will forgive me! No! no! no! You will not die! Sire! I love him!" (p. 109).

Like Cornelius, Massenet has also chosen to juxtapose forcefully the public and private worlds implicit in the story of the Cid. On the one hand we have the investiture, the marches and fanfares, a duel, and battle, but we also have the moments of the human heart, especially in the middle acts where Rodrigue must cope with his dilemma of duty and honor opposed to love, and Chimène must deal with the consequences of his actions. Finally, Chimène must accept the fact that Spain needs the Cid, and recognizes that the public good may sometimes have to subsume the private need. At least this gives Chimène a rationale for her actions in the last scene, for it is clear that above all else she loves Rodrigue.

CLAUDE DEBUSSY, CATULLE MENDÈS, AND
RODRIGUE ET CHIMÈNE (1889–1892)

Claude Debussy was born in 1862 in St.-Germain-en-Laye, studied music in Rome after winning the Prix de Rome at the Paris Conservatoire, and spent most of his composing career in Paris, where he died in 1918.[26] Debussy completed just one opera, but that was the ground-breaking *Pelléas et Mélisande* (1893–1895; 1901–1902). Several other projects were left in various states of incompletion. Debussy seems to have taken little interest in the libretto offered to him by Catulle Mendès, confiding to fellow composer Gustave Charpentier "that the traditional aspects of this subject matter call for music which I cannot call my own."[27] Though small portions of the libretto are missing and Debussy never finished the bulk of the orchestration, enough of the composition has survived to allow for a "reconstruction of the score from the original manuscript."[28]

The opera dramatizes the youthful romance of Rodrigue and Chimène and the quarrel between their fathers, but ends with Rodrigue departing for war, thus avoiding a resolution to the duty/honor/love dilemma. Catulle Mendès's libretto is a mixture of material borrowed from the plays of both Castro and Corneille, with other scenes either invented by the librettist or taken from unidentified sources.

Act 1 begins at night and resembles the "balcony scene" in *Romeo and Juliet*. Rodrigue and Chimène have just been betrothed. They meet in secret, though Rodrigue's brothers and Chimène's confidante keep watch nearby. They embrace, and in a rapturous scene and duet declare their love.[29]

At dawn, as Rodrigue and Chimène part, the Men of Gormaz, belonging to the household of Chimène's father, enter preparing to go to Mass. But before Mass, they get drunk on wine, and then, "for the rest of the day, [they] will be ready for love" (pp. 32–33). On cue, the Daughters of Bivar, the women associated with the household of Rodrigue's father, enter and are quickly assaulted by the amorous, besotted men. Hearing their cries for help, Don Diègue de Bivar enters to assist them. Don Diègue strikes the men and chastises them as "soldiers without honor" (p. 39). Don Gomez de Gormaz enters seeking an explanation for the commotion on his estate. The two men quarrel, and Don Diègue, unable to wield his sword, must endure a slap and insults from Don Gomez. "Accursèd age," Don Diègue exclaims as Act 1 ends, "my honour . . . is no more" (p. 43).

By a quite different route, the first act of *Rodrigue et Chimène* manages to lay out the familiar Cid plot, though in a remarkably unusual way. The scene between the lovers is very Gallic, and very unclassical in its lack of reticence. Even more peculiar is the scene that precipitates the quarrel and slap. Though Mendès's sources are not established, the scene in which the Men of Gormaz assault the Daughters of Bivar does remind one of the third *cantar* of *The Poem of the Cid*, the section sometimes titled, "The Outrage at Corpes," in which the sons-in-law of the Cid strip, tie-up, and beat the Cid's daughters before abandoning them in the wilderness.[30]

Act 2 begins with a scene derived from Castro.[31] Hernando, Bermudo, and Rodrigue—the three sons of Don Diègue—are engaged in a game of chess, but Rodrigue is abstracted and inattentive. This is the first case of an opera employing the three sons. Corneille eliminated Rodrigue's brothers, and the other librettists examined thus far did as well. Don Diègue appears as a beggar, but once the boys have welcomed him and offered him charity, he reveals himself as their father and proceeds to squeeze each of their hands as a test of their courage (pp. 52–55). Learning that his father has been insulted, Rodrigue demands to know the name. At last, his father informs him that it is Don Gomez de Gormaz. Rodrigue laments his fate, much as in Castro and Corneille, and the final line of his aria sums up the scene in sentiments that both playwrights would recognize: "O mon devoir! O mon amour!" [O my duty! My love!] (pp. 58–59).[32] The scene shifts to a mountain pass where Rodrigue confronts Don Gomez in traditional fashion. Don Gomez insultingly refers to him as "enfant," they duel, and Don Gomez is slain (pp. 68–69). As Rodrigue leaves, Chimène rushes on stage to discover her dying father. Don Gomez tells her who has slain him: "Rodrigue!" (pp. 70–71).

As Act 3 begins, war is imminent. Again, the device of a public, external crisis is used to delay dealing with the immediate private problem (pp. 70–73). The king enters, salutes his "warlike barons," and asks where Don Gomez is. The answer is given almost immediately, as Chimène and Don Diègue come forth demanding justice (pp. 74–75). Both prostrate themselves before the king, and Don Pedre de Terruel immediately steps forward as a would-be champion for Chimène. The king preempts Don Pedre, saying that he himself will administer justice. The scene moves to a more private, though unspecified, setting. In a tender aria, Chimène confesses to her confidante that, in spite of all, she still loves Rodrigue. In both music and text there is a reminiscence of their betrothal night, the giddy opening scene of the opera. After only the slightest of struggles with honor and conscience, Chimène allows love to conquer, at least for the moment (pp. 82–83).

The inevitable encounter follows, in which Rodrigue presents his sword to Chimène, still red with the blood of her father, and offers her an opportunity for revenge. Chimène is moved, disturbed by her father's blood, but also enamored in the presence of Rodrigue. She weeps, but dismisses Rodrigue telling him that "obscure revenge" is not a sufficient repayment for public insult. She cannot forgive him (pp. 82–87). Incensed, Rodrigue shouts for others to attend him so that he may be killed in public to accommodate Chimène's desire. Rodrigue's brothers and father respond to his call and urge him not to die but to fight for "Christian Castile" against the "hated paynim" (pp. 86–89). His brothers assure him that in her heart Chimène still loves him. Rodrigue accepts his fate and hopes that he will die for Chimène while triumphing against the enemy (pp. 88–91). And so the opera ends.

One sees why this opera is titled *Rodrigue et Chimène* and not *Le Cid*, since much of the "gloire" surrounding the character of the Cid is still in the future. Though Castro may have called his play *The Youthful Deeds of the Cid*, Mendès's libretto presents an even more juvenile and romantic version of the character.

CONCLUSIONS

Of the parent/child/love/duty conflict in the Cid, George Jellinek writes that it provides for "a dandy operatic conflict."[33] It allows for a vast range of approaches and treatments, and often the individual response to the material says as much about the temperament of those adapting it as it does about the Cid himself. In these four operas alone they range from the seriocomic, satiric rendering of Handel through the quasimystical, Germanic perspective of Cornelius, to the martial/religious approach of Massenet, and the utterly romantic mood of Debussy.

The Cid continues to inspire. Judith Weir, an English composer born in 1954, is the most recent to find the Cid material attractive and inspiring. In 1988 she composed a "music drama" called *Missa del Cid*. The work intermingles a narrator/Evangelist and chorus, juxtaposing quotations—in both English and Spanish—from the *Poema de Mio Cid* with sung sections of the liturgical Latin Mass.[34] Once again, the good, pious, heroic Christian knight has been recreated on the stage; and in the 1980s perhaps another circle reached completion, since Weir chooses the earliest of the Spanish sources as her inspiration, eschewing the later embellishments of the ballads, Castro, and Corneille.

NOTES

1. W. S. Merwin, "Introduction," *Poema del Cid/Poem of the Cid*, Spanish text by Ramón Menéndez Pidal, English verse trans. W. S. Merwin (New York: Penguin/Meridian, 1975), xxv–xxix. Another useful version is *The Poem of the Cid*, trans. Rita Hamilton and Janet Perry (1975; New York: Penguin, 1984).

2. William E. Wilson, *Guillén de Castro*, Twayne's World Authors Ser. 253 (New York: Twayne, 1973), 208.

3. Donald Burrows, *Handel* (New York: Schirmer, 1994). This recent comprehensive biography of Handel lists all of his compositions in the various genres in which he worked. Other biographies include Newman Flower, *Handel: His Personality and His Times* (1923; London: Granada, 1972), and Stanley Sadie, *Handel* (New York: Crowell, 1969).

4. Winton Dean and John Merrill Knapp, *Handel's Operas 1704–1726*, rev. ed. (Oxford: Clarendon Press, 1995), 460. For Handel's *Flavio*, see especially Chapter 21.

5. Consistency of names when working with several languages is a problem. This chapter uses the Spanish versions of the characters' names when referring to "the Cid material." When discussing the individual libretti, however, the names as used in the respective texts are preferred.

6. René Jacobs, cond., *Flavio* by Georg Frideric Handel, Ensemble 15, Harmonia Mundi, 1900. Libretto, trans. Liesel B. Sayre, 48–49. Page references to the libretto of *Flavio* appear in the text.

7. In their massive study, Dean and Knapp note that "in earlier librettos, as in Corneille, the face-slapping incident happens on stage and is a more serious assault.. . . . By banishing this episode and making Ugone come on, furtive and furious, with a red face, Haym and Handel . . . make the disproportion between the injury and the reaction of Ugone and Guido a matter for ridicule." Dean and Knapp, *Handel's Operas*, 464.

8. Ibid., 461.

9. Both Castro and Corneille make use of this device twice, by which Ximena reveals her true feelings as a result of erroneous news of Rodrigo's death. See Guillén de Castro y Bellvis, *The Youthful Deeds of the Cid*, trans. Robert R. LaDu, Luis Soto-Ruiz, and Giles A. Deager (New York: Exposition Press, 1969), 49–50, 65–66; see Corneille, act 4, scene 5, 91–92 and act 5, scene 7, 104–107. For occasional questions the English translations were compared with the texts in their original languages: see D. Guillén de Castro, *Las mocedades del Cid*, ed. Victor Said Armesto, 2d ed. (Madrid: Ediciones de "La Lectura," 1923), and Pierre Corneille, *Le Cid*, ed. Colbert Searle (Boston: Ginn, 1912).

10. According to Scherle, Cornelius saw Wagner's *Lohengrin* in Weimar in 1852 and subsequently became a friend of Wagner. Arthur Scherle, liner notes, Gustav Kuhn, cond., *Der Cid* by Peter Cornelius, Rundfunk-Sinfonieorchester Berlin, Koch Schwann, 1996, 20–21.

11. Kuhn, cond., *Der Cid*, Libretto, trans. Gwyn Morris, 40–41. Page references to the libretto of *Der Cid* appear in the text.

12. Wilson, *Guillén de Castro*, 96.

13. Ibid., 98. W. S. Merwin, in his introduction to the *Poem of the Cid* (pp. xxv–xxix), reprints the portion of a ballad relating this same incident.

14. *Der Cid* had its premiere on May 21, 1865, at the Weimar Court Theatre (Scherle, liner notes, *Der Cid*, 21). *Tristan und Isolde* had its premiere one day less than three weeks later, on June 10, 1865, in Munich. James Anderson, *The Harper Dictionary of Opera and Operettas* (New York: HarperCollins, 1990), 585.

15. Otto T. Salzer, *The Massenet Compendium*, vol. 1 (Fort Lee, N.J.: Massenet Society, 1984), 56, 42, 91. Information on the later operas of Massenet may be found in Volume 2 of this work. General studies of Massenet include James Harding, *Massenet* (New York: St. Martin's Press, 1970), and Demar Irvine, *Massenet: A Chronicle of His Life and Times* (Portland, Ore.: Amadeus Press, 1994).

16. Eve Queler, cond., *Le Cid* by Jules Massenet, Opera Orchestra of New York, CBS Records, 1976. Libretto, trans. Thomas G. Kaufman, 33. Page references to the libretto of *Le Cid* appear in the text.

17. Castro, *Youthful Deeds*, 6.

18. Ibid., 8–11.

19. In Corneille the quarrel occurs in act 2, scene 2, 49–52. Chimène learns that Rodrigue and her father are quarreling in act 2, scene 4, 55, and news of the count's death is delayed until act 2, scene 7, 61.

20. In his memoirs Massenet explains the source of this scene. Recalling that Adolphe D'Emmery "sometime before had entrusted to me an important libretto and that I had found a very moving situation in the fifth act," Massenet obtained permission to make use of that one scene, and "thus d'Emmery became a collaborator. This is the scene in which Chimène find that Rodriguez [*sic*] is her father's murderer." Since the libretto had already been largely written by Louis Gallet and Edouard Blau, it thus acquired a third contributor. Jules Massenet, *My Recollections*, trans. H. Villiers Barneu (1919; Westport, Conn.: Greenwood Press, 1970), 149.

21. The ballet was a theatrical convention of the Paris Opera, and was an obligatory and anticipated part of the performance of every opera.

22. In order, the seven dances are: (1) Castillane, (2) Andalouse, (3) Aragonaise, (4) Aubade, (5) Catalane, (6) Madrilène, and (7) Navarraise. The

Queler recording is not complete and includes only four of the seven dances. The complete ballet music may be heard on Jean Martinon, cond., Massenet, "Le Cid"—Ballet Music and Meyerbeer-Lambert "Les Patineurs" Ballet, Israel Philharmonic Orchestra, London, n.d.

23. In the opera the impact is immediate. In the plays the threat from the Moors happens offstage, between the scenes of the drama. In Castro it occurs as an afterthought on the part of Don Diego, who tells his son, "Serve the King in war, for it has always been a knight's worthy satisfaction to serve a King whom he left offended." In a similar way it appears later in Corneille. Castro, *Youthful Deeds*, 32; Corneille, *The Cid*, act 3, scene 6, 80–81.

24. Massenet, *My Recollections*, 149.

25. Castro, *Youthful Deeds*, 50–55.

26. John Guinn and Les Stone, eds., *The St. James Opera Encyclopedia: A Guide to People and Works* (Detroit: Visible Ink Press, 1997), 197.

27. Letter to Gustave Charpentier, quoted in Orledge, *Debussy and the Theatre* (Cambridge: Cambridge University Press), 18.

28. Kent Nagano, cond., *Rodrigue et Chimène* by Claude Debussy, Orchestre et Choeur de L'Opera de Lyon, MusicFrance/Erato, 1995. Reconstruction of the score by Richard Langham Smith, orchestration by Edison Denisov.

29. Kent Nagano, cond., *Rodrigue et Chimène*, Libretto, trans. Stewart Spencer, 28–29. Page references to the libretto of this opera appear in the text.

30. Merwin, *Poema del Cid*, 232–243.

31. Castro, *Youthful Deeds*, 14–15. Of necessity, the dialogue in this scene of the opera has been radically shortened compared to the play.

32. The comparable scenes are Castro, *Youthful Deeds*, 16–17; Corneille, *The Cid*, act I, scene 6, 41–42.

33. George Jellinek, *History through the Opera Glass* (White Plains, N.Y.: Pro/Am Music Resources, 1994).

34. David Mason, cond., *Missa del Cid* by Judith Weir, included in *3 Operas* by Judith Weir, United, 1994.

3

Bridges of Song: Christian, Judaic, and Islamic Influences in Poetry and Music

Pilar del Carmen Tirado

For centuries, Spain had been homeland to a heterogeneous society of Christian, Muslim, and Jewish peoples. In 1492, with the objective of unifying Spain under a single political and religious allegiance, this pluralistic society was changed forever by the defeat of the last Moorish king at Granada and the expulsion of the Jews. It is understandable that mixed perceptions and feelings would exist among the three groups, especially since their number included those who had intermarried or freely converted during the centuries of coexistence. It is also interesting to note how these perceptions were sustained in later centuries and in other lands. To this end I shall explore the artistic expression of three late fifteenth-century songs, their reflections of the demise of Moorish Spain, and their testimony to the confluence of three cultures.

Too often, literary scholars of fifteenth- and sixteenth-century texts disregard the music scores of the poems they scrutinize, even though many of them were written for or traditionally associated with music. This is not surprising given the complexity of Medieval and Renaissance music, which presents a variety of modalities and scales in a music notation that specifies neither tempo, key, nor harmonies, and whose instrumental accompaniment was improvised from the principal melodic line. In many cases there exists no written music at all, as we find with the traditional *romances* (ballads), whose melodies are still retained in the popular collective memory, transmitted through time by voice and whichever instruments have been available.[1] Not infrequently, music historians who analyze the music and the nuances of performance are daunted by problems of the lyrics, such as lexical adaptations and textual variations of entire stanzas. For the literary specialist, the existence of these is not a problem, but rather a bounty from which to draw. Great poetry can give voice to the seemingly inexpressible, while music has the ability to communicate beyond words and time. In sum, just as every musical performance is but an approximation of its original, every reading devoid of the music of a musically construed poem deprives it of its intended effect. By considering the total artistic expression, one can better appreciate the transhistorical and multicultural perception of the end of Moorish Spain, expressed here in three songs: the *villancico* "Tres moricas m'enamoran," and the *romances* "Una sañosa porfía" and "Abenámar."

At the turn of the fifteenth century, popular and refined secular compositions consisting mainly of *romances* and *villancicos* were compiled in various *cancioneros*, among them the *Cancionero Musical de Palacio* (CMP), a collection of 458 songs used at the household of the Duke of Alba during the reign of the Catholic Monarchs.[2] The piece that has aroused most interest from that collection is the anonymous *villancico* "Tres morillas m'enamoran" (CMP n. 17), whose lyrics gloss and freely adapt to the haunting *estribillo* (refrain): "Tres morillas m'enamoran/ en Jaén,/Axa y Fátima y Marién." Three Moorish maidens go to an olive grove and an apple orchard, only to find the fruits already taken. They return pale and dismayed, without revealing what has transpired to cause such a reaction. The early popularity of this *villancico* is manifested by the fact that in the same collection of songs it is immediately followed by a lesser known version (CMP n. 18) attributed to a certain Diego Fernández, whose identity has been disputed.[3] Here is its lyric as recorded by the Waverly Consort:

Tres moricas m'enamoran	Three Moorish girls made me fall
en Jaén,	in love in Jaen:
Axa y Fátima y Marién.	Axa, Fatima, and Marien.
Díxeles,—¿Quién sois, señoras,	I said to them, "Who are you, ladies,
De mi vida robadoras?	that have robbed me of my life?"
—Cristianas qu'éramos moras	"We are Christians who were Moors
de Jaén,	of Jaen,
Axa y Fátima y Marién.	Axa, Fatima, and Marien."
—Yo vos juro al Alcorán,	I swear by the Koran
en quien, señoras, creéis,	in which, ladies, you believe,
que la una y todas tres	that one and all three of you
m'avéis puesto en grande afán;	have caused me great anxiety;
do mis ojos penerán	where my sorrowful eyes
pues tal verán	see at last
Axa y Fátima y Marién.	Axa, Fatima, and Marien.

Using the same basic refrain as the earlier version, it modifies the encounter and situates it at a fountain, where the poet amorously propositions the three and is rejected.[4] The final stanza of this version, however, is most unusual in a song composed for and played at court because it implies that these new Christian converts still openly believe in the Koran. In fact, the poet swears by that scripture, not by the Bible, in order to add credibility to his amorous intents. In view of the strong Islamic affiliation that the song imparts, it behooves us to consider further its Moorish content in order to fully appreciate the text.

Some scholars believe that the *villancico* "Tres morillas" was based on an earlier Muslim *zéjel*, a song or verse form written in popular rather than classical Arabic.[5] A *zéjel* begins with an opening refrain of two lines, followed by three monorhymed lines, and then a fourth line of verse with the same rhyme and melody as the refrain. This rhyme is repeated in the fourth line of all the stanzas that form the *zéjel*. The *villancico* refrain is attached to the last verse of the stanza, forming with it a single musical phrase and giving it a graceful flowing sound. With regard to the anonymous lyrics of the later version, Menéndez Pidal indicates that its theme comes from an ancient Mid-Eastern song of the ninth century whose male protagonist was Harun ar-Raxid I, the Abbasid caliph of Baghdad. This most sensual ditty, according to Menéndez Pidal, circulated throughout the Islamic world. In southern Spain it was cleansed of all lewdness and reduced to the structure of a *zéjel*, which then evolved into the form of a *villancico*. Thus, the alterations as we find them in the *Cancionero Musical de Palacio* are an echo of the many centuries that Moorish and Christian singers lived together.[6] If this is true, then music is one of the major clues to understanding these two related texts (Figure 3.1).

The music folio for the later version states "*alio modo*," clearly indicating that it is to be performed in the same manner as the preceding *villancico*. Indeed, the intervals and contours of the treble melody line are similar in both versions: an upward fourth, downward second, two successive downward thirds, followed by a stepwise motion upward.[7] A 1992 recording by the Waverly Consort of the later version distills the essence of the Islamic roots by using only the first and fifth stanzas with the traditional refrain. This is preceded by a solo *oud* (Moorish lute) improvisation on the traditional Islamic melody. In this performance of "Tres moricas," one appreciates the expressiveness within the simplicity of style. The musical phrasing closely follows the form of the verse, contributing to a clear and logical structure with well-defined melodic passages that convey sadness and resignation. The *oud* improvisation rapidly builds on the melodic phrasing of the refrain, adding layers of melismas (successions of different notes sung upon the single syllable) in true Arabic style but returning to the

Figure 3.1
18-D°. Fernandez

semicadence or full close that corresponds to the poetic caesura. In contrast to the instrumental improvisation, the addition of these specific lyrics to the music allows for a full impression of the anxiety and sorrow of the male protagonist, which could be attributed either to the implicit amorous rejections and/or to the loss of the three maidens to the Christian faith. This reflects a historical and cultural reality. As the dominion of the Islamic rulers diminished during the long Christian reconquest of Spain, the Moor gained in favor and popularity as a representative literary figure. By the end of Moslem rule, however, he was no longer depicted as an equal in combat but as a subjugated and converted *morisco*. Yet though this might explain the inclusion of this rendition of the traditional *villancico* and an earlier *zéjel* in a songbook (CMP) for the victorious court, it still leaves unanswered how the text could dare to express skepticism that converts would truly abandon their Islamic creed. The answer could be that it reflects the extent to which empathy existed among the victors for the plight of the Moors.

Such clearly is the case with song number 126 from the Cancionero Musical de Palacio: Juan del Encina's *romance*, "Una sañosa porfía."[8]

Una sañosa porfía	A brutal, doomed
sin ventura va pujando.	conflict grinds on.
ya nunca terné alegría	Joy I never had
ya mi mal se va ordenando.	and now my sad fate is ordained.
Ya fortuna disponía	Already Fortune has decreed
quitar mi próspero mando,	an end to my prosperous reign,
qu'el bravo león d'España	for the brave lion of Spain
mal me viene amenazando.	comes to menace me.
Su spantosa artillería,	Its fearful artillery,
los adarves derribando,	demolishing all our ramparts,
mis villas y mis castillos,	captures my towns and my castles
mis ciudades va ganando.	and all my citadels.
La tierra y el mar gemían,	The earth and the sea do groan,
que viene señoreando,	as he masters them imperiously
sus pendones y estandartes	carrying his flags,
y banderas levantando.	his banners and standards.
Su muy gran cavallería,	his imposing cavalry,
hela, viene relumbrando.	here arrive in grand array.
Sus huestes y peonaje	His hosts and infantry
el aire viene turbando.	bring turbulence to the air.
Córreme la morería,	They chase out all my Moors
los campos viene talando;	and devastate the fields;
mis compañas y caudillos	they crush and massacre
viene venciendo y matando;	my companies and my generals;
las mezquitas de Mahoma	they make parish churches
en iglesias consagrando;	of the mosques of Mohammed;
las moras lleva cativas	they take away our women
con alaridos llorando.	amidst cries and tears.
Al cielo dan apellido:	Their shouts go up to heaven
—¡Biva'l rey Fernando!	—Long live King Ferdinand!
—¡Biva la muy gran leona,	—Long live the magnificent lioness,
alta reina prosperada!—	The great and prosperous Queen!—
Una generosa Virgen	A generous Virgin
esfuerço les viene dando.	gives them great courage.
Un famoso cavallero	An illustrious knight
delante viene bolando,	proudly rides before them,
con una cruz colorada	carrying a crimson cross
y un espada relumbrando,	and a sparkling sword;
d'un rico manto vestido,	dressed in a rich mantle,
toda la gente guiando.	he leads forth all the people.

On January 2, 1492, King Ferdinand and Queen Isabella claimed the Alhambra, the last Moorish bastion on the Iberian peninsula. The poet, dramatist, and composer Encina accompanied his patron, the Duke of Alba, Don Fadrique de Toledo, in the siege of the city of Granada.[9] Encina appreciated the gravity of this historic event and wrote several songs to commemorate the passing of Muslim civilization in Spain, none more moving than "Una sañosa porfía," which overtly sympathizes with the unfortunate King Boabdil, who lost his beautiful palace and his prosperous domain. In first person, Encina captures the tragedy suffered by King Boabdil when the latter laments, "Fortune has decreed an end unto my prosperous reign, for the brave lion of Spain comes to menace me." The tension of despair in this monologue is conveyed not only by the use of a minimum of adjectives, a maximum of nouns and verbs, and evocative descriptions of the consequences of battle, but also by its references to the advantage of the Christian side having had the support of St. James (Santiago) and the Virgin. This tension is heightened by the melody, rhythm, and texture of the music, which underscore the pathos of the text (Figure 3.2).

The piece is written in *fa*, a key somewhat similar to our modern scale of A minor, and in duple time (equivalent to 2/4), which allows a slow defined beat for the pensive text. Musical phrase and poetic phrase match each other with a notable aptness and economy. Only the first four lines are set musically; succeeding quatrains are sung to the music of the first. Each line of verse contains eight syllables, with principal stress on the seventh, and every even line is assonated. Thus, the binary rhyme scheme of the text, which is øaøa øaøa, corresponds to musical phrases that are repeated every four verses. The musical phrases that correspond to the rhymed even lines are embellished at the final stressed syllable with melismas, which here musically communicate sorrow.[10] This regularly occurring embellishment complements the rest of the music of repeated solemn root chords formed by the scored four voices in a simple polyphonic style that adds dignity to the lamentation. As a result, "the tone adopted is of such remarkable appropriateness that it is irresistible."[11]

By experiencing its full artistic expression, we can understand how this secular song and poem intended to entertain the victorious court could have enjoyed an enormous popularity with all sectors of Spanish society. Yet as Michel Bernstein points out, their power of evocation was so striking that the singing of certain *romances* had to be banned because of the sorrow and sympathy that they provoked for the losing side.[12] Such might also have been the case for the following traditional poem that reflects an Islamic spirit in its historic relevance and artistic inspiration, yet has been preserved up to the present day by the Spanish Jews:

Abenámar, Abenámar	Abenamar, Abenamar,
moro de la morería,	Moor of the Moorish quarter,
el día que tú naciste	on the day of your birth

Figure 3.2
327-J. Del Encina

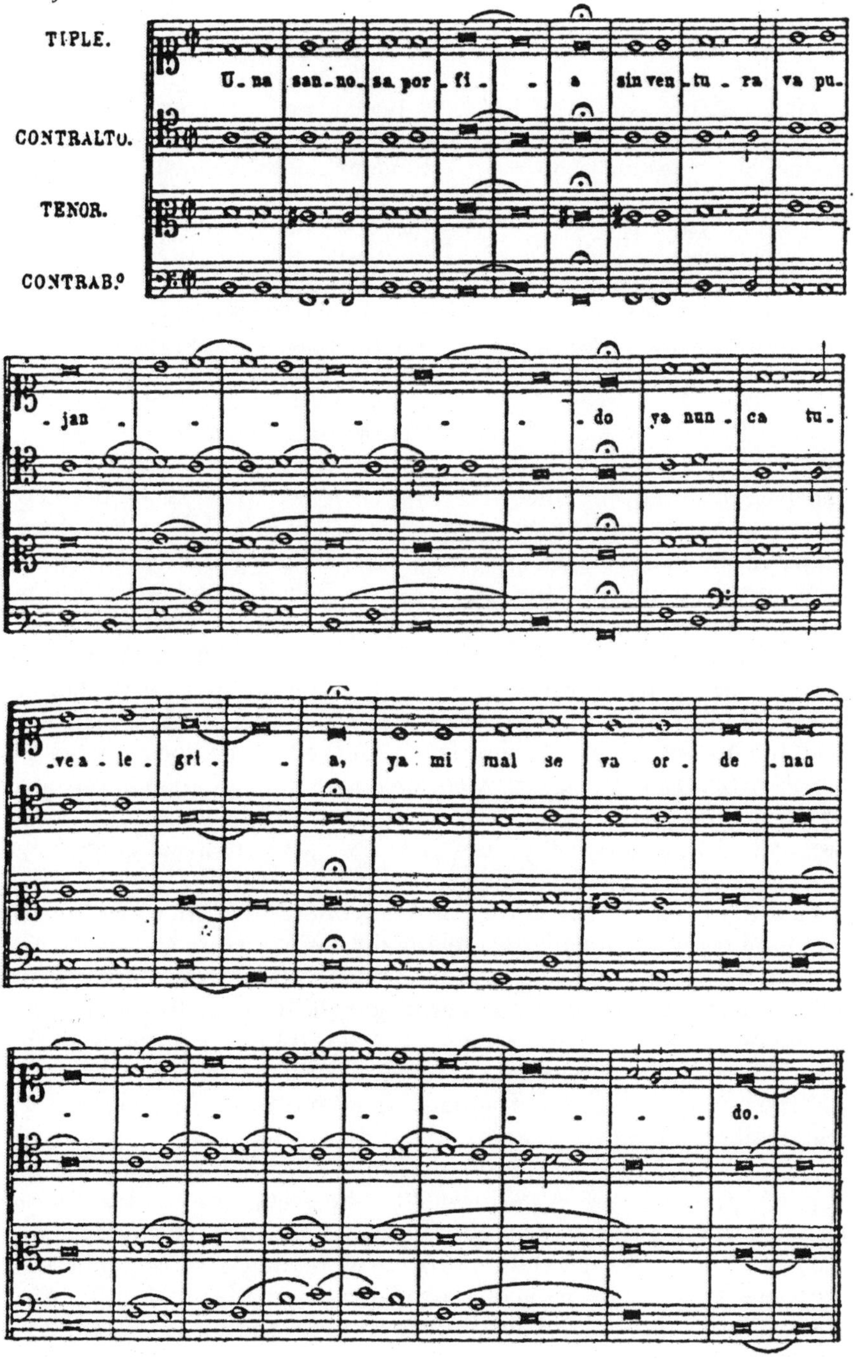

grandes señales había.   great signs appeared.
Estaba la mar en calma,   The sea was calm,
la luna estaba crecida,   the moon was full,
Moro que en tal signo nace   a Moor born under such great signs
no debe decir mentira.   should not tell a lie.
—Y no os la diré, señor   —I would not lie to you, Sire
aunque me cueste la vida,   even at the cost of my life,
que de chico y de muchacho   from my childhood and my youth
mis padres me lo decían: my parents told me
Que mentiras no dijese   that lies I should not say
que era grande villanía.   for it was a great villainy.
Pregunta pués el buen Rey   Ask then, great King,
que la verdad te diría.   for I would tell you the truth.
—¿Qué palacios son aquéllos   —What palaces are those
altos son y relucían?   tall and shining?
—La Alhambra era, señor,   —That was the Alhambra, Sire,
palacio de gran valía . . .   a palace of great worth . . .

A consideration of the historical *romance* "Abenámar," as sung today by the Sephardic Jews of Morocco, allows us to reflect upon the popular perception kept by a people that was also expelled. On March 31, 1492, three months after the final siege of Granada and before Columbus established contact with the New World, Ferdinand and Isabella issued the "Edict of Expulsion" proclaiming that all Jews had to convert to Christianity or leave Spain within four months. More than 8,000 Jewish families are said to have sailed from the port of Cádiz that year. Like the Moors, many of these Jews resettled in the coastal cities of North Africa and the Eastern Mediterranean. Despite their expulsion, they still thought of Spain as their homeland, and they preserved their Spanish culture, especially the music they sang at social gatherings and religious festivals.

Paul Bénichou, in his studies of the Sephardim of Morocco, found that their tradition of ballads is relatively rich in historical *romances*. In general, their tone and style are older than in the modern peninsular versions. One can observe in their usage all the same traits affecting the modern ones: altered endings, gaps, improvisations, and borrowings.[13] But can it not be said that these traits are the property of all oral tradition as it struggles perpetually against oblivion to maintain its value with the passage of time?

The oral Sephardic tradition, according to the informant Clarita Benaim of Melilla and as performed by the group Voice of the Turtle, has preserved only the opening invocation of "Abenámar." It relates the historic moment when the Christian King Juan II, accompanied by the Moor Abenalmao, arrived at the vista of Granada on June 27, 1431, and was able to contemplate for the first time that much coveted city.

Here the Sephardic *romance* presents only the fleeting moment of the contemplation, no more than an episode in the Reconquist that will definitively capture Granada sixty years later via the Catholic kings. In the longer Castilian versions of this ballad, the king "proposes" to the city of Granada in exchange for the already vanquished cities of Cordoba and Sevilla. Granada refuses, and tells him she belongs to the Moors:[14]

Allí habló el rey don Juan.	Then there spoke King John;
bien oiréis lo que decía;	hear well what he said
—Si tú quisieses, Granada,	—Granada, if you wish
contigo me casaría;	indeed would I marry you.
daréte en arras y dote	I'll give you as pledge and dowry
a Córdoba y a Sevilla.	the cities of Cordoba and Seville
—Casada soy, rey don Juan,	—Married I am already, King John,
casada soy, que no viuda;	married, not widowed
el moro que a mí me tiene	the moor to whom I belong
muy grande bien me quería.	well and properly loved me.

What persists through time in a traditional *romance* derives more from the intuitive than the reactive. It is not necessary that the story be told completely and objectively. What is preferred is an emotionally charged, carefully selected communication that is moved by commonly held human values that favor its dramatic presentation. As we listen to the solemn and simple artistic expression of this *romance*, the initial words addressed by the king to Abenámar, "moro de la morería," immediately evoke the entire historical background of the struggle of Christianity and Islam. Christian king and semi-Christian Moor seem to reach a moment of confidence, whereby old recriminations are momentarily forgotten and elements of supernatural signs create a sense of destiny. What would appeal to the Sephardic Jews of Morocco is this sad sense of destiny and the knowledge that what would inevitably be won by force was denied by their rejection of cultural submission, much like Granada's refusal to marry the Christian king. Plaintively sung as it has been by generations of Sephardim, the *romance* "Abenámar" evokes in the Jewish collective memory the tragic circumstances that eventually led to their own expulsion from their Spanish homeland. Understandably, there is great sympathy for the situation of the Moors, who had granted the Jews religious freedom and shared in a similar predicament of exile, loss, and expulsion.

Through the artistic expression of these well-known poems that relate to the end of Moorish rule, we can sense the reciprocal influence of three cultures that fashioned Spain. In the poignant expression of "Tres moricas," whose very form developed from musical Arabic sources, we perceive an Islamic point of view regarding the consequences of Christian acculturation. The stately "Una sañosa porfía" offers further insight into the Christian court's empathy for and fascination with the vanquished Moor. Finally, the moving "Abenámar," as preserved in the folk tradition of the Sephardic Jews of Morocco, provides a glimpse into the mixed sentiments of these people. For all three poems, these bridges of song are powerful articulate vehicles through which cultural history is more audible.

NOTES

1. Even as early as the fourteenth century, Juan Ruiz, in *El Libro de buen amor*, cites no less than thirty-two instruments, many of Arabic origin.

2. References to lyrics and music of the *Cancionero musical de Palacio* are from Asenjo Barbieri's 1890 edition. I number them according to his particular order of the *Cancionero*. Translations are a combination of my own and those provided in liner notes of the recordings.

3. For more on the author, see Stevenson, 1960, 290–291.

4. It was not rare that a peninsular poet sang of passion aroused by either a Jewish or Arabic woman. There are four instances in the *Cancionero musical de Palacio* (nos. 24, 25, 116, and 254).

5. In *Poesía árabe y poesía europea*, Menéndez Pidal (1955) further postulates that the *zéjel* is the prototype of both the refined and popular Castilian lyrics at the end of the Middle Ages.

6. "Este *zéjel* es un eco de muchos siglos de convivencia entre cantores moros y cristianos." Menéndez Pidal, 1955, 42–45.

7. Stevenson (1960) argues that since Arabic melodies were then neither transcribed nor certified, this can never be proven. The Arabist Julián Ribera, however, maintained that the contour of the melody was a prime example of a *zéjel* (Ribera, p. 292). I disagree with the former, in that there is a strong unwritten oral and music tradition in Islamic culture.

8. The *Cancionero musical de Palacio*'s index shows that Encina was originally represented by seventy-five songs, three times as many as any other single composer, so that numerically as well as artistically he dominates the collection.

9. For a full biography on Encina, see R. O. Jones and Carolyn R. Lee (1975).

10. A familiar example of this particular use of melismas at the end of each verse or musical phrase can be found in the *cante jondo* of Flamenco.

11. Michel Bernstein, liner note 17 to the recording *Juan del Enzina: Romances & Villancicos* (1991).

12. Ibid., liner note 13.

13. "La tradición marroquí del romancero judeo español es relativamente rica en romances históricos. . . . En general son de tono y estilo más antiguos (menos modernizados) que las versiones peninsulares modernas. . . . Se observan en esta tradición los mismos rasgos que en toda la tradición moderna: desenlaces alterados (truncos, postizos), lagunas, adiciones mecánicas, contaminación y germinación." Bénichou, 1968, 281.

14. Taken from Díaz Roig, 1988, 61.

BIBLIOGRAPHY

Asenjo Barbieri, Francisco. *Cancionero musical de los siglos XV y XVI*. Madrid: Real Academia de Bellas Artes de San Fernando, 1890.

Bénichou, Paul. *Romancero judeo–español de Marruecos*. Madrid: Editorial Castalia, 1968.

Díaz Roig, Mercedes. *El Romancero Viejo*. Madrid: Cátedra, 1985.

Encina, Juan del. "Una sañosa porfía." In *Juan del Enzina: Romances & Villancicos, Salamanca 1496*. Hesperion XX. Cond. Jordi Savall. Auvidis-Astrée, 1991.

Jones, R. O., and Carolyn R. Lee. *Juan de Encina: Poesía lírica y cancionero musical*. Madrid: Editorial Castalia, 1975.

Menéndez Pidal, Ramón. *Poesía árabe y poesía europea*. 4th ed. Madrid: Espasa-Calpe, 1955.

Ribera, Julián. *Historia de la música árabe medieval y su influencia en la española*. Madrid: Voluntad, 1927.

Stevenson, Robert. *Spanish Music in the Age of Columbus*. The Hague, Netherlands: Martinus Nÿhoff, 1960.

Voice of the Turtle. "Abenámar." Informant, Clarita Benaim (Melilla). *Bridges of Song, Paths of Exile*. Quincentenary Series vol. II. Titanic, 1990.

Waverly Consort. "Improvisations on Tres moricas m'enamoran." Perf. George Mgrdichian. *1492 Music from the Age of Discovery*. Angel Records, 1992.

———. "Tres moricas m'enamoran." Anon./Diego Fernández. *1492 Music from the Age of Discovery*. Angel Records, 1992.

4

The Spanish Muse in Italy: Tirante el Blanco, La vida es sueño, *and* Don Quijote

Pina Palma

To Helene Waysek, in memoriam

In the opening chapter of his landmark work, *La Spagna nella vita italiana durante la Rinascenza*, Benedetto Croce wrote that his book was to be a study of Spanish influences on Italy.[1] A point the critic made immediately clear was that with his work he wanted to "start shaking off that kind of laziness which can be observed in historians and intellectuals every time the topic of Spanish influences in Italy comes up."[2] In the sixty years since Croce made this assertion, there have been copious studies on the literary influence that Italy has had on Spain. The converse is not true. With few exceptions, modern scholarship persists in assessing only the varying degrees to which Spanish literature absorbed and incorporated Italian influences. This scholarship ignores and even belittles the role played by Spanish literature in the development of its Italian counterpart. It implicitly perpetuates the attitude epitomized by Boccaccio, who, in the letter accompanying his *De casibus virorum illustriorum*, affirmed, "Hispani semibarbari et efferati homines."[3]

That Spain was the dominant influence in Italy even before the Middle Ages is a fact long documented by historians. For the scope of this chapter, however, the period of particular literary interest begins with the arrival in Naples of Alphonse of Aragon in 1420 and the establishment of his court. With this began the renewed influx of Spanish customs into Italy. Unlike his father, who had prided himself on "aristocratic ignorance," Alphonse distinguished himself with his sponsorship of arts and letters.[4] This new attitude erased the image of un-cultivated arrogance that had heretofore burdened the Spanish in Italy. Beyond this, it was at the court of Alphonse that the literary and lin-guistic "fusion" of the two cultures took place. A contributing element to this fusion was that only Spanish was spoken at court, since the king was not fluent in Italian. Because the Spanish language was the coin of the realm, it became the language in which the popular litera-ture of the time was written. This state of affairs continued under Alphonse's heir, Ferrante, who was not the literate monarch his father had been and obliged his poets and intellectuals to write mostly mili-tary and political treatises, deemphasizing their poetic works. None-theless, the Aragonese court, through the concatenation of Spanish and Italian literary events, became the center for the Neapolitan poetry that developed in the fifteenth century.[5] The Spanish "colonization" soon expanded to Rome. There, the installation of Alphonse Boda (Borgia) as Pope Callisto III made the hegemony of Spanish culture over Italian an accomplished fact.

Clearly, with the control of the papal state came the infiltration of Spanish customs in Rome, just as had happened in Naples.[6] Callisto was succeeded by his nephew Rodrigo, the notorious Alexander VI, in whose papal court Spanish became the official language, as it had in the Neapolitan court. This is attested to by the fact that Cardinal Pietro Bembo, the most eloquent advocate for an Italian language modeled on the idiom of Boccaccio and Petrarca, had himself taken the time to learn Spanish. In his *Prose della volgar lingua*, Bembo did not hide a certain disdain for this idiom that was permeating the Italian language, although he did admit that both men and women in Rome were imi-tating Spanish terminology, accents, and mannerisms as a fashionable practice: "Poiche' alle Spagne a servire a il pontefice a Roma i loro popoli mandate aveano, e Valenza il colle vaticano occupato avea, ai nostri uomini e alle nostre donne oggimai altre voci, altri accenti avere in bocca non piace che spagnuoli."[7]

With the marriage of Alexander's daughter Lucrezia to Alphonse d'Este in 1502, the Spanish cultural infiltration of the Italian peninsula had effectively taken root to such an extent that it could no longer be thought of as a limited and contained phenomenon. Obviously, the Italian literary landscape of this period fully reflected the sociopolitical environment, making it inevitable that Italian poets would incorpo-rate in their works those Spanish influences and customs that were already part and parcel of their lives.

An examination of the influence of Spanish on Italian literature of this period can begin with Ariosto's *Orlando Furioso*. It is common knowledge that Ariosto wrote his epic poem at the court of the Este family, where he had access to the extensive ducal library. There the poet undoubtedly read Martorell's *Tirante el Blanco* in its Castilian translation.[8] This fact is the undisputable link between Martorell's text and Ariosto's famous Canto V, in which the Italian poet recreated in its entirety, with only minor modifications, the episode of Tirante witnessing Carmesina's alleged betrayal.[9]

In Canto V Ariosto recounts the vicissitudes of Ariodante, who loves (and is loved by) Ginevra. That Ariodante is also highly esteemed by the king inspires the rancor of Polinesso, Duke of Albany and Ariodante's erstwhile friend. Polinesso, who secretly aspires to become the king's son-in-law by marrying Ginevra, orchestrates a scheme to convince Ariodante that she is unfaithful to him (V, 38).[10] With the help of Dalinda, one of Ginevra's maidens with whom he is having a love affair, Polinesso is able to convince Ariodante that contrary to what Ginevra might have told him, at night she awaits Polinesso's embraces. Instructed by Polinesso and unseen by Ginevra, Dalinda dresses in Ginevra's clothes and walks out onto a balcony at night to await her lover. Polinesso arrives and embraces and kisses her profusely in the manner to which, given their amorous relationship, Dalinda is accustomed. Ariodante, observing from a distance, as Polinesso has advised him to do, does not realize that the woman clothed in Ginevra's finery is Dalinda. Deceived by appearances, he takes the embraces of Dalinda and Polinesso to be evidence of Ginevra's faithlessness. Humiliated, he disappears and is believed to have killed himself, while Ginevra is condemned to death by her father. Only if a knight should come forth and attest to her innocence in a duel with Ariodante's brother will she be spared. Having discovered Polinesso's hoax, Dalinda by chance recounts the plot to the knight Rinaldo, who takes up Ginevra's cause and kills Polinesso in a duel. Her honor restored, Ginevra is freed and reunited with Ariodante.

The seeds of this story are undoubtedly rooted in Martorell's *Tirante el Blanco*. With a more intriguing twist, and also with a magisterial play on the names of the characters, in the original version the deception is planned by a woman, la Viuda Reposada. This woman, a widow whose name is charged with the paradoxical ambiguity of "well rested" and "lying down," evokes at once two contradictory images. The first is the image of old age and, consequently, of the amorous apathy that is usually associated with it. The second is of the sexual energy of a woman who has been deprived of any amorous relationship and who now is stirred by the emotions she senses around her. The Viuda Reposada is an attendant of the emperor's daughter, and secretly aspires to Tirante's love. Jealous of the feelings Tirante nurtures for the young princess, Carmesina, she undertakes a series of maneuvers to attract Tirante to herself: "No me maravillo, señor capitán, si el mundo quereys conquistar, que a mí teneys subjeta y captiva. Que la fortuna enemiga de paz, tiene sojuzgado a mi flaco y débil coraçón de puro amor que a vuestra señoría tengo."[11]

Relying upon the old *courtois* language—the only language she can shamelessly use to achieve her goal—she portrays herself as a powerless prisoner of Tirante's amorous indifference. When her ploys fail, she decides to give him "proof" of Carmesina's infidelity, enlisting the help of the guileless Plazer de mi Vida (Pleasure of My Life), another of the princess's maidens. (Here we have another example of Martorell's play on names. This is not an insignificant detail, for it adds an element of humor and subtlety to the rigid ambiance of the courtly ideal. While the Viuda's name, with its contrasting images of old age and reawakened libido, portrays her as torn between physical needs and societal constraints, Plazer de mi Vida's name evokes youthfulness and joy.)

At the arranged time, the Viuda awakens the sleeping Carmesina and under false pretenses leads her naked into the garden. Instructed by the Viuda and playing her part as in a child's game, Plazer de mi Vida appears, disguised as the old black gardener. Recognizing her friend, Carmesina readily welcomes her. Playfully embracing and kissing each other, both Carmesina and Placer de mi Vida continue their innocent amusement. For the hidden and unknowing Tirante, however, the scene he watches confirms the Viuda's insinuations of Carmesina's treachery. Tirante's incredulity becomes horrifying belief when he witnesses Carmesina entering the gardener's hut, accompanied by Plazer de mi Vida, still disguised as the old man. The similarities between Martorell's and Ariosto's plots are so numerous that Martorell's text is in all likelihood the source of Ariosto's episode.

In addition to this, other less conspicuous but just as compelling parts of the *Tirante* found their way into Ariosto's work. An example is the story of the Bella Agnes (the Beautiful Agnes), at whose service Tirante places himself when still learning the rules governing chivalric life (LX). Two attributes make Agnes well-known at court. The first is her beauty. The second is her generosity. She is described as a lady always willing to give to others those things she possesses and which others may desire: "Si estava vestida de ropas que valian una cibdad, y si ella traya joyas o otras cosas, no recibia penas en darlas: tanto era de gentil condicion" (LX). For this reason, when asked for the pin she wears on her breast as a token to the knight who is placing himself at her service, the Bella Agnes does not hesitate. Not only does she comply, but with a gesture that epitomizes her magnanimity, she emboldens Tirante to remove the jewel with his own hands. Agnes's apparent audacity, however, shatters the old courtly ideal. As she allows Tirante to remove the pin, she no longer embodies "the angelic creature" of courtly tradition. Instead, she becomes a woman who can be "touched" by the man requesting to be at her service. For his brazen act Tirante is confronted immediately by Agnes's aspiring lover, the wealthy Señor de las Villas Yermas, who demands the restitution of the jewel, claiming that it can belong only to him, since he has served her well since his youth. Tirante refuses to yield the pin. They duel, and the young, inexperienced Tirante kills the older man.

At the news of his death, Agnes grieves for her lost suitor, but explains that though he pursued her for seven years, she never acknowledged his valiant efforts to win her love. Moreover, she is of a higher lineage than he, being the daughter of the Marquis de Berri and related to the queen by birth. Her explanation is in sharp contrast with her name. In fact, while she is defined as beautiful and generous, her past conduct has proven her insensitive and offensive toward the man who loved her. Thus, the wealthy Señor de las Villas Yermas, whose name literally means "barren domains," becomes the personification of amorous defeat.

With the image of infertility accompanying the unrequited lover throughout his brief appearance in the *Tirante*, Martorell can ridicule the fundamental rules governing courtly love. In fact, with his unchivalrous name, the Señor de las Villas Yermas is presented from the beginning as a character whose ambitions are shadowed by defeat. Acting according to the rules of the old social system, he expects to reap the fruits of his labors and become Agnes's undisputed love. Yet the system within which he acts has changed. Unattuned to the new modalities in which love answers to the individual's preferences rather than to a set of rules, the mature knight is doomed to fail from the onset. He finds death at the hands of a young and to a certain degree inexperienced Tirante, who has learned the rules of the new system and can refuse his rival's demand for Agnes's jewel. Defeated both in love and in combat, vanquished emotionally and physically, the Señor de las Villas Yermas becomes the victim of a new code of love that has as its correlative his own impulsive and jealous anger.

This episode reverberates vividly in a crucial part of Ariosto's poem. Throughout the *Furioso*, the Italian poet warns his readers about the excesses of amorous jealousy. While on the one hand he admits that it is an essential ingredient of love, on the other hand he reveals its disastrous effects. The best illustration of this—one that directly corresponds to the Tirante incident—is found in the scene depicting Orlando's discovery of Angelica's gift to the shepherd at whose house she has stayed with her lover, Medoro. Seeing the shepherd wearing the precious bracelet he himself has given her as a token of his love, Orlando recognizes his amorous defeat. Above all, he is grieved by the fact that his gift has been meaningless for Angelica. This proof of her indifference triggers Orlando's madness (XXIII, 121).

The consuming jealousy that erodes Orlando ultimately destroys the Christian hero both emotionally and physically, albeit for a limited time, while the unpretentious Medoro, much like Tirante after the duel with Villas Yermas, receives Angelica's unequivocal love. In Ariosto's adaptation of the Castilian story, the social discrepancy between the lovers does not carry the same importance as in Martorell's work. Thus, while Agnes de Berri regrets her suitor's death but acknowledges that their different social backgrounds did not make him a suitable husband, in Ariosto's world love disdains all barriers. Accordingly, in a fascinating deviation from its source, the Italian poet allows the royal Angelica to consummate her love with the simple Medoro (XXIII, 120).

Traces of Spanish influence are not limited to Italian works of the sixteenth century. They can be found as well during the following century in the works of Giacinto Andrea Cicognini (1606–1660), one of the first and most enthusiastic imitators of Spanish dramatists. Cicognini's works covered all genres popular in his time: dramas, comedies, and religious representations. During the period in which he wrote, the Italian national and original theater was the Commedia dell'Arte, which had fallen into a repetitive repertoire, limited to common images and motifs. Spanish rule and the predominance of Spanish culture injected new life into the dormant Italian theater. Thus, the "comedia nueva" soon found a whole generation of eager Italian imitators.[12] This type of theater was differentiated from its antecedents and revitalized by an innovative form in which two or more plots unfolded and intertwined to reach a final resolution.

In the introduction to his "Giasone," Cicognini explained the philosophy underlying his work in a manner highly reminiscent of Lope de Vega's *Arte nuevo de hacer comedias*.[13] Following the rules set by Spanish playwrights and patterning his works on theirs, he boldly proclaimed that his goal was to please and delight the public.[14] In his fine investigation, Rosario Verde shows how Cicognini's *Le Gelosie Fortunate del Prencipe don Rodrigo* (Bologna, 1701) was based upon Calderon's *No siempre lo peor es cierto*.[15] In addition, other works by the Italian author point to Spanish plays as their models. Outstanding among these are *La Marlene overo il maggior mostro del mondo*, which imitated Calderon's *El mayor monstruo los celos*, and *La vita e' sogno*, which unambiguously replicated its Spanish equivalent.

Although Cicognini's plays revolved around the same plot, effectively reproducing the model, they were not mere translations of Calderon's originals; rather, they subtly changed the model to suit the Italian public. Following the customs of his times, when the representation and imitation of Spanish works were the norm, Cicognini "Italianized" his version of *La vita e' sogno* through numerous details. Thus, in his version the first striking divergence from the Spanish source is the presence of Arlichino and Pantalone, characters taken directly from the Commedia dell'Arte. In Cicognini's work Arlichino substitutes for Clarín, while Pantalone becomes a servant at court. Given their places in the tradition of the Commedia dell'Arte, these two characters infuse the drama with an unspoken levity absent in the Spanish work. An example of this is the scene that depicts Arlichino asking Sigismondo what he finds to be the most beautiful thing at court. The prince immediately answers, "Women," whom he equates to "small heavens."[16] This exchange does not exist in the Spanish version.

Of the two dramas, the Italian one is substantially shorter and fails to capture the poetic tapestry woven by Calderon's skillful hands. Nevertheless, the Italian playwright, unpreoccupied with finding for every action an origin outside human nature, left his mark both in the scenes themselves and in the touches with which he colored the various parts of his work. A clear example is found in the scene in which Pantalone informs Sigismondo that Stella is Astolfo's promised bride. To this the Italian Sigismondo immediately replies, "Not any more." And when the zealous Pantalone insists that Sigismondo show more respect for his cousin, Sigismondo throws Pantalone from the balcony, killing him. Sigismondo later explains this violence to the bewildered Astolfo with a simple and pungent remark: "I tried, I was able, and he flew." With three verbs Sigismondo affirms his responsibility for the act, emphasizing his princely authority with the repetition of the pronoun "I." According to Sigismondo's logic, it was Pantalone's inability to submit to this authority that brought him his death.

Cicognini believed that human reason must prevail over the evils brought on by destiny; and that even when destiny exerted a destructive power over man's life, it could not change man's feelings.[17] This idea pervades the scene in which Clotaldo reveals that he is Rosaura's father. In Calderon's work the episode is developed as a simple, linear progression of the drama. Learning that Rosaura's new social status makes her immediately eligible to be his wife, the highborn Astolfo simply affirms, "Pues siendo así, mi palabra cumpliré."[18] In the Italian work, on the contrary, Astolfo's discourse is more complex and attests to Cicognini's belief in a realistic concept of life that reflects the Italian mindset. Hence, at Clotaldo's admission of paternity, Astolfo replies that he will marry Rosaura if Clotaldo marries her mother, thus keeping his own promise to the long-abandoned Violante.

In reweaving the Spanish story, Cicognini's work, which borrowed so much from the Spanish model, set the pace for a new Italian theater. Moreover, his works as a whole showed a preoccupation with love that went beyond the fleshly pleasures. Unlike his contemporary Marinisti, Cicognini richly imbued his protagonists with a sense of reality that plainly reflected the character of his people. Fashioning his personages to reflect the Italian identity, Cicognini paved the way to the artistic realism which later dominated and shaped the comedies of Goldoni, an artist who studied him enthusiastically.

The eighteenth century offers another great illustration of the integration of Spanish literature into the Italian literary landscape. Giovanni Meli's (1740–1815) *Don Chisciotti e Sanciu Panza* is a mock-heroic poem of twelve cantos, written between 1785 and 1786 and published for the first time in 1787.[19] In this work, the main characters of the Spanish novel undergo an impassioned metamorphosis. Interestingly, it was this work that, along with Cervantes's original masterpiece, gave Pirandello the literary background for his celebrated essay on "L'umorismo."[20] In Meli's work the first conspicuous change from the Spanish novel is that Sanciu's name appears in the title. What is even more important is that in Meli's epic, Sanciu, unlike his master, is able to learn from experience. He becomes a wise man and a pragmatist, guided by the facts rather than by the universal chivalric rules that impel and ultimately thwart don Chisciotti. It is Sanciu's earnest practical sense which allows him, even early in the poem, to muse:

he whose eyes with science were so filled,
saw giants there; no windmill there at all.
Should I have trusted him or my own senses?
Which of the two would have been less deceptive?
No matter how I think and ponder this,
I still remain perplexed and full of doubt
(. . .)
it was based on faith not on intellect. (IV, 36)

Later Sanciu explains this dilemma:

In spite of such apparent blundering,
that one could almost touch with one's own hands,
his speeches carried such authority
that everything he said seemed pure truth.
It was perhaps the greatness of his worth
or the result of my stupidity,
his words had a virtue, oh so great,
I swallowed every blunder, hook and bait. (IV, 50)

These remarks are imbued with a profound respect as well as an intuitive sense of ambiguity toward Don Chisciotti's actions. They attest to Sanciu's recognition of his master's precarious understanding of reality and clearly illustrate the manner in which the Sicilian Sanciu evolves into a socially conscious savant. Thus, as Cipolla elegantly asserts, "The two works must necessarily be seen as two different manifestations of the same archetype."[21]

In Meli's poem, Sanciu explains in retrospect that the reason he sought learning was that he wanted to be an educated governor of the island his master had promised to him: "Because a governor, so I presumed, should not be stupid or a brutish lot" (IV, 27). Unlike Sanciu himself, who was immersed, at times even submerged, in the boundless sea of don Chisciotti's visionary world, the hypothetical island represented an enticing *terra ferma* upon which to base his desire for self-improvement.

Sanciu's explanation of his absorption with don Chisciotti's words evokes on the one hand a qualitative difference between the master's illusory authority and its intrinsic worth, and on the other hand the squire's declared simplicity juxtaposed with his desire to seek truth. In establishing this binary correspondence between the world of illusion and sophistication and the world of reality and simplicity, Sanciu unearths the fundamental principle that governs his experience. Don Chisciotti's chivalrous world, one of rigid hierarchical control, holds little relevance for the lowly servant, for whom it is removed and impenetrable. Conversely, Sanciu's simplicity encompasses a world that is recognizable to others, complete with its faults and injustices and therefore the world of "collective truth."

Meli himself was a physician who recognized the immense dichotomy in Sicilian society, with its rich and poor placed at extreme poles of the social strata. Realizing the indifference of the aristocrats to the plight of the lower class, Meli advocated social reforms that would transform Sicily into a more equitable society. Thus, his creation of Sanciu reflects his own belief of the power of fate, and for this reason Sanciu affirms, "One thing for sure is evident, that is, if I don't work and sweat, I do not eat, but others sit and eat contentedly" (V, 48). Furthermore, Sanciu's skepticism with regard to his master's chivalric ideals is revealed plainly in his assertion that only for the fortunate few aristocrats is labor not an encumbrance:

In any town, except for two or four
or five or seven persons at the most
who can think straight, the rest is simply mob
and plays no part in the community;
the mob just follows others thoughtlessly,
nor are there any men who reason well.
Born to be crowds, the purpose of the masses,
consists of eating fruits, and meats
and grasses. (XII, 104)

With this awareness, fruit of his experience, the Sicilian Sanciu becomes the true hero of the story, one "remaining always poor, correct and wise," admired as well by his townspeople for the adventures he can recount (XII, 102). In sharp contrast to the wisdom with which

Sanciu is rewarded, and which he has acquired at the expense of his master's illusory world, the erstwhile hero who has presumed to remedy all of the world's evil dies ignominiously of a hernia (XII, 83), a most undignified death, while trying to straighten a misshapen rowan tree.

These few examples, works of Ariosto, Cicognini, and Meli taken from different literary periods, illustrate that Spanish and Italian literature did not develop in isolation from one another. At a time when Spain controlled Italy's political machinery, its church, and, through language, its very culture, Italian writers embraced the new models, fashioning them for their own public. Indeed, the works I have analyzed, all of which owe a profound debt to Spanish literature, have themselves influenced the works of such twentieth-century Italian authors as Pirandello, Sciascia, Vittorini, and, more recently, Bonaviri. For those who choose to ignore Croce's exhortation to explore the lines of Spanish influences in Italy, these few examples may not be convincing. For those willing to explore the myriad possibilities, however, the three works I have presented may serve as the beginning.

NOTES

1. Benedetto Croce, *La Spagna nella vita italiana durante la Rinascenza* (Bari: Laterza, 1917).

2. "Lunghi periodi di intensi amoreggiamenti, seguiti da rotture e ripulse; uno scambio di esperienze e dati, testi; e poi zone bianche di disinteresse ostentato; ora un consegnarsi da discenti ed imitatori di modi e di mode, e ora un dispregio evidente; forse tutti i rapporti interletterari sono altrettanto nevrotici di quelli tra Italia e Spagna." Maria Grazia Profeti, "Importare letteratura: Italia e Spagna." *Belfagor* 41 (1986): 365–379.

3. Giovanni Boccaccio, *De casibus virorum illustriorum* (Rome: Johan Schurener, 1478). See also G. Boccaccio, *Tutte le opera*, a aura di Vittore Branca. (Milano: Mondadori, 1983), 4.

4. "De rebus a Ferdin. Arag. Rege gestis," in *Rerum Hispan. Script.* (Francf., 1579), II, 1071–1072. Valla describes Alphonse's father Ferdinand as "parum excultus literis," although "ut illo soeculo et ut in hispana nobilitate non indoctus" (cf. Capitolo II, n. 1, in *La Spagna nella vita italiana durante la Rinascenza*).

5. Paolo Savi-Lopez, "Lirica spagnuola in Italia nel secolo XV," in *Trovatori e poeti. Studi di lirica antica* (Milano: Sandron, 1906), 189.

6. Paolo da Ponte, "Gregorius," in *Storia della citta' di Roma*, ital. trans. V, 177–178. Describing Rome in 1458, he wrote, "Non vi sono se non catalani." Similarly, Farinelli in *Rassegna bibliografica di letteratura italiana*, II, 138, describes the manner in which in 1455 for the first time in Rome a *corrida* was held in the amphitheater Flavio in honor of the pope.

7. Pietro Bembo, *Prose della volgar lingua* (Milano: Edizioni Sonzogno, 1880), 157. The prominence of Spanish as the language of fashion is also attested by its presence in the comedies of Pietro Aretino. See *La cortigiana* II, 4, 6, V, 6, 7;

La talanta I, 1; and *L'ipocrito* V, 25. See also B. Castiglione, *Il libro del cortigiano,* I, 34, II, 37.

8. The *Tirante* was written in Catalan by Joanot Martorell and completed by Martí Joan de Galba. It was first published in Valencia in 1490. From a 1497 edition an anonymous author made a Castilian translation that was published in Valladolid in 1511. In 1538 Lelio Manfredi translated it into Italian (Martín de Riquer, *Tirante el Blanco: Versión castellana impresa in Valladolid en 1511 de la obra de Joanot Martorell y Martí Joan de Galba*). The first edition of the *Furioso* appeared in 1516. Ariosto therefore was familiar with the Castilian translation owned by Isabella d'Este. See Ludovico Ariosto, *Orlando furioso,* ed. Cesare Segre (Milano: Mondadori, 1976), cf. Canto V, n. 14.

9. As early as 1900 Pio Rajna detected similarities and links between the two episodes. See *Le fonti dell'Orlando Furioso* (Firenze: Sansoni, 1900). See also Paolo Valesio, "Genealogy of a Staged Scene," *Yale Italian Studies* 1 (1980): 5–31.

10. Ludovico Ariosto, *Orlando Furioso,* edizione integra a cura di Nicola Zingarelli (Milano: Hoepli, 1954). All citations are from this edition.

11. Joanot Martorell, *Tirante el Blanco,* ed. M. de Riquer (Barcelona: Planeta, 1990). All citations are from this edition.

12. Rosario Verde, *Studi sull'imitazione spagnuola del teatro italiano del seicento: Giacomo Andrea Cicognini* (Catania: Giannotta, 1912), xiii.

13. Lope de Vega, *Arte nuevo de hacer comedias: La discreta enamorada* (Madrid: Espasa-Calpa, 1967).

14. "Io compongo per mero capriccio: il mio capriccio non ha altro fine che dilettare: l'apportare diletto appresso di me non e' altro che incontrare il genio e il gusto di chi ascolta." Giacomo Andrea Cicognini, "Introduction to *Giasone,*" in Verde, *Studi.*

15. Verde, *Studi,* 26.

16. Giacomo Andrea Cicognini, "La vita e' sogno," in *Le nouveau théatre Italien ou le récueil general des comedies* (Paris: Briasson, 1728).

17. Verde, *Studi,* 26.

18. Pedro Calderón de la Barca, *La vida es sueño,* ed. Ciriaco Morón (Madrid: Catedra, 1982), *tercera jornada,* XIV, versos 3277–3278, 3287.

19. Nino Borsellino, "Don Chisciotte di Sicilia. Note su un poema di Meli," in *Convegno internazionale sul tema: Italia e Spagna nella cultura del 700* (Rome: Accademia Nazionale dei Lincei, 1992), 135–143.

20. Giovanni Meli, *Don Chisciotti e Sanciu Panza,* trans. G. Cipolla (Ottawa: Biblioteca di quaderni d'italianistica, 1986). All citations are from this edition.

21. G. Cipolla, "Introduction," in ibid., xxiii.

BIBLIOGRAPHY

Alvarez Barrientos, J. "La experiencia teatral de Leandro Hernandez de Moratín en Italia." In *Convegno internazionale sul tema: Italia e Spagna nella cultura del 700.* Roma: Accademia Nazionale dei Lincei, 1992.

Ariosto, Ludovico. *Orlando Furioso.* Milano: Hoepli, 1947.

Bembo, Pietro. *Prose della volgar lingua.* Milano: Edizioni Sonzogno, 1880.

Boccaccio, Giovanni. *De casibus virorum illustriorum.* Rome: Johan Schurener, 1478.

Borsellino, Nino. "Don Chisciotte di Sicilia. Note su un poema di Meli." In *Convegno internazionale sul tema: Italia e Spagna nella cultura del 700*. Roma: Accademia Nazionale dei Lincei,1992.

Calderón de la Barca, Pedro. *La vida es sueño*, ed. Ciriaco Morón. Madrid: Catedra, 1982.

Cicognini, Giacinto Andrea. "La vita e' sogno." In *Le nouveau théatre Italien ou le récueil general des comedies*. Paris: Briasson, 1728.

Croce, Benedetto. *Aneddoti di varia letteratura*. Napoli: Ricciardi, 1942.

———. *La Spagna nella vita italiana durante la Rinascenza*. Bari: Laterza, 1917.

Farinelli, Arturo. "Di un antico romanzo spagnuolo relativo alla storia di Napoli." In *Rassegna bibliografica di letteratura italiana*, 1894, n. 5, II, 138.

Martorell, Joanot. *Tirante el Blanco*, ed. M. de Riquer. Barcelona: Planeta, 1990.

Meli, Giovanni. *Don Chisciotti e Sanciu Panza*, trans. G. Cipolla. Ottawa: Biblioteca di quaderni d'italianistica, 1986.

Profeti, Maria Grazia. "Importare letteratura: Italia e Spagna." *Belfagor* 41 (1986): 365–379.

Rajna, Pio. *Le fonti dell'Orlando Furioso*. Firenze: Sansoni, 1900.

Savi-Lopez, Paolo. "Lirica spagnuola in Italia nel secolo XV." In *Trovatori e poeti. Studi sulla lirica antica*. Milano: Sandron, 1906.

Valesio, Paolo. "Genealogy of a Staged Scene." *Yale Italian Studies* 1 (1980): 5–31.

Verde, Rosario. *Studi sull'imitazione spagnuola nel teatro italiano del seicento: Giacomo Andrea Cicognini*. Catania: Giannotta, 1912.

5

The Golden Age Revisited in Twentieth-Century Art Songs

Anna Bartos

There is nothing mysterious about the use of Golden Age poetry by twentieth-century composers of art songs. It is human nature to be fascinated with the past. The past is largely responsible for defining the present; it gives us insight into ourselves and it inspires us as creators of art. In Hispanic culture especially, music and poetry have been closely intertwined for centuries, and their impact has been felt far beyond their borders. So extraordinary is their abundance that more than 460 solo songs with instrumental accompaniment are found in Spanish tablature books, or *cancioneros* (collections of songs) of the sixteenth century, making Spain one of the leading musical nations of the Renaissance. In fact, the emergence of the solo voice accompanied by a stringed continuo, so masterfully handled by the Spaniards, was the forerunner of the "new style of music" of the Florentine *camerata* toward the latter part of the century.[1] In these early Castilian songs we find an intense interest in musical, literary, and human elements, and a charm and variety of expression seldom equalled. The verses of such poets as Garcilaso de la Vega and Juan del Encina vividly and intimately describe the Spanish people in every aspect of their lives, touching us even now with the depth of their joys and sorrows.

Long before the Golden Age per se, the influence and importance of Sephardic and Arabic culture in the Spanish world provides an inexhaustible subject. The story of the Sephardim begins with the Arab conquest of Spain in the early eighth century. For more than 500 years under the Moslem kings, they embarked upon an unprecedented cultural activity with Arabic as their primary medium and wrote exquisite Hebrew poetry adapting the complex prosody of Arab poets. For example, the astoundingly versatile Samuel ibn Naghdela (993–1056) was a linguist, mathematician, philosopher, advisor to the king, and general in the royal army, as well as a Hebrew poet and a patron of poets and scholars. He was not alone. Other notable poet-musicians included Solomon ibn Gabirol (1021–1069), Judah Halevi (1086–1145), and Moses ibn Ezra (1080–1139), whose "Divan" was set for voice and guitar in recent times by Mario Castelnuovo-Tedesco (1895–1968). Many of these works left Spain with the expulsion of the Jews in 1492 and over the years took new forms, both literary and musical, in the diaspora.[2] So has the music of Spain's Golden Age evoked numerous musical compositions, especially during the twentieth century. Let us look now at some of these songs, the poets who created them, and the modern composers who gave them new life.

• • •

"Nani, nani" is an anonymous Sephardic lullaby sung by a mother who is anxiously awaiting her husband's return from the fields, all the while fearing that he has been unfaithful to her. The story evolves amid the interspersed refrain "Ay, dúrmite, mi alma" [Go to sleep, my darling child; so some day you'll be big and grown up. Soon your father will be home].[3] (See Figure 5.1.) When her husband arrives, claiming that he is exhausted from having worked on his land, she accuses him of having spent the time instead with another woman. He sings: "Open the door, my lady":

—Ay, avriméx, mi dama,
Avriméx la puerta,
Que vengo cansado
De arar las huertas.

And she responds: "No, I won't. You've been with your new love":

—Avrir no vos avro,
No veníx cansado,
Sino que veníx
De onde nuevo amor.

Comparing herself to her rival, she complains that the other woman is no more beautiful nor worthy than she, nor even does she wear more jewelry—she isn't even richer!

Ni es más hermoza,
Ni es más valida,
Ni ella llevava
Más de las mis joyas.

Figure 5.1
"Nani, nani"

This song seems to be the ancestor of a *villancico* by the Cuban composer Joaquín Nin y Castellanos (1879–1949) (*villancicos* are short strophic songs of varied subject matter, although often associated with Christmas). Dedicated to the renowned singer Conchita Supervia, it provides an original melody, unlike Nin's other works, which were primarily arrangements of ancient tunes. Here Nin captures the essence of Sephardic music in its melismatic passages (successions of embellishments around a single note), and its lamentative melody in minor key, while consciously imitating the highly contrapuntal instrumental line of Renaissance music.

A composer and pianist, the Havana-born Joaquín Nin wrote for the harpsichord, piano, violin, and voice, devoting himself especially to the old *cancioneros* comprised mostly of amatory, historical, and elegiac *villancicos*. These short songs are also dance related, religious, or specifically associated with church festivals. A good example of these is his setting of the Christmas song, "Un niño nace de flores," dedicated to the Christ child, whom he likens to flowers and the purity of love:

Un niño nace de flores,
todo vestido de amores,
Es de las flores la flor,
Y el amor de los amores.[4]

Here we find the popular *verso octosilábico* (eight-syllable lines with stress on the seventh), in a *rima asonante* (rhyme of the penultimate vowels), a common form of Golden Age poetry. Nin's *villancico*, as well as other early to middle twentieth-century songs utilizing ancient texts, demonstrates the composer's intent to emulate at least in part the melodic lines and rhythmic elements of Renaissance music, and to preserve the poetry in a manner faithful to its original versification. Many of Nin's works have been translated and performed in French.

• • •

Fray Luis de León (1537–1591) and Garcilaso de la Vega (1501–1536) provide the poetic source for our next two songs by the contemporary Mexican composer Salvador Moreno. Fray Luis de León, who was born in Belmonte in the province of Cuenca, Castile, was a descendant of Jewish converts to Christianity. He was a poet, Biblical translator, didactic writer, and indisputably one of the creators of the Spanish Renaissance. Insisting on the primacy of the Hebrew text in his translation and commentary of the *Song of Songs*, he was denounced by the Dominican Inquisition for being critical of the Church and spent four years in prison before he was finally pronounced innocent. Leader of the so-called Salamanca school of poets, Fray Luis was influenced by Horace and Virgil and had the ability to reconcile pagan and Christian teachings in a style that was concise, passionately eloquent, intellectual, and spiritual, yet direct and personal.

Fray Luis's poem, "Cortar me puede el hado," is a tribute to the Virgin Mary, in which he dedicates his life to her, saying that without her he is worthy of nothing. To be unmindful of her, he writes, would be a disservice to himself: "Olvídeme de mí si te olvidare." The versification is a combination of lines of eleven and seven syllables in a *rima consonante* (rhyme of both the vowel and the accompanying consonants) and the musical rendition is in duple time and ternary form. As with Nin, Moreno's treatment displays simple melodic and instrumental lines, in this case reminiscent of a hymn tune, but with a final embellishing melisma. His Mexican heritage is heard distinctly in the sixteenth grace notes that precede each section, recalling perhaps the sound of the *huehetl* (Aztec flute).

Garcilaso de la Vega was of a noble family of Toledo and spent most of his early life at the court of Charles V, where he received a humanistic education. Here indeed was the incarnation of the Renaissance courtly poet-soldier. By arrangement, he married the high-born Elena de Zúñiga, but he fell in love with a Portuguese woman, Isabel Freyre, to whom he addressed his greatest love poems. In 1532 he was banished to the Danube, and then to Naples, for disobedience to his king, but he soon returned to the monarch's graces and was fatally injured while leading an attack on a fortified village in France. Garcilaso's work is important not only for its intrinsic beauty but because it introduced the so-called Italianate style into Spain, with its Petrarchan courtly love tradition and its stylistic innovations.

Salvador Moreno's setting of Garcilaso's "Nadie puede ser dichoso," in *Dos canciones breves*, is in a rather light-hearted Allegretto 6/8 time. The message is simple: No one can be truly happy or even desolate, my lady, unless he has beheld you. In other words, no one can have experienced life without having known your charm.

Nadie puede ser dichoso,
señora, ni desdichado,
sino que os haya mirado.

Moreno (1916–1999), who was born in Orizaba, Mexico, of Spanish parents, resided principally in Barcelona since 1955. He wrote mostly vocal music, several volumes of which have been published in Mexico and Spain.

• • •

Juan del Encina (1469–1539) was a musician, poet, and playwright often called the "Patriarch of the Spanish Theater." His work was a synthesis of medieval Christianity and humanist Renaissance as he contributed to the secularization of the theater, fusing music, poetry, and dramatic action in anticipation of Lope de Vega and Calderón. A court musician in the house of the Duke of Alba, in 1496 he published his *Cancionero*, containing eight plays, sixty-one songs, several unaccompanied lyrics, and a treatise called *Arte de la poesía castellana*. His texts, both lyrical and philosophical, captured the freshness of popular song. One of them, "Más quiero morir por veros," tells of the lover's determination to pursue his beloved though he be ultimately rejected; merely for having aspired to such heights, he will have gained so much.

The poem was set to music by the acclaimed Mexican composer, Manuel M. Ponce (1882–1948):

Más quiero morir por veros
Está firme mi esperanza,
que jamás hace mudanza
teniendo tal confianza
de ganarme por quereros.

Mucho gana el qu'es perdido,
por merescer tan crecido,
y es vitoria ser vencido,
sin jamás poder venceros.

Aunque sienta gran tormento,
gran tristura e pensamiento,
yo seré dello contento,
por ser dichoso de veros.

Born in Fresnillo, Zacatecas, Ponce studied in Berlin, Italy, Paris, and at the Conservatorio Nacional de Música in Mexico. He was a dedicated folklorist and melodist who created musical settings for many Spanish Renaissance poems, masterfully integrating several harmonic and rhythmic styles. His collection, *Seis poemas arcaicos*, in which Encina's work appears, offers a harmonious blend of impressionistic, Moorish, and Spanish folk elements. Of special note is Ponce's transformation of the haunting "Tres morillas de Jaén" (an anonymous song originally called "Zéjel de las tres morillas"), which dates from at least the fifteenth century and made its first printed appearance in the *Cancionero de Palacio* somewhere between 1505 and 1520. Arranged and rearranged by numerous composers, including Federico García Lorca, it takes on an air of mystery as Ponce imbued it with Arabic modes. The poem itself has a possible double meaning, for instead of picking olives (or in some versions, apples), it may be that the girls themselves were plucked or seduced in the fields by their lovers.

• • •

The *villancico*, commonly associated with Christmas songs, has also been the frame for countless amatory, pastoral, and philosophical poems. By the late fifteenth century it was the principal genre in Spanish secular polyphony, and may be considered analogous to the Italian *frottola*. In form it is a short strophic song with a refrain whose typical pattern is aBccaB. The soloist sang the top voice or the principal melody and was accompanied by one to three instruments. *Villancicos* were collected in *cancioneros* and were published as vocal solos with lute accompaniment. Juan del Encina usually ended his pastoral plays with a *villancico*.

A good example of the secular *villancico* is "Con amores la mi madre," written by an early Basque composer, Juan del Anchieta (1462–1523). A leading musician of his day, he made much use of Gregorian melody. Anchieta studied at the University of Salamanca with Encina's brother, and sang at Queen Isabella's court. One of his most memorable pieces was "Tres ánades" [Three Ducks], a three-voice *villancico* to which Cervantes paid tribute in his comic tale *La ilustre fregona*. Another, "Con amores, la mi madre," is a tribute to the healing power of love.[5]

Con amores, la mi madre,
con amores m'adormi . . .
Asi dormida soñava
lo que el corazon velava,
que el amor me consolaba
con mas bien que mereci.
Adormeciome el favor
que amor me dio con amor.
Dio descanso a mi dolor.

In my opinion, the original twentieth-century version by the Barcelonan pianist and composer Fernando J. Obradors (1897–1945), with its more complex metric, melodic, and harmonic structure, is much more beautiful than Anchieta's, and more successful at enhancing the emotional lyrics of this sentimental poem.

• • •

The fragility or inconstancy of women is a subject that has been elaborated upon in literature for centuries, and Spain's contribution to the subject is endless.[6] As Cervantes says in his "Tale of Foolish Curiosity" (Part I, Chapter XXIII of *Don Quixote*), "A woman is made of glass; don't test her to see if she will break, for anything can happen":

Es de vidrio la mujer,
pero no se ha de probar
si se puede o no quebrar,
porque todo podría ser.

In his song cycle, *Las graciosas*, Obradors set this verse in the tempo of a *pavane*, which originated in sixteenth-century Padua, Italy. A stately court dance in a deliberate duple meter, the *pavane* was a European favorite, especially in Elizabethan England. The strutting staccato provides the humor used to describe the fragility of the fair sex, in contrast to the legato of the Renaissance-like contrapuntal line wherein the advice is given not to tempt fate.

• • •

"De los álamos vengo, madre, de ver cómo los menea el aire" [I come from the poplars, mother, where I watched the branches sway in the wind] is the beginning of yet another popular *villancico* by Miguel de Fuenllana (early sixteenth century, ca. 1568), with poetry by Juan Vásquez. Figure 5.2 shows its refrain.[7] A vihuelist and composer, Fuenllana was blind from infancy. He was a chamber musician at the Court of Philip II, to whom he dedicated his book of tablature. His *Orphénica lyra*, published in Seville in 1554, contained mainly borrowed music: motets, masses, and *villancicos* arranged for vihuela, including the texts, which he considered "the soul of any composition." Fuenllana's music has been praised for its "purity of taste" and its concentration. His declamatory style, austere yet eloquent, and his chords so rich in vocal settings have inspired such twentieth-century composers as Falla and Rodrigo to draw from the past. So it was that Rodrigo chose to adapt Fuenllana's "De los álamos" as well as other ancient melodies in his ingenious and enchanting orchestrated songs, "Cuatro canciones amatorias," which he later arranged once more for voice and piano.

The Valencian Joaquín Rodrigo (1901–1999), studied composition in Valencia at the Schola Cantorum and at the Conservatoire and the Sorbonne in Paris, where he lived during the Spanish Civil War (1936–1939). With the success of his *Concierto de Aranjuez*, he became the leading composer of postwar Spain. Rodrigo's neoclassical style has remained constant, marked by its melodic richness, archaic themes, and traditional rhythms, ambience, and color found in French and Spanish nationalist compositions.

• • •

"Feliciano me adora y le aborrezco. Lisardo me aborrece y yo le adoro" begins a poetic setting adapted by Rodolfo Halffter. "Feliciano adores me, and I hate him. Lisardo hates me and I adore him; for him who ungratefully doesn't desire me, I weep, and for him who tenderly weeps for me, I have no desire." These hardly sound like the words of a Mexican Creole nun, least of all one considered to be the greatest lyric poet, essayist, and playwright of the colonial period. Sor Juana Inés de la Cruz (1651–1695) was more than that. She was astonishingly outspoken on a variety of themes, including religious and profane love,

Figure 5.2
"De los álamos vengo"

which marks her as the most notable feminist of her age. Born Juana de Asbaje, daughter of a Mexican woman and a Spaniard, the beautiful and brilliant young woman entered a convent to avoid men and pursue her studies. Renowned for her precociousness as a child, she was taken to live in the viceroy's court in Mexico City, where she was widely consulted and admired for her knowledge and her wit. Although in many ways her poetry continued the Spanish Baroque tradition of Góngora, much of her writing displays a far greater simplicity and a lack of affectation.

Of her 975 verses, the musicalization of her Sonnet 167 by the Mexican composer Rodolfo Halffter in *Dos sonetos* offers a continuation of the question of which suffering is harder to bear, that of love or of hate. "That Fabio doesn't love me while I love him is a grief without equal in my experience; that Silvio loves me while I hate him is a lesser evil, but no less troubling." Halffter's piece, somewhat in the vein of Rodrigo, more Spanish than Latin American in tone and style, makes another charming addition to the collection of modern songs derived from Spanish Golden Age poetry.

• • •

To conclude, I would like to offer a magnificent setting by the Brazilian Heitor Villa-Lobos (1887–1959) of a poem by Gil Vicente (1469–1536). Entitled "Canção do Marinheiro," it is written in the form of a *modinha*, originally an eighteenth-century song that, along with the *lundus*, formed the roots of Brazilian musical nationalism. In its early form, a *modinha* was a lyrical, sentimental song with several distinguishing characteristics: an ornamental vocal line, a romantic lyric character, wide leaps of the melodic line, and modulations to the parallel minor and subdominant key. It is the only Brazilian popular form that is not folk in origin. The first stanza tells of an enamored young woman who had the good fortune to see her lover that day; the second, of three love-struck girls with whom she would share her song:

Hunha moça namorada,
dizia hum cantar d'amôr
e diss' ella: nostro Senhor,
oj' eu fosse aventurada
que visse o meu amigo
como eu este cantar digo, Ah!
Tres moças cantavam d'amôr,
mui fremosinhas pastoras,
mui coytadas dos amôres,
e diss' endunja m'ha sehnor:
Dizede, amigas, comigo
o cantar do meu amigo . . . Ah!

Gil Vicente, whose work was Villa-Lobos's antecedent, was the first of the bilingual dramatists of the Iberian peninsula and one of the most eloquent European dramatists of his time. He wrote plays in Spanish and Portuguese at a time when the two nations were very close, politically and ideologically. In fact, Juan del Encina mentored his early works. Although he sometimes criticized the Church, Vicente's pieces frequently treat of Biblical subjects, liturgy, and the deeds of saints. Other themes and sources of his work include the pastoral eclogues of his predecessors, the plays of Torres Naharro, French mystères, Spanish ballads, novels of chivalry, medieval "dances of death," fairy tales, and popular folklore. Above all, he was a lyricist as well as a musician, and he usually included a *villancico* in his entertainment. Seventeenth-century poets gleaned much from his spirituality and inspiration, which touched the modern genius of such as Villa-Lobos. It is indeed the lyricism and musicality of Golden Age Spanish poetry that has attracted composers throughout the ages, and most certainly of the twentieth century.

NOTES

1. The *camerata* was a historically important group of aristocratic poets, philosophers, and music lovers who renounced the florid art of polyphonic writing with the intent of reinstating *a capella* singing, believed to have been used in ancient Greek drama. Its adherents cultivated lyrical melody, which became the dominant element in song composition and in early operas, subordinating the component vocal or instrumental parts to the melodic line.

2. In this regard we should note that the secular songs of the Sephardim were sung in Ladino, a Judeo–Spanish dialect comprised of old Castilian combined with many Hebrew, Arabic, and Turkish words. Sacred songs, while still Sephardic, would not be considered Ladino since they were sung in Hebrew. In short, as the singer-linguist Nico Castel states, Ladino was the language of their homes, while Hebrew was the language of their prayers.

3. My adaptation.

4. The song, entitled "Jesús de Nazareth," derives from the *Cancionero de Reinosa* (1612). Nin's composition dates from 1933.

5. A vocal and guitar version of this song has been published by Unión Musical Española Editores, Madrid.

6. Consider Don Alfonso's words (via Lorenzo da Ponte) in the first act trio of Mozart's *Cosi fan tutte*: "Woman's famous faith and constancy is a myth and fabrication," and a plot to tempt the ladies' fidelity ensues. Other adaptations of this theme include an entirely new version in London in 1826, *Tit for Tat or the Tables Turned*; a Parisian version in 1863 called *Peines d'Amour Perdu*, based on Shakespeare's *Love's Labours Lost*; and *Die Dame Kobold* in Dresden, 1909, with a libretto taken from Calderón.

7. My adaptation.

BIBLIOGRAPHY

An Anthology of Spanish American Literature, ed. E. Herman Hespelt. New York: Appleton-Century Crofts, 1946.

Appleby, David P. *Heitor Villalobos: A Bio-Bibliography*. New York: Greenwood Press, 1988.

———. *The Music of Brazil*. Austin: University of Texas Press, 1983.

Chandler, Richard E., and Kessel Schwartz. *A New History of Spanish Literature*. Baton Rouge: Louisiana State University Press, 1991.

Chase, Gilbert. *The Music of Spain*. New York: Dover, 1959.

Diccionario de la música Labor. Barcelona: Editorial Labor, 1954.

Enciclopedia de la música, Guía del melómano y del discófilo Casper Howler. Madrid/
Barcelona: Editorial Noguer, n.d.

Grout, Donald J. *A History of Western Music*. Rev. ed. New York: W. W. Norton,
1973.

Livermore, Ann. *A Short History of Spanish Music*. New York: Vienna House,
1972.

Moore, Douglas. *A Guide to Musical Styles from Madrigal to Modern Music*. Rev.
ed. New York: W. W. Norton, 1962.

New Grove's Dictionary of Music and Musicians, ed. Stanley Sadie. Washington,
D.C.: Macmillan/Grove's Dictionaries, 1980.

Peppercorn, Lisa M. *Villa-Lobos* (Collected Studies). Aldershot, Hants, England:
Scolar Press, 1992.

———. *Villa-Lobos: The Illustrated Lives of the Great Composers*, ed. Audrey
Sampson. London/New York: Omnibus, 1989.

Reese, Gustave. *Music in the Renaissance*. Rev. ed. New York: W. W. Norton,
1959.

Rivers, Elias L., ed. *The Renaissance and Baroque Poetry of Spain*. Prospect Heights,
Ill.: Waveland Press, 1988.

Schindler, Kurt. *Folk Music and Poetry of Spain and Portugal* (Música y poesía
popular de España y Portugal). New York: Hispanic Institute, 1941.

PART II

THE UNIVERSAL
DON QUIXOTE

Théophile de Madrazo, *The Imaginary Stroll of Don Quixote*, 1930. Oil on canvas, 25 × 22 inches. Haunted by the images of those who fill his experience and his fantasy, Don Quixote comes upon a carriage-borne Dulcinea, while in the sky above him hover untold definable faces. Meanwhile, a pair of quizzical eyes contemplates the lance-carrying knight from a forlorn tree. (Collection of Mr. and Mrs. Albert I. DaSilva)

6

Don Quixote *on the Western Frontier*

Joann Krieg

Almost 200 years after the advent of Miguel de Cervantes's *Don Quixote* in 1605, the estimable character of the Don made one of his more "Quixotic" appearances on the Western frontier of the newly established United States of America. *Modern Chivalry* by Hugh Henry Brackenridge is one of the first important novels produced in America and is self-consciously styled on the Cervantes work, with numerous direct references to *Don Quixote*, offering as the Don's avatar one Captain John Farrago, who traverses the frontier with his Sancho Panza, an Irish immigrant named Teague O'Regan. Together the two represent the high and low of democracy; blended later into one cultural figure, they will become the ideal frontiersman in whom savagery and civilization meet.

Modern Chivalry had a lengthy publication history stretching from its first installments in 1792 to succeeding volumes in 1793, 1797, 1804, and 1805. Its author, born in Scotland but a resident of Pennsylvania from the age of five, was a Princeton-educated lawyer elected to the Pennsylvania legislature in 1786 and the author of several poems. (One, "The Rising Glory of America," written with Philip Freneau, was considered an important piece in its time.) The dual perspective gained by the combination of Brackenridge's cultured background and his experiences with the rustic settlers in the back country of his state is the underlying structure of *Modern Chivalry*, and the two outlooks remain in tandem, much as do the work's two principals, with the Captain providing a moral view of their adventures and Teague opportunistically seizing every advantage for upward mobility offered by the loosely ordered frontier society. No physical description is offered for O'Regan, save that he has red hair, but he is repeatedly referred to as a "bogtrotter." Despite this, the author's obvious affection for the roguish Teague makes him the more dominant character, and while the Irishman remains unchanged from beginning to end of the sprawling work, the type his character establishes influenced the later development of the virtuous Western hero familiar to literature and film.

Brackenridge's avowed intention in writing *Modern Chivalry* was the education of his backwoods countrymen; "Tom, Dick, and Harry in the woods," as he put it.[1] It made for an important deflection of literary site away from the New England and eastern seacoast literary establishment to the western regions that would not fully claim their literary place until after the Civil War with the rise of regionalism in American literature. The book forecasts this rise, however, in a number of ways, not the least of which is its use of dialect and other reflectors of the diversified American society. While Brackenridge referred to *Modern Chivalry* as a "fable," his style is, as was Cervantes's, realistic. Thus, the details of a rustic democratic background fill his pages in the way that early nineteenth-century American narrative art would. Indeed, George Caleb Bingham's nineteenth-century paintings of electioneering "stump" politicians and of frontier voters eagerly awaiting the results of their suffrage could have come directly from Brackenridge's pages.

The earliest volume of the series is contemporaneous with a period of American history dominated by the absolutely rabid political rivalry between the elitist Federalist Party of John Adams and Alexander Hamilton and the Jeffersonian democrats. Despite the ignorance and chicanery that informs the practice of democracy in *Modern Chivalry*, Hugh Henry Brackenridge was a Jeffersonian and a firm believer in democracy. What he feared were the nefarious uses to which the democratic system could be put by persons of unscrupulous and/or ignorant ambition. He offers numerous examples of such individuals who, posturing as true democrats, do not hesitate to take advantage of their neighbors, of strangers, of native Americans, and of the federal government. More often, however, in the character of Teague O'Regan, Brackenridge shows how ignorant men yield to the temptations provided by democracy to advance themselves beyond their capabilities simply because the opportunity to do so is presented. What O'Regan lacks, of course, is education, and it is this which Brackenridge, in the persona of Captain Farrago, offers to O'Regan and to the reader, to "Tom, Dick, and Harry in the woods."

The Captain is described as "a man of about fifty-three years of age, of good natural sense, and considerable reading," a bachelor who is "unacquainted with the world." "His ideas," we are told, "were chiefly drawn from what may be called the old school: the Greek and Roman notions of things" (p. 42). While his name, Farrago, suggests a confused mix of ideas, this is not borne out by the writing, for the Captain is consistent and clear about his views. The classical allusion is telling, in that eighteenth-century America prided itself on its "Greek and Roman notions" of democracy, a pride exemplified in its public architecture and clearly evidenced later in the building of Washington, D.C. The gap between notions or ideals and the practice of the thing is the subject matter of our American Cervantes, who aims to fill the gap with education, with, for one thing, a knowledge of the classical world and its virtues that will better fit the immigrant, the cobbler, or the backwoods horse trader for the rigors of public service. To emphasize the need for such tutelage Brackenridge fills his tale with examples of democratic mob mentality and cupidity. For this reason, *Modern Chivalry* is not truly a picaresque tale, for attention is focused less on the adventures of Teague O'Regan than on what I have referred to as the "gap" between democratic theory and practice on the Western frontier. It is precisely the same focus as that which Mark Twain later brought, in 1876, to *The Adventures of Huckleberry Finn*, where the rogue-like exploits of the boy are set against the truly villainous behavior of a slave-holding American society.

Unlike Cervantes's Quixote, Captain John Farrago clearly sees the foibles and the misdeeds of those with whom he comes in contact on his travels. The very first episode in Book 1 sets the tone; it concerns a horse race in which Farrago is urged to enter his excellent horse. He declines on the grounds that while his horse is well suited to carrying him at a fine and steady pace, the animal is not a racer and thus will suffer by comparison and be at a sore disadvantage in a contest with his racing superiors. The distinction and the metaphor of a race are lost on the eager competitors, however, who conclude that Farrago is a fool for passing up the opportunity to enrich himself in a race they believe he could win.

In another instance, the Captain and Teague approach a community preparing for an election. The candidates for a seat in the state legislature are a man of education and a weaver. The Captain addresses the assembled crowd on behalf of the educated man, claiming he has been readied by his schooling to represent them, while the weaver has not yet had the time or opportunity to train himself to that end. The voters are torn between the two, and Teague O'Regan, seeing an opportunity, offers himself as a compromise, which the electors are ready to accept, until the Captain dissuades his servant by warning him that the press will only make his life miserable if he is elected. Everywhere they travel O'Regan finds an audience, and his quick tongue and easy

charm bring him rapid acceptance by the crowd. When Captain Farrago declines to be proposed for membership in the American Philosophical Society because of his ignorance of science, Teague is eager to
take his place and the proposers ready to accept the substitution. The
Captain hints darkly of possible scientific experiments to be carried
out on the Irishman's person, and thus dissuades the unworthy
O'Regan. At other times Farrago takes advantage of his servant's ignorance, as when he convinces Teague that a very unattractive but
well-to-do woman who has succumbed to his Irish charm and proposed marriage is really a witch. Comic episodes such as these do not
advance Brackenridge's theme of education, since the Captain is merely
using Teague's ignorance, but they keep the satire moving and went
far toward making *Modern Chivalry* a popular favorite.

Eventually the Captain surrenders to O'Regan's longing for public
service and introduces him (as Major O'Regan) to the president at a
levee, an aristocratic function introduced by President John Adams, of
whom Brackenridge greatly disapproved. When the president appears
ready to appoint the Irishman to high office, Farrago intervenes and
suggests instead a post as excise or tax collector in the backcountry of
Pennsylvania. Once there, Teague is reviled by the populace because
he represents the federal government, which taxes the whiskey produced but refuses to build roads that would enable the backcountry
inhabitants to market other crops. Tarred and feathered in another ritual
of radical democracy, Teague escapes into the woods only to be found
by hunters, brought to Philadelphia, and eventually sent to France,
where the philosophers are to determine whether the feathered creature with an alien form of speech is animal or human. In France, Teague
quickly takes his place in the sansculotte ranks of the revolution, where
he is quite at home.

Later portions of *Modern Chivalry* are not so strongly narrative as
are the earlier, for it is here that Brackenridge attempts to educate the
reader in earnest. The book becomes mostly a series of essays designed
to set forth his ideal of "rational democracy," a midpoint between the
crudity of backwoods demagoguery and the aristocratic airs of the
patrician federal government.

It is in this advocacy of a midpoint between two extremes that
Brackenridge makes his most profound and lasting impression, and
where the influence of Cervantes's novel as a representation of European culture is most felt. Early America was a country of extremes,
with a Puritanical northeast, an elitist mid-Atlantic, and, along the
western settlements, what Brackenridge described as "a kind of Botany
Bay, to the old country, with this difference, that here, the outcasts came
voluntarily" (p. 440). In attempting to define the "American," various
eighteenth-century writers and thinkers sought a median point be-

tween the perceived effetism of those individuals most evidencing European culture and a savagery not only of Indians, but of the ignorant and "uncivilized" specimens who were rapidly filling the western regions. Little hope was entertained for the natives of the country, but the O'Regans who came and would continue to come in such numbers must be made aware of their shortcomings and helped to overcome them. St. John de Crevecoeur, in his 1782 *Letters from an American Farmer*, where he takes up the question "What is an American?" offers a purely economic description: The American, in short, is a displaced European who has found a country that feeds him in return for his labor. Brackenridge aims for a higher definition in proposing a rational democrat who has availed himself of European culture and classical virtues in order to bring these to bear on the practice of democracy. In the process he defines what he believed to be the responsibility of the educated class in America to instruct the ignorant immigrant. Indeed, when at one point in their travels Teague is offered a position as judge, Farrago admonishes those who offer it: "I am shocked at your indiscretion. Have not some of you read Don Quixotte [*sic*]? In the capacity of judge, Sancho Panza made some shrewd decisions; or rather Cervantes made them for him; for, I doubt much whether Sancho ever made one of them. But who is there of you, will make decisions for Teague?" (pp. 389–390). Then to Teague he says, "You have read the Don Quixotte of Cervantes, I presume. But what do I say; you read Don Quixotte! you have read nothing; and yet you would be a judge." Then, assuming his role as educator, Farrago adds, "But I may tell you of him" (p. 392).

The civilizing influence of European culture did not overtake the western frontier as Brackenridge hoped it would; rather, the desire, even the need, to believe in the superiority of America to Europe led to the concomitant belief in the superiority of nature as a civilizing force. A similar instance was the transmogrification, in American art and literature of the early decades of the nineteenth century, of Edmund Spenser's "Faerie Land" into prairie land.[2] The virtues of Spenser's knights and the deficiencies of Cervantes's errant knight and his servant are both subsumed by their exposure to the world of nature, which eventually produced a new creature in the new world, a democrat, educated by his natural environment, a blend of the erudite Captain Farrago and the ambitious Teague O'Regan. James Fenimore Cooper later perfected the image in Hawkeye, the hero of his Leatherstocking tales, and the nation soon chose as its heroes such men as Davy Crockett, Daniel Boone, Andrew Jackson, and Abraham Lincoln, all of them rough-hewn but virtuous products of the frontier, indeed, *frontiers*men not *back*woodsmen in the privileging language of the nation's cultural hierarchy. Eventually the figure moved into popular culture via the "dime novel," movies, and television, and is best exemplified in the persona projected on the movie screen by actors such as John Wayne, who though "rough and tough" maintained a code of honor that upheld the democratic ideal. Brackenridge seems at one point in *Modern Chivalry* to suggest this evolution. Discussing the barter system prevalent on the early frontier, he says that even women were bartered into marriage, and that when they "had been conducted to the bowers mantled with the natural vine, an offspring arose in a few years, such as that from whence the Poets have drawn their best fictions" (p. 437). By his own pointed references throughout *Modern Chivalry*, it is clear that one of those shaping fictions was *Don Quixote*.

NOTES

1. Hugh Henry Brackenridge, *Modern Chivalry*, ed. Claude M. Newlin (New York: American Book Co., 1937), 471. All citations are to this text.

2. See Joann P. Krieg, "The Transmogrification of Faerie Land into PrairieLand," *Journal of American Studies* 19 (1985): 199–223.

7

Don Quixote chez *Donizetti,* chez *Massenet*

Mario Hamlet-Metz

In his interesting article on Don Quixote as "arabesque," in which he explores the relationship between art and nature in the Cervantes novel, Michael McGaha sets out to prove that there is more than just the traditional dichotomous interpretation of the Cervantes character and literary masterpiece found in the writings of Western critics. For them, McGaha states emphatically, "Don Quixote must be either hero or fool, and the novel itself must be seen as embodying either an idealistic or a realistic view of life."[1] How true! But it is also true that this simple, obvious level of interpretation has proven tremendously beneficial to the field of music; opera, in particular, where, until well into the nineteenth century, the prevailing dramatic and musical elements were an unrelenting sense of action and a dearth of psychological complexity. In the case of *Don Quixote,* even when one discards the novel's idealism or the character's constant passage from a state of safe daydreaming to one of total mishandling of reality, the problem of fitting musical characterization is hardly solved. This is due, of course, to the intrinsic difficulty of describing in musical terms the knight's inner sense of virtue, humanity, dignity, and individual freedom, the fundamental characteristics of his psyche. Moreover, despite the fact that Cervantes's original is largely a mockery of the old novels of chivalry, its form is still reminiscent, in many respects, of *Amadis de Gaula.* In the case of opera, this constitutes another problem: Nothing is more difficult for a librettist to adapt or for a composer to set to music than a narrative genre in which the truly dramatic situations, so vital to the lyric stage, occur only sporadically.

Understandably, then, the chapters of Cervantes's *Don Quixote* most frequently used for the seventy-odd operas directly based on it were those filled with action, or at least those with episodes whose clear storyline allowed them to be reshaped in dramatic or comic form: the wedding of the wealthy Camacho, the tale of the man who was too curious for his own good, Don Quixote's adventures in the Sierra Morena, his attack on the windmills, his stay at the Duke's court, his descent to Montesino's cave, the capture of the helmet of Mambrino, Sancho's tossing in the blanket, his trip to deliver the letter to the fair Dulcinea, and his role as governor of Barataria Island. As a result of these choices of plot, it becomes obvious that the large majority of the Quixote-based operas are of the comic genre; some of them are *semi-seria* operas or melodramas and just a few of them fall into the *tragedia lirica* category.

The first reference known to a musical adaptation of *Don Quixote* dates back to the festivities for the beatification of Saint Ignatius of Loyola at the Colegio de la Compañía de Jesús in Salamanca in 1610. The annals of the school describe it as a farce of the triumph of Don Quixote so inventive that it made everyone laugh. The music was improvised and qualified as grotesque.[2] For centuries to come, *Don Quixote* would occupy the musical theater in many distinct forms. The first fully staged Quixote opera, *Il Don Chisciotte della Mancia* (libretto attributed to Marosini, music by Sajon), premiered in Venice in 1680, and the most recent one, *Don Chisciotte* (libretto by Mario Casella, music by Vito Frazzi), opened in Florence during the 1951 season. Between them there are at least a handful that deserve mention here, given the importance of either the librettist or the composer. Among the earliest are *Don Chisciotte in Sierra Morena* (Vienna, 1719), a *tragi-commedia per musica* written by the court dramaturg Apostolo Zeno for the court composer Francesco Bartolomeo Conti, and two works by the composer Georg Philipp Telemann: *Sancio, oder die siegende Grossmuth* (Hamburg, 1727) and *Basilio und Quiteria* (Hamburg, 1761). In less than two decades, Naples saw the premiere of Niccolo Piccinni's *Il curioso del suo propio danno* (1756) and Giovanni Paisiello's *opera buffa, Don Chisciotte della Mancia* (1769). During the 1771 season the Viennese audiences applauded enthusiastically *Don Chisciotte alle nozze di Gamace*, an opera-ballet by court composer Antonio Salieri. Saverio Mercadante presented his *Noces de Gamache* in Paris in 1825 and its Spanish version in Cadiz in 1829. Mendelssohn's comic opera, *Die Hochzeit des Camacho*, opened in Berlin in April 1827. The famous Manuel García (composer, singer, father of primadonnas María Malibran and Pauline Viardot, and author of the most important nineteenth-century manual on voice technique) collaborated in the composition of a *Don Chisciotte* that premiered both in Paris and in New York in 1827. In 1864 the *zarzuela, La ínsula Barataria*, with libretto by Mariano de Larra and music by Emilio Arrieta, had a huge success in Madrid. Jules Barbié and Michel Carré, the successful librettists of Gounod's *Faust*, collaborated with the composer Boulanger in a very popular opera, *Don Quichotte*, unveiled at the Théâtre Lyrique in Paris in 1869. Also worth mentioning are *El retablo de Maese Pedro* by Manuel de Falla, first heard in both Sevilla and Paris in 1823, and, of course, the two operas that are going to be discussed in detail here, Donizetti's *Il furioso all'isola di San Domingo* and Massenet's *Don Quichotte*.

The year 1832 had been an incredibly productive one for Gaetano Donizetti, with his *Fausta* (Naples, January), *Ugo, conte di Parigi* (Milan, March), *L'elisir d'amore* (Milan, May), and *Sanzia di Castiglia* (Naples, November), four operas so diverse in story-lines, characters, and moods. In August of that year he signed a contract in Rome with the impresario Giovanni Paterni for an opera to be performed at the Teatro Valle in the winter season of 1833. The librettist would be Jacopo Ferretti, and the subject chosen was that of *Il furioso all'isola di San Domingo*, an adaptation of the Sierra Morena scenes from Cervantes's *Don Quixote*. Ferretti was not unfamiliar with this subject. In the mid-1820s he had seen in Rome (at the very same Teatro Valle where the opera was to premiere) a *Furioso* that the celebrated actor Luigi Vestri most likely adapted for himself. Seeing the operatic potential of the play, Ferretti suggested the title to Donizetti, who accepted it at once.

Briefly, the Sierra Morena episodes on which the opera is based are found in *Don Quixote*, Part I, Chapters 23 to 28.[3] Beaten and stoned after having freed a gang of ungrateful galley slaves, Don Quixote and Sancho are in the Sierra Morena, looking for a safe haven in those inhospitable mountains. However, instead of peace and calm, they get involved in yet another adventure, this one a tale of love and treachery involving Cardenio, Luscinda, Dorotea, and the Duke Fernando.[4]

The plot of the Sierra Morena chapters has all the necessary ingredients for melodrama: lost and found people, identities and minds, the involuntary seduction of an innocent girl by a cruel seducer, lovers in hiding, disguises, misunderstandings, letters that do not arrive at their destination, daggers, fainting, deceit, violence, and, yes, of course, madness. It is an ideal literary source for a so-called melodramma *lirico*, which is precisely what Ferretti saw in it when he suggested the title of *Il furioso* to Donizetti.[5] But rather than setting the action in the scabrous paths of the Sierra Morena, Ferretti transports it to an exotic island of the Caribbean, with cliffs, stormy seas, bushy vegetation, primitive huts, and aboriginal people. Don Quixote and Sancho are absent, but the contrast between Cardenio, the "Furioso" and Kaidamà, his "moretto" will be of the same kind. Here, two natives, Bartolomeo and his daughter Marcella, protect and nourish the madman Cardenio, who has fled his native Cartagena to seek refuge in Santo Domingo. In melodrama, people and the space they move in invariably fit the needs of the plot. Thus, coincidentally, the two who are looking for the missing Cardenio (Eleonora, his once sinful, now repenting wife, and Fernando, his brother) converge on the island and try to bring the madman back to sanity and a happy marital life. But before the blissful finale, terrible things happen. The desperate Cardenio loses his sight and regains it after throwing himself into the sea. Eleonora is persuaded by Fernando to confess her sin to her husband, and does it eloquently. Loaded pistols fall into the hands of the hero, who decides that death is the only solution for their dilemma. Aghast, Eleonora forcefully declares that she alone is guilty and is willing to die for it, but her noble decision brings about her forgiveness. Along with Fernando, the reunited loving couple returns to their native land.

A musical and dramatic analysis of this opera may be found in William Ashbrook's *Donizetti and His Operas*.[6] There are, however, some interesting additional observations to be made about the Ferretti/Donizetti collaboration, and they have to do mostly with the character of Cardenio. Ferretti, a well-known Roman poet and extremely intelligent librettist, who had written the text for Rossini's delightful *Cenerentola*, met Donizetti as early as 1824, when they worked together on the comic opera *L'ajo nell'imbarazzo*. In a well-documented article, Franca Cella proves that Ferretti had an enormous influence on the stylistic evolution of this composer, awakening in him an interest in linguistics and creative writing.[7] I would like to go a step farther than Cella and suggest that it was the same Ferretti who made Donizetti fully aware of the fact that comic or eccentric characters are not necessarily caricatures or symbols, and that they must behave in such a way that they inspire sympathy and compassion rather than cruel laughter or indifference (we feel sorry for the endearing Nemorino as well as for the odious Don Pasquale, the main characters in *L'elisir d'amore* and *Don Pasquale*).

In the case of *Il furioso*, Cardenio's irrationality and overall disinterest in life could easily have resulted in a dramatically weak, buffoonish character that no one cared about. Yet his sincerity, melancholy, and nobility come across from the very beginning. In fact, even before his entrance, Marcella finds him young and handsome, and describes him as a tormented, wretched, forsaken man who must be protected from peril (I, 1). We understand his predicament with his own very first words: "Like a gleam of love she was / In the prime of her life, / But she was as beautiful as she was an evil / Mistress of deceit" (I, 3). From that moment on, Cardenio slowly emerges as a romantic hero conscious of his fate, very much reminiscent of Hugo's (and Verdi's) *Hernani*: "Everything is poison to me! To me, the order of Nature is upset! / April itself is full of thorns! / The grass is bitter, and very bitter are the fruits!" (I, 7). Later he tells a moved Bartolomeo, "Spare your tears / I don't want them / I have to cry by myself, / As I was cursed by destiny" (I, 7). To Leonora, he says, just as Verdi's Ernani will tell Elvira, "I hate everybody, I hate myself; / I have horror even of the sun!" (I, 15).

During the course of the action, Cardenio has won us over to such an extent that we understand his madness and his resentment of his wife, for whom we do not feel much sympathy and whose erstwhile betrayal seems unnecessary and inexplicable, no matter how eloquent her plea for forgiveness and her promise of fidelity. In the end, Donizetti does succeed in changing our minds about Eleonora via a long closing aria and cabaletta in which she expresses her great joy. Compared with Cardenio, all other characters are of less importance, especially Fernando, whose presence seems justifiable only because an Italian opera without a tenor would be inconceivable. As for Kaidamà, a comic character who is there to receive the "bastonnades" from the deranged Cardenio who terrifies him, he provides that sharp contrast between the hero suffering from a wounded heart and the earthy good-natured servant who does not understand or feel much beyond the purely physical. Indeed, one of the most accomplished moments of the score is the duet between Cardenio and Kaidamà, in which the first tells his sorrows while the latter complains of hunger pains. The exoticism of the setting, the romantic facets of the plot, and especially the felicitous juxtaposition of the comic and the pathetic, both in the text and in the melodic music, accounted for the huge initial success of this three-act opera. After its Roman premiere at the Teatro Valle on January 2, 1833, it was chosen that same year for the opening nights at both the Teatro Carignano in Turin and Milan's La Scala, where it was performed thirty-seven times during the first season. In the twentieth century it was revived in Siena (1958), in Spoleto (1967), and in Savona (1987).

In another time and another place, Jules Massenet would use and adapt in his own fashion Cervantes's masterpiece. In fact, since its spectacular 1910 premiere at Monte Carlo, the Massenet *Don Quichotte* has kept its place in the repertory of important theaters, surfacing whenever top-notch basses with acting abilities express their desire to sing the part of the Knight, initially written for Féodor Chaliapin.[8] Both the great Russian bass and Massenet had enjoyed personal successes at Monte Carlo, so when Raoul Gunsbourg, the Rumanian composer and director of the elegant Monte Carlo opera for almost sixty years approached them for a contract, they were delighted to sign it. Although the relationship between composer and singer was often strained

(Chaliapin's theatrics and constant sobbing irritated the composer during rehearsals), they reconciled after the unanimous acclaim by press and public, and the role eventually became one of Chaliapin's favorites.

Henri Cain, who had previously collaborated with Massenet, was in charge of writing the libretto, whose source was a "heroic play" by Jacques Le Lorrain, *Le chevalier de la longue figure*, which had premiered in Paris in 1904. What Massenet liked about this play was that the author had transformed the coarse Dulcinée into "La Belle Dulcinée," an attractive, sensuous woman, somewhat reminiscent of Massenet's previous courtesans, this one with a distinct Spanish flavor. "It brought to our piece an element of deep beauty in the woman's role and a potent poetical touch to our Don Quixote's dying of love—real love this time—for a Belle Dulcinée who justifies the passion," wrote Massenet in his *Recollections*.[9] For this role, the composer had in mind his favorite female singer of the time, the beautiful Lucy Arbell.

The opera, in five short acts, centers around Quixote's love for La Belle (and coquette, one might add) Dulcinée, who sends the Knight on the "heroic" mission of recovering her necklace, stolen by some bandits. Should he return with it, she promises to love him, and when he does, she embraces him. This inspires a poetic marriage proposal, which she promptly rejects. Her life makes her unworthy of the one she calls "a sublime fool" (IV). Unable to be loved by his Dulcinée, the emotionally exhausted Knight dies, reaching toward a shining star while listening to the distant voice of his beloved: "It is really she! / Light, love and youth. . . . / She . . . to whom I draw near . . . / who beckons me . . . / who waits for me!" (V).

In the Cain/Massenet *Don Quichotte*, the protagonist, still living mostly in his own dream world and still an object of mockery for most, comes across quite differently from his portrayal in other adaptations. This is an idealist in action, who empties his pockets to feed beggars and who would like universal happiness to reign (I); one who, instead of being beaten and stoned by bandits, manages first to make himself heard and forgiven for his intrusion in their territory, then to recuperate the stolen necklace, and, last, to actually move and miraculously convert the rogues to goodness and honesty in an almost Christlike manner: "See the miracle! . . . / Tramps, pillagers, sons of theft and crime / those who live in fear and those oppressed, / the homeless, beggars whose smiles do menace / these have divined my purpose, have understood his meaning." The inspired bandits respond, "Put your unstained hand upon us, / O our knight!" A radiant Don Quixote "holds up his hands in a gesture of blessing over the bandits" (III). (Ridiculed by the villagers, the noble idealist is, ironically, adored by the outcasts, a favorite romantic theme since Schiller.) The relationship between Don Quixote and Sancho is also unique here, as the knight treats his squire like a friend whom he never scolds, one in whom he can confide blindly, and one in whose arms he dies readily. Intellectually and emotionally they are still at opposite poles, of course, but, interestingly enough, their difference in feelings is stressed mainly through their concept of love and women. A kiss thrown by Dulcinée suffices to inspire in the valiant and forgiving knight the purest and most ardent love, while for Sancho women "are all liars and deceivers" and men are but mice "for these cats to play with" (II). Sancho's own nobility and loyalty to his master goes beyond pure rhetoric when, facing a crowd that is cruelly offending Don Quixote, he cries out violently, "You, all of you, have done an appalling deed, in offending this bold hero! / Laugh, go on, laugh at the unfortunate idealist / who walks in a dream and speaks of pastoral simplicity, / of love and goodness as Jesus did once. . . . you low scoundrels, flatterers and sluts, / who should be falling at the feet / of the saint by you ridiculed" (IV). Even Dulcinée is more complex than we are made to believe from her nonchalant femininity. She enjoys her youth, her freedom, her fickleness, her power of seduction, and even her less-than-perfect reputation; yet from the very beginning she seems to be aware of the emptiness of a life without true love: "At twenty, sovereign majesty / has no great appeal for a woman. / She may wear a jewelled crown, / but after that, my friends, after that? / She lives in an exalted state, / surrounded the day long by glory, / yet something is lacking, / or someone, or someone" (I). Later, before her epicurean song about the infinite pleasures of feverish, fleeting hours of love, and bored by her circle of suitors, she tells them that she longs for a love quite different from theirs (IV). Alas, it is a love that still excludes our eccentric Knight of the Mournful Countenance! This Dulcinée is no Carmen; there is a scent of exquisite fragility in her that makes her unique among the many Dulcineas encountered on the opera stage.

Cain's libretto, a free adaptation of another free adaptation of the original, raised the ire of literary critics, especially of Cervantes scholars. Gerardo Diego goes so far as to call the whole work "una disparatada massenética" [Massenetic absurdity] that halfway redeems itself in the last act, with Sancho's weeping and the knight's death standing up. (Gunsbourg's idea originally, it proved most effective.)[10] Yet the often poetic text does include accurate references to the original and recreates beautifully the depth of the hero's convictions, generosity, and overall humanity. In his quasi delirium, the dying Knight whispers, "Sancho, I promised you not long ago / fertile hillsides, castles, / even a verdant isle . . . / Take possession of your island, / for I still have power to give it to you! / An azure wave laps its shores. / 'tis beautiful and pleasing . . . / and it is the island of Dreams!" (V).

I have chosen these two operas by Donizetti and Massenet as my prime focus here because they do not follow the pattern established as early as the seventeenth century of the large majority of Quixote-based operas; that is, a plot built around the knight, his squire, or other characters in ridiculous situations that would make the audience laugh. Cardenio does not make us laugh, not even smile; on the contrary, he is a likable character whose madness is totally understandable, so that when he is cured of it the audience shows signs of relief. (More ridiculous is Kaidamà, a character taken straight out of the Commedia dell'Arte, but one does not really care what happens to him, just as one does not care about what happens to Monostatos in *The Magic Flute*.) In the Cain/Massenet libretto, Don Quixote is also a likable character. Because he does not belong in the "real world," one cannot judge him on the grounds of his awkward behavior, and in the end what transcends is his admirable altruism: "If you had a heart like his, / you would be a fine man," says Dulcinée to another suitor" (IV). Musically, both pieces reflect the taste of their period. While the Donizetti opera, composed at the height of the *bel canto* years, is full of easy-to-remember, contagious melodies, an unprecedented mad scene for the baritone, and an expected finale showing off the soprano, Massenet's *Don Quichotte* has many declamatory pages describing the moods and the inner thoughts and feelings of the knight, often composed in the vein of the fashionable *fin de siècle* French art songs. Having seen the two operas in fully staged performances, I can state without hesitation that while neither one finds the composer at his best, they are by no means to be considered musically or dramatically weak. On the contrary, when sung, acted, and staged well, both come across as aesthetically accomplished works that invariably generate enthusiastic responses from opera-loving audiences. Adapted to their particular medium—the sung theater—both have undoubtedly served as yet another palpable proof of the immortality and universality of Cervantes's admirable Knight.

NOTES

1. Michael McGaha, "*Don Quixote* as Arabesque," in *Cervantes: Estudios en la víspera de su centenario* (Kassel: Reichenberger, 1994), 170.

2. Gerardo Diego, "Cervantes y la música," in *Anales Cervantinos*, vol. 1 (Madrid: Instituto Miguel de Cervantes, 1951), 27.

3. Miguel de Cervantes Saavedra, *Obras completas* (Madrid: Aguilar, 1956), and *The Ingenious Gentleman Don Quixote de la Mancha* (New York: Viking Press, 1949).

4. Having found a rotted saddle pad containing some clean shirts, gold pieces, a notebook with a sonnet, and a letter from a distressed lover, the

Knight's curiosity is stimulated even more at the sight of a madman who is jumping from rock to rock. A goatherd tells him that the suitcase and poem belong to a handsome young man who came there six months earlier looking for the harshest part of the Sierra, where he would stay in isolation hoping only for death. He is still alive, but he acts now like a madman, going from deep depression to uncontrollable fury and constantly railing against "the traitor Fernando." Suddenly, the Ragged One of the Sickly Countenance appears before the Knight of the Mournful Countenance and they embrace. Both men are not too unlike each other, after all. The newfound cavalier, Cardenio, begins to tell the story of his misfortunes. An Andalusian aristocrat by birth, he loved Luscinda since childhood, courted her, and was promised her hand. Before marrying her, however, he was sent by his father to Duke Ricardo's castle, where he befriended the grandee's younger son, the unscrupulous and libertine Fernando, who eventually betrayed his trust and decided to make Luscinda his own. The unhappy girl, ordered to marry Fernando, prefers to die, but faints before committing suicide, right after whispering a weak "yes." Unfortunately, Cardenio, who has overheard this from behind a curtain, thinks that she is unfaithful to him and plunges into the Sierra, with the results we already know. The episode ends with a ray of hope when Cardenio and the priest encounter a lad dressed in rustic garb, who turns out to be the beautiful Dorotea. She too is a victim of Don Fernando, who seduced her and promptly abandoned her for Luscinda. Dorotea tells what Cardenio does not know: that Fernando tried to kill Luscinda when a love letter addressed to Cardenio was found on her person. Since Luscinda has now fled from her home and the marriage was never consummated, Dorotea hopes to reconquer the heart of a repenting Fernando. Joined by Cardenio, now of sound mind, she is determined to find Fernando, and Cardenio, his beloved Luscinda.

5. *Il furioso all'isola di San Domingo*, melodramma in due atti di Jacopo Ferretti, musica di Gaetano Donizetti, texts used in *Tutti i libretti di Donizetti* (Milano: Garzanti, 1993). English quotations from the booklet accompanying the complete recording, Bologna, Bongiovanni, 1987.

6. William Ashbrook, *Donizetti and his operas* (New York: Cambridge University Press, 1982).

7. Franca Cella, "Il donizettismo nei libretti di Donizetti," in *Atti del Primo convegno internazionale di studi donizettiani* (Bergamo, 1993), 46.

8. *Don Quichotte*, comédie héroïque en cinq actes, poème de Henri Cain, d'après Le Lorrain. Quotations from the booklet accompanying the complete recording, Paris, EMI France, 1993.

9. Jules Massenet, *My Recollections* (New York: AMS Press, 1971), 273.

10. Diego, "Cervantes," 30–31.

8

George Eliot's Dorothea in Light of Cervantes's Dorotea

Kevin S. Larsen

At least one important facet of the Hispanic "ancestry" of Dorothea Brooke, the principal female character in George Eliot's *Middlemarch* (1871–1872), has to date been documented. The author patterns her protagonist after Santa Teresa de Avila, suggesting that "here and there is born" such a successor to this saintly individual. Generally, as is the case with the provincial Englishwoman in question, their "loving heart-beats and sobs after an unattained goodness tremble off and are dispersed among hindrances, instead of centering in some long-recognisable deed" (Eliot, 16; cf. 767–768).[1] There is, however, another figure of Golden Age Spanish letters on whose deeds Miss Brooke's are also centered, her namesake in *Don Quixote*, Dorotea, who in her own right figures as one of Cervantes's favorite creations.[2] Eliot makes other direct as well as more oblique references to Cervantes's text, to its protagonist, to various themes and ideas from the novel, and even to the author himself. Nonetheless, her character's Spanish *tocaya* is never specifically mentioned within the elaborately crafted "fabric of quotation" that constitutes *Middlemarch* (Neale, 63–75). The sum of similarities, despite certain significant differences, leads one to suspect that Eliot's selection of the name "Dorothea," and of various parallel circumstances, was purposeful.

Eliot was pointedly skeptical of "questionable riddle-guessing," as she termed the composite work on mythology by Edward Casaubon,

Dorothea's first husband (Eliot, 446). Hopefully this chapter will pass beyond the sort of scholarship where theory "floated among flexible conjectures no more solid than those etymologies which seemed strong because of likeness in sound, until it was shown that likeness in sound made them impossible" (Eliot, 446). Still, as Eliot herself acknowledges, "a vigorous error vigorously pursued has kept the embryos of truth a-breathing" (Eliot, 446). With a bit of luck, my vigor of conjecture shall not prove abortive, though I recognize that zeal may lead to a mixing of error with its converse. I am willing—as were Cervantes and Eliot both—to accept the windmills along with the giants. Indeed, Eliot's admixture of *lo cervantino* is always laden with as potent a level of irony as was her predecessor's text itself. Any analysis of a link between the two must similarly savor its own potential irony, the possible "sinrazón" of its "razón." Of course, the converse could also be true (Cervantes, pt. 1, ch. 1; 20).

Even the most obvious connection between the two novels, the epigraph of Chapter 2 of *Middlemarch*, indicates that Eliot is well aware—as should be the reader—that things are not always as plain as they seem, and they are always more ironic. She quotes, in Spanish and in English, from Chapter 21 (Part I), concerning the "yelmo de Mambrino" (21). The application of this text in *Middlemarch* certainly indicates the pronounced difference of opinion concerning Casaubon. It also suggests that he will not be for Dorotea later on what he is initially. A principal thematic component of the novel is her bitterly disappointing discovery that the clerical scholar, who at first appears to be "the most interesting man she had ever seen" (29), one who seems to have "a great soul" (31), is only a boring old drudge.[3]

Unlike Don Quixote and Sancho after their long dialogues about whether the knight has captured a barber's tin basin or Mambrino's gold helmet, Dorothea is uncompromising and cannot accept any sort of "*baciyelmo.*" For her, Casaubon is a common "*bacía de barbero,*" if he cannot be the enchanting "*yelmo*" of her (day)dreams (see Cervantes, pt. 1, ch. 44, 408; cf. ch. 25, 213–214 and ch. 45, 409–413).[4] Even more than her knightly predecessor, she, at least at the beginning, cannot compromise idealism with quotidian realities. It would seem that Eliot, like Cervantes before her, indeed can, for her text, like the Spaniard's, is laden with nominative polysemy. This constitutes just one expression of a thoroughly polivalent perspectivism, including, of course, the names "Dorothea" and even "George Eliot" itself.[5] We note also in Chapter 21 of *Don Quixote* that it is the idealistic knight errant, not his realist squire, who affirms, "Donde una puerta se cierra otra se abre" (163). In turn, Eliot's Dorothea will pursue her vision of how marriage—and life—ought to be, until she unites eventually, after much travail, with Casaubon's nephew, Will Ladislaw.

In her own right, Cervantes's Dorotea pursues her dream through every obstacle, finally realizing her goals against all odds. As many critics have noted, she is as quixotic—"porque ella había leído muchos libros de caballerías" (pt. 1, ch. 29, 261)—as her supposed champion (see Márquez Villanueva, 19–21; Eisenberg, 8, 90; Hathaway, 32–33). In turn, Dorothea is perhaps as quixotic as either or both of her predecessors. Even while Casaubon is alive, and particularly after his death, she launches herself into a quest seeking nothing less than the vindication of marriage (and of herself as a person). In this regard, Eliot's character clearly recalls Cervantes's Dorotea, whose crusade to confirm her clandestine marriage to Fernando constitutes the bulk of her story in Don Quixote. In some respects the farmer's daughter who will for a time become "la princesa Micomicona" is her own champion, though she plays along with the knight errant, for his "rescue" as much as for her own. In much the same way, Dorothea combines in herself victim and champion. Her generally crestfallen countenance during the course of her crusade suggests the often downcast demeanor of Dorotea, who at one point seems convinced "que será vano el consuelo, pues es imposible el remedio" (pt. 1, ch. 29, 257; cf. Hathaway, 16–17). This woeful cast obtains even in don Quijote himself, who—again within the framework of nominative perspectivism—becomes "el Caballero de la Triste Figura." Still, for all of them, the quest continues.

In a sense, Dorothea unsexes herself while retaining the essence of her femininity. (This recalls her ties to Saint Theresa.)[6] She even brings to mind her creator, a woman (Mary Anne Evans) who adopted a masculine pseudonym in order to facilitate her progress in a largely male-dominated literary world. Like Eliot herself, Dorothea exhibits a particular "eloquence" that can reduce the "masculine consciousness" to "a stammering condition" (365; cf. Oldfield, 63–86; Graver, 68). On the other hand, Cervantes's Dorotea gives away nothing in female attractiveness, even when attired in man's clothing. As the priest, Don Quixote's friend, states (the note of voyeurism, incidentally, should not be lost), "Lo que vuestro traje, señora, nos niega, vuestros cabellos nos descubren: señales claras que no deben de ser de poco momento las causas que han disfrazado vuestra belleza en hábito tan indigno (Cervantes, pt. 1, ch. 28, 242, 245). Then, when she appears dressed as "una rica y gran señora" (pt. 1, ch. 29, 261), even Don Quixote himself may be tempted, if only for a moment, to be unfaithful to his Dulcinea. But for all her "feminidad," Dorotea can hold her own and more in a man's realm of rhetoric and rational persuasion. It is her argumentation and her appeal to Don Fernando's reason(ableness) that finally bring her recalcitrant lover back to her arms, so that "verá el mundo que tiene contigo más fuerza la razón que el apetito" (pt. 1, ch. 36, 332–335). Unable to resist her potent mix of feminine beauty and masculine reason, he must finally confess, "Venciste, hermosa Dorotea, venciste, porque no es posible tener ánimo para negar tantas verdades juntas" (pt. 1, ch. 36, 335; cf. Márquez Villanueva, 34–35; Hathaway, 12–39; Nadeau, 53–61).[7]

Eliot's Dorothea hopes that Casaubon will be her defender, but he never stops being a sort of Alonso Quijano, or at least a staid older man who recalls in various particulars that seminal character. Unlike Cervantes's protagonist, the English scholar never experiences a mid-life crisis to drive him to fabulous exploits (see Johnson). Moreover, he might have learned a lesson from the Manchegan gentleman, that to remain single and "interesting" is perhaps better at a certain age than to marry and merely disappoint. Casaubon cannot leave his books to act out his imaginings in the "real" world or to make reality anew in his own image, as does Don Quixote. In turn, Miss Brooke is reminiscent of the old hidalgo's niece, to whom he is clearly attracted and whom he may "take flight" to avoid (Johnson, 56–78). But Casaubon is not made of the same stuff as Alonso Quijano. Dorothea would never deny that her husband is anything less than "el Bueno," but his actual appelative would more appropriately be "el Aburrido." His studies, like his marriage, remain an unimaginative grind, rather than a labor of love or a crusade charging off on flights of romantic fantasy.

In this regard, one character in Middlemarch terms Casaubon not a "great soul," but, [a] "great bladder for dried peas to rattle in" (65), an apt image for the old cleric, which recalls, ironically, a similar one in Don Quixote. The knight and Sancho encounter a company of actors already in costume on their way from one performance to another. One of them spooks Rocinante by drumming on the ground with "tres vejigas de vaca, hinchadas," fastened on a stick, all the while "sonando los cascabeles" (pt. 2, ch. 11, 541). Don Quixote is thrown from his mount, though as always he gets back on. Casaubon never mounts at all, whether on his own Rocinante or on a Clavileño. He is an unimaginative writer who cannot grasp the immense generative power of words (see Hornback, 32–33, 76–83). But George Eliot does, and so, at least in part, does her Dorothea. Their quixotic philological grounding is secure, whereas the thoroughly pedestrian and pedantic Casaubon is merely grounded.

Incidentally, the images of dryness associated with Casaubon, of which the "bladder" is only one of several, also recall another facet of Alonso Quijano's personality. Concerning his protagonist, the narrator of Don Quixote suggests that "del mucho leer, se le secó el cerebro" (pt. 1, ch. 1, 20). In turn, Casaubon, in the words of Mrs. Cadwallader (the same character who characterizes him as a "great bladder") definitely "does not want drying," as for many years "he has certainly been drying," the result of his arid studies (94). Mrs. Cadwallader further posits that if a drop of Casaubon's blood were examined "under a magnifying-glass," it would be "all semicolons and parentheses" (76). Both Quijano and Casaubon are consumed and desiccated by their respective textual passions. In this regard it may well be that both constitute clear cases of what has been termed the "classic melancholic scholar" (Soufas, 20–22). Certainly, there is influence here on Casaubon of other writers besides Cervantes, from the Elizabethans to the Romantics of Eliot's own century. Nonetheless, of the two characters, Quijano and Casaubon, only the Spanish gentleman has the *ingenio* (and the force of will) to make the equestrian leap to the next plane of existence.

After her second marriage, Dorothea is pleased to follow her husband on his more quixotic forays. At last she has a complement for her own "Quixotic enthusiasm," as Eliot aptly terms it (393; cf. Neale, 95). Ladislaw eventually stands for Parliament: "Since wrongs existed . . . her husband should be in the thick of a struggle against them, and . . . she should give him wifely help" (765–766). Eliot writes that "many who knew her, thought it a pity that so substantive and rare a creature should have been absorbed into the life of another, and be only known in a certain circle as a wife and mother" (766), but this, obviously, is what she wanted.[8] By the same measure, Micomicona, if necessary, will pursue her ends through whichever "knight errant" happens on the scene, as did Dorotea before her. She far outshines the man on whom she focuses her attention(s). We are not told what will become of her—or of them—in the provincial setting to which they will retire, but we can guess that Dorotea will continue to work her own way behind the scenes, while convincing her husband that he figures as the sum of all things (cf. Hathaway, 38–39).

The relationship that exists between Dorothea and Will Ladislaw before their marriage, and their relationship to another married couple, Tertius and Rosamond Lydgate, recall in certain respects the ties (and lack thereof) between Dorotea, Fernando, Luscinda, and Cardenio. What Eliot terms "the stealthy convergence of human lots" with regard to configurations of characters in her novel (98), also describes patterns of association that establish themselves within *Don Quixote*, as well as between the two novels. Fernando has taken Luscinda to wife, though Cardenio has a prior claim, just as Dorotea does on Fernando, who clandestinely promised her marriage. In turn, the Lydgates experience matrimonial discord and, in part to spite her husband, Rosamond feels a real attraction to Will. She recognizes that Dorothea is the "'preferred' woman" as far as Will is concerned, and even to her own husband, whose financial "benefactor" she has been as the wife of Casaubon (728). Dorothea realizes that this constitutes a "turning-point," and that she may be able to rescue Rosamond (and others) "from the misery of false incompatible bonds" (731).[9]

As in *Don Quixote*, this complex knot of relationships is finally unravelled, and each woman ends up with the "proper" mate. This resolution also gives occasion to soulful discourse on the nature of marriage, in words that could just as easily have been penned by Cervantes: "Marriage is so unlike everything else. There is something even awful in the nearness it brings. Even if we loved some one else better than—than those we were married to, it would be no use. . . . I mean marriage drinks up all our power of giving or getting any blessedness in that sort of love" (732). Throughout his literary corpus, though particularly in *Don Quixote*, Cervantes meditates on what constitutes true marriage, to whom, and how.[10] In fact, Dorotea's statement in this regard to Fernando could well serve as a leitmotif for the marriages in *Middlemarch*: "más fácil te será, si en ello miras, reducir tu voluntad a querer a quien te adora, que no encaminar la que te aborrece a que bien te quiera" (pt. 1, ch. 36, 332).

Another thematic strand the two novels in question share is a preoccupation with questions of a social, or more properly, of a genealogical nature. The concern with "limpieza de sangre" in Cervantes's age is well-documented; it is even suggested periodically that the author himself was of *converso* background. George Eliot may well have been aware of such concerns as she depicted Ladislaw of "doubtful" ancestry. One of the objections to Mrs. Casaubon's relationship with him, raised by certain characters in the novel, is that "young Ladislaw [is] the grandson of a thieving Jew pawnbroker" (711). This "tainted" ancestry, of which Will's "social position" (711) becomes a function for some people, will make no difference to Dorothea. Her overarching concern is always justice, to right wrongs done to him or to his ancestors. For that reason she desires to redress the fiscal injustice done to Will's branch of the family by Casaubon's. The fact that certain individuals claim that Ladislaw's grandmother made a "bad" marriage and was disinherited does not mean Dorothea will not follow her best matrimonial inclinations, or at least follow suit, as the case may be (see Beaty, 159–163).

In questions of blood, then, Dorothea lives by the same rationale as her *tocaya*, who argues with Don Fernando, "Y si te parece que has de aniquilar tu sangre por mezclarla con la mía, considera que pocas o ninguna nobleza hay en el mundo que no haya corrido por este camino" (pt. 1, ch. 36, 332). She discourses on the true nature of nobility, which for her consists "en la virtud," rather than strictly in bloodlines (pt. 1, ch. 36, 332; cf. Márquez Villanueva, 30–31; Nieto, 510). Clearly, Cervantes is of like mind, albeit with a potent injection of irony. In this regard, Dorotea further appeals to "la generosidad" of her lover-turned-husband's "ilustre y noble pecho" (pt. 1, ch. 36, 335), until at long last the narrator concedes that "el valeroso pecho de don Fernando, en fin, como alimentado con ilustre sangre, se ablandó y se dejó vencer de la verdad" (336). Perhaps the virtue of this *segundón* (he was only the Duke's second son) does emerge, but the greater virtue, in matters verbal as well as sanguineous, rests with Dorotea, and later with her namesake in *Middlemarch*, who follows her lead to the letter (cf. Wright, 84–92).

As the story of their mutual misfortune unfolds in *Don Quixote*, before all is resolved Cardenio asks Don Fernando's spurned lover, "¿Que Dorotea es tu nombre, señora? Otra he oído decir del mismo, que quizá corre parejas con tus desdichas. Pase adelante, que tiempo vendrá en que te diga cosas que te espanten en el mismo grado que te lastimen" (pt. 1, ch. 28, 250). George Eliot must also have heard these same words and taken them to heart as she created her version of Dorotea in Dorothea. In many respects their misfortunes, as well as their ultimate good fortune, do seem to parallel each other. The author of *Middlemarch* follows Cardenio's lead, narrating in her own fiction exploits both amazing and painful, based at least in part on the life of another character who bears the same name as her protagonist. Cardenio's question could be asked then of either woman to essentially the same effect. Actually, George Eliot is not fettered by her ties to Cervantes's text any more than her predecessor was encumbered by his "imitation" of models (see Riley, 61–67; Robert passim). Her intercalation of a woman whose story itself is intercalated in *Don Quixote* only expands her literary horizons. Dorothea is no clone of Dorotea; their "convergence," far more than a simple question of categories and correspondences, is subtle, and even "stealthy." The two women are much more than just nominally related, though each is independent, even autonomous, within her own sphere and perhaps beyond.

NOTES

1. With reference to Eliot, *Middlemarch*, and Santa Teresa, see, among others, Fraser 400–411; Harvey, 194–195; Wright, 15; Daiches, 7.

2. With regard to Dorotea and her station within the Cervantine canon, see, for instance, Madariaga, 67–82; Márquez Villanueva, 15–75; Combet, 41–49; Márquez, 115–123; Hathaway, 12–39.

3. Concerning Casaubon and his scholarship, see Daiches, 17–18; Mintz, 115–121; Knoepflmacher, 51–58; Harvey, 27–37; Ellmann, 25–26; Hertz, 75–96. In turn, Mills 1994, 1–6) discusses various parallels between Casaubon and Don Quixote.

4. With regard to the perspectivism of this ongoing dialogue, see, for instance, Castro, 82–83, 90; Efron, 77, 172–173; Eisenberg, 140–141.

5. Those few commenting on *Don Quixote* and this part of *Middlemarch* include Miller, 109; Wiesenfarth, 59; McSweeney, 10. Concerning nominative

perspectivism in *Don Quixote*, see Spitzer, 135–187. In his unpublished dissertation, Conner (1977) comments on certain narrative elements in *Don Quixote* that reappear in *Middlemarch*, among other nineteenth- and twentieth-century novels. On the multiple significance of names in *Middlemarch*, see Knoepflmacher, 53–54, 67–68; Harvey, 45.

6. See Oñate, 110; Aspe, 39–43.

7. Concerning Dorotea's dress (and undress), see Madariaga, 67–82; Márquez Villanueva, 22–24; Fajardo, 89–108; Hathaway, 18–20. With regard to the ongoing debate concerning Eliot, *Middlemarch*, and feminism(s), see, for instance, Graver, 64–74; Neale, 147–161; Wright, 72–81.

8. McGhee (1991, 90–95) includes an analytical summary of critical opinions on Ladislaw and Dorothea's marriage. See also Mintz, 111–115, 127–129; Tick, 150–153; Haight, 22–42; Daiches, 42.

9. Concerning relationships between pairs and individuals in this part of *Don Quixote*, see Nieto, 496–527; Márquez, 115–123. With regard to pairings of various sorts in *Middlemarch*, see, among others, Heilman, 47–54; Harvey, 25–37; Hornback, 39–40; Ellmann, 17–38; McGhee, 77–96; Hertz, 75–96. Both *Don Quixote* and *Middlemarch* are aptly described by Neale's term, "multiplot novel." Concerning Dorothea's motivation(s), Daiches writes (linking her once again to Santa Teresa), "In the very first chapter of the novel George Eliot had made clear some of the ambiguities of virtue and showed that the desire to feel good could not be dissociated, even in the most virtuous, from the motives which lead to good and unselfish actions" (cf. Neale, 90–103; Carroll, 7, 88–90. Márquez Villanueva (16–63) and Hathaway (12–39) offer perceptive psychological readings of Dorotea's typically mixed and contradictory motives.

10. Concerning Cervantes and marriage, see, for instance, Cirot, 1–74; Márquez Villanueva, 63–73; Piluso.

BIBLIOGRAPHY

Aspe, María Paz. "Teresa de Jesús o la superación de la feminidad." In *Estudios de historia, literatura y arte hispánicos ofrecidos a Rodrigo A. Molina*. Madrid: Insula, 1977.

Beaty, Jerome. "The Forgotten Past of Will Ladislaw." *Nineteenth-Century Fiction* 13 (1958): 159–163.

Carroll, David. "*Middlemarch* and the Externality of Fact." In *This Particular Web*, ed. Ian Adams. Toronto: University of Toronto Press, 1975.

Castro, Américo. *El pensamiento de Cervantes*. Barcelona: Noguer, 1972.

Cervantes y Saavedra, Miguel de. *El ingenioso hidalgo don Quijote de la Mancha*, ed. Luis Astrana Marín. Madrid: Castilla, 1966.

Cirot, Georges. "Gloses sur les 'maris jaloux' de Cervantes." *Bulletin Hispanique* 31 (1929): 1–74.

Combet, Louis. *Cervantès ou les incertitudes du désir*. Lyon: Presses Universitaires de Lyon, 1980.

Conner, John Joseph. "The Quixotic Novel from the Point of View of the Narrative." Ph.D. diss., University of Florida, 1977.

Daiches, David. *George Eliot: "Middlemarch."* London: Edward Arnold, 1963.

Efron, Arthur. *"Don Quixote" and the Dulcinated World*. Austin: University of Texas Press, 1971.

Eisenberg, Daniel. *A Study of "Don Quixote."* Newark, Del.: Juan de la Cuesta, 1987.

Eliot, George. *Middlemarch*, ed. Quentin Anderson. New York: Collier, 1962.

Ellmann, Richard. *Golden Codgers*. New York: Oxford University Press, 1973.

Fajardo, Salvador J. "Unveiling Dorotea or the Reader as Voyeur." *Cervantes* 4 (1984): 89–108.

Fraser, Hilary. "St. Theresa, St. Dorothea, and Miss Brooke." *Nineteenth-Century Fiction* 40 (1986): 400–411.

Graver, Suzanne. "'Incarnate History': The Feminisms of Middlemarch." In *Approaches to Teaching Eliot's "Middlemarch"*, ed. Kathleen Blake. New York: Modern Language Association of America, 1990.

Haight, Gordon S. "George Eliot's 'Eminent Failure,' Will Ladislaw." In *This Particular Web*, ed. Ian Adams. Toronto: University of Toronto Press, 1975.

Harvey, W. J. *The Art of George Eliot*. London: Chatto and Windus, 1961.

———. "The Intellectual Background of the Novel: Casaubon and Lydgate." In *"Middlemarch": Critical Approaches to the Novel*, ed. Barbara Hardy. New York: Oxford University Press, 1967.

Hathaway, Robert L. *Not Necessarily Cervantes: Reading of the "Quixote"*. Newark, Del.: Juan de la Cuesta, 1995.

Heilman, Robert B. " 'Stealthy Convergence' in *Middlemarch*." In *George Eliot: A Centenary Tribute*, eds. Gordon S. Haight and Rosemary T. VanArsdel. Totowa, N.J.: Barnes and Noble, 1982.

Hertz, Neil. *The End of the Line*. New York: Columbia University Press, 1985.

Hornback, Bert G. *"Middlemarch": A Novel of Reform*. Boston: Twayne, 1988.

Johnson, Carroll B. *Madness and Lust*. Berkeley and Los Angeles: University of California Press, 1983.

Knoepflmacher, U. C. "Fusing Fact and Myth: The New Reality of *Middlemarch*." In *This Particular Web*, ed. Ian Adams. Toronto: University of Toronto Press, 1975.

Madariaga, Salvador de. *Guía del lector del Quijote*. Buenos Aires: Editorial Sudamericana, 1967.

Márquez, Héctor P. *La representación de los personajes femeninos en el "Quijote."* Madrid: José Porrúa Turanzas, 1990.

Márquez Villanueva, Francisco. *Personajes y temas del Quijote*. Madrid: Taurus, 1975.

McGhee, Richard D. "'To Be Wise Herself': The Widowing of Dorothea Brooke in George Eliot's *Middlemarch*." In *Joinings and Disjoinings*, eds. JoAnna Stephens Mink and Janet Doubler Ward. Bowling Green: Bowling Green State University Popular Press, 1991.

McSweeney, Kerry. *Middlemarch*. London: George Allen and Unwin, 1984.

Miller, J. Hillis. "Optic and Semiotic in *Middlemarch*." In *Modern Critical Views: George Eliot*, ed. Harold Bloom. New York: Chelsea, 1986.

Mills, Chester St. H. "Eliot's Spanish Connection: Casaubon, the Avatar of Quixote." *George Eliot/George Henry Lewes Studies* 26–27 (1994): 1–6.

Mintz, Alan. *George Eliot and the Novel of Vocation*. Cambridge: Harvard University Press, 1978.

Nadeau, Carolyn A. "Evoking Astraea: The Speeches of Marcela and Dorotea in *Don Quijote I.*" *Neophilologus* 79 (1995): 53–61.

Neale, Catherine. *George Eliot: "Middlemarch."* London: Penguin, 1989.

Nieto, Ramón. "Cuatro parejas en *El Quijote.*" *Cuadernos Hispanoamericanos* 276 (1973): 496–527.

Oldfield, Derek. "Language of the Novel: The Character of Dorothea." In *"Middlemarch": Critical Approaches to the Novel*, ed. Barbara Hardy. New York: Oxford University Press, 1967.

Oñate, María del Pilar. *El feminismo en la literatura española.* Madrid: Espasa-Calpe, 1938.

Piluso, Robert V. *Amor, matrimonio y honra en Cervantes.* New York: Las Américas, 1967.

Riley, E. C. *Cervantes's Theory of the Novel.* 1962; reprint, Newark, Del.: Juan de la Cuesta, 1992.

Robert, Marthe. *The Old and the New*, trans. Carol Cosman. Berkeley and Los Angeles: University of California Press, 1977.

Soufas, Teresa Scott. *Melancholy and the Secular Mind in Spanish Golden Age Literature.* Columbia: University of Missouri Press, 1990.

Spitzer, Leo. *Lingüística e historia literaria.* 2d ed. Madrid: Gredos, 1961.

Tick, Stanley. "The Very Nature of a Conclusion." In *Approaches to Teaching Eliot's "Middlemarch,"* ed. Kathleen Blake. New York: Modern Language Association of America, 1990.

Wiesenfarth, Joseph. "*Antique Gems* from *Romola* to *Daniel Deronda.*" In *George Eliot: A Centenary Tribute*, eds. Gordon S. Haight and Rosemary T. VanArsdel. Totowa, N.J.: Barnes and Noble, 1982.

Wright, T. R. *George Eliot's "Middlemarch."* New York: Harvester Wheatsheaf, 1991.

9

Cervantes in Bolivia:
The Painter Walter Solón Romero
as Spokesman of Don Quixote

Luis R. Quiroz

In the summer of 1996 I spent two months in Bolivia gathering material for an anthology on the influence of Cervantes and *Don Quixote* on all genres of Bolivian literature. As a result of this trip I was fortunate not only to have found a wealth of information on this fascinating topic, but also to have met with many outstanding writers, literary critics, and painters who have devoted their art to Cervantes and his immortal hero, Don Quixote. Among them were the novelists and short-story writers Francisco Bedregal, Oscar Alfaro, and Gastón Suárez; the poets Gregorio Reynolds, Armando Soriano Badani, Humberto Vicarra Monje, and Abel Alarcón; the painters Carmen Alvarez Daza (also known as Carmen Baptista), Miguel Yapur Daza, and Walter Solón Romero, the subject of this chapter.[1] One of the best known, most admired, and deeply respected Bolivian artists of our time, Solón Romero is a many dimensioned artist, the devoted missionary of a foundation that carries his name, and, above all, the multifaceted spokesman of Don Quixote.[2]

Born on November 9, 1926, in Uyuni, Potosi, Walter Solón Romero was exposed to art since his early and precocious childhood. As a small boy he thought himself "more a musician than an artist," though his drawing of a peacock "just from hearing about it" had him skipped from kindergarten to first grade, where he painted an extraordinary mural at the age of six.[3] In his upper teens he played second violin in the Symphony Orchestra of Sucre, but fearing that he would be "just one more musician," decided instead to pursue the visual arts. In May 1996, in the opening remarks of his last exhibit in La Paz, entitled *Don Quixote in Solón's Work*, the artist tells of how his father would entertain his young family by creating charcoal drawings. One night, he adds, "the magical character of Don Quixote emerged," and the stories that followed the sketches made him identify with that lanky figure of "power, kindness, and justice": "I had not even learned how to read and I already knew Don Quijote. . . . Much later I came to realize that it was a story written by Miguel de Cervantes."[4]

With degrees obtained from the National Academy of Fine Arts of La Paz and Sucre, Solón Romero pursued his studies in Chile, Brazil, Japan, India, Egypt, Greece, Italy, France, and Mexico. In addition, he studied art restoration with Sheldon Keck in New York.[5] In Paris he learned tapestry making with Jacques Brachet, and in Chile he perfected the complex art of mural painting with the Mexican muralist David Alfaro Siqueiros.

Like those of Siqueiros, Solón's murals are meant to reach out and communicate with his people, to capture its history and its sensibility. This can be felt tangibly in his *Portrait of a Town* (*El Retrato de un Pueblo*), which was painted for the University of La Paz. Pablo Ramos Sánchez, rector of the university, speaks of its profound message of "struggle and hope," because "it synthesizes not only the history of the University, but the great popular struggles of many centuries. . . . This mural is the most important contribution that the painter Walter Solón Romero offers to Bolivia and to posterity."[6] Another mural, *A Town in the Wind* (*Pueblo al viento*), from 1958, is described by the scholar Guillermo Francovich as "inspired . . . as all his work, by a profound social and human sensibility; it presents, on the one hand, dramatic scenes of poverty, and, on the other, fierce fights among dogs, bulls, and other domestic animals."[7] These ferocious dogs would appear later in Solón Romero's acclaimed series of drawings of Don Quijote. In all, the seven murals and eight frescoes that reside to date on the walls of public buildings and private homes are eloquent testimony of the artist's ceaseless quest for human dignity and freedom.

In addition to painting murals, Solón Romero has experimented with other modes of expression, creating his own language through a variety of techniques: pen drawing, xylography, stained glass, etching, lithography, oil painting, water color, ink, pyroxiline, woodcarving, fresco, tapestry, and etching on cement.[8] In his constant effort to diversify his work, Walter Solón Romero found another viable medium in tapestry. Using natural materials and techniques, he not only designs but weaves each piece himself. His son Pablo Solón explains, "It is not enough to be an artist. One must also be a craftsman. . . . Solón is in all senses of the word an artisan—which makes the elitists cringe. . . . If

[he] has not delved into other techniques in more depth, it is only because forty years are very little time for an artist."[9] Solón's 1975 tapestry exhibit in La Paz, entitled *In Search of the Lost Art of Weaving* (*En Pos de la Urdidumbre Perdida*), inspired the poet Paz Nery Nava to write a piece in praise of the artist's mastery. The first stanza begins,

To paint with a paintbrush is normal;
but to paint with wool
that comes from graceful highland alpacas,
that indeed is magical.[10]

The critic Teresa Gisbert comments that Solón's tapestry "reveals our world to us with its roots in the land and man, without concessions to international intellectualism or national folklore."[11]

Yet within this immense diversity, which includes even certain strikingly unusual altarpieces, Solón's pen-and-ink drawings of Don Quixote are likely to remain his best known images. Dunia Chávez Gonzáles, writing on "Solón Romero y el Quijote," emphasizes the artist's ability to make the observer see through these drawings "the idealist, the dreamer, the person of courage who is determined to outface life and effect change."[12] Solón Romero himself, noting that many of his colleagues at an exhibit in Spain were "reevaluating Don Quixote's image, but not his spirit," exclaimed, "It is his spirit that I wanted to capture."[13] This has been his lifelong commitment.

As we have noted before, Solón Romero's relationship with Don Quixote dates back to his childhood. Naturally, then, "When I became a painter, I adopted his figure to tell what I have seen and lived in the long journey of so many years, worn out by time."[14] From this point on, Don Quixote became Solón Romero's spokesman, and he, the spokesman of Don Quixote. Actually, in every troubling event of the artist's life, Don Quixote has come to the artist's rescue and given him courage. In his own words, "In his figure I would find the word that I couldn't in my throat."[15] So Solón recounts the genesis of his drawings of Don Quixote. This is his moving story.

In 1947, upon his return from Chile, the young Solón Romero suffered a near fatal airplane accident. In fact, his injuries were so severe that his doctors "very gently" informed him that he was about to expire.[16] But such was not to be. While at a hospital in Sucre, in spite of agonizing pain—he could hardly breathe, much less talk—he drew *Don Quixote, the Physician* (*Don Quijote, Médico*) for the yearbook of the graduating medical students of that year. Goyo Mayer recalls how Solón Romero's hospital bed "turned into a small workshop" and how the excitement of painting again made the artist forget his project of writing *La adaptación a la muerte, o Diario de un hospitalizado*, his memoirs of the crash.[17] Having sketched this first Don Quixote and at last recuperated from his injuries, in 1953–1954 Solón Romero painted for the National Teachers College of Sucre a huge mural entitled *Message to the Teachers of the Future* (*Mensaje a los Maestros del Futuro*), with Don Quixote the Teacher as its central figure. As the artist explains, Don Quixote wears an all-comprehending expression, as if he is looking simultaneously at the past, present and future of Bolivian education.[18]

In 1958, in the private home of a well-known doctor, he painted another mural, *Don Quixote and Tunupa* (the mythological Andean god of goodness, peace, and justice). For his exhibit in New York in 1968, he displayed drawings of Don Quixote, along with "another character as great as himself," to form the series *Don Quixote and Saint Francis* (*Don Quijote y San Francisco*).[19] When asked about this Quixote, Solón answered, "This is a Quixote of peace. I feel that both mythical figures are related by their purity and ideals."[20] Honored by his own government with its highest awards for the arts, feted as well by Chile and Uruguay, and exhibited in fifteen countries, Solón was approaching the height of his career. But the political horizon in his native Bolivia was darkening, and soon his world would irrevocably change.

In 1971 Solón's stepson, José Carlos, was tortured and assassinated at the hands of killers hired by the government. Between 1972 and 1974 Walter and his wife were unjustly imprisoned and exiled, not for being "affiliated with any political party but for thinking like Don Quixote about the value of justice."[21] But all this served only to sharpen his drawing pen, which the poet Jorge Medina Medina likened to "a powerful gun shooting ammunition of light."[22] From exile he drew the series *Don Quixote and the Dogs* (*Don Quijote y los Perros*), in 1972–1974, denouncing the rampages of dictatorship. Despite its refinement of lines and its profound poeticism, this collection would become for many the symbol of man's struggle against oppression. An anthology of writings bearing its name was published in 1979, while some of its authors were still in exile.[23] This volume on political terrorism includes all the drawings of Solón's collection, and its cover is illustrated with one of Solón's paintings, *Death in the Valley* (*Muerte en el Valle*).

Appalled at the massacre of striking miners by the Bolivian army, Solón produced his next series, *Don Quixote in the Mines* (1974–1976), which for obvious reasons could find no way to a gallery at the time. Between 1981 and 1982 he launched his *Don Quixote in Exile*, a collection that has been widely acclaimed, both in Bolivia and abroad. Finally, his latest set of drawings, *Don Quixote and the Angels* (1988–1990) was born when the artist discovered that the assassins who had tortured him and his wife and killed their stepson were declared innocent of all charges. With anguished strokes he denounced through the image of Don Quixote the injustice of courts that exonerated the guilty and punished only those who fought for freedom.

At the start of a talk given in La Paz in 1996, Solón asked his audience, "You must be wondering why Don Quixote is amidst us."[24] Answering from his own perspective, he then concluded by inviting the people in attendance to reflect upon the reality he conveys through his art. In truth, it is by staring at each picture, by watching Don Quixote's many facial expressions and body language, that we realize how masterfully Solón Romero makes his "intimate accomplice" the purveyor of his innermost feelings. Each drawing conveys an extraordinary range of emotions; each one moves the observer in mysterious and magical ways. What adds even more to the portrayal of Don Quixote are the artist's incisive captions, such as one from *Don Quixote and the Dogs*, entitled simply, "Hoy es todavía" [It is still so today] (Figure 9.1).[25]

Here a soldier stands with his tear gas mask, his combat fatigues, and his automatic machine gun, holding by a leash three snarling dogs ready to attack Don Quixote, who has his spear in his right hand and his sword in his left. Behind him there are demonstrators carrying large signs and flags. Don Quixote's courage and determination to stop the dogs and the soldier from attacking the marching group can be seen and felt in his wide-open furious eyes, his arms extended in a fighting position, and his feet firmly planted on the ground. Furthermore, the soldier, surprised by the knight's valor, leans far back to restrain his raging dogs, symbol of the reigning political power. In this scene Don Quixote,

Figure 9.1
Don Quixote and the Dogs

Drawing by Walter Solon Romero.

the tireless defender of the innocent, confirms that things today are still as they were then, when he had to stand up against injustice.

In another instance, Don Quixote is behind jail bars, clenching them with both hands and leaning his head against one of the bars. With his eyes closed, his face wrinkled with pain and sorrow, and his tired lean body, Don Quixote shows not despair or failure, but resignation and hope. He may be physically beaten, but never spiritually defeated. This drawing from the series *Don Quixote in Exile* is deftly captioned: "Freedom will blossom in spring" (Figure 9.2).[26]

In the series *Don Quixote and the Angels*, there is a drawing that epitomizes Solón Romero's understanding of Cervantes and his immortal hero (Figure 9.3). Don Quixote is riding on his Rocinante, and Sancho on his donkey. When they look up to the sky, they see two winged

Figure 9.2
Don Quixote in Exile

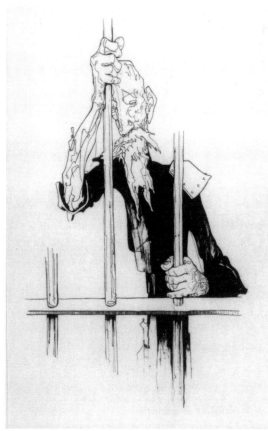

Drawing by Walter Solon Romero.

Figure 9.3
Don Quixote and the Angels

Drawing by Walter Solon Romero.

fully armed soldiers. They carry machine guns aimed at the knight and his squire, and extra rounds of ammunition on their belts and on their chests. Calmly, Don Quixote turns toward Sancho and says, "Do you suppose they are there to *protect* us?" The poignant irony of this statement needs no comment.[27]

In a similar vein, Solón's *The Valley of the Stones*, an animated video featuring the artist and his grandson, portrays Don Quixote's love of beauty. At the end, the child asks his grandfather, "Why did those mean men crush the rose?" "Because those who do not know beauty are always prone to destroy it," the old man answers.[28] At this point Don Quixote's puzzlement equals that of the little boy.

Another quixotic endeavor of Walter Solón Romero has been the establishment of a foundation in 1991 to promote the awareness and recovery of Bolivia's historical and cultural reality and to train young artists and craftsmen in diverse arts and disciplines. In order to achieve these and other objectives, the foundation has had some economic support from the Swiss Labor Union. However, most of its revenues come from the work that the artist, his son, and a few students do in their workshop, creating and selling videos and artwork that deal with education, art, history, and contemporary social issues. Thus, the series of poster-size drawings of Don Quixote and the video *The Valley of the Stones* (*El Valle de las Piedras*), plus fifteen other twenty-minute videos, have become the main source of its income.

In conclusion, Walter Solón Romero, through his life-long relationship with Don Quixote, has learned to cope with adversity in the same way that the fabled hero did. Furthermore, he has imbued himself with the same universal values of love, justice, and beauty that fired the Gentleman of La Mancha. In the process, the artist has left us a worthy legacy that qualifies him as an accurate and eloquent spokesman of Don Quixote.

NOTES

1. The reader may be interested in Juan Francisco Bedregal's "Don Quijote en la ciudad de La Paz" (short story), Oscar Alfaro's "Don Quijote en el siglo XX" (short story), Gastón Suárez's *Las aventuras de Miguelín Quijano* (novelette), and Guillermo Francovich's "Cervantes quiere ser corregidor de La Paz" and *Clavileño* (drama).

2. In recognition of his eminent artistic achievements, the entire edition of *Nueva Universidad. Revista de la Universidad de San Andrés* (La Paz, Bolivia, 1989) was dedicated to Walter Solón Romero. For a complete listing of his works and awards, see p. 3.

3. Luis Ramos Paoli, "Un mural llamado Solón" (*Nueva Universidad*, La Paz, 1989). This information about Solón Romero's childhood is taken from Ramos Paoli's interview with the artist. (All translations in this chapter are mine.)

4. Walter Solón Romero, "El Quijote en la obra de Solón," fragmentos de su discurso en la inauguración de la muestra retrospectiva, *Fundación Mario Mercado Vaca Guzman-Fundación Solón* (La Paz, Bolivia, May 1996) (hereafter "El Quijote") (interview in journal).

5. Walter Solón Romero, "Experiencias sobre conservación y restauración de obras de arte," *Nueva Universidad* (p. 58), praises Prof. Sheldon Keck's Cooperstown Conservation training program and stresses the knowledge and responsibility involved in conserving and restoring works of art. See also Ramos Paoli's comments (p. 10) about the artist's nine-year dedication to these techniques and his trips to Japan, China, Korea, Mongolia, and the Soviet Union in search of more understanding and experience in these areas (interview in journal).

6. *El retrato de un pueblo* (Murales de Solón, La Paz, Bolivia: Universidad de San Andrés, 1989), 2.

7. Guillermo Francovich, *Variedad* (La Paz, Bolivia: Editorial "Juventud," 1988), 194.

8. Etching on cement is achieved through a mixture of resin and cement. A technique developed by the artist, its substantial resistance allows for many imprints.

9. Pablo Solón, "Mensaje Gráfico: Con un nudo en la esperanza," *Nueva Universidad*, 36 (interview in journal).

10. Paz Nery Nava, "Los tapices de Solón Romero," *Nueva Universidad*, 60 (interview in journal).

11. Julia Viotti, quoting Teresa Gisbert de Mesa, "Walter Solón: un Quijote latinoamericano," *Cultura Popular Latinoamericana*, 94. See also Gisbert de Mesa, "Tapiz y dibujo," *Nueva Universidad* (1989): 46.

12. Dunia Chávez Gonzáles,"Solón Romero y el Quijote," *Nueva Universidad* (1989): 33.

13. "El Quijote," 2.

14. Ibid.

15. Ibid.

16. Ramos Paoli, "Un mural," 7.

17. Goyo Mayer, "Cómo se pintaron los murales de la Universidad de Sucre," *Nueva Universidad* (1989): 20.

18. "El Quijote," 2.

19. Ibid.

20. Ibid.

21. Telephone conversation with L. Quiroz, December 4, 1998.

22. Jorge Medina Medina, "Walter Solón Romero," *Nueva Universidad* (1989): 59.

23. *El Quijote y los perros. Antología del terror político*, introduction by Alfredo Medrano (Cochabamba, Bolivia: Editorial Universal, 1979).

24. "El Quijote," 2.

25. *Hoy es todavía*, Serie de videos de reflexión. Permission granted by Fundación Solón Romero, La Paz, Bolivia.

26. From *Don Quijote en el Exilio*. Permission granted by Fundación Solón Romero, La Paz, Bolivia.

27. From *Don Quijote y los Angeles*. Permission granted by Fundación Sólon Romero, La Paz, Bolivia.

28. *El valle de las piedras*. Series de videos de reflexión: *Hoy es todavía*. Fundación Soler, La Paz, Bolivia, 1996.

10

Don Quixote *as Theatre*

Dale Wasserman

In self-defense, I should like it noted that I am not nor ever have been an Hispanic scholar. I am a playwright, one of whose works, *Man of La Mancha*, is enjoying performances in some forty languages, and which seems to have gone into theatrical history as the first truly successful adaptation of the novel *Don Quixote*. I consider this an unfortunate impression. *Man of La Mancha*, strictly speaking, is not an adaptation of *Don Quixote* at all. It is a play about Miguel de Cervantes. I do claim to know a little about Cervantes. That's a fairly safe claim, as there is no one who knows a great deal about him.

For those interested in beginnings, *Man of La Mancha* was born not by design but by accident. The year was 1959. I was in Spain writing a movie when I read in a newspaper that my purpose there was research for a dramatization of *Don Quixote*. That was nonsense, of course, for like the great majority of people who claim to know *Don Quixote*, I had never read it. Spain was a logical place to repair that omission, so I waded in, emerging on the other side of its half-million words convinced that there was *no way* to dramatize this amazing compendium of the good, the bad, and the brilliant.

I was aware that there had been dozens, perhaps hundreds of such attempts—plays, opera, ballet, puppet shows, movies—every dramatic form possible. I was also aware that they had one thing in common—they failed. Having now read the book I wasn't at a loss for a reason. Trying to compress this book into a neat dramatic structure was like trying to force a lake into a bucket: ambitious, but impractical. It was clear that *Don Quixote* was all things to all people, and that no two of them could agree on its meanings. In that, perhaps, lay the power of the book. Each reader seemed to have read something different, something shaped by the attributes the reader brought as personal baggage. No two people with whom I ever had a discussion seem to have read the same book. No two could agree on a precise meaning. One suspects that this may be the most potent reason for the enduring success of the novel—that each may take from it the meaning he personally chooses.

There's my confession: Dazed by the riches of *Don Quixote*, I felt myself quite inadequate to the proposition of adapting it to theatrical form, until that moment that one awaits—and awaits—the moment of revelation that most often never arrives. In this case, however, lightening did strike: It illuminated a single line in the novel, a line which revealed the secret of how a dramatization might be accomplished.

Its prelude lies in an encounter between Don Quixote and the farmer Pedro Alonso, to whom Quixote has spun out a tale of capture by the governor of Antequera and imprisonment in his castle. The farmer is astonished, for he knows Quixote perfectly well as his lifelong neighbor. Says the farmer, "Cannot your Grace see that I am not Don Rodrigo de Narváez, nor the Marquis of Mantua, but Pedro Alonso, your neighbor? And your Grace is merely a respectable gentleman by the name of Alonso Quijana?" Don Quixote replies, "I know who I am, and who I may be if I choose."

Examine that statement. "I know who I am, and who I may be if I choose." That is not the statement of a madman. Nor of one with vacant rooms in his head. To one whose profession is theatre it is instantly recognizable as the statement of an actor, an actor perfectly aware of the role he is playing and quite properly annoyed by any who question his assumed identity.

From this point forward I felt quite comfortable with Don Quixote. I understood him: an actor. That's what he was, first and last, writing his own play, always holding center stage. "In my childhood," he tells Sancho, "I loved plays, and I have always been an admirer of the drama." He also says, "Plays are the semblance of realities, and deserve to be loved because they set before our eyes looking-glasses that reflect human life. . . . Nothing tells us better what we are or ought to be than comedians and comedy."

Of course, there is a Shakespearean echo in these words. They recall the ruminations of another actor, Hamlet, who spoke of a mirror held up to nature, who had a love of theatricals, and who may or may not have been mad. It seems no coincidence that Shakespeare and Cervantes were almost precisely contemporary. Again and again we find evidence that Don Quixote is *acting* his role. We rarely see him alone, but when we do it is observable that he no longer acts the madman but is calm and introspective, the introspection of an actor mentally devising further scenes in the drama. To Sancho he says, "For a knight-errant to run mad upon just any occasion is not meritorious; no, the rarity is to run mad with purpose." Or, as I paraphrased it later, "There's no credit in going crazy by accident, you've got to do it by *design*."

Miguel de Cervantes was passionately and preeminently a man of the theatre. Very logically, his literary creation was an actor quite aware of the role he was playing. Here is where I found an affinity, an identification, and the solution to containment of the novel within a coherent form. The solution, of course, was not to dramatize the novel at all, but to write a play about a playwright and his alter ego. Both of them were actors, fantasists, dreamers of improbable dreams.

Cervantes might have considered a career in theatre before the war but his wounds and the captivity in Algiers intervened. When those harrowing years had passed, he wrote, by his own word, "some thirty or forty plays." Sadly they had little success. In rare lapses from his serene good nature, Cervantes would blame not his own ineptitude at playwriting but his exclusion from the circle of the literati, a circle of sycophants who clung to the shirttails of the very successful Lope de Vega, whom Cervantes called, "That prodigy of comedy." He blamed those who had entrée to the court and to patrons who had little interest in a crippled ex-soldier with theatrical ambitions.

To me it was irrelevant that his plays were not successful. One recognizes the passion for theatre which drives those of us who share it. A playwright has no problem identifying the techniques of theatre in the novel *Don Quixote*. There is the creation of living, breathing characters, the manufacture of a world better than the one we have been born to, the search for concise yet poetic expression of that world, the difficulties of realization which never measure so splendidly as the dimensions in one's mind. And by all means include the love of applause, not from anonymous readers but from a living, breathing audience in the immediate presence of one's creation. The affinity I felt with Cervantes is the same affinity common to all writers of theatre. We *know* each other, in the same moment in which we are ferociously competitive.

To one of the profession Cervantes is instantly recognizable as a playwright, no matter whether he is writing in play form, poetry, or the shape of a novel. *Don Quixote*, the novel, is inherently theatrical. We have mentioned delineation of character, but there is more. Psychological motivations drive the plot. His people change, they *grow*. His stories show the dynamism of the stage. His scenes are pictorial. Depiction of costume and setting are meticulous. Dialogue shows acute observation of behavior; it is terse, muscular, direct.

Most of all, however, Cervantes deals with the matter which is fundamental to all theatre: the collision of reality and illusion. Nowhere is it more eloquently explored than in *Don Quixote*. By no means, though, is it confined to that work. Search all of Cervantes, and you will find it, sometimes expressed overtly, sometimes in the subtext. By the way, those familiar with the *Exemplary Novels* will recognize that I drew upon them as heavily as I did upon *Don Quixote*. They will note that I populated the prison in Seville with raffish characters similar to those in *Rinconete y Cortadillo*. All of them are adrift on their own peculiar seas of illusion.

Partially out of research into those lost years of Cervantes and partially out of my own experience of a lifetime in the theatre, I formulated a vision of his career as a strolling player-playwright. Come, visualize it with me: a troupe of actors always on the move, traveling the dusty roads of Spain, stopping anywhere they might collect an audience. Visualize a painted player's wagon which will unfold its splintery boards to become a stage. The audience, largely illiterate bumpkins but possibly including the local poet or even a grandee or two, applauding, whistling, and, one hopes, tossing coins into the hats passed about by the actors. Cervantes, as the director and actor-in-chief, declaiming versions of his own adventures. His audience doubting those adventures' extravagance even though they had been modified for credibility. Nor let us forget a pudgy little man assembling props, pulling ropes, handling the curtains, the magic, the illusion—a Sancho to Cervantes's Quixote. The days of hunger when it rained or when audiences whistled the players out of town. Nights under the stars when the little band of players drank, roistered, and enjoyed the insular society of strolling players in all ages. And lovemaking, for it was in this period that Cervantes expressed his passion for the actress who gave birth to his natural daughter, Isabel. Here's where I found the courage to approach and interpret Cervantes; for a life in the theatre was my life, too.

One very short chapter in Book 2 of *Don Quixote* was particularly intriguing to me: Chapter 11, in which the knight has an encounter with a theatrical troupe traveling from village to village, performing a play called *The Parliament of Death*. Here the novel invokes devices which are purely theatrical: multiple levels of reality and symbolism with the implication of dark forces which are just beyond the limits of literal vision. Fascinated by the potential of such a scene, initially I developed it at full length, implying the possibility that these players on their trumpery wagon were something other than what they pretended to be. In reply to Quixote's challenge they say they are actors representing, respectively, death, love, a demon, an angel, and the devil himself. Under Don Quixote's challenge, Death removes his mask to reveal an identical skull face beneath. Are these really players, or is Quixote confronting the fundamentals which define each life on Earth? I chose ambiguity, allowing the audience to decide just what he had encountered.

I wrote the scene at some length, falling in love with matters barely implied by Cervantes. But don't look for it in the published version of *Man of La Mancha*, for it was found to be deeply troubling to the audience. The scene was evicted from the play, but I have always missed it. It's a wonderful maze of ideas, of symbolic wheels within wheels. The actor, Don Quixote, encounters a troupe of actors who may or may not *be* actors, leaving both Quixote and the audience wondering where the ultimate reality lay. That is pure theatre. The scene is a house of mirrors—multiple versions of reality—offering the audience a smorgasbord of possibilities from which to choose.

There's the heart of *Don Quixote*: continuous collisions of illusion and reality. Which of them shall overcome? Quite willfully I chose illusion, for illusion is the intriguing choice in a world where reality too often destroys the spirit. The most significant line in my play is a very simple one. Sansón Carrasco informs Don Quixote that there are no knights, no chivalry, that there have been no knights for three hundred years, and these are *facts*. Don Quixote replies, "Facts are the enemy of truth." I do believe that facts are the enemy of truth.

Carrasco adjures Cervantes that one must see life as it *is*. Here is Cervantes's answer, as he speaks in the play:

I have lived more than fifty years and I have seen life as it is. I have heard the singing from taverns and the moans from bundles of filth on the streets. I have been a soldier and seen my comrades die in battle, and I have held them in my arms in the final moment. These were men who saw life as it is, yet they died despairing. No glory, no gallant last words . . . only their eyes filled with confusion, whimpering the question, "Why?" I do not think they asked why they were dying, but why they had lived.

Then Cervantes rallies, his natural buoyancy of spirit asserting itself, and goes on to say,

When life itself seems lunatic, who knows where madness lies? Perhaps to be too practical is madness. To seek treasure where there is only trash. Too much sanity may be madness. And maddest of all, to see life as it is and not as it might *be*.

These are words of conflict, philosophies to be debated. But conflict is at the heart of all theatre, and conflict is inherent in every page of the novel *Don Quixote*. There's a syllogism here: Theatre is at the heart of every page of *Don Quixote*.

In conclusion, we do not know precisely when Cervantes was born. We don't know even where he is buried. But these are merely facts, immaterial to the truth that his literary monuments tower a bit higher with each succeeding century, and that we all are enriched thereby.

11

"Monsignor Quixote": Graham Greene Rewriting Unamuno Rewriting Cervantes

Jack B. Jelinski

In this chapter, I will examine Graham Greene's superb novel as a modern version of Cervantes's masterpiece in which the portrayal of characters, decisive episodes, and themes clearly reflect Miguel de Unamuno's (1964) interpretation of Cervantes's *The Adventures of Don Quixote*. Greene has even expropriated details of Unamuno's life and incorporated them into his own fictional world.

There are a number of references and structural parallels linking Greene's novel to the original. The novel's protagonists are Father Quixote, who is elevated to the status of monsignor, and Enrique Zancas, the communist ex-mayor of El Toboso, nicknamed Sancho for obvious reasons. Together they leave on a short holiday, Father Quixote to momentarily escape his authoritarian bishop, the mayor to escape the consequences of the election victory of his right-wing opponent. Along the way they discuss life's constraints with verve and good humor as they encounter multiple possibilities for adventure. The central characters refer to episodes in Cervantes's novel and occasionally quote from it. The two set off in a dilapidated Seat 600 affectionately referred to as "Rocinante." The Monsignor's novels of chivalry are holy, devotional books, and his squire Sancho makes certain they are well-provisioned with wine. They are pursued by the Guardia Civil (Holy Brotherhood). Monsignor Quixote is chided by his bishop for his madness just as the grave ecclesiastic in the house of the duke and duchess derides Don Quixote for his folly. The Monsignor is brought back to his village as a madman at the end of Part I and dies after a second series of adventures at the end of Part II of the novel. Greene skillfully weaves the threads of the original into the tapestry of his book, but the final pattern that emerges reveals the unmistakable vision of Unamuno.

Reminiscent of Cervantes's humorous inclusion of characters from the apocryphal Part II into his own novel, Greene includes textual references to Miguel de Unamuno in his version. Unamuno is referred to as "one of our great modern philosophers" (206), who was a "professor with a half belief" (98) with whom Sancho studied at Salamanca. In writing his interpretation of Cervantes's novel, Unamuno assumes the posture of a legitimate author of *La Vida de Don Quijote y Sancho*. In the prologue he claims to have the original text of Cide Hamete Benengeli upon which Cervantes based his novel. Just as Cervantes claims that Don Quixote was born for him alone (940), Unamuno makes a parallel claim, also in the last paragraph of his version, that Don Quijote and Sancho were born so that he could explain the significance of their lives (228). The mediations between Unamuno's version of the original and Greene's fiction are not only suggested by the inclusion of Unamuno in the story but are insistent throughout the narrative.

In the first few pages of *Monsignor Quixote*, Father Quixote recalls a reported conversation in which his authoritarian bishop questions the very patrimony of the good father's name, suggesting he could not be the descendent of a fictional character because "Quixote is not even a Spanish patronymic" (Greene, 17). The bishop's incredulity is repeated by Professor Pilbeam, "perhaps the greatest living authority on the life and works of Ignatius Loyola" (205) in the last chapter of the novel: "Don Quixote had no descendants. How could he? He's a fictional character" (209). Father Leopold, a student of Descartes, replies, "Fact and fiction again, professor. So difficult to distinguish" (209). Father Leopold followed the rationalist philosophy of Descartes as a young man in search for absolute truth. In the end, he escaped the doubt of rationalist philosophy by embracing faith (205). Serious students of Unamuno realize at once that he begins his commentary on Cervantes's text by pointing out that the original Don Quixote, in spite of his obscure origin, is as real as any character because his existence has had real consequences (19–21). His fictional existence is paradoxically more real than that of flesh-and-blood persons because his spirit is immortal and he has fathered spiritual descendants (220–226).

Unamuno also draws many parallels between the temperament of Don Quixote and that of "Iñigo de Loyola" (21). Greene refers to Unamuno's comparison in his novel: "You know that one of our great modern philosophers compared Saint Ignatius to Don Quixote. They had a lot in common" (206). Greene is aware that Unamuno was as ardent a student of Saint Ignatius as Professor Pilbeam. The professor and Father Leopold are intellectual alter egos of Unamuno himself. The opposition Greene establishes between Father Leopold and Professor Pilbeam mirrors Unamuno's need to embrace the vitalist philosophy of Don Quixote and reject rationalism, which denies the possibility of immortality; in short, to reject what he refers to as the "duda cósmica" of Descartes in *Del Sentimiento Trágico de la Vida* (86).

The faith of Father Quixote, Greene's simple parish priest of El Toboso, who is elevated to the position of monsignor because he performed a Christian act of charity toward a visiting Italian bishop, reflects the faith born of existential need that Unamuno imputes to the Don Quixote of his commentary. Father Quixote's faith is born of his courage to face doubt and despair. He points out to the mayor that he wants to believe (32), that he has his doubts (55), and that he believes because he must (90), even though he is always aware of the shadow of doubt (173). In explaining the mystery of the Trinity to the mayor, he divides the wine of one bottle into three bottles representing the three persons of the Trinity, explaining that without the Holy Ghost there would not be sufficient courage to continue the journey of life (50). One of the books he carries with him is Augustine's *Confessions*. Thus, the image of the wine suggests the beginning of Saint Augustine's discussion of the Trinity: "Lo, now the trinity appears unto me in a glass darkly" (St. Augustine, 270). The power Father Quixote imputes to the Holy Ghost is, according to Saint Augustine, the gift of love (271). This is the gift Father Quixote imparts to sustain his friend Sancho's faith in the final scenes of the novel when he dies (Greene, 217–221).

Unamuno's Don Quixote reveals a parallel faith based upon his courage to overcome doubt, a courage nourished by love. Unamuno identifies with Don Quixote in his quest for immortality, for meaning that transcends our mortal journey: "Toda vida heroica o santa corrió siempre en pos de la gloria, temporal o eterna, terrena o celestial" (*La Vida de Don Quijote y Sancho*, 27). Unamuno shows how Don Quixote reveals his true mission of conquering the "reino espiritual de la fe" (35) when he challenges the merchants of Toledo to acknowledge Dulcinea as the most beautiful of damsels without seeing her. Like Father Quixote, Unamuno's Don Quixote is motivated by love: "Amó Don Quixote a la Gloria encarnada en mujer" (*La Vida de Don Quijote y Sancho*, 58). He compares Don Quixote's devotion to Dulcinea to Saint Teresa's devotion to Christ (117). The prominent role Unamuno gives to Saint Teresa in his commentary leads Greene to transpose another Saint Teresa, Saint Thérèse of Liseux, "the Little Flower," with Dulcinea, so that Father Quixote too is inspired and comforted by platonic love. "She was dead many years before I knew her and grew to love her" (92). He always thought of her as "Señorita Martin" because it made her seem closer to him (93).

The faith of Unamuno's Don Quixote is also motivated by a vital existential need. Nowhere is this more apparent than in Don Miguel's commentary on the famous words Don Quixote utters in Chapter 58, part II: "Up till now I do not know what I am conquering by the force of my labours" (Cervantes, 839). Here Unamuno identifies with the existential anguish of his hero at a moment when his soul is shaken by a breath of wind from the wing of the angel of mystery; when he doubts, for a moment, the very goal of his mission, "la Gloria" (*La Vida de Don Quijote y Sancho*, 181). However, it is love that sustains Don Quixote even in defeat. For Unamuno, love is the energy that sustains the courage to maintain faith. In his commentary on the death of Don Quixote, Unamuno, like Greene, gives Sancho the gift of faith and transforms him into the heir to the spirit of Don Quixote.

In the course of Greene's novel, Father Quixote receives a "suspension a Divinas" from his bishop for a series of innocent errors born of his basic goodness. Some of these parallel the misadventures of Cervantes's hero. Just as Don Quixote released the galley slaves, Father Quixote contributes to a charitable organization dedicated to looking after the spiritual needs of the imprisoned. He even facilitates the escape of a thief, who steals his shoes in thanks for his trouble. Perhaps the suspension of Greene's character is related to Don Quixote's fear that he might be excommunicated for "laying violent hands on holy things" (Cervantes, 147). However, given the obvious presence of Unamuno in Greene's novel, Father Quixote's suspension from his priestly duties is more likely inspired by celebrated incidents in the life of Miguel de Unamuno indirectly alluded to in the text: "But he went into exile—as he had already done years before" (98). One possibility is his politically motivated suspension from his rectorship of the University of Salamanca in 1914. A more likely parallel is the occasion of his final dismissal and house arrest in October 1936. Luis Portillo, in his moving account of Unamuno's final lecture, recounts that the initial decision Franco sent for the Junta in Burgos to consider was his execution. When Father Quixote first opens his letter from his bishop, he says, "As I thought, it's a sentence of death" (Greene, 182).

As the end of Part I approaches, Father Quixote learns that the bishop, Father Herrera, and the Guardia are all conspiring to bring him home because of his scandalous adventures with the mayor. At the end of their final day spent eluding the authorities, they sleep, and the mayor has a disturbing dream. He is searching for Father Quixote, who is wandering about barefooted. He comes upon some traces of blood and emerges upon a scene where his friend is perched on top of the altar "like a sacred image" (Greene, 144), exposed to the laughter and ridicule of his parishioners. Part II of Greene's novel recounts how Father Quixote was found sleeping, given an injection to calm him, and brought back to El Toboso by Father Herrera. The parallels with

Cervantes's hero, who is brought back to his village under an enchantment fashioned by his friends and in a cage, are obvious. It is the dream of the mayor, which foreshadows his friend's fate, that owes much to Unamuno. Cervantes merely tells us that Don Quixote arrived at midday on a Sunday when all the people were in the marketplace (1950, 455–456). It is Unamuno who suggests that the motivation for bringing Don Quixote back at noon on Sunday was to maximize his exposure to "mayor burla y chacota" (112) of the people of his village. Unamuno draws a clear parallel between the "pasión" (107) of Don Quixote and Christ. He refers to Barcelona, the site of Don Quixote's final defeat, as "la Jerusalén de nuestro Caballero" (166), and compares his antagonists to the Pharisees who persecuted Christ (148). It is Unamuno's commentary on the original text that suggests the mayor's dream of the metaphoric crucifixion of Father Quixote and his exposure to public ridicule on the altar of his church.

The garrulous, worldly Mayor Sancho created by Greene also bears a remarkable series of similarities to Unamuno's recreation of the role of Cervantes's Sancho Panza. In Greene's novel the roles of the two protagonists are transposed, so that it is the mayor who becomes the instigator of most of the adventures they experience. Greene's Sancho is a communist who once studied for the priesthood before going into politics. As we have seen, he even studied with Unamuno at Salamanca, and he suggests to Father Quixote that if Unamuno had lived in the days of Cervantes, "Perhaps he would have followed the Don on a mule called Dapple, instead of Sancho" (98). He goes on to explain that it was the influence of Unamuno that kept him in the church, "with that half belief of his," which he shared for a while before he embraced the materialist philosophy of communism (99). In his reference to the possibility of Unamuno replacing Sancho as the squire of Don Quixote, Greene reveals his awareness of Unamuno's personal identification with the faith of Don Quixote, to whom he refers as "Don Quijote mío" (199) in his *La Vida de Don Quijote y Sancho*. Mayor Sancho's intellectual history mirrors that of Unamuno; only the trajectory is reversed.

Unamuno, as Allen Lacy points out, was not concerned with religious issues during his early years: "His own commitments were to materialistic monism, to science, and to positivism" (xiii). Rafael Pérez de la Dehesa has described in great detail Unamuno's early commitment to the socialist party in Spain and his intimate acquaintance with the materialist conception of history and class struggle of Marxism. However, he points out that after his religious crisis of 1897, precipitated by the severe illness of his son, he turned his attention almost exclusively toward a search for religious faith.

After this religious crisis, Unamuno became preoccupied with his own mortality. As Sánchez-Barbudo tells us, Unamuno sought a faith in God out of the depth of his anguish, but discovered he lacked true belief (205). After his crisis his writing centers around the struggle to resolve the conflict between his need for a faith in God to guarantee his immortality and the torment of doubt born of his intense rationalism. Mayor Sancho, while he was a student of Unamuno, also maintained his faith through this "dialéctica de angustia" (207), which he subsequently abandoned for the security of a life without doubt (Greene, 73–74). Thus, through this ironic biographical inversion, Greene has transformed Unamuno into the squire of Father Quixote in the person of Mayor Sancho.

Mayor Sancho not only represents the early, socialist Unamuno, but is also intimately linked to the materialist Sancho of Unamuno's commentary. Unamuno characterizes him as exclusively interested in his own material well-being, a man as yet without faith, the Simon Peter of Don Quixote (49). Sancho represents the voice of empirical science, of positivism (69). At one point Unamuno employs an extensive Marxist analysis of capitalism to characterize Sancho as a member of the proletariat (213). Greene's mayor is a social class above Sancho, a member of the bourgeoisie, as he illustrates by his Marxist version of the parable of the Prodigal Son (55–58). He is happy, however, to take advantage of bourgeois comfort for as long as it lasts (60). The humble squire of Cervantes, deceived by his greed, is transformed into a member of the proletariat by Unamuno and elevated to the bourgeoisie by Greene.

The conversations between the mayor and Father Quixote link all of their adventures together as a dialogue between faith and belief; between Christian humanism and its promise of immortality and Marxist ideology with its promise of the ideal communist state. As they share experiences, a rhetorical drama enfolds that leads to the redemption of the mayor, who comes to realize both the transformational power of love and the need for faith in something more than Marxist theory. The relationship between the characters and the redemptive ending of the story mirror the pattern of Unamuno's commentary.

Unamuno begins by suggesting that Cervantes's characterization of Sancho as a man of "muy poca sal en la mollera" was mistaken (40). He was Don Quixote's disciple, his chorus, and in the person of Sancho he loved all of humanity (41). Unamuno also discounts the notion that Sancho was motivated by greed, but rather that he follows Don Quixote on their first sally because he admires his faith. René Girard chides Unamuno for his "delirious" interpretation of Cervantes (98). He insists that a spiritual distance always remains between master and squire (9). But Unamuno is not interested in historical criticism. As we have seen at the outset, he is creating his own version of the story. He focuses on textual evidence he finds that confirms the development of a progressively deeper personal relationship between master and squire. Sancho becomes his master's confidant to whom he confesses the secret of his love (Unamuno, 59), just as Greene's Father Quixote confesses the secret of his love for Saint Thérèse to the mayor (93). Greene's Sancho is drawn to Father Quixote because he admired his faith; he thought he was a man without doubts (180). When he discovers that the priest maintains his faith in spite of constant doubt, he touches his shoulder in a moment of mutual understanding. Father Quixote feels "the electricity of affection in the touch," and reflects on how "sharing a sense of doubt can bring men together" (55). Unamuno draws a similar parallel between his characters. He says that the faith of Don Quixote was maintained in the face of constant doubt and that Sancho understood his master very well because, in spite of his own doubts, he too exercised his will to overcome them (124). For Sancho, faith resides "en mantener esa lucha entre el corazón y la cabeza, entre el sentimiento y la inteligencia" (124). The relationship between Unamuno's characters leads to a mutual dependency. When Sancho leaves to assume his governorship, Don Quixote "sintió su soledad" (158). Unamuno points out that Don Quixote is not himself without Sancho, because in him he loved all humanity (158). In a similar confession of love and dependency, Father Quixote confides to the mayor that he no longer has any other home but with him: "El Toboso is no longer home to me and I have no other, except on this spot of ground with you" (183).

In the last chapter of the book, Father Quixote is injured when two Guardias shoot out Rocinante's tires and the little Seat crashes into the walls of a monastery. He is only slightly injured and put to bed with a sedative. He never awakens, but arises while still dreaming, speaking in disjointed sentences about his adventures and quoting passages from Cervantes's novel (212–214). He speaks to the mayor, saying, "I don't offer you a governorship, Sancho. I offer you a Kingdom" (214). He then urges Sancho to follow him down into the shadows of the great church to the altar. Once there, he reenacts a mass consecrating "the non-existent wine in the non-existent chalice" (215). After laying an invisible host on his tongue, he approaches the mayor, addressing him as "compañero" and asks him to kneel. His last act is to administer communion to Sancho (217). Thus, in his final moments of life, he administers the love of Christ to his friend, that he may inherit the Kingdom of Heaven. The following day the mayor discusses with his friends the reality of what happened, whether he had truly received communion or not. In spite of his skepticism about the true nature of the dream, the act of the communion was a moment of epiphany. The love he felt for Father Quixote "seemed now to live and grow in spite of the final separation and the final silence—for how long, he wondered with a kind of fear, was it possible for that love of his to continue? And to what end?" (221). Mayor Sancho has experienced the extraordinary power of personal love, and as Georg Gaston has so perceptively observed, this experience is "so powerful that it can even make us leap into realms of faith where love becomes a transcendent force" (136).

The influence of Unamuno's text on this final chapter is complex and obvious. The descent into the shadows of the church clearly parallels the descent of Don Quixote into the cave of Montesinos. Unamuno compares the dream vision of Don Quixote to the experience of religious ecstasy God grants to mystics (137). He describes the experience within the framework of the theme of "la vida es sueño" (138), which he emphasizes in his moving elegy to the death of Don Quixote, set within verses from Calderón's famous play. The essence of the theme is that one's earthly existence is but transitory. Worldly aspirations are thus a dream, since the true reality for the Christian believer is the immortal life of the soul (Wilson, 74–75). Unamuno extends the parallel between Christ and Don Quixote when describing the death of the latter. In death, Don Quixote revealed the mystery of his life (215). He refers to his death as a sacrifice (218). Christ is always present in the sacrifice of the mass; the celebration of the Eucharist represents his triumph over death (Abbot, 140). Father Quixote is asleep because, as Unamuno suggests, his dream is more real than Mayor Sancho's worldly aspiration to achieve politically the perfect communist world. The mayor has always preferred Marx to the mystery of the possibility of redemption (220). Just as Mayor Sancho is touched by the love of Christ when he receives communion, Unamuno suggests that Sancho Panza is similarly transformed upon the death of Don Quixote. He becomes "filled with faith" as heir to the spirit of Don Quixote (220).

Both Greene's novel and Unamuno's rewriting of Cervantes converge in communicating a final, moving message about the redemptive power of love. Mayor Sancho has now lost his freedom from doubt; he will now live with the possibility of aspiring to the Kingdom of Heaven promised by Father Quixote. Unamuno, in a final supplication to God, asks that Sancho maintain his faith. which will allow him to realize the dream of becoming a shepherd in the infinite pastures of Heaven (225).

Graham Greene's novel has been praised on its own merits as "a moving apotheosis where fact and fiction, belief and faith converge into an acknowledgment of doubt as part of the fabric of belief" (Couto, 202). Clearly, this same description could be easily applied to Unamuno's version of Cervantes's novel. As we have illustrated, these thematic parallels are not coincidental. They reflect Greene's creative integration of Unamuno's commentary, and even Unamuno himself, into the design of the book. It is a beautifully crafted work of fiction in itself and may well be the culminating work in his series of so-called Catholic novels (Gaston, 17). It is also a tribute to two of Spain's most cherished authors, which no student of Spanish literature can read without reading Unamuno rewriting Cervantes.

BIBLIOGRAPHY

Abbot, Walter M.S.J., ed. *The Documents of Vatican II*. New York: Guild Press, 1966.

Augustine, Saint. *The Confessions of Saint Augustine*. Translated by Edward B. Pusey. New York: Washington Square Press, 1951.

Cervantes, Miguel de. *The Adventures of Don Quixote*. Translated by J. M. Cohen. London: Penguin Books, 1950.

Couto, Maria. *Graham Greene: On the Frontier*. New York: St. Martin's Press, 1988.

Gaston, Georg M. A. *The Pursuit of Salvation: A Critical Guide to the Novels of Graham Greene*. Troy, N.Y.: Whitson, 1984.

Greene, Graham. *Monsignor Quixote*. New York: Simon and Schuster, 1982.

Girard, René. *Deceit, Desire, and the Novel: Self and Other in Literary Structure*. Baltimore: Johns Hopkins University Press, 1965.

Lacy, Allen. "Introduction." In *Miguel de Unamuno: The Private World*, translated by Anthony Kerrigan. Princeton, N.J.: Princeton University Press, 1984.

Pérez de la Dehesa, Rafael. *Política y sociedad en el primer Unamuno: 1894–1904*. Madrid: Editorial Ciencia Nueva, 1966.

Portillo, Luis. "Epilogue: Unamuno's Last Lecture." In *Miguel de Unamuno: The Private World*, translated by Anthony Kerrigan. Princeton, N.J.: Princeton University Press, 1984.

Sánchez-Barbudo, Antonio. *El Misterio de la personalidad en Unamuno*. Buenos Aires: Universidad de Buenos Aires Press, 1950.

Unamuno, Miguel de. *La Vida de Don Quijote y Sancho*. Madrid: Espasa-Calpe, 1964.

Wilson, E. M. "On *La Vida Es Sueño*." In *Critical Essays on the Theatre of Calderón*, ed. Bruce W. Wardropper. New York: New York University Press, 1965.

12

The Filmic Quixote of The Fisher King: Sancho as Radio Talk-Show Host

Barbara D. Miller

> . . . and if I talk a lot it proceeds rather
> from weakness than from malice. But he who
> errs and mends, himself to God commends.
> Sancho Panza, in *Don Quixote*, II: 28

In Terry Gilliam's cinematic tour de force, *The Fisher King* (1991), even before the scene in which Parry, the homeless psychotic, proclaims his divinely ordained quest, the alert viewer will have begun to note quixotic motifs. Structural, technical, thematic, and character parallels abound between Miguel de Cervantes's masterwork and the ultrareflexive film. This massive intertextuality facilitates interpretation of *The Fisher King* as a filmic hypertext, vitally influenced by *El ingenioso hidalgo Don Quijote de la Mancha* (1605).[1]

In this chapter Sancho's and Don Quixote's evocations through Gilliam's movie misfits will be treated as particular evidence of "hypertextuality." This critical term designates a major component of Gerard Genette's "transtextual" system and denotes an essentially generative relationship. The indispensable quality of a hypertext is its transformative value. It must modify or elaborate an anterior or "hypo" text. The most obvious forms of hypertextuality involve works overtly based on others, as in textual revisions and retellings, filmic or musical adaptations of literary works, or full-scale movie remakes. However, such direct and inclusive examples are not the only valid representations of Genette's concept. Many of the most fascinating hypertexts, including *Quixote* itself, become the complex transformation instruments of multiple anterior works as well. *Amadís de Gaula* and the Arthurian romance cycles, among the best known hypotexts of *Quixote*, merely top what is actually an extensive list. Some intertextual reference and commentary is integral and profound; some may be found in the merest allusion. The definitive element is that anterior texts are genuinely transformed in the process.

Cervantes modifies his classical, medieval, and Renaissance hypotexts in diverse ways, including description and satirical treatment of the books in Don Quixote's infamous library, as well as through both the frame tale and interpolated stories. Similarly, *The Fisher King* reflects not only *Quixote* but also many other literary, filmic, and other kinds of texts. These range from the Arthurian tale whose title it recycles to movie versions of stage musicals such as *Gypsy* (1962). If the interpreter should take a foucauldian stance, this textual scope would extend from the writings of Nietzsche to newspaper headlines, various song lyrics, imaginary situation-comedy scripts, and beyond.

A key point for the present study is that *Don Quixote* does constitute one of *The Fisher King*'s most significant precursors. In fact, the film's riotous intertextuality, pointing to all manner of other texts and media productions, may comprise its most important structural similarity to Cervantes's novel. Moreover, given the defining generative-transformative nature of hypertextual interaction, the functions of identity and reality transformation, not only as dominant themes but also as narrative catalysts in both works, becomes crucial.

Don Quixote's status as an immense hypertext in its own right draws *The Fisher King* into an artistic spectrum of infinite regression. The film, as much as Spanish literature's ultimate text, comments on an enormous number of literary pieces and also joins in the twentieth-century redefinition of text. The personal collection of Alonso Quixano's library takes the form of Parry's boiler-room archive, the repository of the Grail secret, and, by extension, the secret of the knight's "true" identity. Langdon Carmichael's library, as the Grail vault, becomes an important reflection of the mad knight's epistemological source. Don Quixote's library also has its thoroughly contemporary, technological counterpart in *The Fisher King*. It is the commercial inventory of a video store owned by Jack's Aldonza-like true love, Anne. Filmic self-parody marks this assembly, among which porno flicks entitled *Ordinary Peepholes* and *Creamer versus Creamer* facetiously rename Academy Award–winning dramas.

Similarly, pop-music lyrics and titles, at first controlled from Jack's broadcast studio, seem to escape into the film's soundtrack and then converse with each other independently of the dramatis personae. Rock-and-roll lyrics suggest interior monologue and take on the function of a metanarrator, a phenomenon comparable to the introduction of Cervantes's second narrator, the Moor Cide Hamete Benengeli, in Chapter 9 of part I. Thus, when the audience hears Ray Charles's song, "Hit the Road, Jack," some may recognize the D.J.'s calling to join Parry in the quest, even though at this early point in the story Jack himself does not.

Robert Stam discusses the reflexive device of treating artistic process thematically. Citing the sixty-second chapter of Part II, in which Don Quixote observes the daily business of a Barcelona book-printing shop (including corrections-in-progress on the apocryphal *Quixote*), the critic notes,

Cervantes thus focuses attention on the concrete procedures by which all books, including his own, were produced. Just as a novel can take the production of books as its subject, so a film can focus on the process of filmmaking. . . . Such novels and films necessarily entail a certain measure of reflexivity in that they foreground, in however indirect or idealized fashion, the institutional practices involved in their own production. (71)

Scenes transpiring against the video-store backdrop, including three in which the action involves a customer's search for a particular film genre, figure among several devices through which *The Fisher King* reflects its own filmic nature. This self-conscious aspect is compounded through the integration of various audiovisual technologies and commodities, with Jack as commercial agent. In fact, the connected issues of technology, dehumanization, commercialization, and modern media as nouveau textual forms become personified through Jack, first portrayed as shock D.J., then as video-store clerk. In effect, his technoverbal stocks-in-trade transform him into the perfect incarnation of endless self-referential imagery and discourse.

Jack's manifestation as crass radio talk-show host effects a full revision of the character type embodied in Don Quixote's rustic companion. Talking, like self-indulgence, is no less essential to the Cervantine squire than to the narcissistic announcer. In Part I, between Chapters 20 and 25, Don Quixote, infuriated by his squire's irreverence and incessant string of proverbs, commands that Sancho refrain from idle speech. Having said his piece, the contented knight settles down to enjoy a quiet passage along the road to adventure. But his loquacious sidekick faces an agonizing struggle to comply with the new rule of silence. Finally, the exasperated Sancho begs to abandon the quest and return to his family: "I shall at least be able to talk to them as much as I like. For your worship's wanting me to ride through these lonely parts day and night and never to speak to you when I've a mind to, is like burying me alive" (Cohen, 1950, 199).

Jack's role as professional talker raises the issue of oral versus written cultures, underlying Cervantes's original odd-couple juxtaposition of the illiterate peasant to the more genteel obsessive-compulsive reader. Moreover, Jack's multimedia connection suggests the transitory definition of literacy. For instance, the visual orientation associated with film (as well as with computer "literacy") implies such phenomena as the popular displacement of books by audiovisual means. This trend stands as an historical–contextual antithesis to the rising status of print media that distinguishes Cervantes's time.

Jack's metamorphosis into chivalric squire, like Sancho's, is gradual, yet requires a radically modified perspective. His fundamental change of consciousness plunges him into what he calls his "emotional abyss," a deep alcoholic depression, an utterly profane "dark night of the soul." Its root cause is the tragic outcome of a thoughtless on-air remark to a very literal-minded listener by the name of Edwin Malnick. The unstable Edwin goes on a shooting spree, killing seven people, wounding several others, and ultimately committing suicide by turning the gun on himself.

From a rock-bottom point of despair, at which Desson Howe describes a Jack who looks "as if he might implode with cynicism," the transmutation into squire errant is initiated. Jack is about to hurl himself into the waters under the Manhattan Bridge when the direction of his antiheroic path is abruptly reversed. The Cervantine narrative strategy of multiple interruptions is fundamentally involved in Jack's identity-transformation process. First, a pair of delinquents interrupts Jack's suicide attempt by trying to murder him, then Parry interrupts their interruption. The punks pour gasoline over Jack and are about to light a match when the intervention occurs. Jack's near-deadly baptism, first by water, then by gasoline, and almost by fire, immediately precedes his epiphany as the modern Sancho, for it marks the beginning of his adventures with Parry, a street dweller who fancies himself a knight on a special quest.

Jack's originally egomaniacal personality hinges on his power to shoot barbed verbiage over the Manhattan airwaves. Like Governor Sancho, the radio cult personality has "got the power" of popular persuasion, and blithely passes judgment over the inhabitants of his own mythic isle.[2] His fall from grace is equally as sudden as that of Barataria's ruler, however. If the radio celebrity's flippant advice lacks the wisdom of the surprisingly insightful peasant, perhaps it is because, unlike Sancho, Jack appears not to have learned that responsibility and humility must accompany privilege. Lacking concern for his audience, the showman unwittingly sets up his own tragic fall.

Jack's insolent treatment of his call-in guests is justified as crude entertainment. The savvy caller plays along. Of course, not every caller is even aware of (much less understands) the game. Misunderstanding begets miscommunication, which leads to disaster. In eerie similarity to Don Quixote as befuddled audience member at Maese Pedro's puppet show, caller Edwin Malnick confuses reality and entertainment illusion.[3] He takes Jack the showman's mockery at face value. Speaking of the patrons who frequent the bistro where Edwin has glimpsed his ideal woman, Jack quips, "They're not human! . . . They have to be stopped before it's too late. It's us or them" (LaGravenese, 7). Edwin responds to his idol's tongue-in-cheek edict by opening fire on the Friday-night clientele of "Babbitts." His culminating act of madness, that of shooting himself through the head, creates a hideous parallel to the mangled Charlemagne puppet in the Maese Pedro episode. The most horrible intertextual irony is that Don Quixote's hilarious vandalism of the puppet theater stems from his confused perception that the puppets are real people. The misinterpretation is diametrically reversed in *The Fisher King*. Edwin's massacre is conceived when Jack convinces him to view a crowd of restaurant customers as dehumanized "retards" engendered by what he calls "Yuppie-In-Breeding" (7).

Jack's encounter with Parry three years after the calamity returns the ruined celebrity to the intolerable memory of his fatal error, something from which he has been trying desperately to escape. It brings him face to face with one whose professional and personal identities have been obliterated, however indirectly, because of Jack's careless remarks to Edwin. "Parry" turns out to be the chivalric name adopted by Henry Sagan, a former professor of Arthurian literature. To his utter revulsion, Jack learns that the scholar's breakdown resulted from the catastrophe at Babbitt's. During Edwin's rampage the blood of Henry's beautiful young wife had been splattered grotesquely across their dinner table and over the adoring husband's glasses, the lenses through which he viewed the world. He could not have been more definitively baptized as a "knight of the woeful countenance."

Jack's guilt catapults him into despair and his eventual first meeting out on the streets with Henry, following the professor's sad conversion into Parry, a homeless derelict on a holy quest. Jack, in his alcoholic stupor, interprets Parry's gesture of kneeling grandly and brandishing what appears to be a toy sword, not as that of a heroic knight, but rather of a deranged bum imitating a hood ornament. Despite Jack's failure to perceive it, in that defining moment the vagrant Quixote has met his misanthropic Sancho.

Jack's first attempt to redeem his sin predictably fails, since its method is to give Parry money that might help him get off the streets. As any good reader of Cervantes knows, money is irrelevant to a questing knight. During his second rescue effort, the morosely realistic Jack finds himself being dragged, kicking and screaming, through Parry's fantasy dimension. It is then that the homeless paladin enlists the aid of his newfound Sancho to secure the Holy Grail, which takes the contrasting forms of a silver cup and of an extraordinarily ordinary girl.

As in Part I of *Don Quixote*, the chivalric progress of *The Fisher King*'s heroes is repeatedly interrupted by interpolated stories told by people they meet along the way.[4] For instance, a theatrical drag queen, the "damsel" saved by Parry from being trampled by a horse in Central Park, epitomizes the cross-dressing figures found along Don Quixote's ambivalent landscape. This queen's desire to be a debutante and to go to Venice like Katherine Hepburn in *Summertime* (1955) suggests a bizarre contrast to the situation of Dorotea, Cervantes's dishonored farmer's daughter. Notably, this rescue begins when Parry's initial response to the gay man's cry includes one of actor Robin Williams's improvisationally used paraphrases based on *Don Quixote* (LaGravenese, 133–134) as follows: "Heaven be praised in giving so soon an opportunity for me to fulfill the duties of my profession. These cries are doubtless received from some miserable male or female in need of my immediate aid and protection." The corresponding lines from Cervantes occur at the beginning of Chapter 4 in Part I (Cohen 1982, 47).

The comparison between the drag queen and Dorotea is made all the more compelling by the man's admission that he has become a family outcast by breaking with the predominant code of socially acceptable behavior. His lament for the death of all his friends, an obvious allusion to the AIDS epidemic, exemplifies his disillusioned musings. Dorotea, on the other hand, enters Part I as a young, deflowered, and unmarried runaway wearing boy's clothes, and later transforms herself into the spurious Princess Micomicona, heroine of one of the elaborate fictions devised to trick Don Quixote.

In parallel to Cervantes's numerous interpolated genre-linked segments, one hilarious scene from the movie places Jack as the reluctantly sympathetic listener to the drag queen's tale of woe. His story subtly yet recognizably implies the opening of a picaresque novel: "Well, . . . I'm a singer by trade. . . . Summer stock . . . nightclub reviews . . . that kind of thing. . . . It used to be what I absolutely lived for" (LaGravenese 1991, 57).

Jack's expiation is partially accomplished by reenacting Sancho's stint as lovers' go-between. The aborted delivery of Don Quixote's love letter to Dulcinea is one of Sancho's funniest and most significant failures. According to some, Don Quixote has sabotaged the enterprise himself so as not to admit or reveal Dulcinea's illusory nature. Be that as it may, Sancho's disappointing report on his interview with Aldonza diminishes not in the least his master's pursuit. The purpose of the squire's mission impossible as love emissary was to carry forward a motif central to the knight's identity. This time it failed, but the quest goes on. A knight errant, by definition, must be in love (Cohen 1950, 34).[5]

The comparable scenario to that of Sancho as lovers' messenger occurs in *The Fisher King* when Jack engineers his own elaborate matchmaking communique. Interestingly, Sancho sets out on his errand from the Spanish Sierra, where Don Quixote has been engaging in absurd acrobatics with the intent of proving his love for Dulcinea. Jack's analogous task occurs after Parry removes all doubt about his madness by the eccentricity of what he calls "cloud busting." This performance involves Parry's stripping himself naked in the middle of Central Park, jumping up and down, making wild gestures, howling at the moon, and inviting Jack to join him. The similarity of Parry's antics to Don Quixote's wildman imitation in the Sierra is undeniable.

In any event, many viewers will be driven to stunned silence, or uncontrollable laughter, during a subsequent scene from the film in which the off-Broadway drag queen is dispatched, decked out in full regalia, to deliver a singing telegram. Jack sets out to unite the would-be lovers by luring the lady to Anne's video store, where he plans to introduce her to Parry. For his scheme to succeed, she must be convinced that she has won a free store membership. The function of the outlandish courier is to announce her as the grand-prize winner.

The recipient of this bizarre communication, Parry's "Dulcinea," is Lydia Sinclaire, a mousy little woman who calculates prices for a publisher of (in her words) "trashy romance novels" (LaGravenese, 89).[6] In the best Cervantine tradition, however, her devoted swain hastens to assure her that "there's nothing trashy about romance."[7]

Jack has become aware of Parry's passion by discovering his friend's routine of worship from afar during his lady's lunch hour. Parry dispels any doubt that this unremarkable woman corresponds to Don Quixote's matchless princess of the pearly teeth (Cervantes, 533) with his expression of awe over her own exalted romance-heroine feature: "If anybody ever told me I'd be in love with a woman who chews jawbreakers, I'd say they were nuts. But look at that jaw" (LaGravenese, 45–46). Parry's all-too-brief amatory accolade to his mistress's powerful jaw receives its courtly extension in due time. During the blind date arranged by Jack, Parry serenades his peerless dream girl with a tender chorus of "Lydia the Tattooed Lady."

Just when it seems that Parry's conquest of his long-awaited lady could mark the beginning of the psychological and emotional healing necessary to a restored life, his bliss is viciously curtailed. The only remaining hope is to come through the completion of the Grail quest. At this point thematic reversal once more characterizes *The Fisher King* as quixotic hypertext. In light of this opposition between the film and

Cervantes's prose work, it is well to reconsider Gerard Genette's conceptual keystone, that of transformation. Specifically, the dynamic of suffering and redemption may be interpreted as the catalyst of fundamental change affecting both stories' endings.

Pain and interruption actually demarcate the beginning and the ending of Jack's Sancho-like journey. The violent scenario of the filmic heroes' first meeting, with its double interruption, is reminiscent of Sancho's beatings and blanket tossings, with one important difference. Although Parry's lines and manic behavior when he rescues Jack are absurdly humorous, the danger itself is real. If the punks had been allowed to finish what they started, the grave result would have had little in common with Sancho's comically lamented bruises.

Jack's last squirely endeavor leads to one deliberate salvation and a second spontaneous salvation by interruption. Whereas Jack plays the victim in the earlier street scene, he now switches roles to become the inadvertent savior of the "rich fisher," millionaire Langdon Carmichael, during an attempt to save Parry. Jack's best friend has been beaten into a coma by the same hoods who assaulted Jack himself near the bridge. By this time his fondest wish is to atone for his accidental part in the death of Parry's wife. By scaling the walls of Carmichael's mansion, which Parry sees as the "Grail Castle," and by retrieving from the library the silver trophy cup Parry has insisted is the Holy Grail, God's symbol of divine grace, Jack means to restore his Manichean other half.[8] Carmichael chances to be in the library during the break-in. When a crystal goblet drops from his hand, the sound alerts Jack to the unconscious man's presence, and to his accidental overdose. The emphatic doubling created by the two goblets, both readable as Grail emblems, and by the two unconscious victims, Parry and Carmichael, accentuates the theme of suffering and redemption and underlines the film's moral that all human beings are interconnected, whether rich or poor, strangers or friends. Exiting with the silver cup through the front door of the mansion, Jack is able to escape without being caught yet trip the security alarm at the last second so that help will reach the drugged Carmichael in time.

The theme of transformation through suffering defines the ultimate outcome of *The Fisher King*, although its treatment represents a reversal of the corresponding incident in *Don Quixote*. The Spanish work is read by most scholars as a parody, at least in part, and therefore as a "funny" book. The injuries endured by the knight errant, his squire, and others are outrageously comical, but the ending is not. Don Quixote stops confusing reality with illusion and dies. Sancho, whose worldview has become increasingly fantastic, is devastated. The squire's sadness over his master's death is exacerbated by his disappointment that they will never be able to carry out a plan articulated by Alonso Quixano upon returning home from his chivalric escapades.

The screenwriters and producers of *The Fisher King* transform this ending scenario ingeniously by taking up a story thread suspiciously like the one dropped by Cervantes. The film thus converts its hypotextual comedy-ending-in-tragedy (*Don Quixote*) into a bizarre tragedy-ending-in-comic fantasy. Just prior to the ending of *Don Quixote II*, Don Quixote and Sancho decide to pass their promised year of confinement in their village by dressing up as shepherds and living a pastoral romance idyll. But Don Quixote's return to sanity and subsequent death interrupt this plan, and seemingly disrupt the potential for a never-ending series of sequels. The narrator has clearly had enough of the "endless text" when he cuts it off with his abrupt and famous "basta."

The Fisher King ends when its Don Quixote and Sancho avatars shout a gleeful goodnight to Manhattan and watch the New York skyline light up in colored neon, appropriate to the finale of a stage musical. A cliched "the end" appears on the screen in matching neon. Admittedly this artistically self-conscious and exaggerated happy ending lends a hint of ironic ambiguity. The transformed heroes say their moonlit goodnights from the pastoral green of Central Park (interestingly, Richard LaGravenese's screenplay repeatedly specifies this setting location as "CENTRAL PARK—SHEEPS MEADOW"). The nakedness of the leading duo reminds us of Parry's earlier wildman antics, yet is fitting to the rustic condition of shepherds. The temptation to imagine Parry and Jack as the resurrected Don Quixote and Sancho living out their pastoral dream after all is irresistible. Interpreted this way, the postmodern Quixote has arisen miraculously from his bed, cured of his madness, to assure his musing Sancho that it's the wind, not their minds, that is breaking the clouds apart.

NOTES

1. The movie's Arthurian title tale, central to Chrétien de Troyes's medieval Grail-quest account, is the first obvious intertextual constituent. However, allusions to Perceval's story (and to myriad other texts of every conceivable kind) in no way precludes the presence of Don Quixote and Sancho avatars. Indeed, the simultaneous embodiment of Amadís de Gaula, Lancelot du Lac, and others within a single personage is integral to Cervantes's basic premise.

2. Another of the film's interesting metatextual touches is the pop song "The Power," which passes from radio-show theme to soundtrack background as a sort of floating commentary on Jack's inflated self-opinion and his fluctuating lifestyle and social status. When he has "got the power" he abuses it in the manner of a sorcerer's apprentice. It is not surprising, then, that chaos ensues, in the form of the restaurant tragedy.

3. The suggestion of a puppet show per se—specifically a Punch-and-Judy show—emerges during the very first lines of dialogue (in the edited film version, although this is not developed in the published screenplay), when Jack quips to an enervating caller that someone "ought to hit her over the head." The uncanny coincidence with a Punch-and-Judy scenario is punctuated when Jack concludes his sarcastic abuse by producing a silly boinging sound effect as he hangs up on the listener.

4. Sid, a disabled Vietnam veteran begging in the subway who features himself as a "moral traffic light," evokes El Manco de Lepanto himself. This character's observations on the noble if unappreciated sacrifices of the soldier echo sentiments expressed by Cervantes in the prologue to Part II, as well as in Don Quixote's famous speech on arms and letters in Chapter 24 of the same part. In the film the importance of Sid's supporting role is underscored by its subtle reverberation in the words of another homeless character, the drag queen, when he ironically compares himself to a veteran based on his friendship with several AIDS victims (LaGravenese 1991, 57).

5. Prior to Don Quixote's first sally he deems the following elements as essential to his new identity: clean armor, a completed helmet, an appropriate name for his steed, and, finally, "a lady to be enamoured of." "For a knight errant without a lady is like a tree without leaves or fruit and a body without a soul" (Cohen 1982, 34).

6. This scenario squares with Robert Stam's observations on reflexivity and the process of production. When Parry and Lydia finally meet, their first conversation includes her description of her work in publishing cost calculations, a subject upon which Don Quixote is lectured during his encounter with the Barcelona book printer.

7. This line, spoken by Robin Williams in the film, differs in wording from the published screenplay (LaGravenese, 89).

8. Actually, the mansion is the cleverly employed Fifth Avenue Armory.

BIBLIOGRAPHY

Brown, A.C.L. *The Origin of the Grail Legend*. Cambridge: Harvard University Press, 1943.

Cervantes Saavedra, Miguel de. *El ingenioso hidalgo Don Quijote de La Mancha*. Edited by Juan Bautista Avalle-Arce. 2 vols. Madrid: Editorial Alhambra, 1979.

Cline, Ruth Harwood, trans. *Perceval or The Story of the Grail*. Athens: University of Georgia Press, 1985.

Cohen, J. M., trans. *The Adventures of Don Quixote* (1950). Harmondsworth, England: Penguin, 1982.

Dudley, Edward C. "Don Quixote as Magus: The Rhetoric of Interpolation." *Bulletin of Hispanic Studies* 49 (1972): 355–368.

———. *The Endless Text: "Don Quijote" and the Hermeneutics of Romance*. Albany: State University of New York Press, 1997.

———. "The Wild Man Goes Baroque." In *The Wild Man Within*, eds. Edward C. Dudley and Maximilian Novak. Pittsburgh, Pa.: University of Pittsburgh Press, 1972.

El Saffar, Ruth. *Beyond Fiction: The Recovery of the Feminine in the Novels of Cervantes*. London: California University Press, 1984.

Frappier, Jean. *Chrétien de Troyes et le mythe du Graal*. Paris: S.E.D.E.S., 1972.

Genette, Gerard. *Palimpsestes*. Paris: Seuil, 1982.

Lacy, Norris J. "The Fisher King." In *The New Arthurian Encyclopedia*, ed. Norris J. Lacy. New York: Garland, 1991.

LaGravenese, Richard. *The Fisher King: The Book of the Film*. Introduction by Terry Gilliam. Applause Screenplay Series. New York: Applause, 1991.

Miller, Barbara D. "Movie Merlins of the 1980s and 1990s." In *King Arthur on Film: New Essays on Arthurian Cinema*, ed. Kevin J. Harty. Jefferson, N.C.: McFarland, 1999.

Montalvo, Garci Rodríguez de. *Amadís de Gaula*. Edited by Juan Manuel Cacho Blecua. 2 vols. Madrid: Cátedra, 1987.

Staiger, Janet. *Interpreting Films: Studies in the Historical Reception of American Cinema*. Princeton, N.J.: Princeton University Press, 1992.

Stam, Robert. *Reflexivity in Film and Literature: From "Don Quixote" to Jean-Luc Godard*. New York: Columbia University Press, 1992.

Vauthier, Michèle. "The 'Roi Pescheor' and Iconographic Implications in the *Conte del Graal*." In *Word and Image in Arthurian Literature*, ed. Keith Busby. New York: Garland, 1996.

Reviews

Ebert, Roger. *Chicago Sun-Times*, September 20, 1991.

Forestier, François. *Premiere* [France], October 1991, 26.

Howe, Desson. *Washington Post*, September 20, 1991.

Parent, Denis. *Studio* [France], October 1991, 6.

Jessica D. Winer, *Don Quixote*, 1997. Watercolor on paper, 24 × 36 inches. De-nuded of his armor, Don Quixote is a bold yet pathetic image of humanity drawn to fight against the inevitable certainty of defeat. Still, the challenge remains. The ideal must exist, or where, what, who shall we be?

Part III

THE PERIPATETIC DON JUAN

Jessica D. Winer, *Don Giovanni: Final Scene*, 1997. Watercolor on paper, 36 × 24 inches. Still brazen, still disbelieving, Don Juan is dragged to hell by the sepulchral figure of his victim, the Commendador, who appears to him as the "stone guest." Mozart's opera portrays an almost likeable rogue whose ultimate destiny is easily foreseen, if not relished.

13

Mythic Misnomers: Reinventing Don Juan in Molière and Mozart

Jeanne Fuchs

Adulterer, assassin, atheist, beguiler, blasphemer, hypocrite, liar, libertine, seducer, trickster, and villain are only some of the names used to describe Don Juan in his various incarnations. It is a wonder that he is still with us! Yet the world continues to be seduced by the person whom Molière called a "grand seigneur méchant homme" (great lord and evil man). For nearly four centuries, whatever genre he appears in, whatever form he takes—Don Juan, Dom Juan, Don Giovanni—he has become a riveting symbol of adventure, illicit love, and the unscrupulous individualist who scorns the rules of the establishment and elevates to heroic heights the renegade way of life he has chosen. Without the despised establishment and the social order into which he was born, Don Juan would have little purpose. He remains a figure in constant revolt and for that reason has captured the attention of many who identify with him vicariously or thrill to his exploits.

From his first incarnation in Tirso de Molina's *El Burlador de Sevilla y el convidado de piedra*, which was based on a combination of folktales, legend, and popular ballads, Don Juan has been viewed as a great lover, a dissatisfied lover, a capricious lover, a dangerous lover. In the works I plan to discuss the important accent is not on the lover. The word lover is a misnomer—love has nothing to do with it. Don Juan rapes, attempts rape, kidnaps his victims, and then abandons them in short order. What he demonstrates by his actions is really his need to challenge any authority that tries to limit his spontaneous desires. He lies, cheats, rapes, and even murders when and if he is challenged. "Challenge" is the key word even over "desire" in understanding him.

Each separate rendering of the perfidious aristocrat has to some extent reinvented him to fit the times in which he appears and the particular inner necessity of the author. My concern here rests with his treatment in both the Spanish and French Golden Age literature and in Mozart. To demonstrate how Don Juan was reinvented in Molière and Mozart, I will briefly discuss his treatment in Tirso de Molina.

El Burlador provides the principal source of all other versions. One of the original characteristics of Tirso's protagonist is that he humiliates women; he is unconcerned if their reputations and lives are destroyed. A concomitant of this is the enjoyment he takes in humiliating and/or cuckolding men. In Tirso he says, "In Seville I'm called the Trickster; and my greatest pleasure is to trick women, leaving them dishonored" (Campbell, 173). With aristocratic women, he seduces them while pretending to be someone else—the man each woman loves. This is not seduction but true trickery. He enjoys anonymity. In the opening scene of *El Burlador*, the Duquesa Isabela asks Don Juan, "Quién eres, hombre?" (Who are you, sir?) "Quién soy?" (Who am I?) "Un hombre sin nombre" (A man without a name) (Martel, Alpern, and Mades, 239–240). His response offers a key to unlocking the motives of his character: He does not care about her or any woman after the conquest is achieved. Everything is a game, the game of numbers and combinations and challenges to overcome. After having seduced a woman of high station by pretending to be the Duke Octavio, he has to solve the problem of how to escape from the palace without his identity being uncovered. Duke Octavio, the man who loves Isabela, is accused of having seduced her. His life and love are at once destroyed by the knowledge of the dishonor of the woman he loves. And so it will be with another noble couple, Doña Ana and the Marqués de la Mota. It is during the seduction of Doña Ana that her father, Don Gonzalo (the original Commander), is killed. When it comes to peasants, Don Juan does not hide his identity but rather uses it as a stratagem in his seduction. He promises to marry both Tisbea, a fisherwoman who is loved by Anfriso, and Aminta a shepherdess (on her wedding day). Her husband, Batricio, is left confounded and nearly helpless.

Guilt, remorse, and examination of conscience do not exist for Don Juan. He lacks internality; he lives in the moment and loves movement and action. He is the Baroque incarnate. Julia Kristeva goes so far as to say that he has no ego. He is multiplicity, a polyphony, the harmonization of the multiple (193). Kristeva's remarks apply equally to the three Don Juans in this chapter. Why would a man seduce a woman, pretending to be someone else, if he were seeking ego gratification? Don Juan is adding to his list, which ultimately is full of individually anonymous women. One might say that Tirso opens his play with the Duquesa's unwitting surrender to a stranger to underscore the trickster side of the main character. The disdain of a name for himself raises Don Juan to a universal seducer, a phallus with no identity, quite the opposite of what the mythic name "Don Juan" has come to mean. The other part of the equation always includes the men in love with his victims; the men in the Spanish play, aristocrats and peasants, burn with shame and jealousy. Clearly, Tirso's intention was to paint an unscrupulous cad and lead him in measured steps to his downfall and damnation. Don Juan's blasé attitude is revealed in the refrain he uses throughout the play: "Tan largo me lo fiáis" (You give me a long time to worry about that). In other words, I have plenty of time to repent. His desires of the moment will not be stifled by religious, social, or even political consequences.

In its direct treatment of the theme of sexuality linked with that of punishment and damnation, the Don Juan legend remains one of the most important in Western literature. Don Juan's actions represent unbridled sexuality, but equally they bring about his downfall. In the bifurcation of the story resides its powerful resonance. There is little doubt in anyone's mind that Tirso's play had an example to illustrate. As a priest, Gabriel Téllez, Tirso's actual name, cast his comedia in the tradition of the morality play. Punishment was a crucial part of the equation. The countless incidents of foreshadowing and warning to the protagonist by virtually every character in the play attest to this. The importance of chastisement rings out in his title, which is double, *El Burlador de Sevilla y el convidado de piedra*; the same holds true for Molière, with *Dom Juan ou le festin de pierre*; and Mozart's original title, *Il Dissoluto punito ossìa il Don Giovanni*, reveals an equal preoccupation with the hero's eventual punishment literally at the hand of the Commander, the Stone Guest at the Stone Banquet. The Commander clearly represents society and the father figure against whom Don Juan revolts. Two French treatments of the play that predate Molière's were both entitled *Le Festin de pierre ou le fils criminel* (Rushton 1981, 140).

To continue the concept of the criminal son, I will use the commentary of Otto Rank, who has written extensively on the Don Juan legend. For Rank, the motif of guilt and punishment takes precedence over the motif of sexuality (41). His interpretation of the legend rests on the theme of the murdered man who was mocked getting revenge on the blasphemer (37). Rank traces the notion or superstition of the Stone Guest to many cultures; it invariably contains some sort of mocking invitation (76). Rank notes that forces of overwhelming guilt and punishment are strongly connected with sexual fantasies and are ultimately derived from the Oedipus complex (41). Don Juan denigrates his rivals in all versions of the work and kills the mortal enemy, the father figure who tries to thwart his desire to possess the woman. The many women who are constantly replaced represent the one irreplaceable mother (41). The transformation of Don Juan into a treacherous cynic who has few if any feelings for women—certainly no love or tenderness—occurs through what Rank identifies as "repression" and "displacement" (42). As Rank summarizes the situation,

The characteristic Don Juan fantasy of conquering countless women is ultimately based on the unattainability of the mother and the compensating substitute for her. As the fantasy also clearly reveals, the unattainability does not refer to sexual possession, to which there is certainly no barrier in primitive times and character. It involves the deeply rooted biological wish for the exclusive and complete possession of the mother. The continually repeated sexual conquest of women remains unsatisfying for the reason that the infantile tendency to regress to the mother can only be partially fulfilled. (95)

This analysis holds true, in my view, in *El Burlador*, *Dom Juan*, and *Don Giovanni*. The variations on the theme need to be uncovered.

Remorse is not a component of these dramas. The responsibility for the expression of feelings for the victims rests first and foremost on them, but more often devolves on Don Juan's servant, who acts as a kind of commedia dell'arte Greek chorus: Catalinón, Sganarelle, and Leporello are intimately involved in their respective masters' plots. Though each attempts to persuade his master to change his ways, each is too cowardly and self-interested to leave him. Lack of conscience in the protagonist is nonetheless mediated by the servant. Each servant represents a call for a sense of morality and ethical behavior. The servants form an integral part of the artistic presentation of the hero himself (Rank, 50). What he lacks, they supply, albeit often in a superficial manner. They are the voices of inner criticism, anxiety, and conscience, which is so lacking in their masters. It must be noted that there is no moment in any of the three works when the hero reveals his inner self to the audience; no moment of conflict, no soul-searching soliloquy, no self-questioning or self-reflection. This converges with Kristeva's observation that Don Juan has no ego.

Molière's Don Juan distinguishes himself from the Burlador not through better or different behavior, but through his supreme intelligence, his elegance, his exterior nobility, and above all his command of rhetoric. In Don Juan's first major speech (Act I, Scene 2) he outlines his libertine philosophy and the charms of seduction, while at the same time belittling fidelity and its limitations:

What! Would you have a man tie himself up to the first woman that captured his fancy, renounce the world for her, and never again look at anyone else? That is a fine idea, I must say, to make a virtue of faithfulness, to bury oneself for good and all in one single passion and remain blind ever after to all the other beauties that might catch one's eye! No. Let fools make virtue of constancy. (Molière 1953, 202)

He concludes,

There is no pleasure to compare with the conquest of beauty, and my ambition is that of all the great conquerors who could never find it in them to set bounds to their ambitions, but must go on for ever from conquest to conquest. Nothing can restrain my impetuous desires. I feel it is in me to love the whole world, and like Alexander still wish for new worlds to conquer. (203)

His constant witness, Sganarelle, is impressed by his master's tirade. He says he talks like a book.

Molière's creation is pure virtuosity; his seduction crosses gender as well as class. His extraordinary language ranges in richness from the aristocratic to the common to the tragic. The play marks a turning point in Molière's career: He broke all the rules in *Dom Juan*. The three unities so important in French classical theater are tossed aside. Comedy as one of the noble genres was written in verse, not prose. This was Molière's first comedy written in prose. One critic, Alex Szogyi, suggests that this could have signified a revolt on the part of Molière against the detractors of *Tartuffe*, which was written immediately before *Dom Juan*, caused a great scandal, and was removed from presentation. As Szogyi put it, "La prose en tant que geste et instrument de révolte s'avérait un concept créateur par excellence" (120).

I would add that there is a perfect convergence between form and content in the play. Using the characteristics of revolt—challenge and constant movement—the writer has mirrored these same qualities in his technique and treatment of the material. Each act unfolds in a different setting; the plot is episodic with a sequence of unrelated characters. There are rapid scene changes within each act: seduction, shipwreck, swordplay, and flight are intermingled. Molière's disdain for the rules parallels that of his protagonist. He mixes together a Cornelian father, a Racinian mistress, a commedia dell'arte servant, peasants speaking in a thick dialect, a bill collector who could have escaped from a boulevard farce alongside a ghost, a walking, talking statue and an all-the-stops-out, deus ex machina grand finale in which the hero gets his comeuppance and is dragged down to eternal punishment by the man he has murdered. Instead of placating the devoutly religious who had been so offended by *Tartuffe*, Molière stirred up the opposite reaction. As a result, the play had only fifteen performances, was not published in Molière's lifetime, was rewritten in an inoffensive verse version by Thomas Corneille, and was not seen again for almost 200 years (Classiques Garnier 1962, 709). It was a masterpiece that was not performed.

It is a very modern play. Some critics have suggested that one could only appreciate it fully after the Marquis de Sade, Proust, Gide, and others. What is closer to reality is that Molière's creation possesses such a power and veracity and is so convincingly seductive in his beliefs that it must have frightened many, especially the very devout. While he satirizes perverted nobles of his day, he also targets doctors and those who are falsely devout: hypocrites. He paints what Henri Bremond has called "un libertinage flamboyant" (Classiques Garnier, 710). He is a libertine in mind as much as in body, a cerebral seducer who uses women as a way of restating and reaffirming his liberty. His intelligence has completely dried up his feelings.

In Act III, when Sganarelle and Don Juan are lost in the forest and the servant asks his master what he believes in, he replies, "I believe that two and two are four, Sganarelle, and that four and four are eight" (Molière 1953, 223). Sganarelle's response is most comic: "Now that is a fine sort of faith. As far as I can see then, your religion is arithmetic" (223) (Mozart's famous list is an expansion of this idea). Sganarelle then attempts his proof of the existence of God and uses the arguments of theologians who demonstrate it through rational proofs and the necessity of a first cause. Sganarelle's association of Heaven and God with some superstitious figures particularly infuriated pious people of the day, along with the fact that Molière had put the defense of the existence of God into the mouth of a buffoon and a servant (Molière 1991, 27). Meanwhile, Don Juan the superintellect becomes bored with Sganarelle's raving and changes the subject. After all, he has kidnapped Done Elvire from a convent, caused her to renounce her vows, married her, and then abandoned her. He has also killed the Commander. But unlike in Tirso and Mozart, the event occurs before the curtain goes up. This would seem an attempt on Molière's part to diminish at least one of the evil aspects of his hero's behavior, having only references to the murder in the early part of the play.

Molière's Don Juan is an attractive atheist who has found a worthy adversary in God, or the God that everyone else believes in. Paradoxically, he bets that God does not exist while constantly seeking to provoke the nonexistent being. What Molière created was an astonishing figure of the libertine, a figure by no means limited to seventeenth-century France. Don Juan possesses verve and panache even in his most shocking declarations. Molière's reinvention removes the protagonist from the melodramatic underpinnings of the original story and changes the accent to one of a quest of cosmic proportions of revolt. His Don Juan remains defiantly obstinate in the face of all events. His destiny is a solitary one. He does not resemble anyone else. He breathes a different air from the others.

An important ironic theme in Molière's *Dom Juan* (even more pronounced in Mozart) is the pursuer pursued. Recall in Tirso the same phenomenon. It is both a source of tension and of comedy. In Act I, Don Juan has his first of two scenes with Done Elvire. He has abandoned her; she has pursued him. She vents the rage of the woman scorned; he remains indifferent. At the end of Act II the pursuit begins in earnest. Twelve men on horseback, Elvire's brothers and their comrades, seek to avenge Elvire's honor. In the third act, the brothers actually catch up with him, but because he has saved one of them from bandits in the forest, his fate is deferred. In the last scene of Act III, the climax of the play—the scene in the tomb and the encounter with the statue—the statue becomes still another pursuer.

Act IV has an extraordinary accumulation of pursuers and would-be punishers. There are eight scenes and in each the comic ploy of interruption of another action is used. Don Juan is continuously kept from his supper. The first pursuer is his creditor, M. Dimanche; the scene is comic and provides further proof of Don Juan's mastery of the art of persuasion. He never allows M. Dimanche the opportunity to state the reason for his visit; he literally seduces him into silence and then leaves him (exactly what he does to women, but in miniature). The comic scene is quickly followed by one of great dignity and offense: Don Louis has come to reproach his son for his wantonness. He realizes their mutual discomfort as he reminds his son of his ancestry and of the obligations of nobility:

Don't you blush to be so little worthy of your birth? What right do you think you have to be proud of it still? What have you ever done to deserve the name of a gentleman? Or do you think it is enough to bear the title and the arms of one? What credit is it to be born of noble blood if one lives in infamy? Birth is nothing without virtue, and we have no claim to share in the glory of our ancestors unless we strive to resemble them. (Molière 1953, 236)

He concludes, "Remember that a nobleman who leads an evil life is an offence against nature, a monster, and that virtue is the first title of nobility" (my translation). Finally he threatens Don Juan with the wrath of heaven, which will wash away the shame of having given birth to his son. The scene has immense tragic dimensions and is followed by yet another example of noble suffering: Elvire's second scene with her adulterer husband. She has undergone a purification of her own and has transformed her profane love for Don Juan into a mystical love for God. She appears veiled—a symbol of her return to the convent—to beg him to repent and to avoid the precipice toward which she sees him rushing. Her speech has power, but the reaction of Don Juan to the pleas of both Elvire and Don Louis is the same. He is hostile and arrogant. When his father leaves, he cries, "Die as soon as you can, that's the best you can do. . . . It enrages me to see fathers who live as long as their sons" (my translation). When Elvire exits, he admits to Sganarelle that she began to excite him physically with her lament and tears. The two preceding messengers of warning serve only to announce the final one (in every sense): Le Commandeur. As in Tirso and Mozart, the scene is horrific, but at the same time contains comic elements that are to be found in the servants' actions and reactions. In all three versions Don Juan maintains his dignity and detachment (it is ignoble to fear the dead), and Molière's protagonist remains especially calm.

In Act V, Molière has Don Juan undergo a false conversion. He becomes an avowed hypocrite, which serves to build the case against him. In a false return of the prodigal son, he deceives his own father into believing that he repents of his sins. Then, in a long and violent attack on hypocrisy, Molière seals his character's fate and in many ways the fate of the play. Don Juan informs Sganarelle and us that hypocrisy is fashionable:

Such conduct carries no stigma nowadays, for hypocrisy is a fashionable vice, and all vices pass for virtues once they become fashionable. The role of a man of principle is the best of all parts to play, for the professional hypocrite enjoys remarkable advantages. Hypocrisy is an art, the practice of which always commands respect, and though people may see through it they dare say nothing against it. All other vices of mankind are exposed to censure and anyone may attack them with impunity. (Molière 1953, 243)

Through his pseudoconversion he hopes to avoid a confrontation with Elvire's brothers and being forced back into the role of Elvire's husband. In his usual arrogant manner, he keeps his appointment with the statue, which takes him by the hand and leads him into the abyss.

Instead of several marriages being announced at the end of this comedy, we find Sganarelle scurrying about the stage, bemoaning the loss of his wages, stating that through the death of his master everyone is satisfied: Heaven, seduced women, dishonored families, outraged parents. The supernatural finale and the return to reality have a distinctly modern quality in that they both seem absurd. Molière has Don Juan punished but there was no repentance—not a sign of it. After such a cataclysmic end and Sganarelle's ignoble whining, it is not surprising that virtually all commentators have considered this play the most problematic in Molière's entire oeuvre.

Perhaps the most powerful depiction of Don Juan's downfall is the musical one: Mozart's version. Shaw remarked that the trombones create a "sound of dreadful joy" (Rushton, 89) at the moment when the Commendatore enters Don Giovanni's home. Those instruments, usually reserved for solemn church pieces, appear in the finale of *Don Giovanni*. We are in for a different kind of "folle journée" à la Mozart. It has been noted that if one were to read only DaPonte's libretto, one's sympathy would go, as it often does, to Don Giovanni's victims (Kristeva, 192). Instead, the music, with its vivacity, energy, movement, and quickness, enhances the baroque qualities of Don Giovanni's own nature. Replacing the melancholy claims of his victims, the music bursts forth in exquisite, witty, and often humorous praise of the conqueror himself.

The episodic quality of the Molière play is also present in the opera and adapts equally well to Mozart's genius. There is a sense of fun that gives what Anthony Burgess has called a "champagne sparkle" to Mozart's mature operas (10). The pastiche of the plot did nothing to slow the composer, but only enhanced his own virtuosity. Kierkegaard, in his essay on *Don Giovanni*, states that Mozart's depiction is the greatest embodiment of the character of Don Juan because of the perfect match between medium and subject: music, the most abstract of the arts, is ideally suited to express the principle of sensual desire itself (Rushton, 82). For Kierkegaard, Don Giovanni is a seducer who does not really seduce; rather, "he desires and that desire acts seductively" (83). Thus, he seduces by the force of desire, the sensuality of desire. Zerlina feels this desire and is attracted by it as well as by his rank and wealth. I think it is clear from their behavior toward Don Giovanni that Donna Elvira and Donna Anna have also felt the intensity of this desire.

There seems to be some question as to whether or not Don Giovanni was successful in his attempt on Donna Anna's virtue. There is no real evidence in the libretto. Nonetheless, judging from the violence of her reaction as she pursues him, not only in the opera's opening but throughout, it would seem that he achieved his goal. The anonymity that was sought in Tirso's *Burlador* is also reflected in Don Giovanni's desire to hide his identity. Donna Anna is in a raging fury; he refers to her as "questa furia disperata" who will bring about his downfall, and he is quite correct. Once again there are two distinct stories here: the one describing the womanizer, and the one revealing the murderer who insults the dead. Some commentators on the opera have wondered why it takes Don Ottavio 100 bars to react to his mistress's cries for help, since it is clear that he lives in the palace. These are primarily critics who have found fault with DaPonte's libretto.

As in *Dom Juan*, the opera opens with the servant, in this case Leporello. He, like Sganarelle, paints an unflattering portrait of his master, borne out seconds later by the cries of Donna Anna and the murder of the Commendatore. The opera begins with the word "*notte*" and ends at dawn, after the destruction of the protagonist. There are many similarities in the plots of both Tirso and Molière: The women are more formidable forces in Mozart, and they pursue Don Giovanni more relentlessly than Isabela or Elvire. The psychological development of both women is refined and probing. They both desire vengeance for the crimes committed against them—subjects for great arias. Nevertheless, in their search for vendetta they remain elegant, dignified, and noble. They are certainly articulate; here they join Elvire. Ottavio, who has no counterpart in Molière but does in Tirso, acts as a kind of antidote to the protagonist. Throughout he is faithful, tender, selfless, and noble. Although he personifies the devoted lover, Donna Anna does not seem eager to wed him. Most of Act I reveals the futility of human actions against Don Giovanni. This leads to the graveyard scene, one of pure opera buffa, but as usual it enfolds a serious warning. The finale to Act I has no equivalent in any prior treatment. The seekers of vengeance unite in their determination to destroy Don Giovanni, but even after the attempted rape of Zerlina they cannot stop him and he escapes.

His pursuers neither intimidate nor frighten Don Giovanni, and from the beginning of Act II we know he has no intention of altering his behavior. Don Giovanni is not as much of an amatory strategist as Molière's Don Juan and has no philosophical bent. No aria exists in which he reveals his soul, as there is for the women and Ottavio or even for Leporello, who shares his thoughts with the audience. Don Giovanni is very much in the mold of the eighteenth-century libertine, but, as Rushton has observed, "Mozart is the catalyst whose influence changed the subject from the proper interest of Latin Europe and Catholic morality, and from the status of both vulgar and enlightened entertainment, to the proper interest of Northern Faustian philosophy" (6, 7). Just as Molière's Don Juan appeals to the modern imagination, so too Don Giovanni possesses many qualities of the existential hero. Simone de Beauvoir finds that he is a kind of nihilist, one who denies God and the fetishism of conventional moral approval and social rewards and who lives through free action for its own sake. He combines vitality and skepticism, but unlike the genuine existential hero, he has no sense that freedom is something all should share. In addition, he is dependent on the social institutions that he rejects—wealth and the liberty granted by class (Rushton, 86). In *The Myth of Sisyphus*, Albert Camus states that there is no question that Don Giovanni accepts the rules of the game he plays and expects punishment. In his universe the ridiculous is understood (113).

There are two important elements of the original story absent from the opera: the reciprocal invitation to dinner and the appearance of Don Juan's father. I believe that the father is missing for several reasons. For one, Mozart's pace is quick. To have the dignified favorite of the Spanish king arrive would slow the pace, so Mozart ignores it to sustain the constant movement of his protagonist (similarly, Molière eliminated from the action the murder of the Commander in order to preserve his hero's nobility). In addition, Mozart's own father had died just as he began work on *Don Giovanni*. Biographers and critics have noted that this loss, coupled with the death of his closest friend, caused Mozart to channel all of his creative energy into a frenzy of work, which resulted in the expression of some darker side of his nature and talent. He wrote the overture in one night (Rank, 125). Because of the intensity of the loss and his own conflicted feelings about his father, it is likely that he found it intolerable to write a confrontation between father and son. In short, there were both psychological and aesthetic reasons for not placing the father in the opera.

The second point on which Mozart differs from his predecessors is the single invitation to supper. Don Giovanni invites the statue and it accepts; it does not reciprocate, as does Tirso's stone guest. Clearly, in the context of the operatic form, it provides a much more dramatic and more effective finale to have the Commendatore appear at Don Giovanni's sumptuous dinner party, his own last supper. He wishes to catch his murderer off-guard and unsuspecting (much as Hamlet wishes to catch Claudius carousing or to kill him in his incestuous bed). There is no time for repentance. It would be anticlimactic in the opera to have a second meeting. No one needs to be convinced of Don Giovanni's courage; it has always been there. So when the trombones sound and the voice of doom calls his name, the public in the theater as well as those in the scene are transfixed by their sobering solemnity. The nobleman steps forth, and by taking the Commendatore's hand he admits that the game has ended. Don Giovanni remains defiant and willing to accept the consequences of his actions. The voice of the Commendatore does not necessarily signify the voice of God, but rather the inevitable symbolic consequence of Don Giovanni's life. In fact, since Mozart presents yet another finale with all the other personages coming forward to hear about the fate of their mutual enemy, they do not speak of Christian laws or even a Christian God. Masetto and Zerlina say he is with Prosperina and Pluto, two gods of nature who know something about abduction and dark deeds. The message is mixed as to his fate in one sense. Mozart did not send his hero to Hell but rather to the netherworld of the ancients where he might encounter many with whom he would have something in common. Heaven knows that was not the end of Don Juan by any means.

Along with Hamlet, Faust, and Don Quixote, Don Juan represents one of the great literary myths of the West. Figures not so much to be imitated but to be appreciated in their universality, they continue to thrive and be reinvented in succeeding ages, precisely because they mirror our own foibles, contradictions, and even fantasies.

BIBLIOGRAPHY

Brémond, Henri. In Molière, *Oeuvres Complètes*, Tome I. Paris: Editions Garnier Frères, 1962

Burgess, Anthony. "Introduction." In *Don Giovanni and Idomeneo*. New York: Universe Books, 1971.

Campbell, Roy. *Life Is A Dream, and Other Spanish Classics*. Vol. 2 of *Eric Bentley's Dramatic Repertoire*. New York: Applause, 1985.

Camus, Albert. *Le Mythe de Sisyphe*. Paris: Editions Gallimard, 1942.

Fuchs, Jeanne. *Mythic Misnomers: Reinventing Don Juan in Molière and Mozart*. Classiques Garnier, Paris: Garnier.

Kristeva, Julia. *Tales of Love*. Translated by Leon S. Rudiez. New York: Columbia University Press, 1987.

Martel, José, Alpern, Hyman, and Mades, Leonard. *Diez Comedias del Siglo de Oro*. New York: Harper and Row, 1939.

Molière. *Dom Juan ou Le Festin de Pierre*. Texte établi par Michel Bouty. Paris: Classiques Hachette, 1991.

———. *The Miser and Other Plays*. Translated with an introduction by John Wood. London: Penguin Books, 1953.

———. *Oeuvres Complètes*. Tome I. Edition de R. Jouanny. Paris: Editions Garnier Frères, 1962.

Molina, Tirso de. *The Beguiler from Seville and the Stone Guest*. Translated by Max Oppenheimer, Jr. Lawrence, Kansas: Coronado Press, 1976.

———. *El Vergonzoso en Palacio y El Burlador de Sevilla*. Argentina: Colección Austral, 1946.

Mozart, W. A. *Don Giovanni and Idomeneo* (libretti). Introduction by Anthony Burgess. New York: Universe Books, 1971.

Rank, Otto. *The Don Juan Legend*. Princeton, N.J.: Princeton University Press, 1975.

Rushton, Julian. *W. A. Mozart: Don Giovanni*. London: Cambridge University Press, 1981.

Sneed, J. W. *Don Juan, Variations on a Theme*. London: Routledge, 1990.

Sola-Solé, Josep M., and Gingras, George E., eds. *Tirso's Don Juan: The Metamorphosis of a Theme*. Washington, D.C.: Catholic University of America Press, 1988.

Szogyi, Alex. *Molière Abstrait*. Paris: Librairie A. G. Nizet, 1985.

Weinstein, Leo. *The Metamorphoses of Don Juan*. Stanford: Stanford University Press, 1959.

Whitton, David. *Molière: Don Juan*. Cambridge: Cambridge University Press, 1995.

14

Byron's Don Juan: The Burlador Burlesqued

Alice Levine

Lord Byron's last and greatest poem, *Don Juan*, remained a seventeen-canto fragment at the time of the poet's death in 1824. Nearly all commentaries on Byron's *Don Juan* have concurred on one point: Except for his hero's name, place of birth, and aristocratic Spanish lineage described in the first canto, Byron made very little use of the actual Don Juan source material.[1] However, in 1821, Byron wrote to his publisher, John Murray, of his plans for his epic:

The 5th. is so far from being the last of D. J. that it is hardly the beginning.—I meant to take him the tour of Europe—with a proper mixture of siege—battle—and adventure—and to make him finish as *Anacharsis Cloots*—in the French revolution. . . . I meant to have made him a Cavalier Servente in Italy and a cause for a divorce in England—and a Sentimental "Werther-faced man" in Germany. . . . But I had not quite fixed whether to make him end in Hell—or in an unhappy marriage,—not knowing which would be the severest. The Spanish tradition says Hell—but it is probably only an Allegory of the other state.[2]

As the statement to Murray indicates, although Byron felt free to invent incidents, "the Spanish tradition" was not far from his mind throughout the composition of *Don Juan*, and, in fact, informed the poem more centrally than most critics have allowed. In *Don Juan* Byron in effect reworked the story of Don Juan. The significance of many of the changes he made is illuminated by understanding Byron's personal identification with the legendary hero–villain. Byron's psychology, in fact, provides a deep structure that links the traditional story to its transformation in *Don Juan*.[3]

Before considering the immediate literary sources relevant to Byron's adaptation of the Don Juan legend, I would like to note the ubiquity of theatrical works about Don Juan during the late eighteenth and early nineteenth centuries in England and Italy, where, in July 1818, Byron began *Don Juan*. Goethe, living in Rome in 1787 (the year Mozart's *Don Giovanni* was first produced in Prague), remarked that "nobody lives there without seeing once at least Don Giovanni roasting in hell and the commendador flying like a spirit to Heaven."[4] In addition to the Mozart/Da Ponte opera, the story of Don Juan was the basis of all sorts of serious theatrical works and light entertainments, including a ballet with music by Purcell and a pantomime set to music by Glück.[5] Byron clearly relied on his readers' familiarity with the popular, already burlesqued story when he declared that for his new poem's hero he'd take

our ancient friend Don Juan,
We all have seen him in the pantomime
Sent to the devil, somewhat ere his time. (I, 6–8)[6]

It is quite possible that Byron had seen a performance in Spain of Tirso de Molina's *El burlador de Sevilla*, or of some later Spanish rendering of it. It is probable, too, that he was familiar with Molière's *Dom Juan ou Le Festin de Pierre* and with Carlo Goldoni's autobiographical use of the story in his farce *Don Giovanni Tenorio*, as well as with Mozart's opera.[7]

Three literary works in particular, however, intertwine in a way that relates both to the Don Juan legend and to Byron's use of it, not only in *Don Juan*, but in *Manfred*: Thomas Shadwell's *The Libertine*, Charles Robert Maturin's *Bertram*, and Chapter 23 of the *Biographia Literaria*, in which Samuel Taylor Coleridge denounces Maturin's play by comparing it to Shadwell's, which Coleridge regards as its source. Byron read Coleridge's attack on *Bertram* while he was living in Venice just before beginning *Don Juan*, a poem that is in large part an attack on the poetical system of Coleridge and Wordsworth.

Shadwell's *The Libertine*, first produced in 1676, is an extraordinarily shocking play, whose hero's manic sexual rapaciousness contrasts with Don Giovanni's courtliness and makes iconoclastic Romantic poets like Byron look positively tame. It foreshadows not Byron but de Sade in its unrelenting mixture of violence and sex: "the strangest and wildest and most ferocious Don Juan of them all."[8] Most serious treatments of the Don Juan story seem to flirt with nihilism, but affirmations hover from the classically moral satisfaction at the villain's demise to the

Romantic appreciation of the virtue of self-realization and the triumph over hypocrisy, repression, and superstitious fears. In Shadwell, no political or ideological justification complicates the exhibition of aggressive self-gratification. Shadwell's Don John, with only occasional and transparent self-justification, seduces, kills, commits bigamy, and laughs at the sufferings of the innocent—raping a nun simply to pass the time. Yet the Libertine is attractive, or at least engages the audience's interest, not only because of our eternal fascination with the display of lust and violence, but because his energy, fearlessness, power, and unmediated sexual desire comprise the formula that has consistently lent charisma to the Don Juan character throughout his numerous literary incarnations.

Now, the argument advanced on behalf of Shadwell's play by as high-minded a moralist as Coleridge involves not only our satisfaction at the spectacle of unambiguous villainy receiving its deserved punishment. Coleridge is too astute a critic and imaginative a man not to be aware of the significance of Don John's perverse charm. In the *Biographia*, Chapter 23, written in 1817, Coleridge praises Shadwell for wisely avoiding a certain kind of realism.[9] The Don Juan character type is allowed to appeal to us, Coleridge maintains, when it remains symbolic and makes no claims to verisimilitude, for it symbolizes fundamental realities that are untenable in man's human social condition. The absence of verisimilitude distinguishes Shadwell's Libertine, according to Coleridge, from the outlaw heroes of the *sturm und drang*, with whom their authors invite us to sympathize. Moreover, unlike the *sturm und drang* heroes, Shadwell's Libertine is an aristocrat and behaves like one, an attribute Coleridge considers crucial to elevating his portrayal above the vulgar and to its chief source of wit (as shown, say, in his gentlemanly comportment throughout the dinner invitation/handshake sequence). Don Juan is to Schiller's robbers, Coleridge proceeds, as the "criminal" is to the "mere ruffian."

Coleridge considers Maturin's *Bertram* to be a ludicrous play. Like Shadwell's Don John, Bertram exults in the possession and ruin of an innocent lady who loves him. Though she loves him unlawfully (she is, through events that have compelled her, married to someone she does not love), the audience sees her as more sinned against than sinning, and sees Bertram as heartless, if not sadistic. Unlike Shadwell's Libertine, however, Bertram himself is tormented, and has felt the sting of betrayal, blighted love, and unjust disenfranchisement. The way the audience is therefore invited to identify with him as outlaw/underdog—the naturally endowed individual disempowered by unjust circumstances—is the sort of "moral jacobinism" Coleridge critiques. (Although Coleridge insists his critique is aesthetic and not political, it is easy to see how intertwined in Coleridge's essay are aesthetic, political, and moral biases.)

It is easy to see why Byron, reading Coleridge's attack on *Bertram* in 1817, would have reacted sharply to it. As a codirector of Drury Lane in 1815, Byron had championed *Bertram*, which is itself indebted to Byronic influences.[10] Byron would also have understood (correctly) that a personal attack was intended by Coleridge, whose own *Zaploya* had been rejected in favor of *Bertram*, and whose moralistic position toward the Don Juan/Bertram character would clearly point a finger at the famous libertine poet who had a role in the rejection of his play. *Manfred*, begun in 1816, has much in common with *Bertram*, even to the extent of containing verbal echoes of Maturin's play, which Byron knew well.[11] Understanding some of the personal psychological implications of *Manfred* prepares the reader to observe some of the same implications in *Don Juan*, Byron's in-your-face, "so there!" response to Coleridge.

Manfred tells the story of a brooding, intellectual aristocrat who finds that "knowledge is sorrow." Neither human knowledge nor divine power can alter the past or man's sinful errors, and Manfred, suicidal with guilt, finds it impossible, as well as cowardly and intellectually dishonest, to take comfort from religious forgiveness. The source of Manfred's guilt can generally be identified as his having caused the death of his incestuous lover, Astarte, but the precise details—especially how he caused her death—are shrouded in ambiguity.[12] Neither Bertram nor Manfred exhibit what many would take to be the definitive characteristic of Don Juan: his promiscuity. What they do have in common with Don Juan, however, is the responsibility for seducing, abandoning, and actually harming the women who love them, and for being beyond the reach of conventional morality and religious authority, specifically in their flagrant disregard for sexual taboos (adultery or incest in these works replacing promiscuity).

Byron's drama of the *homme fatal* is easily set in biographical context, as readers from Byron's day to our own have been unable to resist doing.[13] Although typically the poem's love story is taken as referring to the author's scandalous relationship with his half-sister Augusta, Byron's bisexuality, it seems to me, is equally relevant to the poem's psychological resonances. (Bringing this emphasis to *Manfred*, moreover, illuminates Byron's treatment of the Don Juan theme in *Don Juan*, as I will discuss.) On the poem's surface level, Manfred's assertion that "we . . . loved each other as we should not love" (II, i, 26–27) refers to incest. Manfred's description of his beloved, however, is tellingly narcissistic:

She was like me in lineaments—her eyes,
Her hair, her features, all, to the very tone

Even of her voice, they said were like to mine;
But soften'd all, and temper'd into beauty;
She had the same lone thoughts and wanderings. (II, ii, 105–109)

Astarte is not only a blood relation but quite simply a feminized version of himself. Relevant, too, is a passage that suggests that Manfred's guilt concerning Astarte derives less from the violence of outside parties than from a tragic failure within himself, a failure of love itself: "I loved her, and destroyed her / . . . Not with my hand, but heart—which broke her heart— / It gazed on mine, and withered" (II, ii, 118–119). That Manfred failed the female lover the poem names because of some unidentified heart-withering flaw or evil on his part (his "shut soul's hypocrisy" [I, 245], "some half-maddening sin" [II, i, 31]), when taken in the context of Byron's own life suggests a possible encoding of an even greater sexual taboo than incest whose name Byron dare not speak.[14]

Of course, the classical Don Juan experiences no guilt throughout his sexual escapades and, the seeming essence of virility, he is untinged with sexual ambiguity. But the compulsively promiscuous man is surely as preoccupied with avoiding/destroying women as he is with "loving" them. (A good part of the humor of *Don Giovanni*, certainly, derives from Leporello's helping his master escape or hide from women.) It is almost too obviously true that Don Juan—prior to his high Romantic incarnations—is not concerned with love at all, but rather with sex as conquest, as epitomized in the famous catalog aria (the "*mille e tre*") in *Don Giovanni*. Thus, the structure of enmity underlies the relationship between Don Juan and women, a fact that can easily be deciphered as a projection of homosexuality (though the broad appeal of the Don Juan tale suggests that a structure of enmity may be generally relevant to heterosexual relationships).

While Byron is not, of course, consciously reworking in *Manfred* the legend of Don Juan, the shadowing of that legend in Byron's drama is undeniable. By the time of *Manfred*, the story and character of Don Juan had left an imprint on a good deal of literature. Thus, a work like *Bertram*, which bears the stamp of both *sturm und drang* and Byronic influences, is automatically connected by Coleridge to Shadwell's Don Juan adaptation, *The Libertine*. Even the two-part structure of the traditional Don Juan story—the fatal, forbidden attraction; the religious or supernatural reckoning with a male authority figure—is realized in *Manfred*, which concludes with the death of the tormented hero as an abbot who has unsuccessfully tried to convert and save him looks on in a state of mixed dismay and admiration. Reversing the final repentance of Tirso's dramatization, Manfred refuses to repent. However, in a swerve even from the proud and fearless Don Giovanni, Manfred rejects the power of both God and Devil. In this final scene, greatly admired by Nietzsche, Manfred declares the human mind to be its own place of suffering or joy.

Considering *Manfred* then, as Byron's tragic treatment of the Don Juan legend sheds considerable light upon his comic treatment of it in *Don Juan*. The same personal projections and psychological implications of the former poem help explain Byron's particular reworking of the source material in the latter.[15] Now Byron takes up Coleridge's challenge in choosing as an alter ego the famed libertine who so outrages Coleridge's moral sense that he rejects any sympathetic treatment of him as being aesthetically impossible to sustain.[16]

Having cast *Don Juan* as a mock epic, Byron appropriately rejects the list of ancient and contemporary military heroes that immediately suggest themselves, from Agamemnon to Napoleon. Instead, he makes the odd selection of "our ancient friend, Don Juan"—a name associated more with villainy than heroism—and replaces the battlefield with the war between the sexes. The conquest theme is here mocked, as is the idea of heroism itself, which, as Byron sees it, has become yet another illusion of the world:

I want a hero: an uncommon want,
When every year and month sends forth a new one,
Till, after cloying the gazettes with cant,
The age discovers he is not the true one. (I, 1–4)

Well before Andy Warhol, Byron has discovered that the glory and fame of heroes have become a fifteen-minute media event.

But to choose an antihero, a villain, is in some sense still to believe seriously in the heroic, and Byron in this work is committed to the deflationary style. By referring to Don Juan as "our ancient friend," Byron domesticates the larger than life. His hero's pedigree and fate (along with any verisimilitude) are dispatched with a joking rhyme about the popular comic entertainment he has become: "We all have seen him in the pantomime / Sent to the devil, somewhat ere his time" (I, i, 7–8).

Byron takes the character of Don Juan—a fearsome force of masculine energy, power, *droit du seigneur*, controller of his own and others' fates—and stands it on its head. Byron's Juan proceeds, it is true, through a series of sexual adventures, only instead of the grown man, he is a youth; instead of a well-practiced seducer, he is the naif who is seduced and falls in love; instead of a morally jaded cynic, he is openhearted and good-natured; finally, instead of representing the epitome of aggressive virility, he is passive and often takes the feminine role—

as the virginal youth in Canto I seduced by the older woman (of twenty-three); as the cross-dressed stowaway in a sultan's harem; as the happy lover on the run not from the woman he loves, but only from her irate, unfaithful husband or cutthroat father, stock blocking figures to romance. He is repeatedly the victim of more powerful men and women, who either threaten him physically, seduce him, buy him as a slave, or conscript him in their army. When he does oppose the tide of events or venture forth an opinion, it is on behalf of the good Romantic virtues: individual freedom and sympathy with the vulnerable. Byron's Don Juan possesses a natural morality, refusing, for example, during the cannibalism episode to dine "on his pastor and his master" (II, 624), for which he is the only one saved from the ensuing insanity.

Byron's poem, furthermore, differs from earlier Don Juan stories in enlarging the focus on the female characters. In earlier versions the women's characters are developed only as much as necessary to illuminate the character of Don Juan, who is always stage front. The women in *Don Juan* represent a spectrum of types, which is clearly one of the poem's chief concerns. There is the hypocritical, self-righteous, and controlling Donna Inez; the more charmingly self-deceiving Donna Julia, who "whispering 'I will ne'er consent'—consented" (I, 936); Haidée, the child of nature, whose unalienated condition is reflected in her own honest, free, and nonverbal sexual expressiveness, since "never having dreamt of falsehood, she / Had not one word to say of constancy" (II, 1519–1520); the harem women who, through their own subversive actions demonstrate that "love is for the free" (V, 1012); Catherine the Great, powerful and sexually aggressive, but equally a pawn to the mighty forces of nature ("her climacteric teased her as her teens" [X, 373]); the self-deceiving virtuous ladies of the English aristocracy; and finally, a possible soulmate for Don Juan: Aurora, who in her aloofness and intelligence (which she shares with Manfred's Astarte) stands apart from her hypocritical and self-deceiving peers. Byron's poem thus uses the Don Juan story to organize its content as a portrait gallery of women, while Don Juan himself, for all his presence on the scene, remains a not very developed character.[17]

Byron projected his own life and character onto that of his hero in a way that he knew would have been recognized by his inner circle of intimates, who probably numbered in the hundreds. First we must recognize that no matter where geographically the poem takes us, the target of its satire is, first, Regency society, and next, one English lord's life in particular. It is true that, to write it phonetically, Don JOO-an is from SE-vil, that his mother is EYE-nez (to rhyme with "fine as"), and that they live alongside the river, whose name, pronounced to rhyme, is "Gua-dal-KWI-ver." But the funny anglicizations of foreign words and names not only make satirically clear the Englishness of the poem, but satirize implicitly the imperialist mentality embodied in the person and policies of the object of Byron's most vicious satiric thrusts, Foreign Minister Castlereagh.[18]

This is not a poem about Spain and its legendary hero but about Byron's country and Byron himself. Byron uses the original Don Juan's aristocratic lineage in order to mirror and mock that of his own class:

His father's name was Jóse—*Don*, of course,
A true Hidalgo, free from every stain
Of Moor or Hebrew blood, he traced his source
Through the most Gothic gentlemen of Spain. (I, 65–68)

Inez, Don Juan's mother, is a parody of Byron's estranged wife, Annabella Millbanke, in her aptitude for mathematics, her ostentatious moralism, and her having instituted divorce proceedings against her husband, whose personality plays hide-and-seek with the poet's:

He was a mortal of the careless kind,
With no great love for learning, or the learn'd,
Who chose to go where'er he had a mind,
And never dream'd his lady was concern'd;
The world, as usual, wickedly inclined
To see a kingdom or a house o'erturn'd,
Whisper'd he had a mistress, some said two,
But for domestic quarrels *one* will do. (I, 145–152)

In the moralistic upbringing she tries to give her son, moreover, Donna Inez's character draws from Byron's mother as well as wife—a Freudian red flag, of course. The chief attribute of Donna Inez (as of Lady Byron in her lord's view) is a sort of combination of pretentiousness, priggishness, and hypocrisy that is so unattractive that it serves to mitigate anyone else's immorality. Byron's self-conscious inscription of his own biography into the poem is nowhere more evident than in the presence—the ever-presence—of the narrator, who acknowledges that "there is much which could not be appreciated / In any manner by the uninitiated" (XIV, 175–176). In fact, the poet-as-narrator casts a long shadow over the hero (the poet's youthful projection), and in thus doing plays on the servant/Don relationship of the traditional Don Juan story (as well as, by the way, of another important and influential Spanish literary work, *Don Quixote*, to which Byron refers in his own comedy of the world's illusions as "that too true tale / . . . the saddest—and more sad, / Because it makes us smile" [XIII, 63, 65–66]). Byron's preoccupation with the disaster of his own marriage is echoed in the narrator's recurrent, acidic ruminations on the subject:

Marriage from love, like vinegar from wine—
A sad, sour, sober beverage—by time
Is sharpened from its high celestial flavour
Down to a very homely household savour. (III, 37–40)

There's something of "antipathy," the narrator tells us, between the state of love and the state of marriage: "passion in a lover's glorious / But in a husband's pronounced uxorious" (III, 47–48); or, even more famously, "Oh! ye lords of ladies intellectual, / Inform us truly, have they not hen-peck'd you all?" (I, 175–176). Certainly, if "love is for the free," as the harem scene ironically illustrates, then the reason for that antipathy is clear. The antimarriage theme, implicit in all Don Juan stories, here dovetails with the political and social satire.

The two-part structure of the Don Juan legend—that is, the escapades and the embrace with the statue—may also be seen to be shadowed in Byron's poem, even in its incomplete state. The final cantos give Juan's last and perhaps scariest adventures, as, having earlier survived one shipwreck, he navigates the more treacherous waters of Regency society women.[19] Both Lady Adeline Amundeville and the Duchess of Fitz-Fulke alternately vie for his attention as a lover and play the mother to him in trying to marry him off, a not incompatible or even inconsistent behavior in the fast lanes of Regency society and an echo of the mother/wife identification noted before. At the end of Canto XVI (the last completed canto), after hearing a recitation one evening of a gothic tale, "The Black Friar," Don Juan retires to his room, only to be startled by a haunting sound of footsteps. He goes to the door, which opens "with a most infernal creak, / Like that of Hell" (XVI, 969–970). There is a hooded figure all in black, but when the hood is removed, it is no friar—no Commendatore—at all, but "In full, voluptuous, but *not o'er*grown bulk / The phantom of her frolic Grace— Fitz-Fulke" (XVI, 1031–1032). The awful stone guest, figure of religious reckoning, is here replaced with something at least equally nightmarish: the sexually demanding woman, whose very name embeds terrifying etymological possibilities.[20] Of course, the gentle-hearted Juan can do nothing but oblige, but the image of the sexual threat—or perhaps the heterosexual threat—overlapping with and essentially substituting for the stone guest theme reinforces how for Byron hell may indeed be only an allegory of marriage.

In considering *Don Juan*'s transformation of its sources, Byron's sexually obsessed and sexually ambivalent psychology provides a deep structure. After sending bragging letters back to England from Italy about his own "*mille e tre*," Byron also had the gall to complain: "I should like to know *who* has been carried off—except poor dear *me*—I have been more ravished myself than anybody since the Trojan war."[21]

In casting himself as the feminine victim of ravishment here, as he does Juan at the end of Canto XVI, in the cross-dressing scene in the harem, and, generally, in his soft and passive personality, Byron presents an image antithetical to that of the legendary Don Juan, yet one that serves to deconstruct the well-known story along the lines of Byron's own psychology. Byron's last and, in many biographers' views, deepest attachment to a woman, to Countess Teresa Guiccioli, ended when Byron left for Greece in 1823. Yet his departure for Greece was something he chose for himself, having confided to his friend John Cam Hobhouse, "I feel & I feel it bitterly—that a man should not consume his life at the side and on the bosom—of a woman."[22] It is an obvious point that it is as much Don Juan's goal *not* to spend his life by the side of a woman as it is to womanize. (Of course, in Greece Byron is said to have found his final passionate attachment—to his young page, Lukas Chalandritsanos.)

Whatever the implications regarding his ambivalent sexuality, Byron found in the Don Juan story an opportunity to attack Romanticism and marriage at once, even while connecting his own poetic vitality not to the domestic or the higher emotions, as Coleridge and Wordsworth did, but to the raw force of sexuality with which "our ancient friend" Don Juan has always been associated. "As to *Don Juan*," Byron wrote,

it may be bawdy—but is it not good English?—it may be profligate—but is it not *life*, is it not *the thing*? Could any man have written it—who has not lived in the world?—and tooled in a post-chaise? in a hackney coach? in a Gondola? Against a wall? in a court carriage? in a vis a vis?—on a table?—and under it?[23]

NOTES

1. See, for example, Elizabeth Boyd, *Byron's "Don Juan": A Critical Study* (New Brunswick, N.J.: Rutgers University Press, 1945): "For Byron . . . as for Shaw in *Man and Superman*, the legend of Don Juan was merely a framework on which to hang his view of human life and his moralistic philosophizing" (35); Leo Weinstein, *The Metamorphoses of Don Juan* (Stanford: Stanford University Press, 1959): "Byron's Don Juan has so little in common with any of his predecessors that, were it not for his name, he would probably not be thought of as belonging to the Don Juan legend" (79). Hermione de Almeida, *Byron and Joyce through Homer* (London: Macmillan, 1981), in which she considers the myth of Don Juan "ancillary" to *Don Juan*, to which the Odysseus myth is "primary." Jerome J. McGann, "Literary and Historical Background to *Don Juan*," in *Complete Poetical Works*, vol. 5, ed. Jerome McGann and Barry Weller (Oxford: Clarendon Press, 1980–1991), gives as the poem's sources and influences Frere, Pulci, Berni, and Casti (for the mock-serious rhyme); Horace, Chaucer, and Pope (for the conversational manner); the biographical impulse Byron had at the time; and the whole school of poets whom we now take to

represent English Romanticism, which Byron rejects. McGann does not mention Tirso de Molina, whose widely popular play assigned the name Don Juan to the legendary Spanish libertine; brief references to other adaptations of the legend and Byron's relation to them are made in passing toward the end of this section of the commentary.

Two notable exceptions to the list of critics who emphasize the lack of relevance of the Spanish legend to Byron's poem are Candace Tate, "Byron's *Don Juan*: Myth as Psychodrama," *Keats–Shelley Journal* 29 (1980); *Modern Critical Interpretations: Lord Byron's "Don Juan"* (New York: Chelsea House, 1987), and Moyra Haslett, *Byron's "Don Juan" and the Don Juan Legend* (Oxford: Clarendon Press, 1997). Tate's "Byron's *Don Juan*" is regrettably—and surprisingly—not cited by Haslett. My discussion of *Don Juan* is indebted to Tate's insight about the way Byron's psychology may provide a link between the original legend and the differences between it and Byron's poem. Haslett's book came to my attention only during the final editing of this chapter. Surprisingly, it does not cite Tate's excellent article.

2. Leslie A. Marchand, ed., *Byron's Letters and Journals*, 12 vols. (London: John Murray; Cambridge: Harvard University Press, 1973–1982), VIII, 78. All quotations from Byron's letters are taken from this edition.

3. Cf. Tate, "Byron's *Don Juan*," who considers that all the characters in *Don Juan* are the "auxiliary egos" in Byron's own oedipal drama.

4. As quoted in Oscar Mandel, ed., *The Theatre of Don Juan: A Collection of Plays and Views, 1630–1963* (Lincoln: University of Nebraska Press, 1963), 278.

5. Ibid.

6. All quotations from Byron's poetry are taken from Jerome J. McGann, ed., *Lord Byron: The Complete Poetical Works*, 7 vols. (Oxford: Clarendon Press, 1980–1993).

7. Boyd, *Byron's "Don Juan,"* 35; and Haslett, *Byron's "Don Juan,"* 56–57.

8. Mandel, *Theatre of Don Juan*, 167.

9. The chapter was originally published in the form of letters to *The Courier* written between August 29 and September 11, 1816.

10. See Byron's letter to Maturin (IV, 336–337), in which he praises *Bertram*, and Byron's letter to John Murray containing his response upon reading Coleridge's attack of *Bertram* (V, 267).

11. While I have not pursued the source or influence relationship between *Bertram* and *Manfred*, such echoes include "I killed her—but—I loved her" (*Bertram*) / "I loved her, and destroy'd her!" (*Manfred*); "but what avails it" (*Bertram*) / "but they avail not" (*Manfred*); and a reference in *Bertram* to "Manfredonia." Also, compare "He'll curse thee with his pardon" (*Bertram*) with "That curse shall be Forgiveness," from *Childe Harold's Pilgrimage*, Canto IV (1817–1818).

12. This mysteriousness about the given facts of the drama, as well as its "supernatural machinery," is better suited to a symbolic than realistic drama, and perhaps thus contributes to saving *Manfred* from the fault of "verisimilitude" that Coleridge finds in Maturin's work. That Byron was aware of the problem of making *Manfred* work on the stage is clear from his defining *Manfred* as a "closet drama," so perhaps he would not have been unconvinced by some part of Coleridge's critique of *Bertram* as a staged play.

13. Byron was conscious that *Manfred* would be read biographically. See McGann, *Complete Poetical Works*, IV, 466–467.

14. For a discussion of earlier conjectures about the incest guilt in *Manfred* as a disguised reference to homosexual experiences, see Louis Crompton, *Byron and Greek Love: Homophobia in 19th-Century England* (Berkeley and Los Angeles: University of California Press, 1985).

15. *Don Juan* was in fact begun at the same time that Byron began his *Memoirs*, and, as with *Manfred*, Byron was entirely conscious of the autobiographical grounding of his mock epic. See McGann, *Complete Poetical Works*, V, 668.

16. As McGann notes, "Indeed, to this point criticism has failed to see how important Coleridge's book was to the making of Byron's poem." *Complete Poetical Works*, V, 668. Following McGann, Caroline Franklin, in *Byron's Heroines* (Oxford: Clarendon Press, 1992), 99–101, supplies further insightful commentary about the significance to *Don Juan* of Coleridge's essay.

17. Franklin, *Byron's Heroines*, 101.

18. Cf. Peter Graham, "Nothing So Difficult," in *Rereading Byron: Essays Selected from Hofstra University's Byron Bicentennial Conference*, ed. Alice Levine and Robert N. Keane (New York: Garland, 1993).

19. Byron's sources for the shipwreck are discussed extensively in Boyd, *Byron's "Don Juan."* While a shipwreck episode actually occurs in Tirso's *El burlador de Sevilla* and in many of the later versions of the Don Juan story, the shipwreck in Byron's poem is indebted to a variety of sources that have nothing to do with Don Juan. Certainly, Coleridge's critique of the shipwreck in *Bertram* must have been one of the most immediate provocations to Byron to use it. See McGann, *Complete Poetical Works*, V, 668.

20. See Graham, "Nothing So Difficult," 45–46.

21. October 29, 1819 (VI, 237).

22. Letter to John Cam Hobhouse, August 23, 1819 (VI, 214).

23. Letter to Douglas Kinnaird, October 26, 1819 (VI, 232).

15

Don Juan in Hell: *George Bernard Shaw's Perverse Sexual Politics*

Rhoda Nathan

Some of you may be reading this because of one word in the title—"perverse"—especially because the descriptive "sexual" with which it is linked suggests kinky behavior in the boudoir. But let me disabuse you at the outset. Those of you who know Shaw at all will be prepared for the inevitable focus—the noun "politics" that the two adjectives modify. You will recognize the man who expressed perverse theories about every area of quotidian life, many of which are given in the insouciant addendum to the play *Man and Superman*, from which *Don Juan* is extracted: *The Revolutionist's Handbook*. In that nose-thumbing pamphlet, Shaw is perverse in his opinions and advice in every significant area of human or institutional practice: education, child rearing, marriage, government, capital and corporal punishment, and the economy. So powerful was his loathing of poverty, which he himself endured in his youth, that he would probably join the Indian journalists whose praise of Mother Teresa was not unstinting owing to her failure to expend her considerable energy and influence on instructing the poor in ways to rise out of their poverty in addition to ministering to their needs, which were generated by their hopelessness.

The "perverse" in the title of this chapter reflects one single pervading Shavian preoccupation: the uses of sexuality as applied to the institution of marriage and its consequent procreation. (I wish it were more prurient for the purpose of amusement, but, alas, we're interpreting the convictions and positions of a theorist, a futurist, and one of the great intellectual puritans—small "p"—of the century.) For the record, it does appear that Shaw was, in fact, most "perverse" in the areas of sex and marriage, and for a very good reason. As an evolutionist, Lamarckian—that is, creative—as well as Darwinian, a profound advocate of the improvement of the species through positive eugenics—as contrasted with negative eugenics—he was a disciple of Nietzsche, Schopenhauer, and Wagner. He toyed with the *"elan vital"* or Life Force of the French philosopher Henri Bergson and truly believed in the controlled improvement of the species through intelligent breeding. To this end, he created strong women determined to hook into men who would serve their breeding purposes, not unlike Queen Victoria in Stanley Weintraub's stunning biography of Prince Albert, *Uncrowned King* (New York: Simon and Schuster, 1977). The biographer leaves no doubt in his carefully researched analysis of the Victoria–Albert relationship that Victoria chose Albert "who was destined to be a high-class stud, a robust bedroom performer guaranteed to produce plenty of blue-blooded offspring. That was his main duty, indeed it was virtually his only duty." The book leaves no doubt that it was Victoria who was the aggressor in the romance, that she chose Albert not only for his beautiful nose and sweet mouth but as a progenitor for her brood of nine children. How did she know? In the Shavian imagination, she was guided by the Life Force, the same instinct that guided the heroine of *Man and Superman* to home in on her prey, a move that the playwright unromantically calls the spider and fly entrapment ploy.

The sexual politics in *Man and Superman*, the play in which *Don Juan in Hell* is encapsulated as a dream vision—or what Shaw calls a "philosophy"—is just one in a long line of sexually perverse plays. In *Candida*, written before the turn of the century, there is an auction in which a mature woman participates in what was usually called a "white slave" auction in those days, choosing to remain with her weaker husband, who had proved his breeding potential but is in every way intellectually inferior to her, instead of flying off with the handsome young poet, who, like Octavius, the Ricky-Ticky-Tavy, is unfit for the rigors of domestic life. In play after play the female chooses the man who suits her domestic purposes, giving the lie to the Victorian myth that women are passive, must be wooed by a strong man, and are then lost in the domestic confines of the nursery and kitchen. In *Getting Married*, one of Shaw's most audacious plays, we are given an open marriage, a prenuptial contract, and a lesbian heroine who would like a baby but cannot abide the thought of a smelly cigar-puffing man in her bed. In most of his plays it is the woman who is the aggressor, and stripped of any scrap of sentimentality about her function. Shaw gives us strong women, and men who unwillingly or unwittingly lay their heads on the block to serve their primordial needs.

Now to the case in point, in which Shaw spells out most clearly his intention, or rather, the intention of the Life Force, which is instrumental to the shaping and coming of the Superman. *Don Juan in Hell* is always performed as a separate entity, but it really cannot be understood in the abstract. It depends on *Man and Superman* for the transmission of its "message." (In May 1900 Shaw had begun *A Parliament in Hell between Don Juan and the Devil*. The third act was to be called *The Superman or Don Juan's Grandson's Grandson*. The final version, however, completed in 1903, was given the title *Man and Superman: A Comedy and a Philosophy*. The third act became *Don Juan in Hell*.)

The framework comedy dramatizes a chase by a determined young woman to find a suitable father for her children, whose congenital superiority will eventually yield, generations down the pike, a superior human being, or the infant Superman. To this end she has chosen the likeliest prey, an eccentric revolutionary gasbag like Shaw himself, determined never to marry but possessing exactly those qualities which should be bred: vitality, daring, unconventionality, brains, and vision. Her name is,naturally enough, Ann, which is transmuted in the dream vision into Dona Ana; his is John Tanner, a calculated English version of Don Juan Tenorio. The other major characters, who appear in slightly altered form, are Ann's adopted father figure, who, of course, is transmuted into Don Gonzalo, Ana's biological father in the dream play, and a brigand named Mendoza, who shows up as the Devil in the internal dream vision.

The internal play itself is a debate among the four participants, or, in some assessments, a species of oratorio performed by four soloists, who occasionally form a kind of chorale to the accompanying Mozartian strains taken, of course, from his opera *Don Giovanni*. The setting is Hell, properly illuminated by sulfurous leaping flames. An aged woman, newly dead, is surveying her new home, and is appalled to learn that she is indeed in Hell, rather than in the heaven she expected for her eternal home. A conventional Catholic, she is offended at finding herself in the company of bad actors, and the rest of the debate, engaged in by the other denizens, is given over to a spirited argument about the nature of Hell and its polar opposite, the Kingdom of Heaven. The loudest voice, of course, is that of Don Juan Tenorio, Jack Tanner in a previous life, who really is Shaw's mouthpiece. Perverse in the issue of the afterlife as in all things, Tenorio, Shaw's impenitent Don Juan, is hot on going to Heaven, a place of incredible dullness where people do nothing but think to improve their minds, whereas Hell, where they are all immured, is the resting place for artists and pleasure seekers.

Eventually, Tanner persuades the outwardly conventional Ann that Heaven is reserved for those few mortals who have other things on their agenda than mere pleasure: for example, the eventual creation of the Superman. None of this is very logical, but Don Juan, who has left his sexual philanderings behind, is Heaven bent on going to that remote empyrean where he is free of all the earthly temptations and can formulate his blueprint for the superior being to house the superior intellect and spirit. Dona Ana, for once caught up in the spirit of his fantasy, decides to join him in his upward trajectory away from the puerile pleasures and distractions of the underworld and into an ennobling environment where she can concentrate on their shared mission. "Then my work is not done," she exults. "I believe in the life to come. A father . . . a father for the superman!" And the dream vision ends, with Ana persuaded by Don Juan that her immortal future is in Heaven, where serious purpose prevails, not pleasure.

What, you may ask, does all this have to do with sexual perversity? Everything. In Don Juan's effort to persuade Ana to join him, he brushes aside the joys of Hell as a place of love and beauty, where the serious issue of procreation for the purpose of improving the race cannot prevail against all that self-indulgence. The process of creating the Superman, a creature compounded of much mind and little matter, takes all the sexual energy a woman can muster, and the man she chooses must yield himself to her higher purpose like the mate of the praying mantis or the fly to the spider. His sexuality is thus subsumed to her drive, which is directed entirely toward the task before her. In his lecture to Ana, Juan instructs her thus: "Sexually, Woman is Nature's contrivance for perpetuating its highest achievement. Sexually, man is woman's contrivance for fulfilling Nature's behest in the most economical way. She knows by instinct that far back in the evolutional process, she invented him, differentiated him, created him in order to produce something better than the single-sexed process can produce." Naturally, with such an aggrandized goal, Hell provides too much pleasure, too many distractions, too much beauty. Heaven is the proper locale for the process of formulating the coming Superman.

Now, what has Shaw done with the tale of the randy *burlador*, or trickster? Is his version perverse? Damn well told! To abstract sexuality from its conventionalizing cover—love—and present it as a conscious device that the thinking man harnesses to his intellectual goals for the human race is perverse indeed, particularly at the turn of the century, when for the male to subjugate his masculinity for a remote female purpose was turning the entire male–female relationship on its ear. There are other perversities as well: borrowing from the book of Job the image of an afterworld in which the Devil shuttles back and forth between Heaven and Hell for the purpose of selling eternal damnation that he himself hardly believes in, and finally anticipating Sartre's existential Hell as a place not only of other people, but of other people having a fine old time thinking they are reaping the rewards that should rightfully belong in Heaven. But they are all deceived; they are really wasting their substance in Hell.

Did Shaw know he was subverting the Don Juan legend to serve his own futurist theories? Of course. He refashioned the original formula to suit his own prescription, which was itself fashioned of shreds and patches of the Wagnerian, Nietzschean, Bergsonian stew. It goes like this: Woman is the guardian of the Life Force, the bearer of children. Man is the instrument of her purpose. Instinctively she seeks a father and provider for her children. Man desires freedom and is reluctant to bend under the yoke of matrimony. Therefore, he flees, and it is the bounden duty of a woman to pursue, because marriage is something more than a personal affair. Its social purposes are imperative and primary, since the eventual coming of the Superman is no mere accident but the result of carefully planned eugenic breeding. In the framework play, Ann may be conventional in her declarations, but she is the pursuer. She literally reels in her prey with her boa even though she faints when she has achieved her purpose. In the internal dream vision, Dona Ana is also eminently conventional and respectable, and thus expects to find herself in Heaven at the end of a lengthy proper life as a good church-going woman and the mother of many children. But at the end she is persuaded that she belongs in a place not of pleasure and indulgence, the Hell in which she is presently residing, but of serious purpose, where people of vision dedicate themselves to higher purposes, the formulation of the improved race of the future.

Finally, we must remember that we are dealing with Shaw, a genius, who was perverse in all things. Look at what he did in his theatrical transformation of history. Shaw took the historic character of Caesar and turned him into an embryonic Superman in ancient Rome. At the same time he refashioned Cleopatra from a "nursery kitten" on the way to becoming a "New Woman." He took the mythic Pygmalion and transformed him into a clone of Shaw himself, with Eliza Doolittle an incarnation of Ibsen's Nora at the very moment when she slammed that historic door. He even transformed the Salvation Army of *Major Barbara* into an institution that could learn a thing or two from the Krupps Works in Germany or Hershey of Pennsylvania for managing labor relations. The brothel or cat house in *Candida* is presented as a superior working environment to the Dickensian factories of the last years of the nineteenth century. What a perverse playwright—the world has yet to catch up to his perversities. It is just now beginning to enact what he was proposing in his plays more than a hundred years ago.

16

Don Juan Tenorio: From the "Romancero" to Don Juan de Marco

Eliezer Oyola

Of all the cultural contributions that Spain has made to the world, there are three themes that have played an especially significant role: the picaresque, Don Quixote, and Don Juan Tenorio. Just as the picaroon (*el pícaro*) is the antihero vis-à-vis el Cid, so is Don Juan the antithesis of Don Quixote. Next to the Platonic love of Don Quixote for his Dulcinea ("the lady of his thoughts") stands Don Juan's sensual, goliardic love (eros): the saint and the sinner. Don Quixote is faithful to one woman, Dulcinea. Don Juan is faithful, in his manner, to all women at once.[1] That is, he is capable of loving all women through his desire for one, while at the same time loving one ideal woman in the sum of all his conquests—that is, if he is capable of love at all.

But who is he? Where did he come from? And curiously, why is he called Juan? Quite clearly, the title "Don" speaks of his noble ancestry. Unamuno, noting a similarity between the surname "Tenorio" and the Galician-Portuguese name "Tenoiro," deduces that Don Juan is not from Seville but from Galicia. Even if this linguistic argument is not convincing, there are other aspects of the legend that support Unamuno's theory, namely its reference to superstitions, institutions, and customs from Northern Spain: invitations from the dead, banquets in the cemetery, the Santa Compaña (Holy Company), and other folklore.[2]

The character's given name projects a mixed connotation. One of the most common in all Western languages, the name Juan carries in the Hispanic world a dual legacy, that of saint and sinner. On the one hand it speaks of John the Apostle, *el discípulo amado*, the great mystic and author both of the gospel named after him and of the Book of Revelation. Therein as well lies the magical Night of Saint John, where Christian and pagan elements combine in a kind of syncretism (celebrations of love, fertility rites, dreams fulfilled). On the other hand is the Juan of superstition, the *buenazo* and simpleton, object of ridicule, "everyman, all man," more sinner than saint. This is the Juan of countless anecdotes, expressions, and popular omens. Recall Celestina's delight when, on her way to bewitch Melibea, she encounters no less than three men named Juan, two of them cuckolds to boot. Surely, she thinks, good fortune is hers![3] Consider too the Puerto Rican Juan Bobo ("Foolish John"), equivalent to Jack in the universal folktale, "Jack and the Beanstalk," the proverbial Juan sin Miedo ("Fearless John") and so many others. In short, the name Juan oscillates, in both language and cultural patrimony, between the heroic and the ridiculous, between the sacred and the profane.

In the case of Don Juan there is an underlying implication that the sinner is born of the fool. For this there is ample Biblical and literary evidence. "The fool hath said in his heart, There is no God. They are corrupt, they have done abominable works, there is none that doeth good" (Psalm 14:1). Unamuno, commenting on this verse in his *Sentimiento trágico de la vida* (*The Tragic Sense of Life*), says that only the most degenerate of humans can say "in his heart" that there is no God. In this light, Don Juan is a tragicomic blunderer who, like the biblical "fool," mistakes the temporal for the eternal; his heroic side is the thrust of his defiant humanity.[4] Juan, saint and sinner.

The theme or myth of Tirso's Don Juan is the product of a fusion of two literary traditions: (1) the impudent youth who deceives and seduces numerous women and in the process even kills a man (the theme of the scoffer, the defiler, the *burlador*), and (2) the blasphemous, sacrilegious aristocrat who disrespects all that is sacred (the theme of *el convidado de piedra*, the stone guest). Already in the Romancero these two traditions appear together, as we see in the following ballad cited by Menéndez Pidal:

Pa misa diba un galán
Caminito de la iglesia,
No diba por oír misa
Ni pa estar atento a ella,
que diba por ver las damas
las van guapas y frescas.
En el medio del camino
encontró una calavera,
mirándola muy mirada

y un gran puntapié le diera;
arregañaba los dientes
como si ella se riera;
—Calavera, yo te brindo
esta noche a la mi fiesta.
—No hagas burla el caballero;
mi palabra doy por prenda.[5]

What is the power of this tale that invades every genre of literature, music, and art, transcending time, space, and its own cultural-ideological context? How can we explain its proliferation in Spain, Italy, France, England, Russia, Ireland, Denmark, the Americas, and beyond? Why does it surface in so many time frames and with so many faces? We have the medieval Renaissance Don Juan of the *romanceros*; Tirso's Baroque, Counter-Reformation Burlador de Sevilla; the eighteenth-century neoclassical Don Juan of Moreto, Molière, and Mozart's *Don Giovanni*; the nineteenth-century Don Juan of Byron, Zorrilla Espronceda (Don Félix de Montemar), Merimée (Don Juan de Maraña), and Pushkin (*The Stone Guest*). In the early twentieth century we find Valle Inclán's avant-garde *esperpéntico* Don Juan ("Juanito Ventolera" in *Las galas del difunto*), and Unamuno's and Shaw's existential Don Juans in *El hermano Juan* and *Man and Superman: Don Juan in Hell*.[6] Toward its end, and on the heels of a new millenium, there comes a postmodern cinematographic American Don Juan, the New York City–born self-destructive Don Juan de Marco. These offer only a small sampling.[7]

The film *Don Juan de Marco*, which appeared in 1996 starring Johnny Depp, Marlon Brando, and Faye Dunaway, has been classified as a romantic comedy, analogous to some extent to the *dramma giocoso* of Mozart's *Don Giovanni*, itself a fusion of opera sacra and opera buffa.[8] In brief, this is its story: A young man (Johnny Depp) from Queens, New York, has been reading several versions of the Don Juan legend and, like Don Quixote, decides that he is some sort of reincarnation of the legendary Don Juan. Disillusioned with his life as a whole, he decides to have one last conquest before commiting suicide. He enters a hotel lobby, where a young woman is awaiting her male dinner companion. Don Juan approaches her and begins the seduction process. As always, he succeeds in making love to her, just in time for her companion to arrive. He then goes to the top of a tall building with the intention of jumping to his death. The emergency vehicles arrive, along with a psychiatrist (Marlon Brando), who persuades him to come down and submit to therapy. Later on in the psychiatrist's office, the young man relates his life story.

Strangely, the first element of the film that attracts the literary analyst is its fusion of two Hispanic icons, Don Quixote de la Mancha and

Don Juan Tenorio. As we have seen, its protagonist has read numerous versions of the legend of Don Juan, and like Don Quixote, ends up identifying himself with their main character. The theme of books appears at the very beginning of the film, during the opening credits, where the camera focuses on a green volume with the title *El burlador de Sevilla: The Original Tale of Don Juan*. Later, beneath this book appears another, the *Don Juan* of Byron. Obviously, the dementia of Don Juan de Marco is similar to that of Don Quixote. In short, we are about to meet the "descendant" of those two seminal characters, a descendant whose self-indulgence becomes a lust for self-destruction. Another important element that links this film with *Don Quixote* is the pursuit of the action on two narrative planes in a perfect blending of reality and fantasy. Don Juan de Marco, as well as his psychiatrist, oscillates between two worlds. The psychiatrist fulfills the same function as the priest, the barber, and Sansón Carrasco in *Don Quixote*. They all enter the world of the "madman" with the intention of curing him, and ultimately they themselves are lured by the magic of his fictitious creation. But here the fundamental bond with *Don Quixote* stops. It is another literary world that will take over the plot.

In the process of his emotional healing, Don Juan de Marco relates the story of his life. Curiously, everything he recalls of his childhood, his youth, and his current state is taken directly from Lord Byron's mock epic, *Don Juan*. As in Byron's poem, the history of Don Juan de Marco begins with his childhood. Both works mention the love affairs of Don Juan's father and Don Juan's own seduction of an older woman, Doña Julia, when he was only sixteen (in the film and in Byron the name of the married woman and the young man's age are the same). Both works portray the youth's interlude of mystic contemplation after having fallen into temptation, and they both include a scene in which Don Alfonso, the husband of Doña Julia, enters his wife's bedroom and takes Don Juan by surprise. As always, Don Juan escapes. As in Byron's poem, Don Juan de Marco is exiled and finds himself in the harem of a sultan in the Middle East. There is also a coincidence in the occurrence of a shipwreck, although in Byron the shipwreck happens before the episode of the harem and in the film it happens afterward. Don Juan is the only survivor in both. Actually, the shipwreck and the idyll on a Mediterranean island have ties to both Tirso and Byron. In *El burlador*, after the shipwreck Don Juan ends up in the arms of Tisbea, the beautiful but "liberated" fishergirl. In Byron he ends in the arms of the beautiful Haydee. It is this Byronian Haydee who undoubtedly inspired the filmmakers in their re-creation of Doña Ana, originally the daughter of the Commander, and now the girl with whom Don Juan de Marco falls in love after seeing a magazine with her picture taken on the Isle of Eros.

His falling in love without ever having known her is a distinct echo of Alonso Quijano in Cervantes. His ability to experience love at all is an invention of Romanticism, above all of Zorrilla. The only notable difference in the plot is that Byron's Doña Julia, the young Juan's lover, goes into a convent, while in the film it is Doña Inés, Don Juan's mother, who becomes a nun. Significantly, Inés is the name of the heroine in Zorrilla's Tenorio. She too enters a convent and in the end acts as the agent for divine intervention, bringing about Don Juan's redemption through grace. It is no accident that the roles and names of the women here are merged. Inés is a symbol of both mother and bride, recalling thus the Virgin Mary and the Church, the Church as mother (la Santa Madre Iglesia) and the Church as bride (as in the Book of Revelation).

Another intriguing aspect of the film is the name assigned to the psychiatrist, Don Octavio de Flores. The role of Octavio varies in different versions of the Don Juan story. In Tirso's *Burlador* he is the Duke Octavio, betrothed to the Duchess Isabela, whom Don Juan tricks into his arms by disguising himself as her lover. In Mozart's *Don Giovanni* he is engaged to Doña Ana, whom Don Juan tries without success to seduce. It is her father, the Commander Don Gonzalo, whom Don Juan kills and who later returns as the stone statue. In Shaw's *Don Juan in Hell* Octavio is a weak man who is in love with Ann Whitefield, but she rejects him because she is attracted to John Tanner (Don Juan). Why is the psychiatrist called "Octavio"? Perhaps because in one sense he also is seduced by Don Juan; in fact, almost everyone in the story comes under the spell of Don Juan.

On yet another front, we have the recollection of Don Quixote's niece, who shares his home and worries about her uncle's flight from "reality." Don Juan de Marco also has an aunt who lives with him, is scandalized by his adventures, and tries to make him conform to a more standard mode of behavior. In fact, it is she who eventually supplies the psychiatrist with the "reality" of her nephew's life. But a problem remains. We cannot be sure if "reality" lies in what was perceived by her eyes, in what we ourselves observe in the life of this self-destructive Don Juan, or in what he himself relates to the psychiatrist. At the end, in an acutely Cervantine–Unamunian–Pirandellic fashion, what we were led to believe was fantasy (the union of Don Juan with Doña Ana on the Island of Eros) is merged with what we believed to be reality (the retirement of the psychiatrist with his wife on the same island). Can it be that the real Don Juan is the psychiatrist and not Don Juan de Marco?

The epilogue is from the mouth of "the world's greatest psychiatrist," just as the prologue was from the mouth of "the world's greatest lover."[9] This is a kind of redemption for Don Octavio, much as the prostitute Aldonza (who has little to do with Cervantes's Aldonza) is redeemed through Don Quixote in Dale Wasserman's *Man of La Mancha*. Just as Wasserman's Aldonza learns to give and accept true love because of her encounter with Don Quixote, the psychiatrist in the film manages to rekindle the passion in his conjugal relations with his wife because of his interactions with Don Juan de Marco. They are both "born again," so to speak.

Ironically, there is a noteworthy parallel between the time frame of Don Juan and that of his psychiatrist, Don Octavio. The seduction of the woman in the restaurant was to be Don Juan's last conquest before his suicide. So was his case to be Don Octavio's last before his retirement. Like Zorrilla's Don Juan Tenorio, who set himself a limit of five days plus one hour to consummate his seductions,

Uno para enamorarlas
otro para conseguirlas,
otro para abandonarlas,
dos para sustituirlas
y una hora para olvidarlas. (Part I, Act I, Scene XII)[10]

Don Juan de Marco also functions within a self-imposed limitation. Similarly, the psychiatrist has a predetermined number of days, namely ten, for his final conquest, the healing of this suicidal and schizophrenic young man.

In short, Octavio and Juan both confront a final challenge, and they both triumph, but, as always, through deceit. Don Juan's deceits are classic: He either falsely promises marriage or enters the woman's bedroom in the guise of another. In the film the psychiatrist agrees to certify the young man's sanity in spite of evidence to the contrary in order to save him from imprisonment in a mental institution. At the end we find them both on the Island of Eros fulfilling their love dreams. The ploy is to feign sanity in order to persuade the judge that he is cured and can return home. Its implication is that it is as simple to appear sane as it is to appear mad. But what in truth is sanity, and where does one draw the line of madness? *Don Juan de Marco*, like *Don Quixote*, leaves the question unresolved.

In many ways, *Don Juan de Marco* enters the realm of "magic realism" so dear to the Hispanic taste from Cervantes to García Márquez and Isabel Allende. In *Don Juan de Marco*, as in *Don Quixote* and *Cien años de soledad*, reality and fantasy penetrate each other. This curious amalgam exists on three levels. First of all, fantasy penetrates reality, as when Don Juan de Marco easily seduces the woman who waits for her date in a luxurious hotel restaurant at the beginning of the film. This is as improbable an event as the seduction of one engaged to be married, or of a nun. Equally unlikely is the magical influence he exerts upon the nurses of the psychiatric hospital in such a short span of time. Second, reality penetrates fantasy, as when the psychiatrist and his wife go to the Island of Eros and witness the union of Don Juan with his dreamed Doña Ana: Has fantasy become reality or reality become fantasy? Last, fantasy and reality are merged when the nun Doña Inés, the mother of Don Juan de Marco, comes to have a consultation with the psychiatrist. This is reminiscent of the scene where Augusto Pérez (the fictitious character of Unamuno's "nivola," *Niebla*) presents himself before his author-creator, Miguel de Unamuno, in his office in Salamanca. For all this, *Don Juan de Marco* is much more than a "romantic comedy." It is a complex novel in cinematographic form, in which Pío Baroja's "personaje abúlico" and Miguel de Unamuno's "personaje agónico" are fused. It is interesting to note that both Andrés Hurtado (*El árbol de la ciencia*) and Augusto Pérez (*Niebla*) commit suicide in the end.

One key element in the Don Juan theme in the American film is missing: the sacrilegious behavior of the character and his subsequent punishment in the flames of Hell. It has been said that what condemns the classical Don Juan is not his licentiousness with respect to the women he seduces (the theme of the *burlador*), but rather his lack of reverence and respect for that which is sacred (the theme of the *convidado de piedra*). Apart from the fact that Don Juan in the film never faces condemnation, there are other elements of the legend that do not appear in the film. One is the seduction of a peasant girl (Aminta in Tirso, Zerlina in Mozart, Charlotte and Mathurine in Molière). Another is the existence of a servant (Catalinón in Tirso, Leporello in Mozart and others, Sganarelle in Molière).[11] Perhaps the absence of these elements is due to the fact that the cinematographic material is principally of Byronian origin.[12]

There is a final point. In the film the polygamous love of Don Juan (though he is not married) is contrasted with the conjugal, monogamous love of the pychiatrist. Indeed, it is actually through the contagious lover's passion of Don Juan that the conjugal love of the retiring psychiatrist and his wife, which has been dormant for some time, is ignited again.

In conclusion, the theme of Don Juan has been interpreted in countless ways throughout the ages. There is a theological interpretation: Don Juan is an unrepentant sinner (as in Tirso) or a social hypocrite (as in Molière), whereby he receives his eternal punishment in Hell, or he is a repentant sinner redeemed by love and the intervention of divine grace (principally in Zorrilla).[13] There is a philosophical interpretation: Don Juan struggles to find his identity; he faces the ontological dilemma of who he is, faced also by Don Quixote ("Yo sé quién soy"), Segismundo ("Soy un hombre entre las fieras y una fiera entre los hombres"), and Hamlet ("To be or not to be"). There is a psychological interpretation: Don Juan is mentally ill, from which theory the disorder called "donjuanismo" derives its name.[14] There is a political–ideological interpretation: Don Juan is a type of theoretical revolutionary.[15] Finally, there is a sociological interpretation: Don Juan is no longer viewed as a sinner or social delinquent, but as a victim of his societal environment and his genetic makeup, a victim whose last recourse is suicide unless he can be rescued and restored to society through rehabilitation and psychotherapy. This seems to be the thrust of *Don Juan de Marco*, his most recent venture in film. In short, not only does Don Juan lend itself easily to a study of genre in the arts—poetry, drama, opera, the novel, film, and so on—he has also invaded the arena of cross-disciplinary and cross-cultural studies: theology, philosophy, psychology, sociology, and political science.

NOTES

1. This quality is highlighted by Molière, whose Don Juan tells his servant Sganarelle that he would never reject a woman, for they all have the privilege of enjoying his love. In this way Don Juan is not a scourge on women, but rather the fountain of their maximum pleasure and delight.

2. See Víctor Said Armesto, *La leyenda de Don Juan*, 2d ed. (Madrid: Espasa-Calpe, 1968); Miguel de Unamuno, "Sobre don Juan Tenorio," in *Mi religión y otros ensayos* (Madrid: Renacimiento, 1910); Eliezer Oyola, "Aspects of Theatrical Language in Tirso's *Burlador*," in *Tirso's Don Juan: The Metamorphosis of a Theme*, ed. Josep M. Sola-Solá and George E. Gingras (Washington, D.C.: Catholic University of America Press, 1988), 56–73. For a good review of Galician and Basque folk superstitions, see Walter Starkie, *The Road to Santiago* (Berkeley and Los Angeles: University of California Press, 1965).

3. For more popular references to Juan, see Cejador y Frauca's edition of *La Celestina* in *Clasicos Castellanos* (Madrid: Espasa-Calpe, 1945, 156, n. 14).

4. It is interesting to note that in José Zorrilla, *Don Juan Tenorio* (Buenos Aires: Espasa-Calpe, 1940), the turning point for Don Juan comes when he finally acknowleges the existence of God and is thus saved: "yo, ¡santo Dios!, creo en ti; si es mi maldad inaudita, tu piedad es infinita. . . . ¡Señor, ten piedad de mí!" (Part II, Act III, Scene II).

5. Quoted by María Emma Barbería in her critical edition of Zorrilla's *Don Juan Tenorio* (Buenos Aires: Editorial Kapelusz, 1974), 15.

6. Juanito Ventolera is one of the "*esperpentos*" in Valle Inclán's *Martes de Carnaval*. In that work Don Juan is a deceitful, playful type, a soldier of the war in Cuba. Note the deprecatory usage of the diminutive form of this name: Juanito. His last name is even worse, suggesting the vulgar act of passing gas.

In Shaw's *Man and Superman*, Don Juan (John Tanner, "Jack") is presented as a theoretical revolutionary who has written a seditious pamphlet. It is in the second act that the traditional Don Juan appears, supposedly Tirso's Don Juan, in a dream of Tanner and Mendoza. Mendoza is the leader of the insurgents operating in the mountains, but in the dream he takes the appearance of the Devil. Doña Ana has lived to a ripe old age and has now descended to Hell, while her father, the Commander, has gone to Heaven. A dialogue is established between Don Juan, Doña Ana, the Commander, and the Devil. By an ironic transposition of destinies, the Commander is transported into Hell and Don Juan to Heaven. Under the influence of Nietzche, the characters attempt to counter the Life Force as an inexorable fate that pursues them all, especially Don Juan and Doña Ana.

7. Other important authors who have treated the theme include the Spanish Zamora (*No hay deuda que no se pague y Convidado de piedra*), Azorín (*Don Juan*), Pérez de Ayala (*Tigre Juan*), and Marañón; the French Dumas père, Musset, and Beaudelaire; and the British Shadwell (*The Libertine*). There is even another Hollywood classic, *The Adventures of Don Juan*, starring Errol Flynn, following Merimée's character, Don Juan de Maraña. The action is filled with political intrigue during the reign of the House of Hapsburg. We must not forget Valle Inclán's earlier Modernist Marqués de Bradomín ("las hijas de las madres que amé tanto me besan hoy como se besa a un santo") in his *Sonatas*; recall Antonio Machado's lines, "Ni un Bradomín he sido ni un seductor Mañara," in his "Retrato." For a complete bibliography, see Armand E. Singer, *The Don Juan Theme, Versions and Criticism: A Bibliography* (Morgantown: West Virginia University Press, 1988); José Manuel Losada, *Bibliography of the Myth of Don Juan in Literary History* (New York: Edwin Mellen Press, 1997).

8. See George E. Gingras, "Some Observations on the Generic Status of the Don Juan Theme from Tirso de Molina to Mozart." *Tirso's Don Juan: The Metamorphosis of a Theme*, ed. Josep M. Sola-Solá and George E. Gingras (Washington, D.C.: Catholic University of America Press, 1988), 106–126.

9. This epilogue, whose narrator is the psychiatrist, is analogous to the final episode of Don Quixote, where Cide Hamete Benengeli, who purportedly wrote the story, gives his farewell. He warns against those who would desire to falsely continue his creation, and hangs his pen up on the wall forever. It also recalls the epilogue of Unamuno's *Niebla*, in which Orfeo, the dog of Augusto Pérez, utters a kind of moral observation about the destiny of his master, who has just died while eating.

10. José Zorrilla, *Don Juan Tenorio*, 6th ed. (Madrid: Espasa-Calpe, 1965), 35.

11. Byron fuses two characters of Tirso's play: Tisbea, the fishergirl, and Aminta, the peasant girl celebrating her wedding day.

12. Two dramas of Tirso present two opposing aspects of this preoccupation: Paulo is *el condenado por desconfiado* (condemned because of lack of trust in God), while Don Juan is *el condenado por demasiado confiado* (condemned because of too much confidence in himself); the famous line, "tan largo me lo fiáis," is a commentary on his cynical approach to divine judgment. Paulo puts little value on the saving grace of God; Don Juan takes too much for granted. Thus, they are both condemned.

13. For an excellent ontological discussion on these characters, see Miguel de Unamuno, *Vida de Don Quijote y Sancho*, and especially his *Sentimiento trágico de la vida*.

14. See Zelda Irene Brooks and William Heitland, "A Psychological Perspective of the Don Juan Character," in *Tirso's Don Juan: The Metamorphosis of a Theme*, ed. Josep M. Sola-Solá and George E. Gingras (Washington, D.C.: Catholic University of America Press, 1988), 172–177.

15. This alludes to the Jack Tanner of Shaw's *Man and Superman*.

17

Don Juan in the New World: The Erotics of Conquest in Chocano, Fuentes, and Walcott

Ben A. Heller

If there is one thing we as readers never seem to let happen, it is the reduction of Don Juan to a simple libertine who deceives and abuses women and then either receives his due punishment unrepentant, as in Tirso de Molina, or reforms at the last minute and is saved, as in Zorrilla's Romantic remake. These are only two important Don Juans in the Hispanic tradition. Yet there seems to be a Don Juan for every age, country, and creed: Don Juan the blasphemer, Don Juan the criminal, Don Juan the Romantic rebel, Don Juan the narcissist, Don Juan the liberator of women, even Don Juan the woman! We might say that Don Juan always casts meaning far beyond the confines of plot and action. This can be said for many literary characters in the Hispanic tradition, such as the Cid, Celestina, and Don Quixote especially, all of whom have been adapted by subsequent writers. Yet Don Juan seems to exceed these other literary characters in his ferocious intertextuality, his ability to leap from text to text, plot to plot, genre to genre, and culture to culture as easily as he moves from bed to bed.

This supratextual existence has led many critics to speak of the "legend" of Don Juan, thus emphasizing his quasi-historical origins and constant reelaboration in folk culture, while others have preferred to use the term "myth," insisting on his universal exemplarity and eternal presence.[1] Each of these terms has its usefulness, yet given the ease with which Don Juan becomes a motive for meaning in different texts and contexts, I prefer to speak of the "figure" of Don Juan. Like a figure of speech, especially metaphor and metonymy, Don Juan has the ability to stand for something else, and to stand for several things successively—in his case, sinfulness, life force, Eros, rebellion, and so on. While other canonical literary characters (Oedipus, Hamlet, Don Quixote) may also exemplify certain traits, they are more determined by their original formulations and thus are more resistant to refiguration.[2]

In what follows I would like to discuss how three authors, two Latin American and one Caribbean, have reckoned with the figure of Don Juan, what place they have imagined for him in their post-Colonial cultures, and how they have been possessed by him and have simultaneously possessed him in certain specific historical ways. I do not pretend to give a history of Don Juan's escapades in Latin American and Caribbean writing.[3] Instead, I focus on a small suite of twentieth-century texts where Don Juan is seen primarily through the lens of the conquest, making of him a figure synonymous with the *conquistador*, not just of women but of lands and cultures. In these texts Don Juan is a profoundly ambivalent version of Columbus or Cortés, both a violent, violating figure and a paternal, founding one. "Los hijos de Don Juan" are Latin American and Caribbean subjects, "criollos" and mestizos and "indios," left to decipher the physical and cultural signs of violence that lead back to their beginnings. As will become evident, each of the authors chosen for analysis is preoccupied with defining the nature of Latin American or Caribbean culture and asserting its difference from and problematic filiation to Old World culture. Don Juan is a crucial tool in this enterprise.

DON JUAN AS COLUMBUS, BOLÍVAR AS DON JUAN

The Peruvian poet José Santos Chocano treats the figure of Don Juan in an early poem titled *El fin de don Juan* (1893) and makes a passing yet revealing reference to Don Juan in the second part of his later *Tríptico bolivariano* (1923).[4] Both poems associate Don Juan with founding, conquering figures from Latin American history. While these poems no longer hold great interest aesthetically, they have the virtue of making clear the ideological underpinnings of certain more recent resuscitations of Don Juan in the Americas. *El fin de don Juan* imagines a Don Juan who has escaped the usual destinies and is living out his days in seeming sanctity in a monastery as Fray Juan (recall Unamuno's "El hermano Juan"). The poet accuses this Fray Juan of mistaking repentance for boredom and overdoing his asceticism and self-denial, departing from a true Christian, loving attitude. He admonishes him to leave the sterile monastery and to love again, this time for real. Chocano's interpretation of Christianity includes a pure, devoted love that does not contradict faith, an eternal, procreative love between men and women. So he urges Don Juan to approach the Virgin and ask her if it is wrong to have children. She, after all, is a mother.

For Chocano, Don Juan the violator of women was on the wrong track, yet the ascetic Don Juan misses the road as well. Neither of these two extremes conforms to the poet's concept of true love, which is creative and familial. While discussing Don Juan's newfound mystical vocation the poet compares him to Columbus, imagining the tomb as a portal to another world, death, which inspires the aged to reform. The poet does not condemn the mystic impulse at all, although he imagines that others will doubt its sincerity. He exhorts Don Juan to flee the cloister, defy the skeptics (as Columbus did), and love again in a way both holy and human. The result will be a new sense of home, a new rooting: "Cíñete tú las místicas aureolas: / como Colón, altivo y sin temores / rasga del odio las revueltas olas. / Quizás te dé otra América sus flores; / y halles otro árbol en que hacer tu nido; / y halles un nido en que cantar amores (Chocano, 192).[5] This vision of Don Juan as a reformed, monogamous pater familias certainly doesn't mesh well with the classic image of Don Juan. He would cease to be Don Juan as soon as he ceased his passionate self-absorption. And this version of Columbus as intrepid explorer, receiver of blessings from the Americas and founder of New World society, reflects the distance between Chocano's era and our own. This is not the conquistador we came to know during the debates of the quincentenary of the "discovery," a figure much closer to the traditional violator that is Tirso's Don Juan. Nevertheless, the association between Don Juan and the first of the conquistadors, Columbus, is clearly drawn, and the analogy underscores that the problem of Chocano's Don Juan is not the sullying of women's virtue but his inability to accept paternal responsibility. If Don Juan were more like Columbus he would risk all, leave the monastery, and embrace life again, this time founding a New (World) family.

Chocano also places the figure of Don Juan at Latin America's second foundational moment, the nineteenth-century wars of independence. This is explicit in the second part of his *Tríptico bolivariano*, dedicated to (of all things) the great liberator's shirt! The poet meditates on the dual nature of the hero as both conquistador (of armies, men, and lands) and as "conquistado" (at the hands of women): "Imponerse a los hombres con orgullo de artistas / bello es; pero a las damas rendirse ¿no es mejor?" (Chocano, 813).[6] The shirt itself doubles as Christ's shroud, symbol of self-sacrifice, and as the embroidered shirt of that very different figure, Don Juan. Chocano makes of Bolívar a bundle of contradictions: a conqueror who lets himself be conquered, a Don Juan who surrenders to women rather than deceiving them, the very spirit of self-sacrifice who loves carnally and loves to excess. The poet reinforces the connection between male sexuality and political and military prowess. Political power and virility seem to demand each other, and creation of a new body politic or organization of peoples is almost invariably imagined as the creation of a lineage. The founding father of the Spanish-American republics is a *man*, political father and potential biological father of multitudes.

Chocano was an ardent defender of Latin American independence in both his politics and his literary work, and he consistently stressed the importance of both indigenous and Spanish cultural elements in the makeup of Spanish-American cultures. It should not surprise us then that his Don Juan should enfold elements of the conquistador, nor that his Bolívar should contain elements from Don Juan. Of more importance, however, is his embryonic questioning of the riddles of Spanish-American racial and cultural paternity, a questioning taken up much more systematically by authors such as Reyes, Mariátegui, Henríquez Ureña, Paz, and Lezama Lima. These central figures in the discourse of Latin American identity set the stage for the later interventions of Fuentes and Walcott.

TERRA NOSTRA, OR REDEMPTION
THROUGH ART AND EROTICISM

Carlos Fuentes's *Terra Nostra* is a "novel of cultural knowledge" that clearly belongs to the tradition of texts concerned with the nature of Latin American cultural identity, as González Echevarría noted in "*Terra Nostra*: Theory and Practice."[7] Fuentes approaches the issue of cultural identity by revising Spanish and Spanish-American history through a complex intertextual lens comprised of many works, among them three classics of Spanish literature: *La Celestina, Don Quijote,* and *El burlador de Sevilla*.[8] Like his creation Ludovico, the blind student of theology who regains his sight in order to read these three works, Fuentes would claim to see the destiny of Hispanic history anew through the eyes of Celestina, Don Quixote, and Don Juan. He gives these three canonical figures, especially Celestina and Don Juan, new life, weaving them in and out of key events of sixteenth- and seventeenth-century Spain and Latin America. Through this creative refiguring he establishes a certain enigmatic, textual coherence for Hispanic history.

One of Fuentes's major discoveries is the way the figure of Don Juan is inextricably bound to the Spanish royal family, to its odd, incestuous sexual history, and to its administration of the colonies of the New World. Fuentes's Don Juan, like most of the characters in *Terra Nostra*, is fragmented and multivalent, doubled and redoubled by other characters sharing certain traits. Don Juan is one of three identical brothers who are also half-brothers to Felipe, El Señor, a monarch combining traits from a number of Spanish kings. Each of the three brothers dreams the others, while also giving expression to repressed elements in Felipe.[9] Don Juan inflames the desires of the barren queen, La Señora, and is her lover for a time. Leaving her, he goes on to seduce every available female in the palace, including several serving girls, the Mother Superior, a nun, and the initiate Inés, whose father (Don Gonzalo de Ulloa) Don Juan ultimately kills. Don Juan is imprisoned with Inés in the Room of Mirrors, where they make love continuously among multiple reflections. When finally released from their prison of pleasure during the unsuccessful rebellion of the Comuneros (in 1521), Don Juan and Inés embark for the Indies with the theology student Ludovico and the painter-priest Julián to escape the tyranny of El Señor and to mitigate, if possible, the harshness of the king's emissary to the New World, Hernando de Guzmán. As Ludovico later tells the aged king. "Huyeron conmigo. Nos embarcamos disfrazados en las carabelas de Guzmán. Templaríamos, sí, junto con el fraile pintor, los excesos de tu valido; contra tu espada, nuestro arte, nuestra filosofía, nuestro erotismo, nuestra poesía. No fue posible (Fuentes, 745).[10] It turns out that Inés becomes a nun who has a talent for writing verses in the Baroque style, and whose "Piramidal, funesta, de la tierra, / nacida sombra, al Cielo encaminaba" reaches the unappreciative hands of the king. (With a textual sleight of hand, Fuentes has Don Juan's Inés become Sor Juana Inés de la Cruz.) Don Juan, meanwhile, abandons her and takes to impregnating New World women: "Encontró su destino. Abandonó a Inés. Preñó a indias. Preñó a criollas. Ha dejado descendencia en la Nueva España" (745).[11] In short, he returns to his old lascivious ways until he returns to Spain and meets death in Don Gonzalo's stony embrace.

The battle for the New World is ultimately won by the king's representative, Hernando de Guzmán. The painter-priest's art and good works and Inés's poetry are no match for the predations of power. Inés is made to give up her library and her mathematical and musical instruments and dedicate herself to affairs of the soul. Yet the flowering of the Baroque is seen here as a vital force, although its lasting contribution is ultimately in doubt. For Fuentes, the importance of the Baroque to Latin American culture (and to this very Baroque novel itself) cannot be underestimated as both a far-reaching artistic movement and a cultural antidote to the rigors of colonial authoritarianism.[12] Ludovico's description of Julian's art encapsulates Fuentes's concept of the Baroque and points to its sources:

Llámase barroco, y es una floración inmediata: tan plena, que su juventud es su madurez, y su magnificencia, su cáncer. Un arte, Felipe, que como la naturaleza misma, aborrece el vacío: llena cuantos la realidad le ofrece. Su prolongación es su negación. Nacimiento y muerte son para este arte un acto único: su apariencia es su fijeza. (Fuentes, 743–744)[13]

Ludovico's mention of the *horror vacui* ("aborrece el vacío") and of the *"fijeza"* ("su apariencia es su fijeza") are symptoms of Fuentes's indebtedness to Lezama Lima's concept of the Baroque.[14] In "La curiosidad barroca," the second essay of his contribution to the discourse on Latin American identity, *La expresión americana* (1957), Lezama suggests that the New World Baroque differs from the Spanish Baroque in its syncretic incorporation of indigenous and African cultural elements by artisans who themselves carried diverse mixtures of blood in their veins. Thus, Fuentes's mention of Don Juan's taste in New World women ("Preñó a indias. Preñó a criollas") is not just a reflection of the wide range of his desire. For Fuentes, Don Juan himself is a representative of that Spanish *eros* responsible for the fruitful mixtures of the New World. Like the artist, Julián, Juan also leaves a legacy, although it is of a different nature, in the form of human descendants of his sexual dalliances. As the "Barroco de Indias" fuses the European, the African, and the American indigenous cultures into a fertile new art, Don Juan's rampant eroticism carries out a parallel process, creating offspring who reflect all the possible admixtures of races and of cultures. Both aesthetic and racial *mestizaje* are positive consequences of the Conquista for Fuentes, which work against the rigid rule of Guzmán and all the subsequent Guzmanes. In Fuentes's Latin America the centrifugal forces of Baroque art and Don Juanian eros are essential counterbalances to the centripetal, homogenizing power of dictatorship.[15]

Paradoxically, it is Guzmán, the prototypical conquistador, who most closely approximates the original, reprobate, unredeemed Don Juan. The doubling of Guzmán as Don Juan is most explicit in Guzmán's delirious dreams of conquest:

Empiezo a arder en deseos de cruzar el gran mar, plantar mi espada en la ardiente ribera del nuevo mundo . . . conquistar los favores de la dama más inalcanzable y fría, noble y desdeñosa, bañarla de perlas, de oro, de esmeraldas, hacerla mía, mis hazañas, la Señora, el mundo nuevo, conquistada la tierra, conquistada la mujer. (Fuentes, 509–510)[16]

In this conflation of the erotic and the political, in this feminization of the land and territorialization of the feminine, Guzmán reveals himself to be the dark double of Don Juan. He also shows himself to be the anachronistic textual precursor of the *caciques* and tyrants who would torment Latin American nations of the nineteenth and twentieth centuries, and who in turn would become models for central characters in novels such as *Pedro Páramo, El señor presidente, Yo, el supremo*, and *El otoño del patriarca*.

Two series of questions may serve as provisional conclusions to the discussion of Fuentes's Don Juan. First, is it possible for culture (Julián's Baroque art, for example) to mitigate the excesses of political authority? Even if Ludovico does admit that Julián, Celestina, and Don Juan were unable to defeat Guzmán's authoritarianism, we know that Fuentes himself does not give up on the redemptive value of culture.[17] Is this not an exaggeration of the power of the artist? If culture can play a guiding role in civil society, and if the "Barroco de Indias" has an inherently democratic impulse, how will that guidance be exercised, and how does that democratic impulse manifest itself? Second, is it possible to separate Don Juan's supposedly liberating eroticism from the conquering eros of his authoritarian double, Guzmán? Isn't conquest indissolubly bound to this kind of eroticism? If such a separation were possible, what connection is there anyway between physical love—even if conceived as personally liberating—and the achievement of democratic practice in the larger society?

WALCOTT'S *JOKER* AND "THE MUSE OF HISTORY"

Like Fuentes's *Terra Nostra*, Derek Walcott's *The Joker of Seville* also contains a Don Juan who makes his way to the New World and along the way gives occasion to raise the issue of American cultural originality. Yet unlike Fuentes's novel, which enacts a Baroque poetics while self-reflectively questioning the place of that poetics in the social order, Walcott's *The Joker of Seville* exemplifies the author's notion of a Caribbean sensibility without the metatextual framing. That theoretical frame is given, however, in Walcott's journalism and essays, especially in "The Muse of History," which was published in 1974, the very year *The Joker of Seville* was first produced.

With this play, and the productions of the Trinidad Theatre Workshop more generally, many have credited Walcott with creating a true, original theatre in the Anglophone Caribbean.[18] Indeed, such was his explicit intention upon founding the company in 1959. Walcott argued persuasively for a national theatre in Trinidad and a West Indian theatre rooted in local experience in a series of newspaper articles published in Trinidad in the 1960s (Thieme, 62–63). It may seem paradoxical that this should be achieved through the adaptation of a Spanish masterpiece from the seventeenth century, yet I would suggest that this is squarely within Walcott's own ideas on the assimilative nature of the mature artist and entirely consonant with the figure of Don Juan. In adapting Tirso's play, Walcott found a Shakespearean tone that matched the Baroque spirit of the original. Simultaneously, he incorporated the linguistic turns of Caribbean speakers of English, as well as Caribbean cultural and historical elements such as stick dancing and trafficking in slaves. He also took advantage of the structure of the North American musical comedy to enliven the sometimes weighty speeches of the characters. In all, he created a hybrid, Caribbean product that still closely approximates the original. We can even say that Walcott revives Tirso's *burlador* by putting him in contact with the Caribbean landscape, peoples, and culture.[19]

"The Muse of History" is Walcott's central statement on the New World poet's necessary relation to history and tradition, and it provides the theoretical framework in which an adaptation of a European classic can serve as a vehicle for local expression. It condemns those New World poets who would break with the European past, because contesting the past merely perpetuates it. Walcott sees more strength in the position of the classicists who venerate the old, since he understands artistic maturity to be "the assimilation of the features of every ancestor" (Walcott 1995, 370). Nevertheless, these classicists fall into the trap of an "oceanic nostalgia for the older culture and a melancholy at the new" (373). For Walcott, a third position is the most productive, that of the "great poets of the New World, from Whitman to Neruda" (371), whose vision of man is Adamic and elemental, going beyond the confines of ethnic ancestry and historical traumas in a creative apprehension of the present. These poets do not forget the past; neither do they feel a filial dependence on it. Walcott states eloquently,

I say to the ancestor who sold me, and to the ancestor who bought me, I have no father, I want no such father, although I can understand you, black ghost, white ghost, when you both whisper "history," for if I attempt to forgive you both I am falling into your idea of history which justifies and explains and expiates, and it is not mine to forgive, my memory cannot summon any filial love. (373–374)

Walcott sees his Don Juan as a New World poet. When Don Juan first speaks to Tisbea on the shores of New Tarragon, he claims to be both a prince and a poet, and it is his Homeric language and metaphorical pyrotechnics that most seduce the impressionable young fishergirl. More important, when Tisbea makes the mistake of mentioning matrimony, Don Juan makes it clear that he will be neither father, husband, or son: "God, you beasts must love your cages! / Marry a man, Tisbea; I am a / force, a principle, the rest / are husbands, fathers, sons; I'm none / of these" (Walcott 1978, 48). He asserts his independence from all social constraint, and most important, from genealogy and all its power relations. In a sense he is declaring his independence from history itself, or at least from the biological ties that act as its counterpart.

Like Fuentes's Don Juan, Walcott's "joker" reveals himself to be a curious refiguration of the conquistador. Where Tirso has Don Juan flee from Naples to Tarragona after seducing his first victim, Isabella, Walcott's verse adaption has Don Juan flee with his servant Catalinion to Lisbon, and then on to the New World. They shipwreck upon the shores of New Tarragon, where Don Juan seduces Tisbea, a young fishergirl "of mixed race" with a penchant for literature, especially Homer. She is equally impressed by Don Juan's good looks and his command of the classics. Although she fancies herself a virtuous maid, she soon accedes to his advances. Once the deed is done, Tisbea assumes Don Juan will marry her. When he harshly condemns the institution of marriage, Tisbea runs off, threatening to drown herself, while Don Juan vows to make his way back to Spain as soon as possible.

The bare outline of the action gives little indication of the discursive richness of the episode. The scene begins with a high degree of intertextual gaming with the *Odyssey*, specifically the Nausicaa scene. It then quickly moves on to engage the religious discourse of the conquistadors and the anticarnal rhetoric of American revivalism. But it is Don Juan's mocking insistence on viewing the New World as Edenic paradise and Tisbea simultaneously as Eve and as a "native" to be Christianized that makes of him a conquistador with a difference. In a particularly bawdy scene, Don Juan enjoins Tisbea to grasp his phallus (hidden under a basket), comparing it to that "first metaphor of Eden," the serpent that must be cast out. The language here is revealing: Don Juan's legacy is dual; while he would bring the word of God to the New World, he also introduces the agent of sin, the phallus-serpent which takes pleasure in its own casting out. The dialogue makes it clear that Walcott's Don Juan stands as a parodic challenge to a naïve, heroic vision of the Conquest.

Walcott's Don Juan is called a joker because he deceives women by pretending to be the lover they await. As D. L. Macdonald states in his perceptive article, "Derek Walcott's Don Juans," "Walcott's Don Juan is precisely a joker, not a trickster: a wild card that can imitate any of the other cards but has no identity of his own" (105).[20] Walcott's accentuation of this play of identity links his Don Juan to Odysseus, the original "Nobody," as he calls himself in the scene with Polyphemos. Despite this link, Walcott's conflation of Don Juan and Odysseus can seem paradoxical, since Odysseus is the paragon of perseverance, who gives all to return home and reconstruct his marriage, whereas Don Juan wants nothing to do with hearth and home. In fact, he seems hell-bent on destroying any union that might lead to a happy family. Yet the paradox is only apparent, since Walcott makes it clear that Don Juan is in large measure responsible for bringing together Donna Ana and the Marquis, Isabella and Octavio. As the king says at the play's conclusion, "As our souls / blaze in a resurrecting dawn, / we bless these lovers and him, whose / wedding day was his funeral, / who helped us consecrate this aisle / in indivisible marriages. / Donna Ana to her Marquis; / Octavio to Isabel" (149). In this scenario, Don Juan's escapades are not just a stumbling block on the road to social stability. Rather, they are a necessary moment in the creation of the family unit. Only with the death of Don Juan and the exclusion of the unrestrained unscrupulous desire which he embodied can the traditional monogamous couple be consecrated. His death signifies the exile of a ferocious eroticism that lives only for the moment and the inauguration of history and its genealogies.

CONCLUSION

The texts considered here lead us to conclude that Don Juan takes on a special dimension when he arrives in the New World. No longer a blasphemer or a simple, sexual bon vivant living in an eternal present, in the New World he recapitulates the history of conquest. He resonates and melds with the still-unexorcised figure of the conquistador. For Fuentes, Don Juan is the erotic energy that comes to the New World alongside the Baroque, creating the rich mix of peoples that gives Latin America its multiracial and multicultural identity. He also acts as a mitigating factor against the repressive conqueror, with whom he nevertheless shares a secret link. Walcott also sees Don Juan in a stark, post-Colonial light. Both libertine and conquistador, he defiles the pristine shores and fishergirls of the New World, simultaneously introducing and condemning desire, driving the object of his affections to suicide. Yet Don Juan is also the New World poet who lives in the present, aware of history yet free of its domination. As such, he allows Walcott to create what many see as an original hybrid art that epitomizes Caribbean expression. Don Juan is a crucial tool for these two authors as they investigate the difference of Latin American and Caribbean cultures and their problematic filiation to the past. He is a vehicle through which they can apprehend the double edge of conquest, which destroys the past, violates the present, and inaugurates the future. Don Juan gives these writers a way of dealing with history, of reviving it and making it useful to the present. Do these two versions of Don Juan recount his last adventures in the New World? Unlikely. The question of Latin American and Caribbean identity remains open, and will continue to provoke new accomodations with the past and with the cultural heroes that inhabit it. So the figure of Don Juan, conquistador ultimately conquered, founds, and will continue to confound us.

NOTES

1. For a comprehensive discussion of the various critical terms (legend, myth, etc.) used to deal with the theme of Don Juan, see the first chapter (pp. 13–48) of Mandrell's (1992) fine study, *Don Juan and the Point of Honor*.

2. These other characters are inherently so complex that successive treatments of them merely develop what is already there, latent within them. Don Juan, on the other hand, is so easily reduced to one or two dimensions (libidinality, defiance) that he invites refiguration. He is so lacking in interiority (at least in Tirso's original) that he seduces authors into fleshing him out, into recasting him again and again, adding in what is lacking. For more on the original Don Juan's lack of psychological complexity, see Raymond Conlon's "D. L. Macdonald's 'Derek Walcott's Don Juans': Walcott's Debt to Tirso de Molina." Conlon suggests that Tirso leaves his protagonist hollow in order to focus attention on "the actions themselves, their moral implications, and their infernal consequences" (124).

3. For a listing of other Latin American Don Juans, see Armand E. Singer's comprehensive *The Don Juan Theme: An Annotated Bibliography*.

4. Despite Chocano's fame (and notoriety) during the early part of the century, there is a dearth of recent literary criticism on his work. Although acclaimed by many as "el poeta de América" and frequently compared to Darío in the first quarter of the century, his poetry was also judged grandiloquent and declamatory. This latter judgment has prevailed since his death in Santiago de Chile in 1934. Luis Alberto Sánchez's *Aladino o vida y obra de José Santos Chocano* is still the best critical work on this poet.

5. "Bind to yourself the mystic halos: / like Columbus, proud and fearless / slash through the roiling waves of hate. / Perhaps another America will give you her flowers; / and you will find another tree in which to make your nest; / and you will find a nest in which to sing your loves." This and all subsequent translations of Chocano are my own.

6. "Mastering men with the pride of an artist / is beautiful; but isn't surrendering to women even better?"

7. González Echevarría (1982) examines Fuentes's debt to several Hispanic writers concerned with cultural identity and history, particularly Paz, but also Ortega y Gasset and Américo Castro. For a different, friendlier reading of Fuentes's investigation of identity, see Williams, 80–91.

8. Fuentes himself reveals most of his "sources" in the bibliography of his essay, "Cervantes o la crítica de la lectura," which serves also as the novel's bibliography. As Fuentes (1975) states in the bibliography's prefatory note, both the essay and the novel "nacen de impulsos paralelos y obedecen a preocupaciones comunes" [are born of parallel impulses and respond to common concerns].

9. For more on character doubling in *Terra Nostra*, see Swietlicki, "Doubling, Reincarnation, and Cosmic Order in *Terra Nostra*," especially pp. 95–96.

10. "They fled with me. Disguised, we embarked in the caravels of Guzmán. Yes, along with the painter-priest, we would temper the excesses of your favorite: against his sword, our art, our philosophy, our eroticism, our poetry. It

was not possible" (Fuentes 1976, 740). This and all other translations of Terra Nostra are from Margaret Sayers Peden's fine English version.

11. "He met his destiny. He abandoned Inés. He impregnated Indian women. He impregnated those of Spanish blood. He left his descendants throughout New Spain" (Fuentes 1976, 740).

12. For a cogent analysis of Fuentes's views on the redemptive value of culture, see van Delden, 140–147.

13. "It is called Baroque, and it is an instantaneous flowering: its bloom so full that its youth is its maturity, and its magnificence its cancer. An art, Felipe, which, like nature itself, abhors a vacuum: it fills all voids offered by reality. Its prolongation is its negation. Birth and death are the only acts of this art: as it appears, it is fixed" (Fuentes 1976, 739).

14. Fuentes (1992, 205–224) treats the "Barroco de Indias" along similar lines in his history of Hispanic cultures, *El espejo enterrado*, where he makes explicit the syncretism of the New World Baroque. He does not mention, however, his filiation to Lezama on this point, although he later treated Lezama and his theory of the Baroque in a lengthy essay, "José Lezama Lima: cuerpo y palabra del barroco," in *Valiente mundo nuevo* (Fuentes 1990, 213–260).

15. As Faris has shown in her insightful article, "Without Sin, and with Pleasure," Fuentes's idea of the erotic as democratic and antiauthoritarian is similar to that of Bataille and Barthes, and may derive from his reading of these authors in the 1960s and 1970s.

16. "I begin to burn with desire to cross the great sea, to drive my sword into the blazing shore of the new world . . . captivate the favors of the coldest, most remote, most noble and disdainful lady, and bathe her in pearls, gold, emeralds, to make her mine, heroic feats, La Señora, the new world, the land conquered, the woman conquered" (Fuentes 1976, 502).

17. Fuentes (1992, 11) makes similar claims for the saving powers of culture in the introduction to *El espejo enterrado*.

18. For more on the Trinidad Theatre Workshop, see Bruce King's *Derek Walcott and West Indian Drama*.

19. This mode of creation coincides with what Lezama Lima called an American "receptivity." According to Lezama, the American landscape, written over with the knowing gaze of the pre-Columbian natives, accepted the generative impulse of a decaying Europe, reviving it and in the process creating a new American expression. Who better then to represent the paternal European legacy than the peripatetic decadent Don Juan?

20. Macdonald's (1994–1995) article gave rise to an interesting scholarly dialogue. See Macdonald's (1996–1997) "Derek Walcott's Don Juans: A Postilla"; James Mandrell's (1996–1997) "Response to D. L. Macdonald's 'Postilla'"; and Raymond Conlon's (1996–1997) response to the original Macdonald article, "D. L. Macdonald's 'Derek Walcott's Don Juans': Walcott's Debt to Tirso de Molina."

BIBLIOGRAPHY

Chocano, José Santos. *Obras completas*. Edited by Luis Alberto Sánchez. Madrid: Aguilar, 1954.

Conlon, Raymond. "D. L. Macdonald's 'Derek Walcott's Don Juans': Walcott's Debt to Tirso de Molina." *Connotations* 6 (1996–1997): 121–128.

Faris, Wendy. "'Without Sin, and with Pleasure': The Erotic Dimensions of Fuentes' Fiction." *Novel* 20 (1986): 62–77.

Fuentes, Carlos. *Cervantes o la crítica de la lectura.* Mexico, D.F.: Joaquín Mortiz, 1976.

———. *El espejo enterrado.* Mexico, D.F.: Fondo de Cultura Económica, 1992.

———. *Terra Nostra.* Barcelona: Seix Barral, 1975.

———. *Terra Nostra.* Translated by Margaret Sayers Peden. New York: Farrar, Straus, and Giroux, 1976.

———. *Valiente mundo nuevo: épica, utopía y mito en la novela hispanoamericana.* Mexico, D.F.: Fondo de Cultura Económica, 1990.

González Echevarría, Roberto. "*Terra Nostra*: Theory and Practice." In *Carlos Fuentes,* eds. Robert Brody and Charles Rossman. Austin: University of Texas Press, 1982.

King, Bruce. *Derek Walcott and West Indian Drama: "Not Only a Playwright but a Company," the Trinidad Theatre Workshop 1959–1993.* Oxford: Clarendon Press, 1995.

Lezama Lima, José. *Obras completas.* 2 vols. Mexico, D.F.: Aguilar, 1975–1977.

Macdonald, D. L. "Derek Walcott's Don Juans." *Connotations* 4 (1994–1995): 98–118.

———. "Derek Walcott's Don Juans: A Postilla." *Connotations* 6 (1996–1997): 103–110.

Mandrell, James. *Don Juan and the Point of Honor: Seduction, Patriarchal Society, and Literary Tradition.* University Park: Pennsylvania State University Press, 1992.

———. "Response to D. L. Macdonald's 'Postilla.'" *Connotations* 6 (1996–1997): 111–122.

Sánchez, Luis Alberto. *Aladino o vida y obra de José Santos Chocano.* Mexico, D.F.: Libro Mex, 1960.

Singer, Armand E. *The Don Juan Theme: An Annotated Bibliography of Versions, Analogues, Uses and Adaptations.* Morgantown: West Virginia University Press, 1993.

Swietlicki, Catherine. "Doubling, Reincarnation, and Cosmic Order in *Terra Nostra.*" *Hispanófila* 27 (1983): 93–104.

Thieme, John. "A Caribbean Don Juan: Derek Walcott's *Joker of Seville.*" *World Literature Written in English* 23 (1984): 62–75.

van Delden, Maarten. *Carlos Fuentes, Mexico, and Modernity.* Nashville: Vanderbilt University Press, 1998.

Walcott, Derek. *"The Joker of Seville" and "O Babylon!": Two Plays.* New York: Farrar, Straus, and Giroux, 1978.

———. "The Muse of History." In *The Post-Colonial Studies Reader,* eds. Bill Ashcroft, Gareth Griffiths, and Helen Tiffin. London: Routledge, 1995.

Williams, Raymond Leslie. *The Writings of Carlos Fuentes.* Austin: University of Texas Press, 1996.

PART IV

POINT OF CONTACT:
NEW SPAIN

18

A Diverse Legacy: The Hispanic Impact on Mask Use in Mexico

Donald E. Fritz

As soon as one steps through the weathered wooden gate into the walled compound of the Mission San Jose only a few blocks from the busy modern center of San Antonio, Texas, the present disappears and the past returns. A few hundred yards ahead rises the tower of the mission church, which could be moved as is into Spain and fit as harmoniously as if built there. Some of the mission structures are reconstructions, but the whole is much as it appeared 270 years ago when it functioned as one of Spain's farthest outposts on this continent, providing the priests who served it with a base for their efforts to bring Christianity to the indigenous earlier inhabitants of the area.

Significantly, the stone walls are not the only vestige of the early Spanish colonial efforts at this site. This night, as has happened regularly for the past fifty years, members of the mission's parish are to perform *Los Pastores*, an essentially unchanged version of the same religious play initiated by the priests who first ran the mission hundreds of years earlier. In this performance, as before, some of the players will portray innocent shepherds on their way to see the glory of the newly born Christ child, while others will portray Lucifer and various of his devils who try to subvert them from that goal. Now, as before, the simple drama presents the audience with the most basic choice mankind confronts: good or evil. And as before, the shepherds happily choose the good.

The presence of what is essentially a fourteenth-century morality play in the center of a twentieth-century metropolis may seem improbably anachronistic and, to some degree, undoubtedly it is. Yet equally, it is powerful evidence of the lasting vigor of Spanish influence in what was once the New World. The priests and adventurers who poured into North and South America from the sixteenth century on were as clever as they were courageous. Some came with plans to return to Spain once having won gold, glory, or grace from the hostile frontiers, but others came to stay, to plant their world, their ways, and the Christian word firmly into the new lands. And, of course, many did stay, as did their legacies.

Still, as the buffeting of weather altered even the durable stone of the early colonial buildings, time also altered the less solid—but, to the priests, more important—legacy, the teachings of the church. The Spanish spoken by the current players is decidedly a modern vernacular, undoubtedly quite altered from that first used. Similarly, the costumes are now modern: The shepherds would be essentially indistinguishable from other parishioners if all were in a local grocery store; Lucifer, though, does wear the rather more elaborate Western apparel one sees at rodeos and Western dances, but appropriately, of course, all in black, including the obligatory black Stetson hat.

Of equal significance from the point of view of one interested in the continuity as well as in the changes that have occurred in the Hispanic legacy, although the devils, as is traditional, are wearing masks, the masks now are more like those one sees at Halloween parties, rubberized movie devils of a grotesque but somehow banal appearance. These masks, while adequately effective in the performance, lack both the art and substance one finds in masks used in versions of the same drama still performed in parts of Mexico, masks less modern, more linked to older traditions of design and imagery. Masks can, in fact, serve admirably to illustrate both the strength of the influence of Spain in the New World and, as well, the limitations of that influence.

As anyone who is even slightly familiar with Spain's conquest and colonization of the Americas knows, the small bands of Spanish adventurers encountered not only primitive tribal peoples but highly advanced cultures whose sophistication and achievements rivaled those of the invading Europeans themselves. Certainly in Mexico, the existing indigenous cultures, especially that of the dominant Aztec people, had firmly entrenched traditions and beliefs that might be abhorred by the Spanish who wished to establish Christianity in the New World, but which unquestionably could not be ignored by them. Despite the Spaniards' amazingly swift and thorough military subjugation of the native Mexicans and the subsequent ravaging of indigenous populations by disease, the Spaniards remained a small minority in the midst of a numerous and potentially dangerous majority. Consequently, the history of the spread of Spanish influence in Mexico can be considered as much an acculturation by accommodation as one by elimination: the priests and others would often of necessity alter existing cultural practices rather than wholly replace them, cleverly substituting new Christian beliefs in place of the previous religious beliefs while leaving much of the actual activities unchanged. Thus, many churches were built on top of the ruins of temples considered holy by the locals; similarly, many dances were initiated using the times and locations previously established by local custom. The idea was to alter the spiritual significance of activities and thus move souls away from pagan damnation to Christian salvation. Generally, at least apparently, that goal was achieved (Martinez-Hunter, 71–72). But "generally" is not the same as "entirely," nor "apparently" the same as "certainly."

Mexico is a huge and staggeringly diverse land and the indigenous people whom the Spaniards encountered were numerous, varied, and widely dispersed throughout that vastness. The extent to which the Hispanic/Christian culture replaced the existing local cultures was never uniform, nor is it so now. Much of Mexico is today as wholly Christian as Spain itself, but some areas are essentially unchanged as to the pre-conquest practices and beliefs of their people. Then, again, there are areas where the Christian and pre-conquest religions are intricately fused with varying degrees of dominance or subordination of one of the two. What one finds varies as to where one is, and when.

Three factors that significantly influenced the success and duration of the transmission of the Spanish culture into Mexico were, of course, the nature of a cultural activity itself, its location, and the duration of the Spanish attempts to replace or alter it. As a rule, any nonreligious and nonthreatening activity was ignored, or often even adopted by the Spaniards, with foods being one major example. Obviously, the location of an activity was significant. If the activity, even though offensive to the Spaniards, was rarely—or even never—seen by them, it could continue essentially unchanged for years or even centuries. The duration of the Spaniards' attempt to replace an activity similarly played a role, in that the more time the new culture had to work on the old culture, the more completely any changes were likely to be achieved. Predictably, therefore, the closer a cultural activity was to a population center dominantly Hispanic, especially the more clearly religious it was seen to be, the more Hispanicized it became and, conversely, the more remotely distant an activity was from the Spaniards, even if essentially religious, the more Indian it remained.

As noted, the masks of Mexico nicely illustrate these varying degrees of cultural transmission, dominance, fusion, and continuation (see Figures 18.1 and 18.2). Some masks are unmistakably European in

Figure 18.1
Mask of a Paraguero or Catrin
character. State of Tlaxcala. Photo by
Donald E. Fritz.

Figure 18.2
One of the "Moros y cristianos," a
character from the Dance of the
Conquest. State of Mexico. Photo by
Donald E. Fritz.

appearance; some show no European influence at all; some straddle or fuse the two cultures. Typically, the degree of Hispanic, Indian, or fusion imagery in a mask can be traced, in part at least, to the factors just listed, especially the proximity and duration of the contacts between the mask users and the Spanish culture.

As one would expect, the areas closest to Mexico City, which was built on the site of the Aztec capital city, Tenochtitlan, conquered initially by Cortes in 1521 and the center of Spanish occupation ever since, have numerous dances and masks that are clearly Spanish in origin and imagery. The peoples of the states of central Mexico—Tlaxcala, Puebla, Morelia, Michoacan, Vera Cruz, Guanajuato, and Guerrero— produce masks that rival in their realistic depictions of European features the masks still used in folk rituals in Europe itself. More Indian-influenced masks are also produced in these states, but usually in the smaller villages tucked away in mountains or other areas relatively inaccessible (and/or undesirable) to the Spaniards. European masks are found far away from Mexico City as well, but almost invariably in areas long settled and controlled by the original Spaniards or those who later spread its culture (see Figures 18.3 and 18.4).

Figure 18.3
This devil mask, possibly from the
Danza de los Siete Vicios (Dance of
the Seven Vices), shows the mixture
of the Hispanic horned devil with
the Indian animal/nagual imagery.
State of Guerrero. Photo by Donald
E. Fritz.

Figure 18.4
Another mask from the Dance of the
Seven Vices, with only animal/
nagual imagery. State of Guerrero.
Photo by Donald E. Fritz.

The opposite is also as expected: Those areas most distant from the center, such as the northern and western states of Nayarit, Sinaloa, Sonora, Chihuahua, and parts of Jalisco, retain traditions and masks that are at best a strange fusion of cultures or are virtually purely Indian (see Figures 18.5 and 18.6). However, once again Europeanized exceptions can be found in some of the more readily accessible or desirable of the distant areas, thus appropriately reversing the pattern seen in the central states. The masks of the Yaqui and Mayo Indians, for example, are totally different from any other masks in the world and as uniquely locally culture-based and as easily identifiable as any tribal mask from Africa or Micronesia.

Probably the most interesting masks to consider in a study of the effects of Spanish culture on the people of the New World are those that show no full dominance by either culture, but rather differing degrees of syncretic fusion. Devil masks are often of this type: The

Figure 18.5
A Tigre (Tiger) mask: Olínalá. State of Guerrero. Photo by Donald E. Fritz.

Figure 18.6
A Yaqui "Pascala" mask with Indian imagery, used during Christian Holy Week dances. State of Sonora. Photo by Donald E. Fritz.

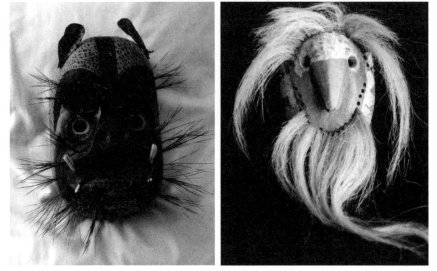

faces of the horned devil traditional in European imagery are often enriched with serpents, lizards, protruding tongues, or fangs, all imagery with traceable pre-conquest origins. Presumably, the Spaniards did not mind having the old gods transformed into devils, nor, one gathers, did the Indians mind carrying their old gods forward in whatever way possible. For the Indians the nature of the gods—good or evil—was of less concern than their attributed powers, powers that needed recognition and respect, if not open reverence.

Certainly one of the most fascinating examples of the complexities involved in the cultural interactions that have produced the Mexican masks as we now know them are the masks used by the Cora Indians of Nayarit. Donald Cordry in *Mexican Masks* relates succinctly how what was at one time a reenactment of the Passion Play taught to the Coras by Jesuit missionaries reverted more or less fully to its pre-conquest nature after the influence of the Jesuits was removed upon their expulsion from Mexico early in the nineteenth century (99). The mock combat still uses Christian terminology, but virtually all of the imagery and action is as it was before the Spaniards came, or as if they had never come. In addition to wearing fantastically bizarre masks made out of papier mâché, the participants paint their entire bodies in startling patterns and conduct themselves with truly pagan abandonment.

After the reenactment is over, the participants go into the river and wash away their body paint and cast their masks into the water, where they disintegrate (123; Luna Parra and Romandia, 126–127). A similar example of the Indians retaining much of their own culture despite putatively Christian themes and narratives is seen in the Easter-season ceremonies of the Mayo Indians of Sonora. Those who portray the Chapayekos, the masked persecutors of Christ, are rebaptized at the ceremony's end and their masks are piled together and ritually burned as a rite of purification. The whole enactment is more that of an earlier Indian celebration of a cyclical drama of human existence than the linear human narrative of Christianity (Markman and Markman, 187).

While these two examples of the intricate interplay between the Hispanic and pre-conquest cultures are more dramatic than most, they are so only in degree. The same interplay exists in some ways in virtually every mask found in Mexico. Mask use was important in Mexico before the Spaniards came, and the Spanish used masks to further their own purposes. Paradoxically, the masks became both bridges that joined the two cultures and walls that forever isolated them. The great majority of mask use in Mexico today is linked with Spain and/or Christianity; even the most purely Indian ceremonies, such as dances based on overcoming the threat of a *tigre* (jaguar), are in some ways connected with the Church or its calendar (Momprade and Gutiérrez, 216). Nevertheless, as Charles Gibson argues, although the surface of the dances is Christian, their central core and the energy that keeps them viable remains Indian (Markman and Markman, 166). For example, even when held within Church sanctuaries, the directional orientation used in the dances parallels that of the pre-Hispanic cosmos and its natural forces (Covarrubias, 1). In short, masks may look Spanish, but virtually all those who wear them are Indian.

After centuries of such syncretic interactions, the exact nature or extent of cultural fusions, replacements, concealments, inversions, or whatever else is far too complex and varied to yield certainties about origins from analyses. The Hispanic impact on mask use in Mexico is inescapably clear, from the European imagery one sees in so many of the masks to the Church-based uses for most of them. As Frances Toor remarks in her seminal study of Mexican folk culture, the early Spanish missionaries were superb teachers, to the extent that most Mexicans today know much more about Church history than about that of their own country prior to the conquest (216). Still, as noted earlier, beneath and along with the Hispanic influence run the ancient indigenous currents as well; nonverbally, even unconsciously in most cases, yet nonetheless powerfully present. The masks, as well as the dances, plays, or rituals in which they are used, are now neither Spanish nor Indian, only purely Mexican. They remain an engaging physical presence in our modern world and an enigmatic record both of the lost worlds of the pre-conquest Indian peoples and of those proud, clever, and incredibly intrepid Spaniards who came across the ocean to bring to the new world their own ways and God's word.

BIBLIOGRAPHY

Cordry, Donald B. *Mexican Masks*. Austin: University of Texas Press, 1980.

Covarrubias, Luis. *Regional Dances of Mexico*. Mexico, D.F.: E. Fischgrund, 1960.

Luna Parra de García Sáenz, Georgina, and Romandia de Cantu, Graciela. *En el mundo de la máscara*. 2d ed. Mexico, D.F.: Fomento Cultural Banamex, 1979.

Markman, Peter T., and Markman, Roberta. *Masks of the Spirit*. Berkeley and Los Angeles: University of California Press, 1989.

Martinez-Hunter, Sanjuanita. "The Development of Dance in Mexico: 1325–1910." Ph.D. diss., Texas Woman's University, Denton, Texas, 1984.

Momprade, Electra L., and Gutiérrez, Tonatiuh. *Danzas y Bailes Populares*. Buenos Aires: Editorial Hermes, 1981.

Toor, Frances. *A Treasury of Mexican Folkways*. New York: Crown, 1947.

19

Poetry of Praise to the Virgin of Guadalupe

RoseAnna Mueller

According to a legend first published in 1648, the Virgin Mary appeared to the Indian Juan Diego at the hill called Tepeyac, once sacred to the Aztec goddess Tonantzín. This apparition of the Virgin in the New World happened in 1531, just ten years after Cortes's conquest of Tenochtitlan. The Virgin instructed Juan Diego, a neophyte, to deliver a message to Juan de Zumárraga, bishop-elect of Mexico City, conveying her desire to have a church built on the site. The bishop demanded proof, so during the fourth apparition the Virgin instructed Juan Diego to gather roses and take them in his *tilma* (cloak) to the bishop. When Juan Diego unfolded his *tilma* the Virgin's image was imprinted on it. The *tilma* now hangs behind the altar of the Basilica of Nuestra Señora de Guadalupe in Mexico City, a much-visited shrine and site of pilgrimages.

Although it is possible to study the devotion to Our Lady of Guadalupe through religious, historical, artistic, anthropological, cultural, and other lenses, this presentation will focus on the representative poetry of praise written to Guadalupe shortly after the apparition, ending with some contemporary hymns.

The Mexican image of Mary, who appears in the New World as a *mestiza* to those indigenous to the land, has been recorded in historical accounts, eyewitness accounts, sermons, hymns, and poetry. The descriptions of the miracle often merged Biblical quotations from *The Song of Songs* 6:10 and *Revelations* 12 with imagery and symbols associated with Aztec female deities. Eventually the image itself and its associations took on political significance in the nation-building of Mexico. Contemporary hymns emphasize the religious and cultural significance of the miracle, and virtually equate belief in Guadalupe with ethnic identity. Some of the poems to be examined include the earliest known verses written by the transplanted Spaniard González de Eslava, representative verse from the prodigious seventy-eight-stanza *Primavera indiana* (1662) by Carlos Sigüenza y Góngora, a sonnet by the nun Sor Juana Inés de la Cruz, another by José Manuel Sartorio, and a few recent hymns. The poetry often forms the verbal counterpart to the image and its associations, which combine elements of faith, spirituality, baroque *ingenio*, and the symbolism contained within names, emblem books, occult messages, and the Bible. Then there is the enigma of the freshness and longevity of the image itself, beginning with the question of who painted it. (Figures 19.1 through 19.7 show various concepts of the Virgin of Guadalupe found in the art of today.)

According to the *Album conmemorativo*, the first recorded poem to the Virgin of Guadalupe was written by the Spaniard Hernán González de Eslava (b.1534). He arrived in Mexico in 1588, where he was ordained. The "Canción a Nuestra Señora," although not directly addressed to the Virgin of Guadalupe, shows clear references and allusions to the miracle. The first line,"Sois hermosa, aunque morena," borrows from *The Song of Songs*—"Dark am I but lovely" or "I am dark but I am beautiful," depending on the translation—a biblical reference that is repeated in many other poems to the *mestiza Virgin*. This borrowing clearly establishes the Virgin as dark skinned, with its political implications for the history of Mexico's indigenous and *mestizo* population. It also establishes the Virgin as the intercessor sent by God to the inhabitants of the New World. The second stanza associates the Virgin with the sun, whose rays always appear as the background of the image. The sun, of course, was worshipped by many of the Amerindian peoples, including the Aztecs, whose ritual worship of the sun god included elaborate songs, dances, and human sacrifices. The third stanza notes Mary's privileged position, since she alone was conceived without original sin. The poem concludes with its emphasis on the color of the Virgin's skin, having Guadalupe herself repeat and rephrase the biblical allusion to *The Song of Songs*: "I am dark but I am beautiful, daughters of Jerusalem."

Carlos Sigüenza y Góngora's seventy-eight-stanza *Primavera indiana* retells the story of the miracle in his typical Baroque and *cultista* manner. This highly stylized and erudite poem is replete with classical allusions to Phaeton, Mt. Olympus, and the reign of Calixtus, and is full of the requisite elaborate conceits and arch witticisms. In stanza 47 the

Figure 19.1
A mural in Pope Pius V Church on Ashland and 16th Street in Chicago
tells the story of the miracle that occurred to Juan Diego in 1531. Photo by
R. Mueller.

poet begins by describing the harmonious sounds that preceded the apparition. It is interesting that the current missal (from which the later examples of hymns are taken) is called *Flor y canto*, which is what the Aztecs called oratory or poetry, a combination of flower and song. This, too, forms part of the oral legend, for as the story goes, the first phenomenon that Juan Diego noticed was the birdsong: "En la madrugada del sábado 9 de 1531 cuando Juan Diego emprendió su camino habitual a Tlatelolco, a pasar junto al cerro del Tepeyac se percató de que ese día ocurría algo especial, pues el trino del coyoltotol, del txinizcan y de otros pájaros era hermoso. Se detuvo un momento a deleitarse del hermoso trinar y en ese preciso istante escuchó una dulce

Figure 19.2
A roadside chapel near the Maya ruins in Muyil, Yucatan. The cult of the
Virgin, centered at first near Mexico City, grew to encompass much of
Latin America. Photo by R. Mueller.

voz que le decía: Juanito, Juan Dieguito." This quote, along with a
story of the apparition, a brief biography of Juan Diego, and a chronology of events associated with the Guadalupe legend is printed on
the reverse side of a calender sold at Tienda Guadalupe in San Antonio, Texas. This folk-art store sells many articles in many mediums
with the image of the Virgin, and attests to the popularity of devotion
to the Virgin by the inhabitants in the U.S. southwest.

In his poetry, Sigüenza y Góngora calls the song a harmonious concert that elevates Juan Diego to an ecstatic state. The next stanza describes the light emitted, as brilliant as many diamonds, a light
appropriate to queens. Mary addresses Juan Diego in the next stanza:
"I am Mary, the humble mother of omnipotent God." She continues to
describe her mission, which is to give hope to Mexico. Again we have
a reference to Mexico as the chosen country for the Virgin's apparition
in the New World, consonant with the theme of "Grandeza Mexicana."
Juan Diego, still in his altered state, hastens to tell the bishop (the sacred shepherd), who of course does not believe him. Juan Diego returns to the "eriazo monte," where he once again sees the Queen. The

Figure 19.3
A mural on the side of Taquería Vega in Pilsen, a predominantly Mexican neighborhood of Chicago, seems to be promoting two popular Mexican imports as well. Photo by R. Mueller.

bishop demands proof: "de la virgen intacta, intactas señas." This is the kind of writing the critics point to when they claim Sigüenza y Góngora "out-Góngorad Góngora himself."

It is ironic that Sor Juana Inés de la Cruz, who herself was dubbed "La Décima Musa," dedicates her only poem to the Virgin of Guadalupe in a collection called *La octava maravilla y sin segunda milagro de México*. The anthology was compiled by a Jesuit from Madrid, Francisco de Castro. In this sonnet written in 1680 but not published until 1729, Sor Juana includes the flower imagery and establishes Mary's role as protector of the Americas. The bishop demanded proof of Mary's appearance to Juan Diego. The Virgin instructed Juan Diego to gather roses and present them to the bishop. Part of the miracle at Tepeyac was the blooming of the roses, since the hill on which the Virgin appeared was a dry and barren area and it was unlikely that roses would be growing there. But several versions of the legend mention that roses suddenly bloomed on the hill, and that they were the same kind as those which grew in Castile, hence Sor Juana's play on "Rosa de Castilla." In her

Figure 19.4
A mosaic at the entrance of the Paulina elevated train station in Chicago blesses the commuters. Photo by R. Mueller.

poem, Sor Juana transforms the European roses into "la Rosa Mejicana." This sonnet is packed with additional references and allusions: to Patmos, where St. John the Evangelist wrote of his apocalyptic vision, to the beast or dragon linked to the Apocalypse, and to the mystery of how the copy of the celestial image was made.

An anonymous poem of 1756 (fifty-two *cuartetos*) tells how the Virgin appears to Juan Diego: a woman crowned with stars, clothed by the sun, with the moon at her feet. It is as if her image has been painted by the stars' own light, as though through a flash of celestial luminescence. This is followed with a description of the roses that miraculously appeared on Tepeyac, and a description of the *tilma*, which has endured for centuries. The line, "No hizo con otras naciones fineza tan extrema," echoes the quotation that established Mexico as being singled out for the Virgin's appearance in the New World, and to the privileged position Mexico occupies because it alone was granted the apparition. "Non Fecit Taliter Omni Nationi" [He hath not done so for any other nation] was the quote that became linked to the image in

Figure 19.5
An image near Chicago's St. Vitus Plaza is surrounded by Aztec symbols, the roses that the Virgin asked Juan Diego to gather, and the stars that appear on the Virgin's cloak. Photo by R. Mueller.

paintings and engravings and speaks to the need for establishing a national identity, of moving away from colonial status into a proper nation. The need to establish a feeling of *patria* became basically a *criollo* preoccupation, and now all the inhabitants of Mexico were linked as one through worship of the Virgin of Guadalupe. The last line in the example calls the Virgin "Patrona de Nueva España." Through the ages, Mary's rank progressed from Patroness of Mexico City, to Patroness of all of Mexico, to all of New Spain, and she was eventually proclaimed Empress of the Americas. Many contemporary feminists refer to Guadalupe as "Goddess of the Americas", which is the title of Ana Castillo's 1996 anthology.

José Manuel Sartorio's sonnet to the Virgin of Guadalupe is one of twelve he published in 1812. This coincides with the era of the Mexican War of Independence. The sonnet proclaims that all of Mexico reveres the lovely and divine image of Mary, who is adorned with stars and the rays of the sun. Historically, this is important, because some have argued that the cult of Guadalupe was originally a localized one, and was not embraced by all of Mexico until quite later. Father Hidalgo, for example, carried the image of Guadalupe on his standard in the

Figure 19.6
The Tienda Guadalupe in San Antonio, Texas, offers all manner of
objects, even temporary tattoos, bearing the image of Mexico's patron
saint. Photo by Donna Nay Cade. Used by permission.

struggle for Mexican independence. Sartorio claims that the image the
entire nation worhips is of Guadalupe, a modest and gracious maiden.
After this statement comes a series of questions and answers. What is
this image, the poet asks? It is a divine copy of the Mother of God,
who, through her love, has allowed herself to be depicted. The final
stanza is addressed to the "beloved Indians," who should see in this
miracle (spell or enchantment) the gift of maternal love that fills the
entire world with wonder. This, of course, is a restatement of the
premise that since the Virgin first appeared to an Indian, it was a sign
to facilitate the indigenous conversion to Catholicism. Three questions
follow: Who assures it? Who conceived the design? Who painted it?
The answers follow: We have the Virgin's own words. Divine Love
conceived the design. Eternal God himself painted the image.

In the search for the origins of the image, God is often referenced as
the artist. One painting by an anonymous colonial eighteenth-century
painter, *El padre eterno pintando a la Virgen de Guadalupe*, depicts God
the father in his atelier painting the image as he confers with St. Luke,
the youngest Evangelist. Luke was reputed to have been an artist.
Angels hold up the canvas as God paints the image of the Virgin of
Guadalupe.

Figure 19.7
A mural painted by Jeff Zimmerman above the Lavandería Pilsen in Chicago depicts Mexican families making the dangerous crossing into the United States under the watchful eye of the Virgin of Guadalupe. Photo by J. Zimmerman. Used by permission.

The question of the image's provenance and its fresh colors and longevity through the centuries is one that continues to puzzle us. It withstood a fire. As recently as 1984, the *tilma* is visited by millions. It has been the object of several scientific Turin shroud–like examinations from which different conclusions have been drawn. Manuel Sartorio's sonnet and the anonymous painting both establish God as the artist.

Moving to the contemporary scene, *Flor y canto*, a Spanish language hymnal, contains many hymns devoted to the adoration of the Virgin of Guadalupe. Hymn 215, "Las Apariciones Guadalupanas," tells the Guadalupe story, describing the Virgin's descent to Tepeyac with her hands joined in prayer. It insists on her "Mexicanness" through her very appearance on Mexican soil and the features of her face, the face of a *mestiza*. Stanza 3 describes the peace and harmony of the Anáhuac valley, which is the central valley of Mexico surrounding Mexico City, once the cradle of Aztec civilization. Stanza 4 tells how as Juan Diego approaches the hill he is distracted by the singing. The Virgin tells "Juan Dieguito" (this is supposedly how she addressed the poor peasant, whom she refers to as "the smallest of my small ones"), that she has chosen this site for her altar. Stanza 5 describes how she leaves her imprint on his *tilma*. The heart of this hymn is stanza 7, conflated to "Desde entonces para el mexicano ser Guadalupano es algo esencial." To be Mexican *is* to be Guadalupan. It is a cultural and religious marker. Stanza 8 addresses Mary as the mother of Mexicans, and ends with an invitation to bend one's knee and lift one's eyes toward Tepeyac.

Hymn 209, "Morning Song to the Virgin" is a version of the traditional *mañanitas*, or wake-up song, usually sung on the occasion of one's birthday. The traditional chorus alternates with eleven stanzas: the first greets the Virgin and situates her in the Anáhuac Valley, the third calls her the mother of all Mexicans, the fourth recounts her appearance to Juan Diego, the sixth sets up the premise, "because I am Mexican, I am yours." In the eighth stanza the singer claims to be envious of the angel at her feet, who has formed a footstool, as it were, for the Virgin for the past 400 years. The singer would like to trade places with the angel so as to be closer to the Virgin. The ninth stanza greets Mary as the spotless Virgin, unparalleled in her beauty, whose name is Guadalupe and whose throne is Tepeyac. The "Morning Song" ends as the Virgin is compared to the morning star that announces a new dawn, and the singer implores Mary to cast her gaze on her children, who weeping approach her altar.

Hymn 246, "O Virgin of Guadalupe", is a song of greeting as the singer approaches the Virgin's altar, her throne. Again, the legend of Juan Diego's roses is referenced. The third verse is an appeal to the Virgin not to abandon the faraway homeland, portrayed as victimized and in need of the Virgin's help. This hymn is meant to be sung by Mexican emigrants on December 12, because verse 5 states, "This is the day you visited us on our soil, and we lovingly prostrate ourselves on your altar." Verse 6 greets the Virgin as unblemished and unparalleled in her beauty: "Guadalupe is your name, Tepeyac your throne." Verse 7 compares the Virgin to the morning star announcing a new dawn. The tenth and final verse is sung by the Virgin herself: "I wish to be your mother, here build me a temple, and as a loving mother I will always listen to you."

Moving as I have from the sixteenth century to the present leaves a large gap as far as Guadalupan poetry is concerned. This study has attempted to reconcile only some of the poetry as a counterpart to the images. I have touched on no other literary genres, and I have had to leave out a substantial corpus dealing with the apparition and its importance in the history of Mexican national and religious identity. The roots of the cult of the Virgin of Guadalupe were set in the sixteenth-century clash of Spain and the New World. To appreciate the importance of the apparition and its psychosocial and religious impact is to understand the clash of Spanish and Aztec and the submergence of the latter. Perhaps the most profound aspect of the conquest was the spiritual devastation, as Spanish missionaries were urging the indigenous to believe in one Christian God while wiping out Indian gods and goddesses. But both the image of the Virgin of Guadalupe and the legend of her apparition blend elements of the New World with the Old. The image itself is consonant with European depictions of the Immaculate Conception by Spanish artists such as Zurbarán and Velázquez, with added indigenous symbolism in elements such as the incorporation of the sun in the Virgin's mandorla, her darkened skin and *mestizo* features, her star-studded cloak, and the floral decoration of her robe. The Mexican apparition story also shares elements of previous European legends. The Virgin appears to a humble person, the witness's honesty and integrity are first questioned by the authorities, tangible proof is sought and is miraculously provided, and the Virgin insists on having a church built on the spot where she appeared. In the case of Guadalupe, the spot happens to be one that was formerly sacred to the indigenous population. Truly, both the image and the legend are syncretic, and devotion to the Virgin of Guadalupe has spread beyond Mexico, across the Mexico–U.S. border and into all of Spanish-speaking America. She is a consoling, compassionate mother to all, offering a link between the pre-Hispanic Aztec past, the colonial period of evangelization, and contemporary beliefs in her ability to intercede and to strengthen religious and ethnic identity.

The cult of Guadalupe and the demographic makeup of her devotees changed substantially during the course of the colonial era to take in the *criollos*, who reinterpreted her appearance as a legitimization of their national aspirations. Throughout its history Guadulupe has been a malleable and manipulated symbol, and she continues to be so today. There is an ongoing attempt to rediscover the meaning of Guadalupe, depicting her as an embodiment of Tonantzín-Coatlique, goddess of the cosmos, sacred guardian and mother image for the Mexican nation (Peterson, 46). She is a multifaceted symbol for believers and nonbelievers alike. In the words of Octavio Paz, "There are two beliefs deeply embedded in Mexican consciousness: belief in the lottery and belief in the Virgin of Guadalupe."

BIBLIOGRAPHY

Alstott, Owen, ed. *Flor y canto*. Portland, Ore.: OCP, 1991.

Aguilera, D. Franscisco, et al. *Album Conmemorativo del 450 aniversario de las apariciones de Nuestra Señora de Guadalupe*. Mexico, D.F.: Ediciones Buena Nueva, 1981.

Castillo, Ana, ed. *Goddess of the Americas [La Diosa de las Americas]*. New York: Riverhead Books, 1996.

Cawley, Martinus. *Anthology of Early Guadalupan Literature*. CARA Studies on Guadalupan Devotion 8. Lafayette, Ore.: Guadalupe Abbey, 1984.

La Reina de las Américas: Works of Art from the Museum of the Basilica of Guadalupe. Chicago: Mexican Fine Arts Center Museum, 1996.

Paz, Octavio. *The Labyrinth of Solitude*. Translated by Lysander Kemp. New York: Grove, 1985.

Peterson, Jeannette Favrot. "The Virgin of Guadalupe: Symbol of Conquest or Liberation?" *Art Journal* (Winter 1992).

Poole, Stafford. *Our Lady of Guadalupe: The Origins and Sources of a Mexican National Symbol, 1531–1787*. Tucson: University of Arizona Press, 1996.

20

Century XX: Legacy of the Spanish Exiles in Mexican Music

Consuelo Carredano

In the summer of 1937 the Spanish Levant became the scene of the Second International Congress of Anti-Fascist Writers. The meeting in Valencia was attended by a Mexican delegation consisting of Carlos Pellicer, José Mancisidor, and Octavio Paz. After the close of the conference, a new delegation joined them, this time composed of members of LEAR (the League of Revolutionary Writers and Artists of Mexico), whose mission was to show their solidarity with the Spanish people in their fight for the Republican cause. Among this group of writers and painters was one musician, the great Silvestre Revueltas.

The various activities of the solidarity group included public presentations, exhibits, meetings, and concerts, in which Revueltas himself presented some of his works and conducted the Symphony Orchestra of Valencia. At the end of one of these well-attended concerts in the Conservatory, whose program included the debut of his *Tribute to García Lorca*, Revueltas received the enthusiastic acclaim of the audience, "the creme de la creme of Spanish music," as he would say in a letter to his wife. Also appearing with him were Bartolomé Pérez Casas, Salvador Bacarisse, Palau, and Casals-Chapí.

History does not specify whether it was on that night or on some other that Revueltas met Rodolfo Halffter, a Madrilian composer of German surname, who years later, in very different circumstances for both musicians, would recall the first time he was introduced to Revueltas. He told of their meeting, of their visits to the front, and of the strong musical bond that developed between them as they sat at a piano and played with four hands the compositions of the vigorous young Mexican. This could well be called the first "real" encounter between Spanish and Mexican music. If with his *Tribute to Federico García Lorca* Revueltas was showing the world what a Spanish poet had inspired, his work, with all its strength and vigor, revealed at the same time to the Spanish musicians a musical Mexico they had never known before, proclaimed so eloquently through the genius of Revueltas.

The degree of mutual familiarity between these two cultures was at best unequal, to say the least, in those days. As Octavio Paz says in his book *Itinerarios*, nothing that was happening culturally in Republican Spain was alien to the Mexican intellectuals. The magazine *Occidente*, headed by Ortega y Gasset, had become, according to Octavio Paz, "the great provider of theories and names."[1] Among its contributors was Adolfo Salazar, one of the foremost figures of Spanish art and culture in that period. Salazar was considered in his country the intellectual leader of the Generation of '27, given his close ties to Federico García Lorca, José Ortega y Gasset, Juan Ramón Jiménez, Pablo Picasso, Ramón Menéndez Pidal, Manuel Azaña, Miguel Salvador, Gerardo Diego, Vicente Aleixandre, León Felipe, and many other artists and writers with whom he lived in the Student Residence of Madrid before the Civil War. His thinking had a decisive influence in the shaping of Spain's musical life, just as it would on Mexico's during the years of his exile. Perhaps it was an omen that in 1921 he had published his first book, *Andrómeda*, in Mexico, with a prologue by the Dominican intellectual Pedro Henríquez Ureña, even before having set foot on its soil. To quote the words of the Mexican musician Salvador Moreno shortly after Salazar's death,

Adolfo Salazar's first book was printed in Mexico many years ago, and it is in Mexico where he has now left his last breath. With a man like him, for whom writing and speaking, thinking and living are all as one, that was tantamount to a kind of birth. And so we can say that Adolfo Salazar was born and died in Mexico, and with all due respect to Madrid, this was his true native land.[2]

On the contrary, in Spain the names of Mexico's most prominent writers were hardly known. They were read very little, even those like Alfonso Reyes or Jaime Torres Bodet, whose works were appearing sporadically in Spanish literary reviews.

If that is what was happening in the field of letters, Spain's lack of familiarity with Mexican music was almost absolute. It is not difficult to assume that before the legendary trip of Revueltas to Spain, Spanish musicians were totally unaware of the work of their fellow Mexicans. One of the first Spaniards of the time, if not the first, to call attention to Mexican music was the poet Rafael Alberti, who in 1934, during a seven-month stay in Mexico, had come to know Silvestre Revueltas—the man, not his work. It wasn't until 1937 that Alberti heard his music in Valencia, was captivated by it, and published a highly laudatory piece that same year in the weekly La voz.[3] Alberti's example was followed some time later by the Catalonian critic Otto Mayer Serra and the composer Rodolfo Halffter, who would make musical criticism and chronicling one of the principal pursuits of their lives in Mexico. It is impossible to ignore the work of these two scholars, whose pens were placed exclusively at the service of Mexican music and musicians.

Rodolfo Halffter claimed that he first heard the name of Carlos Chávez in Paris in 1931. It was at a concert of the American musicologist Nicholas Slonimsky, which included the world premiere of Energía, a work written by Chávez in 1925 for a small instrumental group. Thanks to Slonimsky, Halffter wrote, "Europe has just discovered that on the other side of the Atlantic a very new kind of music is being composed, one worthy of serious consideration."[4] Little did Halffter know on that night that not only would his own life end in Mexico, land of that unknown musician, but that together they would form an unbreakable friendship and professional association that would bring immeasurable benefits to the music of that country.

The echoes of Isaac Albéniz, Enrique Granados, and Manuel de Falla reached Mexico in 1919 with the first visit of the young pianist Arthur Rubinstein. Until then, Carlos Chávez later explained, the existence of a composer called Manuel de Falla was known in Mexico, but very few knew anything about his compositions.[5] Unfortunately, this first presentation turned out for naught. Although Rubinstein's rendition of the Ritual Fire Dance displayed an astounding virtuosity, his performance was not well received, and Falla would not be heard again in Mexico for some time to come. During a trip to France in 1923, Chávez had the opportunity to meet with Paul Dukas in his old home in Paris. On that occasion, he recalls, the French musician spoke to him about the enormous treasure that lay undiscovered in Falla's Siete canciones populares. Urging him to look at them and study them well, he held them as a model of what Mexican composers could do with their own rich heritage of folklore. Needless to say, on his return to Mexico Chávez debuted Falla's Seven Songs in one of his concerts of new music.[6] From 1928 on, when he founded the Symphony Orchestra of Mexico, he would introduce to Mexican audiences all the major works of the Spanish composer: Noches en los jardines de España [Nights in the Gardens of Spain], El amor brujo [Love the Magician], El sombrero de tres picos [The Three-Cornered Hat], and El retablo de Maese Pedro [Master Peter's Puppet Show].

The composers of the generation after Falla, that is, the so-called Group of Madrid or the Musical Generation of '27, were not known in Mexico until some of them arrived to begin their lives in exile. It is common knowledge that by the end of the Civil War a large portion of Spanish artists and intellectuals were living outside the Peninsula. The author Gonzalo Torrente Ballester speaks of 90 percent, and of those a great many, including Rodolfo Halffter, Salvador Bacarisse, Rosa García Ascot, and Gustavo Pittaluga, took up residence in Mexico. Quite clearly, the Spanish exiles would initiate a fruitful new era in the cultural life of Mexico.[7]

It would be well to recall here the situation of Mexican music at the time of the refugees' arrival. At the start of the 1940s, Mexico was enjoying a moment of intense musical activity, both in its creation and in its dissemination. During the second and third decades of the century, Chávez had been the prime mover in a series of actions designed to organize the various branches of music. The creation of the Symphony Orchestra of Mexico was a major landmark in the cultural development of the nation. Now for the first time there was a permanent musical organization, with a conductor dedicated to renewing and modernizing the repertoire, creating new audiences, and refining their tastes. The orchestra had contributed to increasing noticeably the composition of symphonic pieces. So, by the early 1940s, Carlos Chávez, Silvestre Revueltas, José Pablo Monayo, Blas Galindo, and Luis Sandi, to mention just a few, were in high gear and reaching their stride.

But there were two fields of music that were still being neglected in Mexico at the moment of the defeat of the Spanish Republic: (1) good editions of music were almost nonexistent, and (2) musical criticism and analysis were notoriously weak, due to the provincial and exceedingly conservative vision of those who practiced them. The active and successful participation of the emigrés in these areas has now been fully recognized. The establishment in 1946 of the publishing house Ediciones Mexicanas de Música is only one example. In 1996 the publishing house celebrated its fiftieth anniversary with a catalogue containing nearly 300 titles. And this was not the only contribution of the exiles, who extended their efforts into teaching, interpretation, film, radio, and television.[8] One of the greatest accomplishments of the musical collaboration of Spaniards and Mexicans was the formation of the Grupo Nuestra Música, a nonprofit organization whose goal was to publish the concert works of its members. It also sought to create a review with articles, scholarly studies, and critiques of contemporary music. The first issue of the magazine *Nuestra Música* in the spring of 1946 was the ultimate realization of the project conceived by this splendid group of composers. In the seven years of its existence, it was in essence the depository of new trends in Mexican music.

Since the dissemination of their works was as important to the founders of the Group as their publication, they organized a series of "Monday Concerts," given generally on the last Monday of every month to let the public hear the new composers and to offer a contemporary international repertoire of chamber music, with which few were as yet familiar.

• • •

As the undisputed leader of Mexican music, Carlos Chávez, with his prestige as a composer and as a cultural administrator, could and did manifest in diverse ways his sympathy for the Spanish Republic. In addition, he had sufficient vision to take immediate advantage of the intellectual initiatives and the solid formation of the recent arrivals. The affinity of purpose between the Mexican composers headed by Chávez and the nucleus of emigrés would form the base for a close professional relationship. Under his leadership, these Spanish musicians, along with other philosophers, scientists, writers, and artists, were able to continue and consolidate their work in Mexico.

It is impossible here to delve into the contributions of all of the leading musician exiles in Mexico. Nevertheless, we cannot fail to mention the composer Rodolfo Halffter, whose importance in the cultural world of his adopted land was not only multifold but prolonged. Since his arrival in Mexico in 1939, his teachings introduced into Mexico the study of new currents in European composition, such as polytonality and twelve-tone systems. Through his classrooms in the Conservatory passed several generations of musicians, among them many who would later enjoy substantial international careers.

Two questions remain: What did the Spanish exiles derive from Mexico? And how did this new land affect their work? It would seem from the foregoing that their reception in Mexico was idyllic, and that they encountered nothing but immediate acceptance from their Mexican peers. Actually, this was not true. There were also groups—almost all of them second-rate—that consistently rejected the presence and the activities of the Spanish emigrés. There were even instances of their being insulted openly and disqualified professionally simply for being foreigners. For these reactionary enclaves, just as for Franco's Spain, a nation's culture should remain uncontaminated, protected by means of censorship from such corrupting agents as cosmopolitanism, which threaten its spiritual personality. Starting from the premise that an idea was valid simply because it was theirs, not because of its instrinsic validity, they considered anything foreign an aberration.

It is now abundantly clear that for Spanish and Mexican artists the reciprocal influences were undoubtedly enriching. They produced a dialogue, an interchange of ideas that probed deeply into the imagination and the spirit. The music and poetry of these artists offered fertile ground for sharing their own imaginary universes. So, while Revueltas and Chávez sang to García Lorca and Blas Galindo to Juan Ramón Jiménez, Halffter was doing the same with Sor Juana Inés de la Cruz and Simón Tapia Colman was evoking pre-Hispanic poetry. In more recent times, the Mexican Joaquín Gutiérrez Heras has been setting to music poems by the Spaniard Emilio Prados, and the Spaniard Carlos Cruz de Castro is paying tribute to Mexican poetry in the voice of Octavio Paz.

This dialogue established among Mexican and Spanish artists, uninterrupted to this day, was born of a healthy and legitimate curiosity to recognize and understand what each other was doing and thinking. What better example is there than to recall the opening of *Don Lindo de Almería* on the night of January 9, 1940, when Halffter was making his debut in Mexico? Reliving this event, the composer wrote, "When the piece ended, Carlos Chávez, Silvestre Revueltes, and Blas Galindo came over to me, impelled by a sincere interest in the kind of music that I, the newly arrived Spaniard, was writing."[9] Many years later, in 1968, when Halffter was named to the Mexican Academy of Arts, Chávez conducted in his honor that very work, the first by a Spanish emigré to be heard in Mexico. In short, the arrival of Spanish intellectuals and artists in Mexico was one of the most significant moments in the history of the two cultures. Despite those who would cling to the past, these master creators knew that one's own tradition can blend with another's, and that originality is not stifled by the sharing of ideas.

NOTES

1. Octavio Paz, *Itinerarios* (México, D.F.: FCE, 1993).
2. Ricardo Miranda, *Detener el tiempo. Escritos musicales de Salvador Moreno* (México, D.F.: INBA-CENIDIM, 1996), 91.
3. This article appears in a book by the composer's sister, Rosaura Revueltas, *Silvestre Revueltas por él mismo* (Mexico, D.F.: Ediciones Era, 1989).
4. See Rodolfo Halffter, "Crónica del trasladado," acceptance speech on being admitted to the Academia de Artes de México, *Pauta* 1 (1982).
5. See Carlos Chávez, "Falla en México," lecture delivered in the Colegio Nacional, July 23, 1970, *Pauta* 7 (1988).
6. The work was given its debut performance by the singer Lupe Medina.
7. Although every other aspect of the cultural and social phenomenon of the Spanish emigrés in Mexico has been given serious and profound study, to date their musical contribution has produced very few scholarly efforts. To my knowledge, the only monograph on the subject is Arturo Souto Alabarce, "Musica y danza," in *El exilio español en México* (Mexico, D.F.: Fondo de Cultura Económica, 1982). Aside from that, there are only short articles, notes, or com-

ments inserted in panoramic studies of the history of Mexican music or in monographs on certain national composers whose paths crossed those of the exiles. Given the meager published documentation, I would recommend Josefina Estrada, "El exilio español y la música," *Novedades*, October 7, 1978, which contains an interview with the musicologist José Antonio Alcarás, who was closely connected with the emigrés.

8. In 1994 the Centro de Investigación, Documentación e Información Musical de México published my book *Ediciones Mexicanas de Música: historia y catálogo*, which describes the work of this publishing house founded more than fifty years ago by Spanish-Mexican musicians. At present I am preparing an edition of the letters of Adolfo Salazar.

9. See Halffter, "Crónica del trasladado."

PART V

SPANISH ROMANTICS ET AL. IN OPERA AND BALLET

——————————— 21

La Forza del Destino: *Destiny as Portrayed by Rivas and Verdi*

David G. Burton

The relationship between Giuseppe Verdi and the Spanish Romantic drama continues to intrigue those Hispanists who are fond of the opera. It is well-known that Verdi, the major composer of Italian opera during the mid to late nineteenth century, chose texts by two early nineteenth-century Spanish dramatists as the source for three of his operas. *Il Trovatore* (1851) and *Simon Boccanegra* (1857, revised 1887) are based on plays of the same names by Antonio García Gutiérrez (1813–1884), and *La Forza del Destino* (1862, revised 1869), is derived from *Don Alvaro o La fuerza del sino* by Angel Saavedra, Duke of Rivas (1791–1865). In the Italian translations of these works Verdi saw potential for three very different operas. *Il Trovatore* provides all the elements of great opera: passion, envy, and revenge set in the Spanish Middle Ages to some of the composer's best-loved music. *Simon Boccanegra*, although somewhat less familiar, offers tender moments of filial love against a turbulent period in Genoese history. *La Forza del Destino*, seemingly less unified and more episodic than the other two operas, appears to be epic in form; that is, comprised of vast lyrical scenes that seem to be sewn together with only the slightest thread of plot. Given its structural difference as compared to *Trovatore* and *Simon Boccanegra*, as well as the importance of *Don Alvaro* as the defining Spanish Romantic drama, this chapter will focus upon the transformation of *Don Alvaro* into *La Forza del Destino*.

Angel Saavedra, Duke of Rivas, wrote his *Don Alvaro* during the last years of his exile in France. He, like many other liberal intellectuals, had been forced to leave Spain in the 1820s when the reactionary Ferdinand VII began his reign. Ferdinand died in 1833, and soon thereafter an amnesty permitted the exiles to return. *Don Alvaro* had its premiere in Madrid on March 22, 1835, a year after Rivas returned to Spain (Rivas, 9–11, 62). In 1850 Faustino Sanseverino translated the play into Italian, and it was this translation that Verdi read (Brown, 37; Budden, 430).

In the summer of 1861 Verdi received a commission from the Imperial Theater at St. Petersburg for an opera to be staged during the following winter season (Budden, 427). He was given a free-hand in the choice of texts and selected Victor Hugo's *Ruy Blas*. The Russian censors, however, rejected the idea, and Verdi began looking for another play (428). He had read the Italian translation of Rivas's work and immediately set about to find it (428). Verdi chose Francesco Maria Piave, his collaborator on *Rigoletto* and *La Traviata*, as the librettist to mold the drama into operatic plot (Brener, 103; Budden, 431). The opera was completed by the fall of 1861 and Verdi, along with his wife, traveled to Russia to direct the première (Budden, 433–434). Problems with singers forced the first performance to be postponed until November 1862 (434). Soon thereafter Verdi went to Madrid for the Spanish première (435). Almost from the beginning Verdi was dissatisfied with the finale of the opera, and made several attempts at revising the score (436; Godefroy, 94–95). It was not until 1869, however, that he and Antonio Ghizlanzoni, future librettist of *Aida*, came together to revise the opera for La Scala (Brown, 42–48; Budden, 437–438; Godefroy, 101). He added the now-famous Overture and reworked Act 3 and the Act 4 finale (Verdi, 34–35). The *Forza* that we know and see today is the revised version of 1869. Curiously enough, Hispanists would instantly recognize Verdi's 1862 ending. It follows the Rivas play exactly.

Rivas	Verdi/Piave
P. Guardián: ¡Padre Rafael!	Guardiano: Padre Raffaele . . .
D. Alvaro: (*Desde un risco, con sonrisa diabólica, todo convulso, dice.*) Busca, imbécil, al padre Rafael. . . . Yo soy un enviado del infierno, soy el demonio exterminador. . . . Huid, miserables.	Alvaro: Imbecille, cerca il Padre Raffaele . . . . Un inviato dell' inferno io son . . .
Todos: ¡Jesús! ¡Jesús!	Melitone: L'ho sempre detto . . .
D. Alvaro: ¡Infierno, abre tu boca y trágame! ¡Húndase el cielo, perezca la raza humana; exter-	Alvaro: Apriti, o terra, M'ingoi l'inferno. . . . Precipiti il ciel . . . Pera la razza humana. . . . (*He climbs*

minio, destrucción. . . ! (*Sube a lo más alto del monte y se precipita.*)

P. GUARDIÁN Y LOS FRAILES: (*Aterrados y en actitudes diversas.*) ¡Misericordia, Señor! ¡Misericordia! (Rivas,179)

higher and throws himself into the void.)

ALL: Orrore! . . . Pietà signor. . . . Misericordia! (*All kneel.*) (Verdi, 110)

Without doubt, *Forza* is an opera in which words, music, stage actions, and scenery combine to express in epic fashion the theme of destiny. William Weaver writes that this opera is "a work of great variety, vast scope, juxtaposing comic and tragic, employing a number of unusual characters. . . . It is perhaps Verdi's boldest attempt to portray an entire, complex, contradictory world" (135). In the same article, Weaver calls this "Verdi's most Shakespearean opera" (135). With all due respect for Weaver's encyclopedic erudition in the realm of opera, especially Italian opera, his reference here to Shakespeare is arguable. *Don Alvaro*, and by extension *Forza*, are the very essence of Romantic drama. What could be more Romantic than presenting a complex and contradictory world that is subject to the whim of "*sino*"—destiny, fate. *Sino* is the idea that especially informs Rivas's play and Verdi's opera. Rivas's title states it clearly; Verdi's is even more direct. It therefore seems appropriate to focus on those scenes in both works where this unrelenting "force of destiny" begins to express itself as a major player in the action. It is in Verdi's Act 3, corresponding to Rivas's Acts 3 and 4, where music and language come together in a powerful presentation of that which haunts Alvaro and the other principal characters, from the first notes of the overture.

Rivas's play and Verdi's opera have challenged critics and viewers to consider just what this term "destiny" means. Richard Cardwell, in his 1973 article on *Don Alvaro*, equates it with cosmic injustice. Cardwell writes that the end of the eighteenth century brought with it a metaphysical crisis that challenged long-held traditional values, especially religion, in Western Europe. Alvaro, then, represents the person who has lost faith in any sort of "benevolent pattern of existence" (162). Alvaro's life seems to be guided not by Providence but by a meaningless game of chance (Rivas, 20). Deprived of the love of Leonor, first by her family's exaggerated sense of honor and prestige and then by the accidental murder of her father, Alvaro becomes a restless wanderer trying to escape reality. For Alvaro, like other Romantic heroes, a world without love is intolerable. Alvaro laments at the beginning of his soliloquy in Act 3,

¡Qué carga tan insufrible
es el ambiente vital

para el mezquino mortal
que nace en signo terrible! (Rivas, 891–894)

The escape that he seeks is death. Over and over again he repeats his desire to die: "y yo, que infelice soy, / yo, que buscándola voy, / no puedo encontrar con ella" (918–920); "pues busco ansioso el morir / por no osar el resistir / de los astros el furor" (988–990). But that for which he so yearns always lies just beyond his grasp. Alvaro cannot die. He is imprisoned in a world from which there is no escape.

Verdi's Alvaro sings, "la vita è inferno all'infelice . . . Invano / Morte desio!" (Verdi, 82). He has entered the world of war (the Austrian War at Velletri) in search of death as a means of escaping his world void of love. Verdi communicates Alvaro's "angst" through music as well as words. The extended clarinet solo that precedes his "romanza" evokes the hero's state of mind. Recollection of all that he has lost brings on melancholy. Destiny has robbed him of everything except death:

Chè senza nome ed esule,
in odio del destino,
Chiedo anelando, ahi misero,
La morte d'incontrar. (82)

Sounds of quarreling interrupt these reveries, and now begins a series of scenes in both play and opera fraught with the greatest of dramatic ironies. Donald Shaw calls this "el episodio central de la obra" (Rivas, 32). The comment applies to the opera as well.

Alvaro, known in the army as Fadrique de Herreros (Verdi's Federico de Herreros), rushes to a call for help. He saves the life of Felix de Avendaño (Felice de Bornos), who is the general's aide, a recent arrival to the Italian front, and, as we soon find out, none other than Leonor's brother Carlos. Felix, having heard about the legendary prowess of Fadrique, has wanted to meet him. Destiny grants him that wish. Fadrique and Felix are immediately drawn to one another in friendship and go off to fight side by side. Verdi expands their chance meeting. In the first of three duets in this act, singing in thirds, the two men clasp hands, swearing,

Amici in vita e in morte
Il mondo ne vedrà . . .
Uniti in vita e in morte
Entrambi troverà. (Verdi, 84)

But eternal friendship will prove to be short-lived. Circumstances have brought together two enemies whose true identities are unknown to each other. One, Alvaro, is the murderer of the Marquis of Calatrava and the would-be husband of Leonor, the marquis' daughter. The other, Carlos, is the son of the murdered marquis and brother of Leonor, who has escaped his wrath to find peace as a hermit in the Convent of Santa María de los Angeles.

Fate now turns the tables and the irony increases. Carlos saves the life of his newfound friend on the battlefield. The wounded Alvaro, upset that his life has been spared, hopes that his desire to die will at last be granted. Carlos tries to console Alvaro by stating that for his bravery he will be awarded the Cross of Calatrava. Alvaro, quite naturally, due to his precarious relationship with the family, reacts strongly against such a move. This causes some concern to Carlos. Alvaro informs him that certain secrets contained in sealed letters must die with him, makes Carlos swear to destroy them, and entrusts the letters to his friend. In Verdi's hands the scene becomes one of the most celebrated of tenor–baritone duets in all opera: "Solenne in quest'ora." The beauty and simplicity of the melody convince us that the two are indeed friends.

What follows is surely one of the great theatrical recognition scenes. Alvaro has been taken off to surgery. Carlos, distraught over his friend's wound, muses on the reaction to the name of Calatrava, begins to doubt his friend, controls himself, and finally addresses the packet of letters:

Salid caja misteriosa
del destino urna fatal,
a quien con sudor mortal
toca mi mano medrosa. (Rivas, 1252–1255)

He wavers, then refuses to open the sealed letters, but suddenly finds a locket. Since he has not sworn to its sanctity, he opens it, and finds, of course, a portrait of Leonor, thus proving beyond all doubt that the wounded man is Alvaro. Destiny has again granted him his wish: It has delivered his enemy into his hands. At last he can avenge the death of his father:

¡Cuán feliz será mi suerte
si la venganza y castigo,
sólo de un golpe consigo
a los dos dando la muerte! (1332–1335)

When the surgeon announces that Alvaro will live, Carlos exclaims jubilantly,

Feliz me hacéis;
por ver bueno al capitán
tengo, amigo, más afán
del que imaginar podéis. (1344–1347)

Verdi, following the Rivas text closely, creates a highly dramatic scene for baritone. Carlos wavers between friendship sworn to this man and duty to his family name. He controls himself in the aria, "Urna fatale del mio destino." He cannot break his vow, but the temptation is too strong. He wants Alvaro to live so that he can have the pleasure of killing him. When the surgeon announces that Alvaro will live, Carlos erupts into a *cabaletta* exulting in his good fortune at being able to avenge his father at long last.

Rivas's Act 4 treats the mounting tension between Carlos and Alvaro. Carlos maliciously and with pointed irony tells Alvaro that he is pleased that he is recovering from his wounds. He insistently asks Alvaro about his ability to fight, which leaves the wounded man confused. Carlos seditiously asks, "¿Habéis recibido carta / de don Alvaro el indiano?" (Rivas, 1422–1423) Alvaro is outraged that his "friend" violated an oath. Carlos informs him that the portrait of Leonor gave away his secret, and that he is Carlos de Vargas. Carlos demands a duel, but Alvaro tries to persuade him that he too is noble, that they are friends, that destiny killed the marquis, who with Leonor looks down from heaven. All is to no avail. Carlos announces that Leonor is not dead, but that he will continue his search until he finds her and kills her. Alvaro sees a glimmer of hope that love is not lost. But his hope is in vain; Destiny has other plans for him. The two must duel to the death; the murder of the marquis deserves no less. Alvaro gives in and the two rush off to fight. Alvaro kills Carlos, is imprisoned for having violated the law against dueling, and will be executed. Yet again Destiny intercedes and frees him from death when the Austrians attack the Spanish camp. Alvaro rushes off promising God to "renunciar al mundo / y de acabar mi vida en un desierto" (1870–1871).

Verdi's original and revised versions follow the play up to the point of the duel. He has a patrol enter just in time to break up the fight and take Carlos away. Alvaro vows to God to enter a cloister and find peace at last. Verdi concludes the act with a scene drawn from Schiller's *Wallensteins Lager* in which he adds comic relief in Fra Melitone's sermon and patriotic fervor in the stirring "Rataplan" chorus (Conrad, 8).

Rivas did not allow Alvaro to find peace in the monastery. He is constantly assailed by a past he cannot escape. Alfonso, Leonor's other brother whom Verdi eliminates and coalesces into Carlos, arrives and taunts him yet again. Alvaro is at last unable to resist the world and duels with his adversary, whom he fatally wounds. Alvaro calls for the nearby hermit to hear the confession of a dying man. When the hermit appears, it is none other than Leonor. Alvaro is finally united with her, but only briefly. Alfonso lives long enough to kill her, thus attaining his desired vengeance. In a final rejection of a world that is senseless without love and without the hand of Providence, Alvaro leaps to his death. This was also Verdi's finale in 1862, but in 1869 he and Ghislanzoni changed things drastically. Alvaro, redeemed by the intervention of Leonor with God, seems to accept the advice of Padre Guardiano to a life of prayer and penitence. At long last Alvaro is at peace in his world. In Verdi, the force of Destiny at last has been mitigated by Providence.

BIBLIOGRAPHY

Brener, Milton. *Opera Offstage: Passion and Politics behind the Great Operas*. New York: Walker, 1996.

Brown, Bruce A. "That Damned Ending." In *The Force of Destiny/La Forza del Destino*. Opera Guide 23. London: John Calder; New York: Riverrun Press, 1983.

Budden, Julian. "*La Forza del Destino*." In *The Operas of Verdi*. New York: Oxford University Press, 1979.

Cardwell, Richard. "*Don Alvaro* or the Force of Cosmic Injustice." *Studies in Romanticism* 12 (1973): 559–579.

Conrad, Peter. "War and Peace." In Giuseppe Verdi, *The Force of Destiny/La Forza del Destino*. Opera Guide 23. London: John Calder; New York: Riverrun Press, 1983.

Godefroy, Vincent. "Alvaro and the Vargas." In *The Dramatic Genius of Verdi: Studies of Selected Operas*. New York: St. Martin's Press, 1977.

Rivas, Duque de. *Don Alvaro o La fuerza del sino*. Edited by Donald Shaw. Madrid: Castalia, 1986.

Verdi, Giuseppe. *The Force of Destiny/La Forza del Destino*. Opera Guide 23. London: John Calder; New York: Riverrun Press, 1983.

Weaver, William. "Aspects of Verdi's Dramaturgy." In *The Verdi Companion*, eds. William Weaver and Martin Chusid. New York: W. W. Norton, 1979.

22

García Gutiérrez's Bequest to Verdi: Il Trovatore *and* Simon Boccanegra

John Louis DiGaetani

When one thinks of Spain and opera, Bizet's *Carmen* immediately comes to mind. But *Carmen* is an opera in French by a French composer based on a French short story by Merimée, despite its lush ambience in the setting of Seville. One would also be tempted to suggest Rossini's *The Barber of Seville*, but this is by an Italian composer, uses a libretto by Sterbini, and is based on a play by the French playwright Beaumarchais. *The Marriage of Figaro* takes place in Spain as well, but it is by Mozart, with a libretto by Lorenzo Da Ponte, and derives from *Figaro*, a trilogy of French plays all by the same Beaumarchais. Beethoven's *Fidelio* employs a Spanish locale, although the text by the German Josef Sonnleithner is taken from a French literary source, Bouilly's *Leonore, ou L'Amour Conjugal*. Jules Massenet's *Cherubin* revives the commedia dell'arte character Cherubino, but places the action in Spain. Finally, Richard Wagner, who was extraordinarily interested in Lope de Vega and in Spanish legends of the Holy Grail, set his last opera, *Parsifal*, in Monsalvat, Spain.

Certain premier composers indeed did turn to Spanish literature for their operatic flights: Mozart in his *Don Giovanni*, Massenet in his *Don Quichotte*, Pedrell in his *Celestina*, Ginastera in his *Don Rodrigo*, and others. But it was Verdi who showed the greatest interest in Spanish drama and who used works from the Spanish romantic theater for at least three of his most popular operas. Verdi's *Il Trovatore* is based on the Spanish play, *El Trovador*, by Antonio García Gutiérrez (who incidentally was born in the same year as both Verdi and Wagner, 1813, and lived until 1884). His *Simon Boccanegra* comes from a play by the same name, again authored by García Gutiérrez. *La Forza del Destino*, arguably one of the finest of Verdi's middle operas, adapts the Spanish *Don Alvaro, o La fuerza del sino*, of Angel de Saavedra, Duke of Rivas. He worked extensively on yet another play by García Gutiérrez, *El tesorero del Rey Don Pedro*, but eventually had to abandon the project. And he brought to fruition his *Don Carlo*, which derives from a variety of sources, both Spanish and German, but deals with a moment of Spanish history.

Let us look first at *Il Trovatore*. The year was 1851, and at the age of thirty-eight, Verdi was savoring the triumph of his *Rigoletto*. His creative energies were at their peak, despite the difficulties he was undergoing in his personal life. His mother had just died, he was embroiled in a lawsuit against his father, and he was living scandalously "in sin" with his common-law wife. Having composed two operas per year, he now proposed a new piece for the following fall: an opera based on García Gutiérrez's *El trovador*, for which he had begun to negotiate from Venice in January of the previous year with his librettist Salvatore Cammarano. Apparently he did not include the Spanish author in these negotiations, for he neither contacted him nor paid him a fee. As late as 1861, García Gutiérrez would have to sue Verdi for royalties on both this opera and *Simon Boccanegra*.

El trovador, an unfettered melodrama of love and vengeance, had been produced in Madrid in August 1836 with extraordinary success. How Verdi actually got hold of the Spanish play is still a mystery. No Italian translation has ever been discovered. We do know, however, that Verdi was interested in the theater and would attend wherever and whenever possible. Also, Madrid was on the international operatic circuit and it was not uncommon for singers who were friends of the composer to send him plays and libretti from foreign parts. It seems that Verdi was immediately attracted to *El trovador*, with its tragic, ironic twists, and that he had it translated for him by Giuseppina Strepponi, his common-law wife (Budden, 59). Personally involved with the Spanish text, he offered his new project to his impresario in Bologna, insisting that the libretto "be my responsibility, and I hope, by Cammarano" (59).

Briefly, this is the argument of the play: As the servants of Don Nuño, the Count de Luna, recount a tale of many years past—of a gypsy who was burned at the stake for having bewitched the Count's older brother, of the child's disappearance, and the discovery of an infant's ashes—we learn that the noble lady Jimena, who is being ardently pursued by the Count, is in fact desperately in love with the mysterious and valiant "troubadour" Manrique. Civil war is raging, and Manrique is also Luna's prime political enemy. Hearing that Manrique has been killed in battle, Leonor decides to enter a convent rather than marry a man she despises. But Manrique appears and the lovers flee together. Meanwhile, we have discovered that Manrique was raised since infancy by the gypsy Azucena, who reveals to him that some twenty years before, in revenge for her mother's death, she stole the old Count's son, intending to throw the child into the flames. Somehow, in the madness of the moment, she threw her own son into the fire instead. Retracting her story, she now says that indeed she did murder the son of the Count and that Manrique is really hers. Ultimately, Azucena is captured and sentenced to death by the Count's men, Manrique is captured while trying to rescue her, and Leonor agrees to marry the Count if only he will free her lover. But she makes a nefarious bargain. Instead of marrying the Count, she plans to take her own life. The Count discovers the plot, but too late. Leonor dies, and as the executioner's ax falls on Manrique, Azucena, with her last breath, tells the horrified Count that he has killed his long-lost brother. Only in the high noon of the romantic era could such a premise have been tolerated. But indeed it was, not only for much of nineteenth-century Spain but for Giuseppi Verdi and his many disciples.

Cammarano and Verdi altered the source considerably, using the revenge theme more significantly than in the original. For some reason they made Manrico the younger rather than the older brother, thereby diluting the subplot of Nuño's lifelong search for his older brother, the rightful heir of their estates. They also developed the main characters more fully, gave them longer monologues to suit the opera's aria structure, eliminated certain minor characters, and made the libretto a more unified and simplified plot. But the more serious themes of the play deeply fascinated Verdi and these remained in the opera. Verdi's story centers more around the two women—Leonora and Azucena, who is actually its prime mover—and eliminates the issue of class distinction, which looms significantly in the rivalry of the two political opponents, Manrico and Don Nuño.

Verdi completed *Il Trovatore*, and its premiere in Rome on January 19, 1853, was very successful. Staged in New York two years later, it again was an instant success, despite attacks on its libretto for its obscurity and its complex narrations. Meanwhile, Gutierrez's play, with the same complexities, continued to be well received by nineteenth-century Spanish audiences. On the other hand, it is interesting that in Spain a group of comic parodies of these "revenge" dramas were written and became popular themselves. In fact, García Gutiérrez himself published a parody of *El trovador*, which he called *Los hijos del tío Tronera* [Uncle Tronera's Children] (Gies, 285). A century later the Marx brothers would make their own spoof in *A Night at the Opera*. Complexities notwithstanding, Verdi was not to be daunted. He still responded to melodramas of dire revenge, and so did much of his audience.

Verdi's *Simon Boccanegra*, which premiered in 1857, is based on another play by Antonio García Gutiérrez, this one written in 1842. *Simón Bocanegra* is the fictionalized history of a fourteenth-century Genoese corsair, his rise to power, and his death at the hands of a former friend and ally. Since the Spanish drama was never published in Italian, we may assume once again that Giuseppina Strepponi made the translation. But what led Verdi to another play by the same author? Perhaps it was the hope of repeating the success of *Il Trovatore*. Like its predecessor, *Simon Boccanegra* encompasses a huge time span; much of the action takes place against the background of a civil war—in this case a Guelph rebellion—and the plot revolves about a long-lost child. Possibly it was because he himself had such affection for the Genoese setting, where he often spent his vacations.

But what had led the Spaniard to embark on such a theme? William Mann explains that Gutiérrez wrote the play after serving as Spanish consul in Genoa and learning something about its history. For dramatic purposes, he merged into one personage two Boccanegra brothers who lived in the fourteenth century. One was Egidio, a seafaring man reputed to be something of a buccaneer and to have rid Italy's sea lanes of African pirates. The other was Simon, who was first elected doge by the Genoese in 1339 and then again in 1356 after a period of voluntary retirement. History recalls him as a ruler of great clemency who strove to keep the peace, even among the feuding Guelphs and Ghibellines. A man of the people, Simon was opposed by the arrogant patricians, and actually died from a dose of poisoned wine given him by one of them during a banquet in 1363. (In Verdi's opera he is done in by a fellow plebeian.)

The theme of the lost child recurs in both operas, and according to Mary Jane Phillips-Matz also occurred in Verdi's life (though this remains a controversial theory). The original librettist, Piave, altered the Spanish original to emphasize even more the Italian setting. Piave also provided more monologues for the main characters and eliminated certain secondary characters. As in *Il Trovatore*, the opera combined Gutiérrez's acts 3 and 4 into only one act.

If *Il Trovatore* has been criticized for its intricate plot and confused identities, in *Simon Boccanegra* the confusion is compounded. Two characters appear, each with two different names. Maria Boccanegra, Simon's daughter, passes as Amelia Grimaldo (her mother's surname) so that the estate of the exiled Grimaldo family might not be lost. Then Maria's grandfather, Jacopo Fiesco, changes his name after the Prologue to Andrea and continues under that name until the end (Mann, 25). For that reason, among others, *Simon Boccanegra* failed at its premiere on March 12, 1857. Despite this setback, Verdi did not forget the opera nor lose faith in it. He asked Arrigo Boito to revise the text and

simplify the plot, which the new librettist attempted with little success. Julian Budden, who has written at length about Boito's revision
of the opera, comments,

It was not until they came to work on the last act that librettist and composer
began to realize that with the altered incidents of the new finale to Act I they
had created difficulties for themselves. The plan of the original Act III was a
digest of Gutiérrez's Act IV: victory chorus in honor of the Doge, announce-
ment by Boccanegra of rewards to the victors and the marriage of Gabriele
and Amelia; exchange of Paolo and Pietro about the poisoning of the Doge;
wedding chorus; final dialogue between Fiesco and Paolo, who has admitted
the old man by the same secret door into the ducal palace so that he and his
men can turn the tables on the victors. But Fiesco's men have deserted him
and Paolo also flees. Duet Fiesco/Boccanegra and reconciliation: death of Doge.
All this would need to be modified. (2, 262–263)

Verdi and Boito modified accordingly, greatly altering and attempting to simplify Gutierrez's plot. Boito expanded several of the scenes,
again eliminated a number of minor characters, reemphasized the
theme of revenge, and reduced the secondary action. Most critics argue that the argument of the revised version is as complicated as the
earlier one, but many of Boito's changes did try to clarify both character and storyline. Certainly his revision added some strong drama to
the opera, especially in the famous Council Scene, but the problem
was never fully resolved. Nevertheless, the revised version of the opera premiered at La Scala in Milan on March 24, 1881, and from then it
succeeded admirably, though it did not reach New York until the Metropolitan Opera's production on January 28, 1932.

The many popular objections to the first version of Verdi's opera
seem strange to modern readers. Both versions of the opera have been
staged in modern times—most recently the first version at London's
Royal Opera at Covent Garden during the summer of 1997—and both
have succeeded with modern audiences. In fact, some critics and conductors prefer the Piave libretto to the revised Boito version. Many
contemporary critics have objected to the general gloom of the plot,
but this also appears in Gutiérrez's play and in many other Italian
melodramas of the nineteenth century.

It is unfortunate that no Spanish composer has entered the standard
repertory of opera, but Spain has certainly given opera some of its
greatest singers. In our own time, to name the most obvious, we have
had Placido Domingo, Jose Carreras, Monserrat Caballé, Teresa
Berganza, Victoria de Los Angeles, Alfredo Kraus, Juan Pons, and
Francesco Araiza. Earlier in the twentieth century great Spanish singers included Maria Gay and Julian Gayarre. Manuel Garcia—a great
tenor and a minor composer— was also famous for his method of teach-

ing the bel canto style of singing. His three children—Maria Malibran, Pauline Viardot, and Manuel Garcia II—all had very successful operatic careers in the nineteenth century.

Spain, Spanish culture, and Spanish literature have clearly all been major influences on opera. Both Madrid and Barcelona had important opera companies by the nineteenth century, and the Spanish colonies in the New World soon had opera companies of their own. In fact, Madrid's own beautiful opera house was newly restored and reopened in 1997. For centuries Spanish culture has been a breeding ground for opera composers and opera singers. Giuseppe Verdi's fascination with the plays of Garcia Gutiérrez remains a special example of the Spanish influence on Italian operatic culture.

BIBLIOGRAPHY

Budden, Julian. *The Operas of Verdi*. Oxford: Clarendon Press, 1992.

DiGaetani, John Louis. *An Invitation to the Opera*. New York: Anchor/ Doubleday, 1991.

Freedley, George, and Reeves, John. *A History of the Theatre*. New York: Crown Press, 1968.

Gies, David Thatcher. *The Theatre in Nineteenth-Century Spain*. Cambridge: Cambridge University Press, 1994.

Mann, William. "Verdi on Politics and Parenthood." In brochure and libretto with *Simon Boccanegra* recording, conducted by Claudio Abbado. Deutsche Grammophone Geschellschaft, 1977.

Phillips-Matz, Mary Jane. *Verdi: A Biography*. New York: Oxford University Press, 1993.

Warrack, John, and West, Ewan, eds. *The Oxford Dictionary of Opera*. Oxford: Oxford University Press, 1992.

23

The Fatal Triangle: Don Carlos, King Philip, and Elizabeth of Valois in Literature and Opera

John Dowling

The life and death of the sixteenth-century Spanish prince Don Carlos became a myth, thanks first to malicious propagandists and then to imaginative writers. As a result, serious historians have been hard pressed to separate fact from gossip, fiction, and unfounded allegation. In a general way, one may say that Spanish writers have stayed close to history and have emphasized politics. Foreign writers have given preference to malice and romance. It is my purpose to pay special attention to Spanish treatments of a story best known to us through the 1787 play by Friedrich von Schiller (1759–1805) and the 1867 opera by Giuseppe Verdi (1813–1901) and his librettists.

Don Carlos of Austria (1545–1568) was the first-born son of Prince Philip (1527–1598), heir of Charles I of Spain (Charles V of the Holy Roman Empire). Philip had married Maria of Portugal when he was sixteen. With the birth of the Infante Carlos, he became a father at the age of eighteen. Four days later, Maria died of childbirth fever, and Philip was left a widower. Carlos, though grandson of the Emperor Charles, was reared in Spain by men and women of the retinue of Prince Philip, heir apparent to a world empire.

Philip remained a discreet widower for nine years in the arms of his mistress, Isabel Osorio. Then, obedient to the *Realpolitik* of the emperor, he left his son behind in Spain for five years (1554–1559) and, at age twenty-seven, took as his second wife Mary Tudor, Queen of England, who was thirty-eight. The marriage ended, without issue, four years later when Mary died in 1558. Meanwhile, Charles V ceded to Philip sovereignty over The Netherlands and subsequently the crowns of Castile, Aragon, and Sicily. The emperor himself retired to the monastery at Yuste in Extremadura, and there he died just two months before Mary Tudor. As king, Philip II stayed a widower for two years. In 1560, again in obeisance to international politics, he took as his third wife Elizabeth of Valois, daughter of Henry II of France and Catherine de Medici. By then Philip was thirty-two; the bride was not quite fourteen, which was the age of her new stepson, Carlos. When the two were children, about six years old, there had been a plan for them to marry, but, like many such plans among European monarchies, it had been abandoned.

The father–son relationship has had enduring appeal as a dramatic subject. With the presence of a third person, especially a woman, events assume ominous tones. Such were the mythical stories of Oedipus, son; Laius, father; and Iocasta, mother; and of Hippolytus, son; Theseus, father; and Phaedra, stepmother. Euripedes gave top billing to the son in *Hippolytus* (428 B.C.); Seneca to the stepmother in *Phaedra* (ca. A.D. 50). In modern times, Racine took up the theme in *Phèdre* (1677). In our own century, Eugene O'Neill, in *Desire under the Elms* (1924), presented the absorbing drama of Eben, son; Ephraim, father; and Abie, stepmother. Attesting to the relevance of the theme is the catharsis that audiences have experienced in these versions.

Schiller, when he created his play, knew the 1672 historical novel *Dom Carlos* by César Vichard, Abbé de Saint-Réal (1643–1692), who, more than a century after the death of the stepson and the young stepmother, imagined a love relationship between the two. Historians have not been able to document a love affair. Rather, the conflict between father and son that historians can affirm was one of empowerment, possibly treason. That is what we find in Spanish versions of the Don Carlos story prior to the diffusion of the Saint-Réal novel. Beginning with the abbé's novel, politics was enhanced with a forbidden romance until the love story became ascendant.

Although Carlos grew up without a mother and with an absent father, both Philip and grandfather Charles took a long-distance interest in his health and education. For a while he lived at Alcalá de Henares, a short distance from Madrid and seat of the Renaissance university founded under the auspices of his great grandparents Ferdinand and Isabel. His closest companions were his uncle Don Juan de Austria (1547–1578), the bastard son of his grandfather the emperor; and his cousin Alessandro Farnese (1545–1592), heir to the dukedom of Parma. Don Juan was two years younger than his nephew Carlos, and the prince and his cousin Alessandro were the same age. Both Juan and Alessandro later fought at Lepanto (1571) and lived on to distinguish themselves on the field of battle, Don Juan quelling the Moorish rebellion in Spain, Farnese fighting Protestant forces in The Netherlands.

Carlos was slight of build; nor did he have a thirst for learning. Observers of the time have left an unflattering picture of him. In portraits of the teenager by Sánchez Coello, his eyes are langourous and weary. Notable is the fashionably erect codpiece of his short, flared breeches (Bernis, 70). Eyes and *bragueta* lend credence to stories of his womanizing on nocturnal excursions through city streets.

Serious historians and biographers of Carlos, Philip, and Elizabeth discount a romantic relationship between stepson and stepmother. However, the conflict between father and son was real. In the son's teenage years, ambassadors from Paris, Venice, and Vienna sent stories home of his erratic behavior.[1] An event that occurred in 1562, when he was sixteen, was a turning point. On his way to a night assignation with a girl, he fell down a spiral staircase and injured his head. Treatment of the day included trepanning, and the injury exacerbated behavioral problems already determined by the royal genes (Cotarelo, 523–524).[2]

Luis Cabrera de Córdoba (1559–1623), a reliable historian who served Philip II in the years after the death of Don Carlos and then wrote the king's biography (1619), relates incidents that he had heard spoken of. On a night prowl through Madrid streets, Carlos was under a balcony when someone emptied water into the street and got the prince wet (469–470). He ordered the house burned and the inhabitants killed. (His guardsmen spared the house and covered up by feigning that, when they arrived, the Holy Sacrament was being brought to a person who was dying inside.) On another occasion a member of the prince's retinue failed to respond promptly when the prince rang for him. Carlos seized the man and tried to throw him out a palace window (470). Carlos was displeased with the boots that a cobbler delivered to him. He ordered the man to cut them into small pieces, cook them, and eat them (Cabrera, 470; Brantôme, 105–106; Gachard, 1, 163). Carlos wanted the actor Alonso Cisneros to perform for him. When Cardinal Diego de Espinosa, the Grand Inquisitor, more than forty years Carlos's senior, forbade the show, the angry prince seized the prelate by the collar and threatened, "You scurvy little priest, how dare you forbid Cisneros from serving me? I swear by my father's life I'll kill you!" (Cabrera, 470). These incidents or references to them figure in the Spanish plays.

When Carlos became eighteen and then twenty, he was impatient to marry and to have a place in government. The logical step in his education would have been to place him under the tutelage of experienced administrators and in charge of one of the empire's many provinces so that he might learn to govern. In fact, Philip thought seriously of sending him to the Low Countries where he himself had been, but the youth's irrational behavior caused the father to hesitate. Furthermore, Protestantism was making inroads into those northern provinces, and the king and his ministers were themselves in a quandary about how to deal with rebellious subjects.

At the end of 1567 Philip had reason to believe that Carlos was conspiring in Madrid with representatives from Holland and Flanders, among them the marquis of Berghes (d. 1567) and Florence de Montmorency, seigneur de Montigny (d. 1571) (*Diogènes* 1865, 31, n. 1). The king moved decisively. Late on the night of January 18, 1568, he and his advisers presented themselves in the prince's quarters, and there they confined him for the next several months. Even under arrest, Carlos continued his habitual abuse of his health. He suffered from intermittent fevers and sought relief drinking ice water, bathing in it, putting ice in his bed, and going naked. The ordeal for son and for father ended with the death of the prince on July 24. The letters that Philip sent to the courts of Europe were equivocal; they raised doubts rather than allaying them.

Less than three months later, on October 3, 1568, Elizabeth of Valois died in childbirth. The scandalmongers set to work. Their efforts became especially effective some twelve years after the two deaths, as Protestant propaganda in The Netherlands spread the "black legend" of Philip II. In June 1580 Philip issued his ban against William of Orange, and the next year William answered with his *Apologie,* in which he charged Philip with murdering his wife and son (43–46, 150–169). That same year the embittered Protestant author of a poem, *Diogènes,* who searched for a good Catholic and did not find one, repeated William's accusation and boldly added that the relationship of Don Carlos and Elizabeth was not "chaste et honneste" (32).[3] Philip's detention of the Princess of Éboli in her palace at Pastrana (Muro, 188–207) and the arrest and eventual flight abroad of his secretary Antonio Pérez (Marañón 1954, passim) fueled the creation of the "black legend" around the figure of the monarch.

In Spain, Cabrera de Córdoba's biography of Philip II appeared in 1619, two decades after the monarch's death, half a century after the death of Carlos and Elizabeth. It was followed in 1625 by Lorenzo Vander Hammen's *Don Filipe el prudente, segundo de este nombre.* The Spanish theater was at its height, and in the next few years at least three writers brought the story of Don Carlos to the stage.

The best of the three plays was *El príncipe Don Carlos* by Diego Jiménez de Enciso (1585–1634), a younger contemporary of Lope de Vega. His *comedia*, printed in 1631, had likely been performed by 1628, more than sixty years after the events on which it is based, thirty years after the death of Philip II, and nine years after the publication of

Cabrera's biography of the king.[4] Two critics of our time, Wilson and Moir, assert that Enciso's play "is for dignity and refinement of characterisation better than Schiller's *Don Carlos* and only surpassed by Verdi's opera" (78).

Displaying true dramatic instinct, Enciso opens *El príncipe don Carlos* with a royal reception (*besamanos*) attended by leading figures of the court, the main characters of the *comedia*, among them King Philip II, the Duke of Alba, the Grand Inquisitor Cardinal Espinosa, Ruy Gómez de Silva, Prince of Éboli, and Don Diego de Córdoba, the king's equerry. They have come to kiss the king's hand. Missing is Don Carlos. Alba goes in search of the prince, who was on the point of leaving for the university town of Alcalá de Henares. In a private audience with his son, Philip delivers a *relación*, a long speech that can be a triumphal feat when recited by a skilled actor. Both expository and accusatory, it in turn evokes a defensive *relación* from Carlos. Their positions reveal the conflict between parent and teenager: The prince wishes to marry and be entrusted with governance; the father distrusts his son's abilities to govern.

While Enciso rearranges historical events, episodes in the play may be dated mostly in the period from 1560 to 1562, when Carlos was between fifteen and seventeen. His father had just married Elizabeth, but in the play Elizabeth does not have a speaking part. Ruy Gómez de Silva, counselor for Carlos during the absence of his father, and recently created Prince of Éboli by the king, enjoyed ascendancy among the king's counselors (Boyden, 63–66). The Duke of Alba, having returned from successful diplomatic missions in Italy and France, was destined to go to the Netherlands and hence was a potential rival of Carlos (Maltby, 121).

In the *comedia*, Enciso exploits these latent political conflicts. The prince's interaction with each of the characters emphasizes his capricious conduct. The responses of King Philip to his son's deeds accentuate his paternal and political concerns. The secondary characters, such as the equerry Don Diego de Córdoba or the comic Tejoletas, enhance the dramatic quality of the characterization. The role of the Flemish delegate Montení, who conspires with Carlos, serves to produce a shocking climax in the third act when the curtain on the inner stage is suddenly drawn to reveal him murdered.

The love interest revolves around two cousins, Violante and Fadrique, niece and nephew of Alba, who suffer Carlos's brutish behavior. Early in the play even the duke is obliged to come to Violante's rescue. The prince precipitates the final crisis when he finds Fadrique in Violante's apartment and pursues him with his sword onto the balcony. It collapses under their weight, and Carlos is mortally injured. In the dénouement, Philip cries in anguish, "God knows, the more I loved him the more I chastened him" ("sabe Dios que le amaba / más, cuanto más le reñía" [ed. Hurtado and González Palencia, 155]). In his anguish, the king appeals to the Blessed Diego de Ávila to save the prince, and, in accord with the spirit of Counter-Reformation Spain, Carlos recovers to witness a superb baroque emblem staged by the actors in which the prince sees a vision of the future succession: Beneath a revolving tree stands Philip II, a torch in one hand, the other holding his queen's hand (the only appearance of Elisabeth); above him, Philip III hand in hand with Queen Margaret; and farther above, Philip IV and his queen. Carlos himself does not figure in the chain, but for the present he survives. Philip blesses the marriage of Violante and Fadrique and promises that he will ask the Pope to canonize Diego de Ávila. The courtiers of 1562 end the play with a shout of "Viva Carlos."[5]

Within a five-year period, 1627 to 1632, Spanish audiences witnessed the father–son conflict in two other plays. Juan Pérez de Montalbán (1601?–1638) sympathetically portrayed Philip II in *El segundo Séneca de España*, which had as its subtitle *El príncipe don Carlos*.[6] Luis Vélez de Guevara (1579–1644) gave prominent roles to both father and son in *El águila del agua y batalla de Lepanto*, which featured Don Juan de Austria, their half-brother and uncle, respectively. The battle of 1571 occurred after Carlos's death, so that the prince appears only in the first two acts. The intent in all three plays is similar: to portray Philip as a strict but loving father, hard pressed to cope with the erratic behavior of his son while bearing the responsibility of monarchy. By exhibiting to a high degree the kingly virtue of prudence in affairs of state and in his personal life, he earns the epithet, Philip the Prudent. In this respect the stage reflects a theme prominent in contemporary books on the art of government.

In the plays by Montalbán and Guevara, Elizabeth of Valois does not appear at all. As in Enciso's play, the love interest is borne by secondary characters. In the next century, when José de Cañizares (1676–1750) rewrote Enciso's play for another generation of playgoers around 1720, he cut out even the brief appearance that Elizabeth had made in the tableau near the end of the original.

Indeed, the French princess, who earned the affection of her Spanish subjects in her brief reign as Queen of Spain, is not featured in Spanish literature until the 1805 dialogue poem of Manuel José Quintana (1772–1857), *El panteón del Escorial*. By then, Saint-Réal's novel had begotten works by writers both great and obscure, among them Thomas Otway (*Don Carlos, Prince of Spain*, 1676), Marquis de Ximènes (*Don Carlos*, 1761), Francesco Beccatini (*Don Carlos, Principe di Spagna*, 1774), Pierre Lefèvre (*Elisabeth de France*, 1781), Vittorio Alfieri (*Filippo II*, 1783), Alessandro Pepoli (*La gelosia snaturata*, 1784), and the most influential of all, Friedrich Schiller (*Dom Karlos, Infant von Spanien*, 1787). Quintana, the nineteenth-century liberal, using the mausoleum of the Escorial as his setting, presents a tableau, much as Enciso had done, except that Quintana's is spoken. In the 304-verse poem, royal figures, from Philip II to Carlos II, emerge from their tombs to reflect on how the Hapsburg royal line went wrong. Philip II is not the caring father struggling with an errant son; he is, as the "black legend" painted him, the cruel husband and barbarous father, the religious fanatic bent on stamping out heresy; he is not the prudent king but the tyrant who resorts to poison to save the state.

In the eighty years between the publication of Schiller's *Dom Karlos* at Leipzig in 1787 and the première of Verdi's *Don Carlos* in Paris in 1867 more than fifty versions of the story appeared in print or on stage in German, Dutch, English, French, Italian, Portuguese, and Spanish. Most were dramas, including several operas.

In the nineteenth century, scholarly historians were at work. Their research confirmed the presence on the scene of Cardinal Espinosa, who was indeed the Grand Inquisitor; the visits to Madrid of Flemish emissaries; and the intervention of the temperamental Princess of Éboli, whose eyepatch lent mystery to her character. They could not confirm a love affair between Carlos and Elizabeth. Louis Prosper Gachard, a Belgian sympathetic to the cause of the Spanish Netherlands, wrote in detail of the father–son conflict in his 1863 biography of Don Carlos. Antoine Théodore Marquis du Prat, in his 1859 life of Elizabeth de Valois, found the queen without blemish, and his scholarship is confirmed in our time by González de Amezúa's three-volume biography of a queen who died at the age of twenty-three.

By the 1860s, however, when Verdi's two librettists, Joseph Méry and Camille du Locle, prepared the text for the opera, they went not to the historians but to the creative writers, and, of course to Schiller in first place. The result was "Verdi's finest opera," in the words of Sir Denis Forman, who sets aside banter to give his serious judgment: "We can believe in the ruthless King, the terrifying Grand Inquisitor, the tormented Carlos," in Eboli "the liberated woman," and in Elizabeth and her "tremendously inconvenient passion for Carlos" (149). We are in accord with his summary: "*Carlos* is the grandest of grand operas and an alpha-plus through and through" (150).

In the period between Schiller and Verdi, the Spanish contribution is slight. Aside from Quintana, there is only José Lorenzo Figueroa's *Isabel de la Paz* (1839). However, five years after the Verdi première, in 1872, the poet Gaspar Núñez de Arce (1832–1903) presented *El haz de leña*. The reference is to a bundle of wood that could be used to burn a heretic. It has been called the finest historical play of the century, and, like the Golden Age *comedias*, it adheres to facts provided by the historians Cabrera and Vander Hammen. A stern Philip II is torn between his paternal instincts and his duty to church and monarchy. His statement, which comes from Montalbán's play, is believable: "If my son were a heretic, I myself would bring the wood to burn him."[7] Carlos is presented with failings that justify his father's reservations. Elizabeth does not appear at all, and there is no love affair between her and Carlos. But there is a love interest, and Arce's achievement is the creation of the character Catalina, a woman of the people, who loves and understands a young prince who grew up without a mother's love (Gies, 259–261). This resolution sets *El haz de leña* apart from all other treatments of the myth. With grace and intuition, Arce avoids the fatal triangle of misbegotten love that Saint-Réal had imagined, that Schiller turned to such good account, and that Verdi's music has fixed forever in our imagination.

NOTES

1. Among such "investigative reporters," the Seigneur de Brantôme (1535?–1614) was in Madrid in 1564 (Levi 1913, 855) when Don Carlos was nineteen. He left a repertoire of tales, one of which was the story of the cobbler that is found in Cabrera.

2. Some historians, among them Gachard (1803, 1, 72–77), place the event in the Royal Seat of El Pardo; others say it happened at the archbishop's palace in Alcalá de Henares.

3. An echo of previous denials of this early charge is to be found in Verdi's *Don Carlos*, when the prince declares in the first scene of Act I, "Dieu bénit nos chastes amours!"

4. Williamsen (1973, 42–43) describes the earliest known text, which appeared, attributed to Lope de Vega (1631), in a collection of Lope de Vega plays: *Las comedias del Fénix de España Lope de Vega Crapio* [sic]. The volume appears to be a re-edition of a book that was originally published in Zaragoza. Subsequent editions were Huesca, 1634 (attributed to Enciso), described by Profeti (1988, 75–76); Madrid, 1667 (erroneously attributed to Juan Pérez de Montalbán); and Madrid, 1925(?), (based on Huesca, 1634). The attributions to Lope and Pérez de Montalbán were discounted well before the 1914 study by Cotarelo y Mori; since then the authorship of Jiménez de Enciso has not been questioned.

5. An audience of around 1630 may have thought the "Viva" with which the play ends was intended for the baby, the Infante Baltasar Carlos, who was born October 17, 1629, son of Philip IV and Isabel (Elizabeth) de Borbón (de Francia), who were being portrayed in the tableau that the public was witnessing.

6. In placing Montalbán's *El segundo Séneca de España* within the period 1627 to 1632, I have relied on the studies of Bacon (1910), Dixon (1961, 1964), and Parker (1952). For the variant spellings of Montalbán's name, see Parker (1975, 135, n. 1).

7. The words appear at the beginning of Act 1 in the Montalbán text (1942): "si mi hijo / hereje fuera, yo fuera / quien la leña le pusiera" (511). Núñez de Arce (1882) has his character Carlos quote Philip as follows: "Si como vos mi

hijo fuera, / . . . no dudaría: el haz de leña echaría, / para quemarle, a la hoguera" (Act 2, Scene 8, p. 339). Historians attest that on Philip's return to Spain in 1559, from England via The Netherlands, the thirty-two-year-old king attended an auto de fe at Valladolid in the company of his fourteen-year-old son. At that time an exchange of words occurred with the condemned heretic Don Carlos de Seso (or Sese), an Italian nobleman who had married Doña Isabel de Castilla, of royal descent. Having embraced the Protestant faith, Seso proselytized in the Valladolid area and was denounced and condemned. At the auto de fe, according to Cabrera, Seso encountered the king on his way to the stake and asked him, "cómo le dejaba quemar"; Philip replied, "Yo traeré leña para quemar a mi hijo si fuere tan malo como vos" (Book 5, ch. 3, p. 236). Colmenares (1637) cites almost the same words (2, 259; Cap. XLII, Sec. 3]).

BIBLIOGRAPHY

Bacon, George. "La comedia *El segundo Séneca de España* del Dr. Juan Pérez de Montalbán." *Romanic Review* 1 (1910): 64–86.

Bernis, Carmen. "La moda en la España de Felipe II a través del retrato de Corte." In *Alonso Sánchez Coello y el retrato en la Corte de Felipe II*, ed. Alfonso E. Pérez Sánchez. Madrid: Museo del Prado, 1990.

Boyden, James M. *The Courtier and the King: Ruy Gómez de Silva, Philip II, and the Court of Spain*. Berkeley and Los Angeles: University of California Press, 1995.

Brantôme, Pierre de Bourdeille, seigneur de. *Vies des grands capitaines estrangers. Oeuvres complètes*. Edited by Ludovic Lalanne. Vol. 2. Paris: Ve Jules Renouard, 1866.

Cabrera de Córdoba, Luis. *Filipe Segundo, Rey de España*. Madrid: Luis Sánchez, 1619.

Cañizares, José de. *Refuncación de la Comedia famosa: El príncipe don Carlos de Don Diego Ximénez de Enciso*. Valencia: José y Tomás de Orga, 1773.

Colmenares, Diego de. *Historia de la insigne ciudad de Segovia y compendio de las historias de Castilla*. 3 vols. 1637. Segovia: Academia de Historia y Arte de San Quirce, 1969–1974.

Cotarelo y Mori, Emilio. "Don Diego Jiménez de Enciso y su teatro." *Boletín de la Real Academia Española* 1 (1914): 209–248, 385–415, 510–550.

Diogènes, ou du moïen d'establir, après tant de misères et de calamitez, une bonne et asseurée paix en France, et la rendre plus florissante qu'elle ne fust jamais. Liège, 1581. In *Recueil de poésies françoises des XVe et XVIe siècles: morales, facétieuses, historiques*. Edited by Anatole de Montaiglon. Bibliothèque Elzevirienne, vol. 9. Paris: A. Franck, 1865.

Dixon, Victor. "Juan Pérez de Montalbán's *Para todos*." *Hispanic Review* 32 (1964): 36–59.

———. "Juan Pérez de Montalbán's *Segundo tomo de las comedias*." *Hispanic Review* 29 (1961): 91–109.

Du Prat, Antoine Théodore, Marquis. *Histoire d'Elisabeth de Valois, Reine d'Espagne (1545–1568)*. Paris: Tehener, 1859.

Figueroa, José Lorenzo. *Isabel de la Paz. Drama en cinco actos y en verso*. Sevilla: Mariano Caro, 1839.

Forman, Denis. *A Night at the Opera*. New York: Random House, 1994.

Gachard, Louis Prosper. *Don Carlos et Philippe II*. 2 vols. Bruxelles: Devroye, 1863.

Gies, David Thatcher. *The Theatre in Nineteenth-Century Spain*. Cambridge: Cambridge University Press, 1994.

González de Amezúa y Mayo, Agustín. *Isabel de Valois, reina de España (1546–1568). Estudio biográfico*. 3 vols. Madrid: Gráficas Ultra, 1949.

Jiménez de Enciso, Diego. *El príncipe don Carlos*. [Comedia famosa de Lope de Vega Crapio [*sic*]]. In *Las comedias del Fénix de España Lope de Vega Crapio* [*sic*]. [Parte veynte y cinco. Corregidas y enmendadas en esta segunda impresión. Dirigidas al Doctor Ivan Pérez de Montalván, natural de Madrid.] 1631. Con licencia, en Barcelona, por Sebastián Cormellas. Fols. 92r–113v.

———. *El príncipe don Carlos*. [Comedia famosa de Don Diego Ximénez de Anciso [*sic*]]. In *Parte Veynte y ocho de comedias de varios autores*. Con licencia, en Huesca, por Pedro Blusón. 1634. Fols. 175r–196r.

———. *El príncipe don Carlos*. [Comedia famosa. Del Doctor Ivan Pérez de Montalván]. In *Parte Veinte y ocho de comedias nuevas de los mejores ingenios desta corte*. [Dedicada al señor D. Lvis de Gvzmán, Cavallero de la Orden de Santiago, Prior de Aroniz en el Reyno de Nauarra, secretario del Excelentissimo Señor Duque de Alva]. Año 1667. Con licencia, Madrid: Joseph Fernández de Buendía. Fols. 1r–43v.

———. *El príncipe don Carlos*. Edited by Juan Hurtado and Ángel González Palencia. Letras Españolas, 18. Madrid: Bruno del Amo, 1925.

Levi, Ezio. "La leggenda di Don Carlos nel teatro spagnuolo del seicento." *Rivista d'Italia* 16 (1913): 855–913.

Lieder, Frederick W. C. *The Don Carlos Theme*. Harvard Studies and Notes in Philology and Literature. Cambridge: Harvard University Press, 1930.

Lope de Vega. *Las comedias del Fénix de España Lope de Vega Crapio* [*sic*]. *Parte veynte y cinco. Corregidas y enmendadas en esta segunda impressión*. Barcelona: Sebastián Comellas, 1631, fols. 92r–113v.

Maltby, William S. *Alba: A Biography of Fernando Álvarez de Toledo, Third Duke of Alba, 1507–1582*. Berkeley and Los Angeles: University of California Press, 1983.

Marañón, Gregorio. *Antonio Pérez (el hombre, el drama, la época)*. 2d ed. 2 vols. Madrid: Espasa-Calpe, 1948.

———. *Antonio Pérez: Spanish Traitor*. Translated by Charles David Ley. London: Hollis and Carter, 1954.

Muro, Gaspar. *Vida de la Princesa de Éboli*. Madrid: Mariano Murillo, 1877.

Núñez de Arce, Gaspar. *El haz de leña. Drama en cinco actos y en verso. Autores dramáticos contemporáneos y joyas del teatro español del siglo XIX*. Edited by Pedro Novo y Colson. Vol. 2. Madrid: Fortanet, 1882.

Parker, Jack Horace. "The Chronology of the Plays of Juan Pérez de Montalván." *PMLA* 67 (1952): 186–210.

———. *Juan Pérez de Montalván*. Boston: Twayne, 1975.

Paulson, Michael G., and Alvarez-Detrell, Tamara. *Lepanto: Fact, Fiction and Fantasy, with a Critical Edition of Luis Vélez de Guevara's El águila del agua, a Play in Three Acts*. Lanham, N.Y.: University Press of America, 1986.

Pérez de Montalbán, Juan. *El segundo Séneca de España y el príncipe don Carlos.* *El teatro español. Historia y antología.* Edited by Federico Carlos Sainz de Robles. Vol. 4. Madrid: Aguilar, 1942.

Profeti, Maria Grazia. *La collezione "Diferentes autores."* In *Teatro del Siglo de Oro: Bibliografías y Catálogos*, vol. 6. Kassel: Reichenberger, 1988.

Quintana, Manuel José. *El panteón del Escorial.* 1805. *Obras completas.* Biblioteca de Autores Españoles, 19. Madrid: Atlas, 1946.

Sacks, Zenia. "Verdi and Spanish Romantic Drama." *Hispania* 27 (1944): 451–465.

Saint-Réal, César Vichard, abbé de. *Don Carlos: La Conjuration des espagnols contre la République de Venise.* Edited by Andrée Mansau. Genève: Droz, 1977.

Schiller, Johann Christoph Friedrich von. *Don Carlos, Infant von Spanien.* Edited by H. B. Garland. 1787. London: Harrap, 1949.

———. *Don Carlos, Infante of Spain.* Translated by Charles E. Passage. New York: Ungar, 1959.

Vander Hammen y León, Lorenzo. *Don Filipe el Prudente, segundo deste nombre, rey de las Españas y Nuevo mundo.* Madrid: Viuda de A. Martín, 1625.

Vélez de Guevara, Luis. *El águila del agua.* Edited by A. Paz y Meliá. *Revista de Archivos, Biblioteca y Museos*, Tercera época, año VIII, tomo 10 (enero–junio 1904): 180–200, 307–325; tomo 11 (julio–dic 1904): 50–67.

Verdi, Giuseppe. *Don Carlos.* Compact disc. Libretto by Joseph Méry and Camille de Locle, based on Friedrich von Schiller. Five acts in French. Edited by Ursula Günther and Andrew Porter. Chorus and orchestra, Teatro alla Scala, conducted by Claudio Abbado. Hamburg, Polydor International, 1985.

———. *Don Carlos.* Compact disc. Edited by Ursula Günther and Luciano Petazzoni. Five acts in French. Chorus, Théâtre du Châtelet, Orchestre de Paris, conducted by Antonio Pappano. Milano, Editions BMG Ricordi, 1996.

———. *Don Carlo.* Videocassette. Three acts in Italian. The Metropolitan Opera, conducted by James Levine, March 26, 1983. Bel Canto Paramount Home Video.

William, Prince of Orange. *The Apologie of Prince William of Orange against the Proclamation of the King of Spain.* Edited by H. Wansink. Leiden: Brill, 1969.

Williamsen, Vern G. "Lope de Vega: A 'Missing' *Parte* and Two 'Lost' *Comedias*." *Bulletin of the Comediantes* 25 (1973): 42–51.

———. *The Minor Dramatists of Seventeenth-Century Spain.* Boston: Twayne, 1982.

Wilson, Edward M., and Moir, Duncan. *A Literary History of Spain: The Golden Age Drama, 1492–1700.* London: Ernest Benn, 1971.

24

El sombrero de tres picos *and*
Its Projection in Opera and Ballet

Fernando Barroso

In the preface to his novel *El sombrero de tres picos*, Pedro Antonio de Alarcón points out two things: his story's origin and his reasons for writing it. He says that it was a common tale known to everyone. He heard it first at a farmhouse feast from the lips of a coarse shepherd called Repela, "one of those unlettered rustics by nature sly and comical who play such an important role in our national literature under the rubric of *pícaros* . . . , the kind who enlivened every local occasion, be it a wedding, baptism or solemn celebration of the masters, with his tricks and jokes and clowning, with the ballads that he sang and the stories he recounted" (73). In short, it was an old, bandied-about tale related by a shepherd half rogue and half minstrel, and told in "tragicomic, tantalizing and terribly epigrammatic tones" (74). The theme and the novel are pure entertainment, which is not the same as saying "meaningless" or "lacking in seriousness." Alarcón notes that years later he heard many different versions of that same adventure of the miller's wife and the Corregidor, always from the lips of village and country jokesters. And even though the theme was always identical, its form was perverted by "gross-tongued bumpkins" (75) who made the story vulgar and tasteless.

Alarcón's purpose in this novel is to reestablish the essence of a venerable tale whose character had been tarnished at the hands of the masses. But he goes beyond that. He also seeks to recreate a world long gone by, which he recalls with affection. A touch of nostalgia interspersed with humor permeates the novel, as has been remarked by all who have studied the work. Emiliano Diez Echarri and José María Roca Franqueza reiterate the general consensus that *El sombrero de tres picos* makes us think on the one hand of the eighteenth-century scenes of Goya and Ramón de la Cruz; on the other it continues the sound tradition of the Spanish realistic novel of the Golden Age. Alarcón reveals his feelings in a tongue-in-cheek adaptation of Don Quixote's speech about the Golden Age, in which he exalts in similar words the idyllic existence of those times past. Classical references abound and recur throughout the novel. The personality of tío Lucas is likened to "un don Francisco de Quevedo en bruto" and to "un Otelo de Murcia, con alpargatas y montera" (85). The scene in the vineyard is reminiscent of one in *Fuenteovejuna*, despite the difference in time frame and the absence of the old grandeur. The repeated thrashings accorded to the Corregidor by error and in the dark recall those received by Don Quixote. The majestic Corregidora, like the great ladies of old, determines to resolve the conflict much in the way that disputes were settled in the Middle Ages. And the constant confusion created by misunderstanding brings to mind the dynamics of the old farce. In all these ways, as well as in its graceful caricature, wit, and simple-faced humor, *El sombrero de tres picos* sustains and replenishes the Spanish literary tradition of the anecdote. Alarcón delights and entertains. With a refined yet popular elegance he lays before our eyes an album of old illustrations and makes them live with all the color of sunny Andalusia. His episodes are tinged with dialogues so masterfully construed that they seem to us witty, roguish, and full of charm, when in reality he has reserved the craftiness and grace for the narrative. So perfect is his union of dialogue and act that we are led as if by mirage to find the spoken words funny.

The descriptive part of the novel is neither precise nor detailed. The geographical setting is rural: a small episcopal city of the provinces. Alarcón carefully observes the people, their drive, their loves, and their melancholy, collecting the hues and colors that lie therein. And still, despite the realistic observation, a subjective projection enfolds this world and its characters, enveloping them as it were in a haze of suggestion evoked by fallible memories. He places his story somewhere between 1804 and 1808 in a Spain of continued isolation, one that ignored Europe as if "el Pirineo se hubiese convertido en otra muralla de China" (77). Alarcón himself is omnipresent, palpably directing all that his characters do, but delving only into the mind of Lucas. For the most part, the Corregidor, the mayor, the constable Garduña, the farmhand Toñuelo, perhaps even the Corregidor's wife, are contrived figures whose mental processes are very similar. More than real people, provincials both empowered and plebeian, they are essentially caricatures, and the ambience is roguish and merry despite its tinge of irony and tragicomedy. But the cheerful tone does not erase the poetic breath nor the larger motivation of the novel, for the merriment is overshadowed by the dark suffering of Lucas's doubts, which at one point seem to move toward murder, and the aura of pleasantness is sullied by the contemptible behavior of the Corregidor and his cohorts. Above all, the action, confined to a small episode in the life of a miller and his spouse, reaches far beyond the anecdote, displaying a portrait of corruption and abuse that can be halted only by the victim's astute reaction. While preserving for all time the fundaments of Andalusian tradition, it opens a window of popular intervention. Cruelty and abuse may exist, but there is a ray of hope in the integrity of tío Lucas and his wife, Frasquita, of the Corregidora and of the Bishop. Alarcón's blending of characters from different social classes creates a feeling of social homogeniety, even of democratic populism.

Many references have been made to this novel's symmetry and balance. Belic studies its structure and points out its scheme of classical comedy (159–185). The action takes place in a time frame not longer than twenty-four hours, and its events move chronologically, with only one exception (Chapters 20 to 22, where the narrative backtracks to explain how the Corregidor actually landed in Frasquita's bed, minus her presence, to be sure). Dynamism is one of its most notable characteristics, as is its density. Alarcón recounts episodes that are filled with secondary incidents. Still, their proliferation does not create an obstacle, for all elements of the work are so aptly proportioned that we can easily understand the characters and their circumstances. In a sense, this multiplicity of incidents related to the main episode serves as the primary content of the novel. The action, densely constructed, seamlessly linked, and devoid of superfluous scenes, is almost cinematographic in its development. The suspicion surrounding the Corregidor and his designs on the miller's wife is its nucleus, and the chapters that are not essential to the central anecdote either provide the antecedents of each character or their ultimate destiny. The storyline flows constantly, with but a single pause—when the miller gets to the mill and suspects his misfortune. Rather than a digression, this interruption gives the author the opportunity to penetrate the mind of his protagonist, revealing how Lucas actually thinks and what he proposes to do to avenge his dishonor. Here we are made party to his intimate agony, and he elicits our profound sympathy. At last, the argument leads to its happy denouement, and its course is completed.

As one can well imagine, the popularity of this tale gave rise to other versions in the nineteenth century, amply documented by Cook, Belic, and others. Even before Alarcón, a dramatic dialogue called *Una nueva farsa en un acto: El Corregidor y la Molinera* was published in Barcelona in 1855. Its theme reiterates the need for a representative of the king to safeguard the people from predatory public officers, as it repeats the tale of the innocent woman rescued from the menace of violation or forced adultery. Shortly thereafter came a *sainete* written in 1862, a song, and a *romance* that appeared in several versions in the *Romancero* of Durán. The story also became the source of two operas. One, *Der Trekantede Hat* by the Danish composer Frederic Rubn, was adapted by E. Christiansen and staged for the first time by the Royal Opera of Copenhagen in 1894. The other, a more recent Italian opera by Ricardo Zandonai, *La Farsa Amorosa*, was based on a text by A. Rossato and premiered in Rome in 1933. But the most significant operatic work on this theme is the German Hugo Wolf's *Der Corregidor*, which derives essentially from Alarcón's original. Here is how it came to be.

Hugo Wolf, looking for material for an opera, refused several serious subjects that were suggested to him, among them a script based on the life of Buddha. In his private correspondence he explains, "Do we always have to offer people sackcloth and ashes? Leave the salvation of the world for those who have a strong urge for it. For myself, . . . if a hundred people can laugh with me, I am content" (Cook, 43). As Cook describes the genesis of the opera, in 1894 Wolf received a libretto written by Rosa Mayreder, which he accepted after a second reading. Again following information from the composer's personal correspondence, we learn that the composition of the opera itself took from March 1895 to early July of that year. Its premiere, after several abortive attempts in Berlin and Vienna, was held at last in the Mannheim Theater on July 7, 1896, to the great disappointment of the composer himself, who found the singers inadequate. But public acceptance was far less sparing. As the music and the action unfolded, the work met with increasing enthusiasm, and by its end the opera was received with fervent acclaim.

In creating his adaptation of Alarcón's novel, Wolf introduced into his text certain small changes that facilitated its staging and allowed for a better psychological delineation of the characters. The most radical change is the one involving Garduña, who, under the name of Repela, is elevated here to the classical category of the old *gracioso*. In all other respects, Mayreder's libretto displays a notable verisimilitude to the original novel, preserving faithfully its Spanish flavor.

Criticism of *Der Corregidor* has been varied. From the very outset, its musicality and dramatic value have been appraised in divergent ways. Cook, for example, states,

It can be fairly concluded that the music of the *Corregidor* is music of genius and as such commands hearing. The text, although not of the highest poetical quality, contains a great deal that is amusing, apt and uncomplicated—more than can be said for many an opera book established in the repertory. The dramatic qualities of the work are no doubt its weakest feature, but those who experienced the work on the stage have by no means rejected it on this account. A sympathetic producer using imagination and modern projection techniques can devise a satisfying presentation for a theatre audience and yet preserve the musical expression by which Hugo Wolf communicates his unique artistic power. No artist of his talent can go unrecognized in such an important part of his work. (168)

Wolf's opera, which has had qualified success, has been regularly staged in German theaters up to the present. Nevertheless, despite the Germans' interest in the theme, it was Manuel de Falla who knew best how to interpret the work with a more acute sense of what is truly regional and Spanish. He ultimately did so in his own *El sombrero de tres picos*.

Actually, Falla's version has a strange history of its own. The dramatic richess of Alarcón's novel had made the composer think at first in terms of a comic opera, which led him to conversations with Carlos Fernández Shaw about the creation of a libretto. But the collaboration ran into an unexpected obstacle, for Alarcón himself, fearing a poor adaptation of his work, had inserted certain clauses into his will that precisely prohibited its dramatization. Once the words were eliminated, the heirs could no longer object to the transformation. And so the novel was turned into dance.

The literary presence that the ballet carries with it is visible throughout this final work of Falla. The anecdotes follow closely those of Alarcón's novel, and the ballet concludes with the miller's happiness and the Corregidor's disgrace as he is tossed in effigy in a blanket. For his stage settings, Falla used the brilliant comedic specialist Gregorio Martínez Sierra, and with this the great Spanish composer Falla rendered homage to a great novelist, Alarcón. *El sombrero de tres picos* has taken new form through the happy collusion of music and the arts.

BIBLIOGRAPHY

Alarcón, Pedro Antonio de. *El sombrero de tres picos*. Madrid: Colección Austral, Espasa-Calpe, 1984.

Belic, Oldrich. "*El sombrero de tres picos* como estructura épica." In *Análisis de textos hispanos*. Madrid: Prensa Española, 1956.

Cook, Peter. *Hugo Wolf's "Corregidor."* London: Staples Printers, 1976.

Díez Echarri, Emiliano y Roca Franqueza, José María. *Historia de la literatura española e hispanoamericana*. Madrid: Aguilar, 1968.

Valbuena Prat, Angel. *Historia de la literatura española*. Vol. 3. Barcelona: Gustavo Gili, S.A., 1968.

25

Albéniz's Pepita Jiménez: The Strange Expropriation of Juan Valera's Novel

Salvador Anton Pujol

No aficionado can overlook the importance that Spain has had for the world of opera. Spanish texts have provided the basis of such emblematic and canonized works as Mozart's *Don Giovanni*, Verdi's *Simon Boccanegra, La forza del destino*, and *Il trovatore*, and Massenet's *Le Cid*. Spanish culture has been reflected at its most stereotypical in Bizet's *Carmen*, its land has provided the setting for Wagner's *Parsifal*, and its history has found its way into music and words in Verdi's *Don Carlos*, Donizetti's *María Padilla*, and Ginastera's *Don Rodrigo*.

Indeed, Spanish romantic plays have been rifled by opera composers, with remarkable results. Still, Spanish nineteenth-century realist novels, which offer fertile ground for operatic notions, have been essentially ignored. One often wonders what Verdi could have done with some of Spain's realist works. Couldn't Galdós's *La de Bringas* or *La desheredada* have equally inspired Puccini's *Manon Lescaut*, a tale of social downfall taken from a novel by the Abbé Prévost? So it is not surprising that Isaac Albéniz (1860–1909), a composer known for his orchestral pieces and for such piano works as *Iberia*, should look into realism and find in Juan Valera's *Pepita Jiménez* (1874) an opera composer's dream come true. What is surprising is that Albéniz's final product bears only a superficial resemblance to Valera's original work. Concentrating on its two protagonists and on the middle part of the novel, called "Paralipómenos," this oratorio–opera deprives the text of some of its most enticing qualities: its narrative ambiguity and perspectivism, its depiction of social roles, and its gentle ambience and sentimentality. At the same time, its minimalism, both from a lyric and musical point of view, allowed Albéniz to create a work that quietly advanced some of the techniques that the listener would encounter through the remainder of the twentieth century.

For those not familiar with Valera's novel, a key work in the canon of Spanish realism, this brief review of the plot will help us note the materials that the opera excises. Luis, a young seminarist under his uncle's spiritual guidance, spends a few months in the house of his father, Don Pedro, the *cacique* of a town somewhere in Andalusia. His father's love object is a beautiful young widow, Pepita Jiménez. Through a series of letters that Luis writes to his uncle, we learn that the initial animosity that Luis feels toward Pepita turns slowly into love. With the help of Pepita's confidante and servant, Antoñona, Luis and Pepita find themselves alone during a Carnival night, and the inevitable happens. (Lou Charnon-Deutsch describes this as a "process of masculinization," through which Luis learns how to become a man, according to nineteenth-century Spanish social standards.) Now Luis must confront such ghosts from his past as his illegitimate birth, as well as the prospect of taking control of his father's estate. Luis's rivalry with his father soon fades, since the father, as the reader suspects, has been behind all the romantic machinations, and the story ends happily.

Quite clearly, the novel offers many attractions to an opera composer, above all a complicated love story between the soprano and tenor, a Verdi-like baritone father, and a maid who, as usual, is sung by the mezzo-soprano. The novel also contains duels, self-doubting soliloquies, and such local scenes as the Carnival that provides the context for the lovers' meeting. All these novelistic constructs provide enough ingredients to fill many pages of music with arias, duets, and choral and ballet music. The novel unmistakably reminds us of some of the best-known operas of Verdi.

The gestation of Albéniz's piece, however, was burdensome from the start. Even though the composer was most recognized for his symphonic work, it seems that he was always laboring on some "opera, zarzuela, lyrical drama or incidental stage music," as one of his prominent scholars, Jacinto Torres attests (8). Unfortunately, of almost thirty vocal works, the majority have been lost. After Albéniz scored a shy success with an opera titled *Henry Clifford* (1895), an English banker named Francis Money-Coutts encouraged the composer to create an opera on Valera's *Pepita Jiménez*. The Englishman ensured "a substantial personal pension" in return for which Albéniz would commit himself to setting Money-Coutts's words to music (Henderson, 985). The project was begun, but problems were in the offing. The novelist Juan

Valera voiced his discontent and tried to discourage the composer from using his literary masterpiece. He even proposed to write a libretto on a story other than *Pepita Jiménez*, but the Money-Coutts project went on (García Rosado, 57). Albéniz himself hampered its development by drafting numerous revisions before the final English libretto was completed. (Actually, since the end product was later complicated by several opera directors' own versions, it is extremely difficult to speak at this point of one definitive book. This is not an uncommon problem in opera, as witnessed by several of Verdi's works, especially the two versions of both *Simon Boccanegra* and *La forza del destino*, and the multiple bilingual versions of *Don Carlos*.) Money-Coutts attempted to bring the English *Pepita* to Covent Garden in June of the following season, even offering to defray all the costs, but the performance failed to materialize and the work would not reach the public for many years to come. Today it has been recorded and performed, and from there stems this analysis.

Money-Coutts's libretto focuses sharply on Pepita's character, a radical departure from the novel. In Valera's original, Pepita is more a masculine construct than a full-fledged character, viewed from Luis's perspective at the beginning of the novel and ultimately portrayed through Don Pedro's letters. In the opera she takes center stage and is given her own singular voice. Instead of stressing Luis's antagonism, as in the early part of the novel, the first act of the opera is devoted to Pepita's conversations with the vicar and her self-revealing confessions. The soprano's first aria works as an excellent recapitulation of the novel's thrust:

Do you remember, one
Day, reckoning for fun
How many suitors seek
My fortune, week by week?
You praised my modest mood,
My love of widowhood!
But they were not denied
By modesty, but pride!
From where I soared, serene
In secret realms of rest,
These cavaliers were seen
Unworthy and unblest!
And now my very scorn
Its punishment has borne!
Myself am I possessed
By the vile spirit of the Unholy Love!
Alas he is betrothed already!
The Church herself is waiting to espouse him!

Don Luis de Vargas! (*She covers her face*)
And I am so wicked that I can't regret
That once, just once, our very lips have met! (Albéniz, 26)

Musically, the aria resembles Tatiana's in the famous letter scene of Tschaikovsky's *Eugene Onegin* (1879). The setting conveys the same mixture of pathos and broken hope as does the Russian piece. But there are various elements in conflict in Albéniz's score. Those intended to convey Andalusian color, or what we have learned to identify as such, are present only in the orchestral parts. Meanwhile, the characters' vocal lines, drawn with minimalistic cacaphony, portray them as highly tortured individuals, a trait that their counterparts in the novel exhibit to a far lesser degree. This makes the opera difficult to follow, since it points in two very different directions: on the one hand, the familiar, almost joyous rhythms of the accompaniment; on the other, the anguished discord of the voices. Could it have been the composer's sardonic scheme to make the conflict more dramatic?

The problem is exacerbated in the second act. After Luis decides to leave town to become a priest, Antoñona arranges a secret meeting between him and Pepita. While waiting, she sings a short prayer. Then Luis enters and sings about the guilt he feels for loving a human being. The end of the opera consists of a long duet between Luis and Pepita, in which she tries to convince him that their love is stronger than any celestial bonds. Luis finally surrenders when Pepita threatens to commit suicide if he leaves:

Farewell for ever!
And when I lie beneath the sod,
God grant that no distress affray
Your conscience for the soul you slay. (Albéniz, 40)

Even though the story ends well, the violence of the vocal score is a far cry from Valera's pleasing novel, especially during some parts of the final scene where the vocal section seems to bear the pathos of Greek tragedies.

Albéniz's first version of the opera (in one act and two tableaux) opened in 1896 at the Liceu in Barcelona in an Italian adaptation. Subsequently, it was performed in Prague in German. After numerous changes, it played in Madrid, Nice, and Monte Carlo, and finally in Brussels in 1905, each time with different translations, revisions, and reorchestrations by the composer. An extensively revised French version saw the light in 1923 at the Opéra Comique, and the piece returned to the Liceu in 1926 with a new Italian libretto. The 1964 revision by Pablo Solozábal, featuring Pilar Lorengar and Alfredo Kraus, opened in Madrid to a mixed critical reception. On the one hand, José Luis Téllez safely calls it an "artisan work," but Jacinto Torres, while admiring it, reproached Solozábal for his "recomposition" of Albéniz's music, of the text, and of the dramatic structure, "since the result was very different from Albéniz's musical and dramatic intentions, particularly in the treatment of the voices and the manner of their thematic and rhythmic integration into the orchestra" (10).

In 1995, Josep Pons, conductor of the Orquestra de Cambra Teatre Lliure, known for its commitment to giving rarely performed twentieth-century works a chance to be heard, recorded what seems to be a definitive version, at least for the time being. Pons has taken a few liberties in the recording, making such changes as the omission of Don Pedro, Luis's father, and of Antoñona's intervention in the lovers' romance. Focusing on the drama involving Pepita and Luis, he has highlighted the modernity of the score, avoiding at the same the repetitions that are vital for any stage version (Torres, 11).

The reviews of Pons's recording and of a subsequent production in 1996, conducted by Pons with his own arrangements and directed by Lluis Homar, have not been encouraging. García Rosado in *Opera Actual* spoke highly of the instrumental part of the score, but rejected the vocal component as "unbefitting" (57). Robert Henderson, in the influential British magazine *Opera*, wrote that "[Pons's] concert suite makes for discreet, uncomplicated listening," and ended the review by adding that "its main source of interest is still likely to be addicted collectors of the marginalia of Spanish music" (986).

Pepita Jiménez, the opera, in this final Pons version, explains Valera's reasons for discouraging its composition. Apparently, the lack of popular acceptance throughout its reincarnations has more to do with Albéniz's intentions than with the text itself. Any Spanish audience is probably familiar with the novel's plot, in the same way that a French audience knows *Madame Bovary* or a Russian knows *Anna Karenina*. It is common knowledge that the novel does not dwell on the unpleasantness of life. On the contrary, as Valera himself wrote, his prime objective was to depict life as prettier than it really is, moving away from tragic stances, and always providing a happy ending (Oleza, 61). The topic seems to be ideal for a *zarzuela*, the Spanish light opera or operetta, along the lines, perhaps, of *Don Pasquale* by Donizetti. But Albéniz, the composer, was too sensitive a musician to fall into old nineteenth-century opera clichés, and he definitely was not interested in *zarzuela*. His sophisticated modern musical vision clashed with a text that belonged to another era, and so he ended up by defying Valera's novel.

Though the opera was first performed in 1896, Albéniz's most important revisions were undertaken between 1903 and 1905. The composer certainly tried not to fit each character into a single musical line.

Instead, the different melodies, the clear rejection of *leitmotifs*, and the free form suggest that the music follows an impressionistic or modernist style, in which "greatly expanded resources of instrumental tone color and harmony are employed, including free treatment of dissonance, parallel chords, and pitch collections" (Randel, 235). Even the opera's brevity, a constant throughout its many different revisions, puts it in a category closer to more contemporary works than any of the nineteenth-century works the audience was used to seeing on the stage of the Liceu.

In my opinion, the expropriation of Valera's novel by Albéniz and Money-Coutts is but a reflection of the musical currents of the times. On listening to it repeatedly, one notices the disorientation that the music conveys. A simple, happily resolved love story becomes tragic in its musical recasting when the last bars of Luis's final aria fall. It os not surprising, then, that Henderson wonders why the opera is described on the sleeve note as a comedy, since "little evidence of the comic survives in [the] music" (986).

Herbert Lindenberger tries to explain why this opera will never be part of the standard repertoire, even in Spain. For him, the clarity of Valera's novel clashes with the density of Albéniz's orchestrations and lyrics. Again, he finds it closer musically to contemporary pieces, while thematically it relates more to works by Verdi or Donizetti, and to the *zarzuelas*. He notes that the "modernist impulse toward achieving intensity by means of suggestiveness rather than explicitness manifests itself in works . . . of considerable more brevity than one finds in earlier centuries" (39). Valera's novel is far from the modernity that the music conveys, and it is not a brief novel. Negotiating a thin line between the source and the product, the music ends up by ultimately betraying its textual source.

In short, *Pepita Jiménez*, the opera, forces us to broaden our conceptions of the lyric art in the same way that Francis Poulenc's *La Voix humaine* (1959) or Igor Stravinsky's *Oedipus Rex* (1927) do. The operatic canon is known for its stagnation, and works like *Pepita Jiménez* take a long time to become a part of it, if ever. Added to the obstacles facing the canonization of Albeniz's opera is the difficulty of its staging, given the paucity of action so common in modernist works. Again, in the words of Lindenberger, "[The] impulse towards brevity (and austerity) also conflicts with the desire of the opera audience for a sustained illusion, for a prescribed period in which it can submit itself passively to the overpowering auditory and visual forces that emanate from the stage" (39).

An opera audience familiar with Valera's novel is bound to reject Albéniz's work on the grounds that its musical style is too complicated, tumultuous, and contemporary for such an unaffected story.

But there is much to be said on its behalf. It may well be that Albéniz's genius lies in the very fact that he uses a traditional work that looks back in order to create another that points toward the future. His expropriation of the novel—focusing on the raw feelings of the characters and discarding most of the stereotypical color with which Valera endows his settings—has less to do with the novel itself than with what he intended to accomplish musically. Whether one agrees with Albéniz and Money-Coutts's choices or not, the work certainly deserves another hearing.

BIBLIOGRAPHY

Charnon-Deutsch, Lou. *Gender and Representation: Women in Spanish Realist Fiction*. Philadelphia, Pa.: John Benjamins North America, 1990.

Albéniz, Isaac. *Pepita Jiménez*. With Susan Chilcott and Francesc Garrigosa. Cond. Josep Pons, Orquestra de Cambra Teatre Lliure. Harmonia Mundi, 1995.

García Rosado, Francisco. Review of *Pepita Jiménez*, by Isaac Albéniz. *Ópera Actual* (Diciembre 1996–Febrero 1997): 57.

Henderson, Robert. Review of *Pepita Jiménez*, by Isaac Albéniz. *Opera*, August 1996, 985–986.

Lindenberger, Herbert. "From Opera to Postmodernity: On Genre, Style, Institutions." In *Postmodern Genres*, ed. Marjorie Perloff. Norman: University of Oklahoma Press, 1989.

Oleza, Juan. *La novela del XIX: Del parto de una ideología*. Valencia: Bello, 1976.

Randel, Don Michael. *A New Harvard Dictionary of Music*. Cambridge: Harvard University Press, 1986.

Téllez, José Luis. "*Pepita Jiménez*, una ópera española reencontrada." *Ajoblanco* (Enero 1996): 51.

Torres, Jacinto. "The Long Sleep of *Pepita Jiménez*." Jacket notes for *Pepita Jiménez*, by Isaac Albéniz. Cond. Josep Pons, Orquestra de Cambra Teatre Lliure. Harmonia Mundi, 1995.

Part VI

MODERN WRITERS IN
MUSICAL TRANSCRIPTION

26

Federico García Lorca and His Influence on Music and Dance

Sara Vélez

Federico García Lorca was born in 1898 in Fuente Vaqueros, a small village near Granada, Spain. He frequently spoke of his early years and of his love for the countryside, the meadows, the fields, the live-stock, the people of the Vega, recalling that his "oldest childhood memo-ries have the flavour of the earth."[1] Ian Gibson, in his book *Federico Garcia Lorca: A Life*, concurs:

In the Vega no linguistic and few social differences separated wealthy and poor, peasants and landowners. Lorca inherited all the vigour of a speech that springs from the earth and expresses itself with extraordinary spontaneity. Indeed, one has only to hear the inhabitants of the Vega talk and observe their colorful use of imagery to realize that the metaphorical language of Lorca's theatre and poetry . . . is rooted in an ancient, collective awareness of nature in which all things—trees, horses, mountains, the moon and the sun, rivers, flow-ers, human beings—are closely related and interdependent.[2]

In August 1936, at the height of his literary career, Lorca was assas-sinated by the Falangists in Viznar, a village near Granada. Viznar had become a Nationalist military outpost and place of execution for those whom the insurgents felt were opposed to their cause, especially those of Republican or leftest persuasions. This included people from all walks of life: rofessors, teachers, doctors, and artists, as well as work-ers and trade unionists. Actually, Lorca was not a political person, and when asked on various occasions to what party he belonged, he would simply reply, "I am on the side of the poor."[3] In 1932 he had become the artistic director of La Barraca, a traveling theatre company composed of university students. The goal of La Barraca was to bring classical Spanish theatre to the peasants and other working people of the Spanish countryside. Lorca wanted to clear the Spanish stage of "false sirens . . . sawdust hearts, and superficial dialogue" and create a theatre that would capture the social pulse, the historical pulse, the drama of its people, and the true color of their countryside and spirit.[4] This was the life that was abruptly curtailed at the age of thirty-eight.

From his earliest years, Federico was musically inclined and learned to play both piano and guitar. In 1909 he moved with his family to Granada, where he continued his piano studies with Don Antonio Segura Mesa, who also taught him solfeggio, harmony, and composition. In time the poet began giving concerts and composing piano pieces and incidental music for a musical comedy. At this point it was thought that he would eventually pursue a career in music. But in 1916, as his university semester ended, his beloved music teacher died and his parents refused to allow him to continue his music studies in Paris. Thus, he became more involved with literary figures at the university and his creative urges turned increasingly to writing, although he still played the piano and sang for gatherings.

Along with his growing love for literature, Lorca was developing a great interest in Spanish folk songs, and he collected and arranged many for piano and voice. Among them are the celebrated "El Café de Chinitas" and "Zorongo gitano" from his *Canciones populares antiguas*. In 1931 he would record for Spanish HMV Gramophone a selection of these songs with himself at the piano accompanying Argentinita (Encarnación López Júlvez), one of his dear friends and favorite artists, who sang, danced, and played the castanets.

He also had a profound love and appreciation for the *cante jondo* or "deep song" of his native Andalusia. (*Cante jondo* is the older body of Andalusian vocal music from which flamenco is derived.) After all, the famous gypsy caves of Sacromonte were in Granada and he had grown up surrounded by this music.[5] Together with his friend, the composer Manuel de Falla, the poet made an extensive study of *cante jondo*, observing, "The essential difference between 'deep song' and flamenco is that the origins of the former must be sought in the primitive musical systems of India . . . while flamenco, a consequence of 'deep song', did not acquire its definitive form until the eighteenth century. 'Deep song' is imbued with the mysterious color of primordial ages; flamenco is relatively modern song whose emotional interest fades before that of 'deep song'. Local color versus spiritual color, that is the profound difference."[6] The two men, joined by other colleagues, decided to create an annual competition of *cante jondo* singers as a way to draw attention to what they felt was one of Spain's greatest folk arts. The first competition, held in Granada in 1922, was a notable success.

Meanwhile, in 1921 the twenty-year-old poet had produced his first major work, *Poema del cante jondo.* In these poems Lorca's musical rhythms, striking imagery, and passionate intensity (*duende*) create a moving evocation of the sounds and emotions of the ancient vocal form. Three pieces from this collection, "La guitarra," "El grito," and "El silencio" are expressively read by Germaine Montero on an LP entitled *Lament on the Death of a Bullfighter and Other Poems and Songs of Federico García Lorca.* Montero was an actress and singer who worked with García Lorca in the 1930s and eventually went to France, where she became noted for her interpretations of French and Spanish songs.

Lorca had a deep concern for social justice and was particularly sensitive to the cries of the downtrodden and the outcasts of society. He especially sympathized with the Gypsies of his native Andalusia, and in 1924–1927 published his *Romancero gitano.* This series of poems contains some wonderfully evocative expressions of the mystery and sadness of the gypsy soul, "the black sorrow," as García Lorca called it in his "Romance de la pena negra." One poem from this collection, "Romance del prendimiento de Antoñito el Camborio," the story of a gypsy lad who was arrested by the Civil Guard while on the road to Seville to see the bulls, can be heard on an album entitled, *Archivo de la palabra,* read by Margarita Xirgu, the Catalan actress who was a great favorite of García Lorca and to whom the poem is dedicated.[7]

In the decades that followed, many premier musicians were captivated by the rhythms, the passion, and the mystical metaphors of Lorca's poetry. Here are just a few of the works they inspired:

Francis Poulenc, the French composer whose songs are greatly admired for their sensitive integration of vocal line and accompaniment, created musical settings for three short poems of Lorca in 1947: "L'enfant muet [El niño mudo / The mute boy]," "Adelina a la promenade [Adelina de paseo / Adelina on a Stroll]," and "Chanson de l'oranger sec [Canción del naranjo seco / Song of the Withered Orange Tree]." Scored for baritone and piano, these songs all derive from Lorca's *Canciones 1921–1924.* Poulenc also composed a sonata for violin and piano "to the memory of Federico García Lorca" in 1943.[8]

On other shores, the Italian composer Luigi Nono, renowned for his electronic, aleatoric (random), and serial music, was another great admirer of the martyred poet. Like Lorca, Nono was an advocate for social reforms, but unlike him, he was an avowed Communist and far more active politically. Nono composed two works inspired by Lorca: *L'Epitaffio per Federico García Lorca* (1952) for voice and orchestra, which includes "Tarde" from *Canciones 1921–1924*, and a ballet, *Il mantello rosso*, based on *El amor de don Perlimplín*. The ballet, with choreography by Tatiana Gsovsky, was first staged in Berlin in 1954.[9]

George Crumb, the American composer known for his innovative techniques in the use of sonorities obtained from an enormous range of instrumental and vocal effects, made various musical versions of García Lorca's poems. In fact, almost all of his vocal compositions are settings of verses by Lorca, which the composer views as an extended cycle. The influence of Lorca's imagery can also be noted in his instrumental works. Two expressive vocal pieces based on Lorca's works are from Crumb's 1963 work, *Night Music I*, which is scored for soprano, piano-celesta, and percussion. Crumb's unusual use of timbre, register, and rhythmic patterns, as well as his highly colored chromaticism (notes not on the diatonic scale) heighten the effects of the poems "La luna asoma," from Lorca's *Canciones 1921–1924*, and "Gacela de la terrible presencia," from his *Diván del Tamarit*, a series of poems written in honor of the Arabic poets of Granada.[10]

In 1965 the Belgian composer, cellist, and conductor Eric Feldbusch composed his *Trois poèmes de Federico García Lorca*, setting to music three sections of Lorca's "Llanto por Ignacio Sancho Mejías," the poet's searing lament upon the death of the bullfighter Mejias, one of his close friends. The three sections, scored for speaker and orchestra, are "La prise et la mort" [La cogida y la muerte / The Goring and Death], "Le sang répandu" [La sangre derramada / The Spilled Blood], and "Ame absente" [Alma ausente / Absent soul].[11]

In 1969 the Russian composer Dmitri Shostakovich, in his *Symphony No. 14*, scored for soprano, bass, and chamber orchestra, created intense settings for eleven poems, all dealing with the same subject: death. Describing this symphony as his protest against death, he heightens the sombre imagery of the poetry with stark orchestral colors, strident atonality in the strings, and darkly passionate declamations of the singers. The two opening poems in this symphony are "De Profundis" and "Malagueña" from Lorca's *Poema del cante jondo*. In "De Profundis" the Russian reproduces with bass and strings Lorca's verse, "Los cien enamorados duermen para siempre bajo la tierra seca."[12] In "Malagueña," the verse, "La muerte entra y sale, y sale y entra la muerte de la taberna," is sung by soprano accompanied by strings and castanets.[13]

More recently, in 1985 the Puerto Rican composer Roberto Sierra, also known for incorporating elements of folklore and popular music in his compositions, wrote a piece for soprano and wind quintet based on the Act 1 monologue, "Romance de las tres manolas" from Lorca's play *Doña Rosita la soltera o El lenguaje de las flores*, subtitulada "*Poema granadino del novecientos, dividido en varios jardines con escenas de canto y de baile*."[14] In speaking of this play at its opening in 1935, García Lorca said, "*Doña Rosita* is the outwardly gentle but inwardly parched life of a Granadan maiden, who little by little gets transformed into the grotesque and touching thing that is a spinster in Spain. . . . Did I call it a comedy? It's better to say the drama of Spanish tastelessness, of Spanish hypocrisy and of our women's need to repress by force into the depths of their blighted dispositions any desire for personal pleasure."[15] Felicia Hardison Londré, in her book, *Federico Garcia Lorca*, calls this play, "Lorca's finest achievement of a synthesis of music, visual design, and folk entertainment in one wholly theatrical work."[16]

Even more than his poetry, Lorca's pieces for the stage are truly a synthesis of several art forms. Christopher Maurer, in his introduction to three plays by Garcia Lorca, speaks of their extraordinary blend of dramatic devices and musicality: "There are two areas in particular in which Lorca's theater differs radically from that of his predecessors: his idea of poetic drama and the musical nature of his work. . . . In Lorca's work, drama and poetry seem inseparable. His poetry often has the dramatic quality that he admired in traditional Spanish songs and narrative ballads, and his drama has the metaphorical density, the attention to rhythm, the ring of 'memorable speech' one normally associates with poetry."[17] Unquestionably, one of the most musical of Lorca's plays is *Bodas de sangre*, which contains choral and solo singing as well as instrumental background. To quote again from Maurer, "Nowhere is musical form more apparent than in *Blood Wedding*, where the characters' speech is 'orchestrated' in a highly stylized, rhythmic manner that sometimes borders on liturgical chant."[18] The actress Josefina Díaz de Artigas, who played the bride in the 1933 Madrid premiere, remembers that Lorca staged certain scenes rather like the conductor of an orchestra, "so that there wouldn't be a single voice that didn't blend with the others. . . . He combined the voices, their special timbres and strengths, as a composer puts together sounds."[19]

Through his use of Spanish folk songs, to which his strophic forms and verse structure can be traced, García Lorca's dramas are infused with music. In turn, many musicians have been inspired by his poetic dramas. Four operas have been based on *Bodas de sangre* alone: one, a chamber opera by the American composer Hale Smith; another by the German composer Wolfgang Fortner; the third by the Yugoslavian composer Kresimir Fribec, who also composed an opera based on *Yerma*; and the fourth by the Hungarian composer Sandor Szokolay, who also composed an opera based on Lorca's *El amor de don Perlimplín*.

Szokolay, who was invariably drawn to dramatic themes and ancient folk expressions and traditions, was immediately taken with Lorca's *Blood Wedding*. He spoke of being terribly moved when he first saw it produced in Paris in 1962: "I literally trembled, wept, suffered throughout the play. I went through the ordeal of the play's vengeance:

an annihilating crush. For it is unrelenting and merciless,"[20] and he dedicated himself to its musical transformation. Szokolay's opera premiered in Budapest in 1964.[21]

Blood Wedding is the story of a bride who runs away with a married lover on her wedding day. Her bridegroom follows after them, and the two men kill each other. All the women are now left to mourn the deaths of the new bridegroom and of Leonardo, the bride's lover. The closing scene of Szokolay's moving opera is called "The Weavers' Scene." Closely paralleling the original play, it brings all the women together in a stark white room. Two girls are winding skeins of red wool and singing about the thread of life, much like a tragic Greek chorus commenting on the action. The beggar woman (Death) arrives with the news that both the bridegroom and Leonardo, the lover, are dead. The groom's mother enters in tearless despair as the bodies of her son and Leonardo are carried in. The neighbors are crying. The bride enters, asking to be punished, but the mother in her deep grief is calm. She has no more fear, since her last son has been killed, as were her husband and her other son, in violent vengeful encounters. This scene is reminiscent of the final scene of another folk tragedy, *Riders to the Sea* (1904), a play by the Irish author J. M. Synge, in which Maurya, the mother, sits calmly while her neighbors keen over the death of her last son. As they lament and sway, the women pull red petticoats over their heads. The mother is calm, for she has lost all of her men, husbands and son, not to human violence but to the raging sea. Both mothers, at one with their harsh environments, accept their fates stoically, and in the end, for all of them, there is only silence: "¡Silencio!," and a heart-wrenching scream.

The dance world has also been greatly attracted to Lorca's poetic dramas and dramatic poetry, much as Lorca himself was always interested in the dance. He had a long collaboraton and close friendship with the dancer and singer Argentinita, using her in 1920 in his first play, *El maleficio de la mariposa*. In 1931 he recorded with her his arrangements of Spanish folk songs. In 1932 he again collaborated with her to found the Ballet Madrid, and helped organize a production of *El amor brujo* at the Teatro Español de Madrid.

Many choreographers have created a diverse body of works inspired by Lorca's genius. In the 1940s, Doris Humphrey staged for the great dancer José Limón a piece called *Lament*, based on Lorca's "Llanto por Ignacio Sánchez Mejías." In 1953 the South African choreographer Alfred Rodrigues created a dance version of *Bodas de sangre* for the Sadler Wells Ballet, and in 1958 Mary Anthony offered another on the same theme. In 1962 Alvin Ailey premiered his work *Feast of Ashes*, derived from Lorca's *La casa de Bernarda Alba*, which also inspired the British choreographer Kenneth Macmillan's *Las hermanas*, created in

1963 for the Stuttgart Ballet. Anna Sokolow, the famed modern dance choreographer, premiered in 1974 her *Homage to Federico García Lorca* with the José Limón Dance Company. In Germany, in 1992, Lorca's *Yerma* was the inspiration for the ballet of the same name by Krisztina Horvath, who is now creating a dance trilogy based on *Bodas de sangre, Yerma,* and *La casa de Bernarda Alba*. This is just a sampling of the many dance pieces that have sprung from Lorca's works.

Two powerful films of choreographic works derived from Lorca are *Bernardus hus* and *Bodas de sangre* (see Figure 26.1). The first is a modern Swedish ballet version of *La casa de Bernarda Alba*, in which the role of the tyrannical matriarch is powerfully portrayed by a man.[22] On the death of her second husband, Bernarda keeps her five daughters, aged twenty to thirty-nine, severely dressed in black mourning clothes and locked in the house. Only Adela, the youngest, tries to break loose, daring to put on a bright green dress and furtively taking a lover. Tragically, it is Adela who kills herself at the end, victim of her family's frustration and repression. The music of Johann Sebastian Bach, Heitor Villalobos, Isaac Albéniz, and Francisco Tárrega is used brilliantly throughout the ballet to reflect the varying emotional states and personalities of the characters. The choreographer also has the dancers utter shouts, Spanish words, and animal sounds and adopt stylized

Figure 26.1
Climactic moment from the Spanish film of the ballet *Bodas de sangre*.
Used by permission of Brepi Films.

facial expressions and movements, all of which add markedly to the dramatic impact.

The second film, *Bodas de sangre*, is a flamenco recreation of the Lorca play. Originally choreographed by Antonio Gades in 1974 for his Spanish Dance Company, it was later redone for the 1981 Spanish film directed by Carlos Saura. It shows the dancers, who include Antonio Gades and Christina Hoyos, rehearsing their version of Lorca's play. Their powerful performance highlights the mounting tensions between the rival suitors and La Novia, the bride. These passions reach their apex in the knife duel of the two men, which is filmed in slow motion and in such excruciating silence that the audience is mesmerized by the drama unfolding before them. Luigi Rossi, in his article, "Danzando Lorca," in *Musica & Arte: Quaderni del Museo Teatrale alla Scala*, also talks of being deeply moved by this scene and speaks of its incredible dramatic tension. Comparing to Michelangelo's *Pieta* the scene in which La Novia gives the dead men her final embrace, he speaks of the omnipresent duality of life and death in the gypsy soul.[23]

This duality of love and death (amor y muerte / sangre y silencio) is featured prominently in the works of Lorca. One could almost say that it is the force which drives his creation. Perhaps it stems in part from his own suffering in love, being unable to express openly his homosexuality. Thus, he understood only too well the torments of repressed love and rigid societal attitudes toward "outsiders." In his works the impassioned voices of these "outsiders" can be heard in the mournful cries of the Gypsies, the barren wails of Yerma, the parched sighs of Doña Rosita, the yearning arms of Bernarda's daughters, the hopeless sobs of La Novia for her "flores rotas . . . flores secas" [broken . . . withered flowers].[24] This is the poetic legacy that Lorca has left us, a marvelous musical mosaic of dark pathos and flaming passions, of love and death "bajo la luna gitana" [under the gypsy moon].[25]

NOTES

1. Ian Gibson, *Federico García Lorca: A Life* (New York: Pantheon Books, 1989), 22.

2. Gibson, 23.

3. Felicia Hardison Londré, *Federico García Lorca* (New York: Ungar, 1984), 36.

4. Ibid., 30.

5. There have been many theories as to the origins of *cante jondo*, and references have been made to the Moslem occupation of Spain, 711–1492, to the Gypsy migration from India in the fifteenth century, and even to Byzantine chant and early Hebrew liturgical music. The influence of Asian sources appears to be the most profound, and the Gypsies, who settled prinnarily in Andalusia, played a large part in the development of songs and dances derived from *cante jondo*.

Gilbert Chase, in his introduction and notes to the 1956 Folkways album, *Spain: Flamenco Music of Andalusia* clearly identifies *cante jondo* with the Orient rather than with Europe: "European music in general has a harmonic and instrumental basis. Even its melody is largely derived from harmonic structure. But in *cante jondo*, as in Oriental music, melody predominates and determines the essential features of the style." Turning to the specifics of flamenco, he adds,

Although dancing and guitar-playing are important aspects of the flamenco tradition, its soul is in the singing voice. What the voice does is what makes flamenco different from European music. The distinguishing traits of flamenco music are . . . 1) a melodic range that seldom surpasses the interval of a sixth; 2) the reiterated use of one note . . . frequently accompanied by *appoggiature* [dissonant grace notes] from above and below; 3) the use of profuse ornamentation . . . ; 4) frequent use of *portamento* (sliding from one note to another); 5) *enharmonic modulation* . . . the alteration by less than a semi-tone of certain notes of the scale. An analogy would be the slightly flattened "blue" notes of Afro-American music (third and seventh degrees of the scale). (2)

6. Federico García Lorca, *Deep Song and Other Prose*, ed. and trans. Christopher Maurer (New York: New Directions Books, 1980), 24–25.

7. Xirgu played the premiere performances of the mother in *Bodas de sangre* and the title roles in *Doña Rosita la soltera, Mariana Pineda*, and *Yerma*. The recording referred to here was originally made in the 1930's and reissued on CSIC Publicaciones de la Residencia de Estudiantes, 1989.

8. These pieces are beautifully performed by Gerard Souzay, baritone, and Dalton Baldwin, pianist, on a record issued by La Voix de Son Maitre EMI, 1973.

9. Both *L'Epitaffio per Federico Garcia Lorca* and "Casida de la rosa" from *Diván del Tamarit* were exquisitely recorded by soprano Lidia Marimpietri and the baritone Mario Borriello with the Symphony Orchestra and Chorus of Radio Rome, conducted by Bruno Maderna on the record label Arkadia in 1992. (*Casida* is the Arabic word for a type of short fixed rhymed verse.)

10. *Diván* is Arabic for "collection of poems," and *tamarit*, which means "an abundance of dates" is the ancient Arabic name of a place near Granada where Lorca's family had a country house. Soprano Louise Toth and an instrumental ensemble conducted by George Crumb give an expressive performance of these poems on a record produced by Composers Recordings Incorporated, 1967.

11. Germaine Gerin plays the speaker and Julien Ghyoros conducts the Symphony Orchestra of Liege on a record made by Cultura, 1967. Germaine Montero, the remarkable artist who worked with Lorca, movingly recorded the same poem in the original Spanish on the record, *Lament on the Death of a Bullfighter and Other Poems and Songs of Federico Garcla Lorca*, which Vanguard issued in the 1960s.

12. Federico García Lorca, "De Profundis," in *Poem of the Deep Song / Poema del cante jondo*, trans. Carlos Bauer (San Francisco: City Lights Books, 1987), 68–69.

13. Ibid., 88–89. We recommend the recording of this work with Mark Reshetin as bass, Galina Vishnevskaya as soprano, and Mstislav Rostropovich conducting a chamber ensemble from the Moscow Philharmonic. The record label is RCA Victor Red Seal, 1971.

14. Puli Toro, mezzo-soprano, gives a haunting rendition of this work with the Bronx Arts Ensemble on the record label New World, 1989.

15. Quoted in Hardison Londré, *Lorca*, 163.

16. Ibid., 162.

17. Christopher Maurer, "Introduction," in *Federico García Lorca, Three Plays: Yerma, Blood Wedding, The House of Bernarda Alba* (New York: Farrar, Straus, and Giroux, 1993), xiii.

18. Ibid., xvi.

19. Ibid.

20. Péter Várnai, Liner notes, *Vernasz/Blood Wedding*, Sandor Szokolay, Qualiton, 1968, 42.

21. The opera was beautifully recorded by the Hungarian State Opera House, soloists, chorus, and orchestra, conducted by Andras Kórody, Qualiton, 1968.

22. The choreographer is Mats Ek and the company is the Cullbergbaletten. A video of this ballet was originally produced for Swedish Television in 1986.

23. Luigi Rossi, "Danzando Lorca," *Musica & Arte: Quaderni del Museo Teatrale alla Scala*, June 1996, 67.

24. Federico García Lorca, *Bodas de sangre*, eds. Allen Josephs and Juan Caballero (Madrid: Ediciones Catedra, S.A., 1988), 160–161.

25. Federico García Lorca, "Romance sonámbulo," in *Selected Verse*, vol. 3, ed. Christopher Maurer (New York: Ferrar, Straus, and Giroux, 1996), 178.

BIBLIOGRAPHY

Allen, Rupert C. *Psyche and Symbol in the Theater of Federico García Lorca: Perlimplin, Yerma, Blood Wedding*. Austin: University of Texas Press, 1974.

Auclair, Marcelle. *Vida y muerte de García Lorca*. Mexico City: Ediciones Era, S.A., 1975.

Babín, María Teresa. *Estudios lorquianos*. Riopiedras: Editorial Universitaria, 1976.

Chase, Gilbert. Liner notes. *Spain: Flamenco Music of Andalusia*. Folkways Records, 1956.

Duran, Manuel, ed. *Lorca: A Collection of Critical Essays*. Westport, Conn.: Greenwood Press, 1962.

García Lorca, Federico. *Bodas de sangre*. Edited by Allen Josephs and Juan Caballero. Madrid: Ediciones Cátedra, S.A., 1988.

———. *Deep Song and Other Prose*. Edited and translated by Christopher Maurer. New York: New Directions Books, 1980.

———. *Mariana Pineda, Doña Rosita la soltera o El lenguaje de las flores*. Madrid: Espasa-Calpe, S.A., 1979.

———. *Mariana Pineda, La zapatera prodigiosa, Bodas de sangre*. Madrid: Novelas y Cuentos, 1968.

———. *Poem of the Deep Song/Poema del cante jondo*. Translated by Carlos Bauer. San Francisco: City Lights Books, 1987.

———. *Poet in New York*. Translated by Greg Simon and Steven F. White, edited by Christopher Maurer. New York: Noonday Press, 1988.

———. *The Public & Play without a Title*. Translated by Carlos Bauer. New York: New Directions Books, 1983.

————. *The Rural Triology: Blood Wedding, Yerma, The House of Bernarda Alba*. Translated by Michael Dewell and Carmen Zapata. New York: Bantam Books, 1987.

————. *The Selected Poems of Federico García Lorca*. Edited by Francisco García Lorca and Donald M. Allen. New York: New Directions Books, 1955.

————. *Selected Verse*. Vol. 3. Edited by Christopher Maurer. New York: Farrar, Straus, and Giroux, 1996.

————. *Three Tragedies: Blood Wedding, Yerma, Bernarda Alba*. Introduced by Francisco García Lorca, translated by James Graham-Luján and Richard L. O'Connell. Westport, Conn.: Greenwood Press, 1977.

————. *Yerma*. Edited by Ildefonso-Manuel Gil. Madrid: Cátedra, S.A., 1993.

Gibson, Ian. *Federico García Lorca: A Life*. New York: Pantheon Books, 1989.

Hardison Londré, Felicia. *Federico García Lorca*. New York: Ungar, 1984.

Honig, Edwin. *García Lorca*. New York: New Directions Books, 1963.

Rossi Luigi. "Danzando Lorca." *Musica & Arte: Quaderni dei Museo Teatrale alla Scala*, June 1996, 65–68.

Sadie, Stanley, ed. *The New Grove Dictionary of Music and Musicians*. London: Macmillan, 1980.

Synge, John M. *The Complete Plays*. New York: Vintage Books, 1960.

Várnai, Péter. Liner notes. *Vérnász/Blood Wedding*. Sándor Szokolay. Qualiton, 1968.

27

A Composer's Journey with the Poetry of Federico García Lorca

David H. Macbride

As we approach the 100th anniversary of his birth, Federico García Lorca remains one of the greatest writers of the twentieth century and the most translated modern Spanish writer of all. His sensual imagery and sonorous use of the Spanish language have not only gained universal acclaim, but have also attracted numerous composers from around the world, all intent on integrating Lorca's words into their own distinct forms of musical expression.

I first discovered Lorca's work in 1977 when, as a doctoral student at Columbia University, I happened upon a secondhand copy of *Poet in New York*, written while Lorca himself was at Columbia in 1929–1930.[1] To this day I find myself coming back to his work regularly, always identifying most sympathetically with his strong sense of solitude, his omniscient manchild vision for and of the world, and, most of all, the beauty of the work itself. Using excerpts from my work, I will recollect some of the compositional considerations and share personal associations. In so doing, I hope not only to illuminate a significant thread in my opus, but to help cast a new light on Lorca's work.

Poet in New York (1977–1983) is a setting of two poems from Lorca's collection previously mentioned: "Vuelta de paseo" [Back from a Walk] and "Niña ahogada en el pozo" [Little Girl Drowned in the Well].[2] The first poem is from a suite titled "Poemas de la soledad en Columbia University" [Poems of Solitude at Columbia University], the second is subtitled "Granada y Newburg."[3] My identification with Lorca's emotional state, as expressed in these poems, was immediate and complete. I too felt totally alone, I too had walked the streets of the Upper West Side, I too felt unappreciated, both as a person and as a composer; I imagined *myself* a poet in New York.

Having studied Spanish in public school, the idea of setting these poems in their original Spanish was appealing for three reasons. First, I enjoyed the idea of being able to "speak" musically—dangerously— in the safety of a "foreign" language. Second, I felt my music would be better served if understanding the sung text were not an issue (at least for most of the audience). Third, and most important, I wanted to work with the sound and imagery of the original poems themselves, as Lorca wrote them.

My *Poet in New York* exists in three versions: (1) tenor, two vielles, and two lutes, (2) tenor and string quartet, and (3) tenor and string orchestra. The tenor should have a lyric, quasi-countertenor quality, as this is how I imagine Lorca's own singing voice to have sounded. My approach to these poems specifically, and to his poetry in general, is to faithfully represent, in music, the emotional qualities that I perceive in the text. While the voice is preoccupied with the dual role of transmitting the text and personalizing the poet's voice, the ensemble is mainly responsible for communicating both the emotional subtext and the musical imagery. Often instrumental ideas were conceived first, then revised to accomodate the vocal line. At other times instrumental motives were incorporated into the vocal material. For instance, the opening five measures, which present the main motive G-A-F#-(F) (as shown in Figures 27.1, 27.2, and 27.3), become the basis of much of the first song's vocal material, as exemplified by the framing "Asesinado por el cielo" [Heaven-murdered one].[4]

"Vuelta de Paseo" contains many instances of pathetic, even self-pitying lines, such as "Con el árbol de muñones que no canta" [With the tree-stump now tuneless] or "mariposa ahogada en el tintero" [butterfly drowned in the inkwell].[5] One clearly hears these lines portrayed in the music as well.

Note the "tuneless" vocal line in Figure 27.4, and note the musical depiction of beating butterfly wings in the violin parts in Figure 27.5; the butterfly's "tune becomes tuneless."

The use of stanzas complete with the recurring mantra, "(Agua) . . . que no desemboca" [(Water) . . . that never disgorges], made "Niña ahogada en el pozo" seem very suitable as a song.[6] Even more attractive was the clarity of its vision as exemplified by the following lines: "Las estatuas sufren por los ojos" [The eyes of the statues convulse] and "lloras por las orillas de un ojo de caballo" [you weep on the shores that encircle the eye of a horse].[7] The theme of a little girl drowning in

Figure 27.1
"Vuelta de Paseo": Opening Five Measures

Figure 27.2
"Vuelta de Paseo": Letter B

Figure 27.3
"Vuelta de Paseo": Final Six Measures

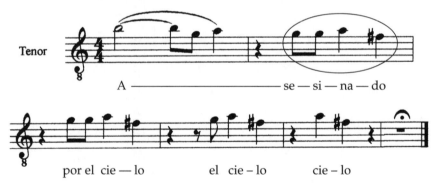

Figure 27.4
"Vuelta de Paseo": Six Measures after C

Figure 27.5
"Vuelta de Paseo": Letter E

a well is found repeatedly throughout Lorca's work. It is the inevitable silence, the still point, that I also wanted to capture.

The final stanza in "Nocturnos de la Ventana" [Nocturnes: The Window] recapitulates this theme of a small girl drowning, which provided me the chance to continue to explore the musical tone of *Poet in New York*.[8] I was attracted to this poem's sharp contrasts and conflicts, innocence and violence, the corporeal coupled with the spiritual. My setting, also called *Nocturnos de la Ventana*, composed in 1986, again uses the tenor voice, but I hear a more dramatic edge to it, in keeping with the first-person narrative used in the poem. I chose a chamber orchestra accompaniment for its expanded possibilities of volume and color. Although the text is laid out in four numbered stanzas, I decided early on to join stanzas 2 and 3, as their visceral, frankly sexual tone naturally formed a middle section for the piece.

The poem's lines, sometimes structured in short couplets, sometimes in descriptive single phrases, inspired my response. In particular, "Las voces de dos niñas" [Voices of two small girls] provided much of the piece's first section as exemplified by the piano's principal idea (Figures 27.6 and 27.7).[9]

Perhaps not coincidentally the Eb–C–D motive of the prayerful "Sálvate" (Figure 27.8) is similar to the "heaven-murdered" motive mentioned earlier (see Figure 27.2).[10]

Another less veiled connection between text and music occurs at "veo como quiere cortarla la cuchilla del viento" [I see how the knife of wind wants to cut it off], where the percussionist draws a serrated knife over the rim of a glass (Figure 27.9).[11]

The final line "¡ay! sobre la mar salada" [hai! on the salty sea] becomes an extended coda to the piece, its repeating, floating harmonies

Figure 27.6
"Nocturnos de la Ventana": m. 24–25

Piano

Figure 27.7
"Nocturnos de la Ventana": m. 60–69

forming the sea of tears on which the "two small gourds" (and the tenor) are rocking.[12] This idea found its way into *Deep Song* (1988), a setting of Lorca's "Poema de la Siguiriya Gitana" [Poem of the Gypsy Siguiriya].[13] In "El Grito" [The Cry], Lorca alternates the narrative description of the cry with the sound of the cry itself ("¡Ay!").[14] My setting employs two voices, narrator (spoken) and soprano (sung), in order to convey these two levels of meaning. The narrator is storyteller, while the soprano joins the instrumental ensemble in exploring the poem's emotional and sensual imagery. Given the length and multifaceted nature of the set of poems, I was reluctant to set it solely with pitched voice. The use of a narrator also allows the text to be read (and heard) aloud (as Lorca wrote it). Often one finds beautiful poetry that would be disserved by putting it to notes.

Figure 27.8
"Nocturnos de la Ventana": m. 193–195

Figure 27.9
"Nocturnos de la Ventana": m. 128–135

My composition *Night* (1993) develops this relationship of spoken and sung text. Taking my cue from the subtitle, *Suite for Piano and Poet's Voice*, *Night* reverses the traditional relationship of voice and accompaniment.[15] The baritone (poet's voice), with its sparse lines, actually accompanies the more continuous piano part. The poet scans the night, the night sky, the night creatures, the night sounds, feeling at one with and apart from his universe. He is not only an observer, but wants to be seen and understood as well. But he can't. This is "la gran tristeza" [the great sadness]:[16]

La gran tristeza	The Great Sadness
No puedes contemplarte	You can't really see yourself
en el mar.	in the sea.
Tus miradas se tronchan	Your glances dissolve
como tallos de luz.	like slim stalks of light.
Noche de la tierra.	Night on earth.

The entire cycle is structured around this dichotomy or conflict be-tween the observer and the observed. I use four of the short poems as spoken interludes with percussion accompaniment. *Un lucero* [A Star] is an example of one of these (Figure 27.10).[17]

These interludes not only help break the possible monotony of thir-teen consecutive songs at slow tempo; they heighten the sense of the aforementioned duality of the poet's voice. The use of percussion in the audience suggests the "slim stalks of light" in the night sky (*Night on earth*).[18] In *La gran tristeza*, the reprise of the wheel-like material of *Total* (*The Whole Works*) is inspired by the words "again and again"; and in *Recuerdo* [Memory], "playing ring around a wheel" suggests eternity, while also providing closure (Figure 27.11):[19]

Two other cycles focus on another side of Lorca's poetry, his child-like innocence reflected in his love of children, games, fantasy, and nonsense. *Children's Songs* (1981) is a setting of four poems from *The Cricket Sings*, Lorca's poems and songs for children.[20] The bilingual setting enables children to understand and fully appreciate the mean-ing and sound of the poetry, regardless of their native tongue. Musical games abound; squeaking rat toys and lizard masks are both props and instruments. Similarly, *Balanza* (1986) for soprano at the piano fo-cuses on three modest poems of innocence.[21] The dual role of the per-former not only helped determine the direct and simple style of both voice and accompaniment, but gives the performance a more informal and intimate feeling. The piano often acts as a reflective repository for the voice's utterances, an idea expanded upon in *Night*.

I hope these brief musical examples have helped illuminate my read-ings of some of Lorca's poetry. A composer, much like a poet, spends a lifetime trying to refine his or her voice into its essence. My music has always tried to find the silence, "un silencio ondulado" [a rolling si-lence].[22] In Lorca, many composers including myself have found the means to speak with their own voices. I am confident that Lorca him-

Figure 27.10
Night: *Un lucero*, Complete
BARITONE: (spoken) Hay un lucero quieto, un lucero sin párpados. [There is a star lying still, a star that never blinks.]

PIANO: ⌢•
            ○   ⌢• (spoken) ¿Dónde? [Where?] ⌢•
            (triangle)

BARITONE: Un lucero . . . En el agua dormida del estanque. [A star . . . In the sleeping waters of the pond.]

PIANO: ⌢•
            ○   ⌢•

Figure 27.11
Night: *La gran tristeza*, m. 1–2

self, as musician, visual artist, and writer, would have been pleased to know that he had created this safe haven. Lorca, like Schubert, like Kahlo, is the quintessential artist: a martyr who, above all, gave his spiritual life to the heartache of an imperfect world and the vision of a better one. We not only identify with him wholeheartedly; we know that therein lies the salvation of mankind.

SCORES AND RECORDINGS BY DAVID MACBRIDE

Balanza (1986). Christine Schadeberg, soprano, at the piano. Studio recording. Score unpublished.

Children's Songs (1981). Anni Baker and Caroline Rockwood Saslow, sopranos, with Gageego. Performance cassette. Score unpublished.

Deep Song (1988). Joanne Scattergood-Reeves, soprano, and the New World Chamber Ensemble. Performance cassette. Score unpublished.

Night (1993). (1) Fredric Moses, baritone, and Irma Vallecillo, piano, with assistance from the Hartt School Percussion Ensemble. Performance cassette; (2) Fredric Moses, baritone, and David Macbride, piano (with assistance from Benjamin Toth, percussion. Studio recording. Score unpublished.

Nocturnos de la Ventana (1986). Frank Hoffmeister, tenor, and the Prism Orchestra, Robert Black, conductor. Owl (Starkland) Recording, Inc. (CD #34). Score unpublished.

Poet in New York (1977–1983). Frank Hoffmeister, tenor, and the Heights String Quartet. Performance cassette. Score unpublished.

NOTES

The translations in this chapter are by David H. Macbride and Zenia Sacks DaSilva.

1. Federico García Lorca, *Poet in New York*, trans. Ben Belitt (New York: Grove Press, 1955).

2. Ibid., 3, 79.

3. Ibid. The poet is referring to Granada, Spain, and Newburg, Vermont.

4. Ibid., 79.

5. Ibid.

6. Ibid.

7. Ibid.

8. Federico García Lorca, *Poems of Federico García Lorca*, chosen and trans. Paul Blackburn (San Francisco: Momo's Press, 1979).

9. Ibid. (note that there are no page numbers in *Poems of García Lorca*).

10. The word *Sálvate* was derived from "te salve," and was added by the composer for emphasis.

11. Lorca, *Poems of García Lorca*.

12. Ibid.

13. Federico García Lorca, *Poem of the Deep Song* [Poema del cante jondo], trans. Carlos Bauer (San Francisco: City Lights Books, 1989), 10–11.

14. Ibid.

15. Federico García Lorca, *Collected Poems*, vol. 2, ed. Christopher Maurer, trans. Jerome Rothenberg (New York: Farrar, Straus, and Giroux, 1993), 183.

16. Ibid., 191 (my translation).

17. Rothenberg, 187 (my translation).

18. Ibid., 187.

19. Ibid., 189.

20. Federico García Lorca, *The Cricket Sings*, trans. Will Kirkland (New York: New Directions, 1980).

21. *Eco, Balanza*, and *Caracola*, from Lorca, *Poems of García Lorca*.

22. Lorca, *Poem of the Deep Song*, 12–13.

28

Poetry to Song: Modern Spanish Poetry Set to Music by Twentieth-Century Composers

Roderick S. Quiroz

BACKGROUNDS

The problem of translating a poem into a vibrant musical form has fascinated composers over the centuries. With special insights and resources, the composer of music can provide a fresh view of a poetic text already subject to diverse interpretations. Highly sensitive to the lyrical and dramatic qualities of the poetry, the composer creates a new work of art, further triggering the curiosity of the reader. This new conception may follow closely the structure of the poetry or may develop impressionistically under different lines.

Composers often identify closely with their chosen poets, and some, like Juan del Encina (ca. 1468–1529), have even set their own poetry to music.[1] For music and poetry, in the words of the German composer Robert Schumann, "spring from the same source and have the same function" (Ostwald, 24). Yet with so much in common, their stylistic course may differ strikingly, even in musical settings of the same poem. Take, for example, the settings of García Lorca's poem "El niño mudo" by the current American composer George Crumb and by the Catalonian Federico Mompou, or Lope de Vega's *Cantarcillo* ("Pues andáis en las palmas"), set by Brahms, Hugo Wolf, and the modern Spanish composers Eduardo Toldrá and Angel Mingote.

Because of the vast dimensions of the material at hand, this chapter will focus essentially on only one aspect: modern Spanish poetry employed by twentieth-century Spanish composers, with emphasis on compositions for voice and piano. This is not meant to detract from the abundant contributions of contemporary composers from other nations. In fact, the international music on the texts of García Lorca alone is so great as to require separate investigation. Neither do we wish to ignore the musicalization of earlier Spanish works by such non-Hispanic composers as Brahms, Schumann, and Wolf, especially the spiritual songs in the latter's *Spanisches Liederbuch*. Nor should we overlook the many musical adaptations of poems by the Marqués de Santillana, Juan del Encina, Gil Vicente, Garcilaso de la Vega, San Juan de la Cruz, Góngora, Lope de Vega, Quevedo, and others by composers of Spain. For our purposes, then, it would be well to glance briefly at a few of these antecedents before pursuing our survey of Spanish twentieth-century poetry turned into musical form.

As a general observation, it is interesting to note that in settings of early poetry there is often a strict convergence of musical and poetic structures, in contrast to music based on later works. For example, in the setting of a mystical poem of San Juan de la Cruz (1542–1591), *Cantar del alma* [Song of the Soul Happy to Know God through Faith], by the late Federico Mompou, there is literally one note for each syllable of the text:[2]

Qué bien sé yo la fuente que mana y corre,
aunque es de noche, . . .
Aquella eterna fuente está escondida,
qué bien sé yo dó tiene su manida,
aunque es de noche, . . .

How well I know the fountain that springs and flows,
although it is night, . . .
That eternal fountain is hidden,
how well I know its dwelling,
although it is night. . . .

Mompou adheres closely to the poetic structure, yet attains the highest musical perfection, the notes rising and falling in parallel with the poetic imagery ("cosa tan bella," "noche," etc.), and with alternating passages of piano solo and unaccompanied voice.

Not surprisingly, no poet of the Golden Age has been set to music so often as Lope de Vega (1562–1635). More than 100 renderings by composers of his time have been identified by musicologist Miguel Querol, and our own survey shows more than twenty song settings by modern composers. There is even a modern *zarzuela* by the composer Joaquín Rodrigo based on a play by Lope, *El hijo fingido*. A fine example of music from Lope's own time is the deeply felt polyphonic work by composer Francisco Guerrero on the devotional poem, *Si tus penas no pruevo*, from *Los soliloquios de un alma a Dios*.[3]

Si tus penas no pruevo, Jesús mío,
vivo triste y penado.

If I do not share your suffering, O Jesus mine,
My life is sadness and grief.

Very different in style, but still with basically congruent poetic and musical structures, is a modern song by the composer Eduardo Toldrá based on another poem by Lope.[4]

Madre, unos ojuelos vi,
verdes, alegres y bellos.
¡Ay que me muero por ellos,
y ellos se burlan de mí!

Mother, such handsome eyes I've seen,
green, smiling, and lovely.
Oh I shall die without them,
but they only make fun of me.

This conception, with its natural and gracious melody, seems in total accord with the intentions of the poet. So too does the attractively set *Tu pupila es azul*, Joaquín Turina's version of *Rima No. 13* by the post-Romantic Gustavo Becquer, at the threshold of modern poetry. As we approach the poetry of the twentieth century, the musical spectrum will become much more diverse.

In order to obtain a comprehensive idea of the available musical settings of modern Spanish poetry, we made a survey of the vocal works of thirty Spanish composers, ranging from Enrique Granados (1867–1916) to Antón García Abril (born 1933).[5] The results show that these composers have set to music some 250 poetic texts by twenty-seven modern poets, including 60 by Rafael Alberti, 43 by Antonio Machado, 40 by García Lorca (not counting the music for his theater and many miscellaneous works), 28 by Juan Ramón Jiménez, and approximately 80 by the remaining poets. Not included in this tally are many anonymous poems and poems of popular origen, even though Manuel de Falla, Felipe Pedrell (composer of the opera *La Celestina* [1904]), and others have demonstrated the successful fusion of popular and artistic traditions. In short, simply because the number of collections of popular Spanish songs, whether in folkloric or cultivated versions, is so extensive, these will not appear among the examples offered here. Only settings of original verses by some of the greatest modern poets will be our concern.

MUSICAL SETTINGS OF SELECTED WORKS

As we have noted, extraordinary attention has been given to the works of Rafael Alberti, with sixty songs by ten Spanish composers based on his poems. Certain composers (e.g., Salvador Bacarisse, Oscar Esplá, and Ernesto Halffter) have used Alberti's early lyrics from *Marinero en la tierra* and *El alba del alhelí*, still somewhat influenced by traditional poetry. On the other hand, Riesco Grey has chosen a number of dark, difficult, surrealistic poems from *Sobre los ángeles* (1929), written by the poet at a time of emotional crisis and poor health. Gustavo Pittaluga has composed a cycle based on eighteen poems from *Metamorfosis del clavel* (1939–1940), and from this same book, the Argentine composer Carlos Guastavino wrote a delightful song to the poem "Se equivocó la paloma, / por ir al norte fue al sur" [The dove was mistaken, instead of going north, she flew south].[6]

Perhaps the most touching song composed to an Alberti text is Ernesto Halffter's (b. 1905) *La corza blanca*. (Alberti's title was "Mi corza," from *Marinero en tierra*):

Mi corza, buen amigo,
mi corza blanca
los lobos la mataron
al pie del agua.

The white doe, good friend,
my white doe,
the wolves have killed her,
at the water's edge.

Formerly in the recital repertory of Victoria de los Angeles, this song does not appear to have been recorded. A recorded song of similar appeal, however, *El pescador sin dinero*, is found in the cycle *Canciones playeras*, of Oscar Esplá (b. 1898), all on texts from *El alba del alhelí*.[7]

Pez verde y dulce del río
(. . .)
sal, y escucha el llanto mío.

Green, sweet fish of the stream,
come and hear my piteous weeping.

The music, somewhat impressionistic, maintains a simple and direct melodic line and is faithful to the text as it intensifies the fisherman's sense of desolation.

Alberti also contributes the text "Cuando mi madre llevaba un sorbete" to Xavier Montsalvatge's well-known group of songs, *Cinco canciones negras*, which also contains two striking pieces by the Cuban Nicolás Guillén, from his *Poemas mulatos*. One of these is *Chévere* ("Chévere del navajazo") and the other is *Canto negro* (¡Yambambó, yambambé!), set in dynamic rhythmic patterns by the composer. This cycle, as it happens, has acquired greater fame for its *Canción de cuna para dormir a un negrito* [Lullaby for a Little Black Child], based on a poem by Uruguayan poet Ildefonso Pereda Valdés, who published his *Antología de la poesía negra americana* in 1936.[8]

Composers throughout the world have particularly favored García Lorca. Compositions based on his texts run into the hundreds, but these include operas of his plays, choral works, ballet, popular and flamenco pieces, and even a part of a symphony by Shostakovich (see Tinnell). The number of *cultivated* songs by Hispanic composers, however—those with a good representation of Lorca's texts—is only around forty, mainly by the Spaniards Julián Bautista, Antón García Abril, Jesús García Leoz, Federico Mompou, and Carlos Suriñach, and by the Mexicans Carlos Chávez and Silvestre Revueltas. Not counted in this tally are the thirty-five pieces of incidental music specified by Lorca for his plays, pristinely realized in 1960 by composer Gustavo Pittaluga. In addition, the famous "Llanto por Ignacio Sánchez Mejías" has been set to music a number of times by Spanish and other composers.[9]

Lorca's poems on the theme of children have been treated by various composers, among them the American George Crumb and the Spaniard Xavier Montsalvatge. Crumb's cycle, *Ancient Voices of Children*, starts with a song entitled *El niño busca su voz* (Lorca's "El niño mudo," from his *Canciones*, 1921–1924). In a recording of this song performed by singer Jan de Gaetani, it is difficult to make out a single word.[10] The composer explains that he was seeking to capture Lorca's imagery by having the singer project odd syllabic sounds into the interior of an amplified piano. The result, fascinating but possibly distanced from the poet's original concept, is quite different from other songs in the series, such as *Todas las tardes en Granada . . . se muere un niño* (*Gacela V* from *Diván del Tamarit*, 1934), with its clear and moving convergence with Lorca's lines. In all, despite their wide range of musical treatments, Crumb's songs provide an imaginative and touching interpretation of the substance of Lorca's verse. In contrast, Xavier Montsalvatge's rendering of Lorca's *Canciones para niños* offers a more traditional approach, and it may be argued that his elegant artistry captures the spontaneous world of children only in his delightful last piece, *Cancioncilla sevillana*.[11]

Doce canciones infantiles by the composer Angel Mingote is yet another group of songs on the theme of children, these based on the poetry of Unamuno, Gerardo Diego, Juan Ramón Jiménez, Antonio Machado, and others. The enchantment of childhood is gratifyingly portrayed in Mingote's more artless but convincing pieces, which were awarded the Spanish Premio Nacional de Música in 1956. One can readily believe that Unamuno would have been pleased with Mingote's exquisite adaptation of his poem, "A mi primer nieto," with its opening verse, "La media luna es una cuna."

For the poetry of Juan Ramón Jiménez (1881–1958) there exists vocal music by five Spanish composers (Mompou, Rodrigo, Mingote, Salvador Bacarisse, and Manuel Castillo), aside from orchestral and guitar settings of *Platero y yo*. Quite beautiful is a setting of the poem "Llueve sobre el río" by the extremely sensitive composer Mompou, to be found in a recording by Montserrat Caballé.[12]

It should be noted that numerous works have been composed by Mompou and others with texts in Catalonian, Galician, Basque, and Portuguese. An outstanding example in Galician is *As froliñas dos toxos* [The little flowers of the gorse bushes], set by Eduardo Toldrá. The poet is A. Noriega Varela (1869–1936) and the text begins with, "Not the white roses, nor the red carnations, do I like as much as the delicate yellow flowers that timidly smile among the thorns."[13] Further songs in Galician, set by many of Spain's most outstanding composers, are contained in a volume dedicated to the musical historian and critic Antonio Fernández Cid (Orense 1982).

Finally, the great Castilian poet Antonio Machado has been remembered with forty-three songs by nine classical Spanish composers. In 1971 Joaquín Rodrigo, known throughout the world for his *Concierto de Aranjuez*, concerto for guitar and symphony orchestra, composed ten songs for voice and piano based on Machado's poetry. (A few years earlier, the popular singer-composer Joan Manuel Serrat had conceived a group of popular songs also based on poems of Machado.) Rodrigo's ten songs, titled *Con Antonio Machado*, are remarkable for their ability to capture much of the intimate and reflective, often somber, character of the poet's verses. There is heightened drama in the setting of Machado's "Amada, el aura dice" (no. XII in Machado's works; Rodrigo's title was *Mi corazón te aguarda*), where we hear the sound of dissonant bells in the piano.[14]

En las sombrías torres
repican las campanas. . . .

No te verán mis ojos;
¡mi corazón te aguarda!
Los golpes del martillo
dicen la negra caja.

In the gloomy towers
the bells are pealing. . . .
My eyes shall never see you,
yet my heart is waiting!
The sounds of the hammer
belie the dark, black coffin.

Another song, *Tu voz y tu mano* [Your voice and your hand] (Machado; "Soñé que tú me llevabas," CXXII) is moving for its recollection of the poet's young wife, Leonor, but also for the evident appreciation of the composer Rodrigo, blind from the age of three, for the companionship of his own wife:

Sentí tu mano en la mía,
tu mano de compañera.

I felt your hand in mine,
the hand of my companion.

This cycle ends with a jubilant, more conventionally Spanish *Canción del Duero*, based on Machado's lighthearted "Molinero es mi amante" (CLX, I).

The Machado songs of Serrat (first recorded with guitar, later with orchestra) are based on a different grouping of eleven poems, including five from *Campos de Castilla*. There is an effective and stirring setting of "La saeta" (CXXX): "¡Oh, la saeta, el cantar / al Cristo de los gitanos."[15] Other songs on such poems as "Retrato," "Guitarra del Mesón," Las Moscas," and others enhance the collection, yet in several of Serrat's renderings one perceives a certain blandness and inadequate attention to important nuances, symbols, and meanings in the poetry. An example is "A un olmo seco" (CXV), in which a dying elm tree, torn asunder by lightning, miraculously sprouts a few green leaves with the warmth and rains of spring. The poem ends with three affirmative and moving verses, in which the poet's own heart looks to the light and to life, awaiting another miracle of spring. Nevertheless, in his setting of the text, Serrat scarcely contrasts these life-affirming words with the forlorn mood of the earlier verses.

Quite moving, on the other hand, are Serrat's own poem and song, *En Colliure*, dedicated to Machado, in which he visualizes the poet in his French grave, and sings,

Profeta
ni mártir
quiso Antonio ser.
Y un poco de todo lo fue sin querer.

Neither a prophet
nor a martyr
did Antonio wish to be.
Yet despite that a little of all was he.

In sum, a wealth of music by modern composers has been found, based on the texts of Alberti, García Lorca, Jiménez, Antonio Machado, and more than twenty other modern poets. The thirty composers whose works we surveyed have also devoted much attention to early poets, such as Lope de Vega and San Juan de la Cruz, and they have shown a strong continuing interest in the use of traditional poetry as well. A wide range of approaches to the process of translating poetry into music is evident, often with results of great beauty. It is hoped that the few examples presented here may stimulate professors to look into music that would prove useful in their own teaching of Spanish poetry.

NOTES

References to recordings of songs are given as follows: Song // Poet / Composer / Performers / Recording number, date. Where an earlier recording exists, the latest known reissue is listed.

1. The great Viennese composer Franz Schubert (1797–1828) wrote only one song based on his own poetry, but magically transformed into song about 600 texts by more than fifty poets. Although there is minimal allusion to Spanish themes in Schubert's songs, three of his major stage works—one based on a play by Calderón de la Barca—have Spanish settings.

2. *Cantar del alma* // San Juan de la Cruz (1542–1591) / Federico Mompou (1893–1987) / Montserrat Caballé / Vergara LP 701-TL, ca. 1975 (all translations are mine).

3. *Si tus penas no pruevo* // Lope de Vega (1562–1637) / Francisco Guerrero (1522–1599) / Cor de Cambra del Palau de Música de Barcelona / CD HMI 987005, 1992.

4. *Madre, unos ojuelos vi* // Lope de Vega (1562–1637) / Eduardo Toldrá (1895–1962) / V. de los Angeles / CD Testament SBT 1087, 1996.

5. In addition to my own scores and recordings, holdings of the Library of Congress were consulted, along with a special listing given by Federico Sopeña in his work on contemporary Spanish music (1958, 339–384). For a variety of reasons, special detective work was sometimes needed to identify poetic texts in musical scores: The name of the poet may not be given, the title given by the composer may differ from the original title, or the composer may abridge or rearrange the text. On the other hand, many composers show a special sen-

sitivity by using such concrete allusions as "Cuatro sonetos," "Tres poemas de Antonio Machado," and the like, or the general title for a book of poetry applied to a selection of poems from that book, as with songs composed by C. Riesco Grey (b. 1923) to texts from Rafael Alberti's *Sobre los ángeles*.

6. *Se equivocó la paloma* / / Rafael Alberti (1902–1984) / Carlos Guastavino (Argentina) / José Carreras / Phillips LP 411 478-1, 1984.

7. *Pez verde y dulce* / / Rafael Alberti (1902–1984) / Oscar Esplá (1889–1976), *Canciones playeras* / / V. de los Angeles / CD EMI 742 5-65061-2, 1993.

8. *Canción de cuna para dormir a un negrito* / / I. Pereda Valdés (1899–?) / Xavier Montsalvatge (1912–2002) / V. de los Angeles / CD EMI 742 5-65061, 1993.

9. The recording of the *Llanto* by singer and actress Germaine Montero (Vanguard LP 6536), part recital and part song, borders on a nightclub style and does not always appear faithful to Lorca's intentions.

10. *El niño busca su voz* (Lorca's "El niño mudo") / / George Crumb (b. 1929) / Jan de Gaetani / Nonesuch LP H-71255, 1971.

11. *Canciones para niños* / / J. Montsalvatge (1912–2002) / M. Caballé / EMI Odeon LALP 668.

12. *Llueve sobre el río* / / Juan Ramón Jiménez (1881–1958) / Federico Mampou (1893–1987) / M. Caballé / LP Vergara 701-TL.

13. *As froliñas dos toxos* / / A. Noriega Varela (1869–1936) / Eduardo Toldrá (1875–1962) / V. de los Angeles / CD EMI 7243 5 65061, 1993.

14. *Mi corazón te aguarda* (Machado's "Amada, el aura dice") / / Antonio Machado (1875–1939) / Joaquín Rodrigo (b. 1901) / María Orán / CD EMI Odeon CDM 7243 56641-7, 1997.

15. "La saeta" / / Antonio Machado (1875–1939) / Joan Manuel Serrat / Serrat / CD RCA BMG 74321-20241-2, 1969. Titled *Dedicado a Antonio Machado, poeta*.

BIBLIOGRAPHY

Alberti, Rafael. *Poesía (1924–1967)*. Madrid: Aguilar, 1977.

García Lorca, Federico. *Collected poems*. Edited by C. Maurer. New York: Farrar, Strauss, and Giroux, 1991.

Guillén, Nicolás. *Nueva antología*. Mexico City: Mexicanos Unidos, 1979.

Jiménez, Juan Ramón. *Libros de poesía*. Madrid: Aguilar, 1987.

Macri, Oreste, ed. *Antonio Machado. Poesía y prosa*. Vol. 2, *Poesías completas*. Madrid: Espasa-Calpe, 1989.

Orense, Excelentísima Diputación Provincial. *Treinta y cuatro canciones gallegas dedicadas a Antonio Fernández Cid*. Orense, 1982.

Ostwald, Peter. *Schumann: The Inner Voices of a Musical Genius*. Boston: New England University Press, 1985.

Pereda Valdés, Ildefonso, ed. *Antología de la poesía negra americana*. Montevideo: Organización Medina, 1936.

Querol, Miguel. *Cancionero musical de Lope de Vega*. 3 vols. Barcelona: Inst. Esp. de Musicología, 1986–1991.

Quiroz, Roderick S. "Versiones musicales de la poesía del Siglo de Oro: desde

Boscán hasta Lope de Vega." *Hispania* 79 (1996): 491–501.

Rodrigo, Victoria Kamhi de. *Hand in Hand with Joaquín Rodrigo*. Translated by E. Wilkerson. Pittsburgh: Latin American Literature Review Press, 1992.

Sopeña, Federico. *Historia de la música española contemporánea*. Madrid: Rialp, 1958.

Tinnell, Roger D. *Federico García Lorca: Catálogo-discografía*. Durham: University of New Hampshire Press, 1986.

Vega Carpio, Lope de. *Obras escogidas*. Vol. 1, 2d ed. Edited by F. Sainz de Robles. Madrid: Aguilar, 1952.

29

From the Composer's Viewpoint: The Dialogue between Music and Poetry

Mario Lavista

During the past few years I have been very involved in writing chamber music, series of instrumental pieces in which I have explored some of the new technical possibilities that traditional instruments still offer the composer. At the same time, in most of these works I have tried to establish some kind of relationship between music and literature, especially between music and poetry. When writing this music I never had the intention of composing tone poems, that is to say, pieces that narrate stories or describe the psychology of the characters. The relationship between my music and other arts such as poetry or painting is less anecdotal, less scientific, more poetic, more arbitrary, more subjective, and removed from any kind of realism.

It is quite clear to me that our preferences for certain authors depend exclusively on some sort of inexplicable affinity. I believe that everything we read during our lifetimes has an influence on all our actions and activities, including the making of music.

Reading molds us and directs us in a very significant way, and musicians express these influences mysteriously through a unique and totally different language, the language of sounds.

Music, just like verbal exegeses, cannot embrace the multiple meaings of a poem or story, but as a composer one can enhance its meaning by highlighting certain facets, emphasizing images, or trying to establish some structural connection. I would like to offer two pieces that clearly illustrate the work I have been doing in this field. In them you will find references to Hispanic literaure as well as some of the new instrumental techniques I have been studying.

The first piece, *Marsias*, was written for oboe and eight tuned crystal glasses. Here I drew my inspiration from a story of the same title by the Spanish poet Luis Cernuda and from the legend of the fabled Phrygian satyr. The *aulos*, considered the ancestor of the oboe, was a double-reed instrument invented by the goddess Pallas. According to the legend, Pallas was playing her instrument by the lake one day when she saw her face reflected on the water. She did not like what she saw. She looked ugly because she was playing the *aulos* and her cheeks were full of air. So she immediately dropped the instrument and ran away. Some time later, Marsias passed by and saw it. He picked it up and started practicing until at last he succeeded in mastering it. Soon he realized that the sounds he was producing came from the innermost voice of his self. It was the secret voice of his heart. When he played, every living creature became silent and listened to his music. Heartened by this reception, he decided to challenge Apollo, the god of music, to a competition. Apollo accepted the challenge, and the contest was held before a jury, with Marsias playing the *aulos* and Apollo the lyre.

Marsias played first, and the audience was captivated by the unique sounds he produced on his *aulos*. When Apollo's turn came, he played his lyre with a purity and perfection that never had been heard before. The god was declared the winner, and Marsias was flayed alive as punishment for his arrogance and his defeat. It is said that the River Marsias in Asia Minor was born from his blood and tears. According to Cernuda, the satyr represents the poet who is eternally seeking the right word, the only word, the perfect expression. In their attempts at approaching divinity through perfection, poets and artists are always doomed to fail.

In this piece I have explored the interaction between an oboe, which represents Marsias's *aulos*, and a set of eight crystal glasses, which stand for Apollo's world. The glasses provide a harmonic environment based on perfect fifths, intervals of perfect consonance that were usually identified with divinity. These perfect fifths are linked by tritones, an interval that in ancient times was regarded as the sound of the devil in music; an imperfect interval associated with earthly matters. At times the oboe blends with the harmonic environment, and on other occasions it conflicts with it. Throughout the piece the harmonic environment created by the tuned glasses works as a kind of bubble, inside of which the oboe roams freely. The score of *Marsias* bears an epigraph taken from Luis Cernuda's story. It says, "Marsias blew and sighed from time to time through the entwined reeds, obtaining sweet and mysterious sounds that were like the secret voice of his heart."

The second piece I would like to describe to you is a string quartet entitled *Reflections of the Night* that I wrote for and dedicated to the Latin American String Quartet. When writing this piece, one of my main purposes was to eliminate fundamental tones and use only harmonic sounds—the audible reflections of the fundamental pitch or note, not the note itself. This is how it works:

From a physical perspective, a fundamental pitch vibrates at a specified frequency. For instance, the pitch "A" vibrates at a frequency of 440 cycles per second. That is called the fundamental pitch. The fundamental pitch also causes overtones or harmonics to vibrate in a pattern called the *harmonic series*. On a string instrument you can easily hear the overtones by touching the string in different places. If you touch the string at the halfway point, you will hear the octave above the fundamental pitch. If you divide the string into three parts and touch it at the 1/3 or 2/3 point, you will hear the fifth above that. If you divide the string into four parts and touch it, you will hear two octaves above the fundamental pitch. These pitches are called natural harmonics, and they have been used only sporadically in music. The enormous technical difficulties inherent in producing these sounds explain the need to use a simple musical form, one that is comprehensible to both listeners and performers.

My quartet *Reflections of the Night* never uses the fundamental pitches of the violin, viola, or cello. It uses only the harmonics that are created by touching the strings at various points, which allows the listener to hear the overtones very clearly. The title of this piece was taken from the collected poems published in 1926 of Xavier Villaurrutia, a Mexican poet and playwright. I was particularly taken with the poem "Echo," one of eight brief pieces in his *Insomniac Suite*. The poet says,

Night plays with noises
copying them into its mirrors
of sounds.

I have tried to capture both the nocturnal mood and the idea of reflection that the poem suggests. According to my personal interpretation, everything we hear at night is but an echo, the refracted sounds of the noises we hear during the day.

In a way, using harmonic sounds is just like using reflected sounds. Each of these tones is a mirror sound produced by a single generator, a fundamental pitch we never actually hear. We hear only its partials, its harmonics, its reflected sounds. On the other hand, the overall form has also been conceived as a mirror. The piece is in one continuous movement that can be divided into three parts, and each of these can be subdivided into two: A–(a–b)–B–(c–d)–A–(b–a). As you can see, the first two and the last two parts are identical, but they have been placed in a different order. Therefore, the piece ends just as it began, creating the illusion of a mirror form. These are some of the techniques that I have applied as well to others of my works, among them my opera based on Carlos Fuentes's *Aura*, and my rendering of Jorge Luis Borges's enigmatic tale, *The Approach to Al-mutasim*, described in the essay by Jeannine Wagar (Chapter 30 of this volume).

I would like to conclude by saying that throughout history the association between music and poetry has always been the rule, not the exception. This includes vocal music and music without words that still has literary references. The relationship between music and poetry belongs to the realm of dreams. It ultimately remains a mystery, and it is probably best that it remain so. This intense relationship, comparable to that of twin sisters, illustrates the way in which two artistic disciplines can explore their mutual unknowns.

Ezra Pound once said that when he felt like learning more about poetry, he turned to Stravinski. In the same way, we musicians should approach poetry to expand our knowledge of our profession, our art, and the essence of music itself.

NOTE

This chapter was derived from a keynote address and musical performance.—ed.

30

Harmonic Mirrors within Circular Time: A Study of Mario Lavista's Ficciones

Jeannine Wagar

Mario Lavista, one of Mexico's foremost contemporary composers and an undisputed leader in current innovative techniques, was born in Mexico City in 1943, where he lives to this date. Most of Lavista's music is greatly influenced by poetry and fiction, which he uses as inspirational sources for his own expression. This chapter is an analysis of one of Lavista's symphonic pieces, entitled *Ficciones* ("Fictions" or "Stories"). Completed in 1980 and premiered in June of that year by the Orquesta Sinfónica de Minería under the direction of Herrera de la Fuente, it has recently been performed by the Pittsburgh Symphony Orchestra and has achieved international acclaim.

Lavista's *Ficciones* is based on a short story by Jorge Luis Borges, titled *El Acercamiento a Almotásim*. In this story, Borges reviews a nonexistent book in which is mentioned an actual twelfth-century Persian poem, "The Conference of the Birds" by Farid ud-Din Attar, a Sufi mystic. The story of the birds is about the spiritual search for self-identity. According to Sufi belief, our life on earth is a journey toward conscious realization of the divine within ourselves. This journey toward the divine is always arduous and many are lost in the process. In the poem, hundreds of thousands of birds gather to travel across seven valleys to find Simurg, the king of birds. Most of the birds give up or are killed along the way. The few survivors find, after encountering innumerable trials and difficulties on the journey, that Simurg is a mirror of themselves and that the god they sought is within.

Although the inspiration for *Ficciones* came indirectly through Borges from "The Conference of the Birds," *Ficciones* is not a narrative symphonic poem. The development of the compositional ideas and harmonic language is purely musical, though Lavista frequently creates musical connotations that reflect the story and philosophy of the poem.

Lavista's musical language in *Ficciones* includes the use of harmonic and melodic mirrors. The system is based on twelve sets of fifths and their corresponding tritones. The first six sets are the exact mirror images of the final six sets. The sound of the interval of a fifth is stable and consonant. The superimposed tritones create the dissonance that questions the fifth's static stability. This creates a harmonic "answer" to the first question of "why should the birds leave safety to undertake a perilous journey?" The dissonance of the tritone urges them to travel from the safety of the fifths into the unknown. The musical mirrors point out that though the birds travel a great distance, they arrive back at the beginning (Figure 30.1).

This mirrored compositional style also creates a sense of circular time. *Ficciones* moves through time by ever-changing "archetypal" intervals that self-generate and then mirror back on themselves. This system is in contrast to much of Western music.

Western music evolved by using a system of harmonic tension and release, thereby creating a sense of linear time. By the eighteenth century, Western European music had created an elaborate and complex harmonic language that used twelve major and minor key centers. This harmonic language was based on the premise that there is a "home" or central key. The eighteenth- and early nineteenth-century composer could travel through modulation to other keys, but was obligated through formal structure based on Western harmony to return home once again.

As Western harmonic language grew more complex, composers modulated so far from the original home key that the ear couldn't hear the necessity of the return. Thus, a whole new system was created by which going forward (linearly) could just as easily be heard as going backward. The sense of forward motion was lost.

Twentieth-century composers devised many different "solutions" to this problem. Lavista's solution of a self-generating system was influenced greatly by the impressionist composer Debussy. Thus, Lavista's musical system corresponds directly to Borges's own nonlinear literary style and alludes to the journey of the birds. The birds have searched across seven valleys for Simurg only to discover he was with them all the time. Simurg was a mirror of themselves.

The formal structure of *Ficciones* is composed of two contrasting sections of approximately equal length. The first section is characterized by slow melodic movement and an almost static sense of rhythmic

Figure 30.1

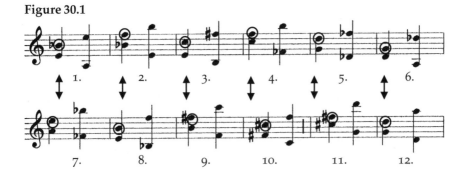

and harmonic movement. This introduction can be seen as a musical depiction of the birds' motionless and embryonic state of consciousness, the state of consciousness that exists before they decide to undertake their spiritual journey of self-discovery. The second section of *Ficciones* is marked by sudden rhythmic, dynamic, harmonic, and textural changes. This section represents the "journey," filled with unexpected dangers and perils. Rhythmic complexities, introduced through use of 7/8 meters and alternating 3/4 and 4/4 bars subtly allude to the birds' quest through the seven valleys referred to in the poem.

The first section (prejourney) of *Ficciones* begins with the fifth E and B, whose corresponding tritone A and E is superimposed upon it. He modulates by using the B as the generator for another fifth, B and F, with its superimposed tritones E and B. By modulating in this manner, Lavista can easily reach the mirror groups of the original six sets of fifths and tritones. The listener can actually begin to "hear" the mirrored images that Borges creates with words and that only later become apparent.

In the second (journey) section of *Ficciones*, a different type of modulation results by using the E of the opening fifth as the generator for transposing down a minor third. This creates another group, the fifth C and G, with its respective tritones, G and D. These pitches become increasingly important throughout the composition, until finally the fifth C and G achieve an equal status with the original fifth E and B. The listener who follows this musical path both literally and intuitively can ask, "Why is this new modulation so important? What is the meaning of the dual presence of two tonal centers?" Or intuitively, "We have gone to a new place but are still at the beginning. How is that possible?" (Figure 30.2). The melodies in *Ficciones* are derived from the same harmonic system (Figure 30.3). By filling in the larger intervallic leaps in the basic fifths and tritones with adjacent notes, melodies are formed that are cantabile and expressive. Lavista then uses these melodies both contrapuntally and in inversion, once again mirroring each other in the same manner as the underlying harmonies.

Figure 30.2

Figure 30.3

Harmonic activity during the second (journey) section is increased by rapid interchanging of fragmentary motives from the initial fifths and tritones over a new static pedal of C and G. There is a gradual slowing of harmonic and rhythmic motion accompanied by the introduction of a long pedal on G. In spite of the distance traveled and the emphasis placed on a "new" tonal center, the original presence of the E is still felt. As the piece closes, harmonic motion becomes even slower, until the climax reinstates the E to a position of equal importance with G. Lavista then closes the work with the superimposition of both harmonic groups.

Finally, the listener can hear the importance of both tonal centers. The music itself has been transformed by the journey. The listener can relate the presence of the two tonal centers to the transformed self-identity of the surviving birds. Though their journey led them to the realization that Simurg was actually within themselves, the birds' spiritual consciousness has been affected by the experience of the journey and by the realization of God within. They had "arrived" back to the beginning of their journey (E /B), but were intrinsically changed by that journey (C-G).

Throughout *Ficciones*, Lavista humorously uses one final technique that plays with our imagination in the same manner in which Borges plays with us in his novels. Lavista quotes his earlier piano piece, *Simurg*, which quotes composer Gerhart Muench, who quotes Scriabin's *Op. 74* as perceived by Muench. Thus, in *Ficciones*, Lavista alludes to the work of composer Muench, who in turn alludes to Scriabin. This is, of course, a musical comment that imitates Borges's own literary humor, which quotes and reviews existing and nonexistent books with references to both.

In short, through the application of similar techniques, through the blending of their poetic and musical conceptions, Lavista and Borges reflect and translate each other, and the artistic impulse emerges as one. Literature becomes music even without the blatant word.

31

Of Echoes and Clones: Mirror Images in Borges's The Approach to Al-Mu'tasim

Nora de Marval-McNair

Ficciones.
Seventeen stories spawned by dreams.
Seventeen dreams clothed as stories.
Stories and dreams peopled by writers and librarians, by gauchos and pilgrims, by philosophers and theologians, by detectives, by wizards, by assassins, by traitors, by heroes . . .
Stories and dreams nourished by books and by labyrinths, by circular towers and wicked swords, by masks, by myths, by mirrors, by moons . . .
Stories and dreams about time and the absurd, about pantheism and idealism and, ultimately, about chaotic and chimerical worlds devoid of order and absolutes and governed by relativity, by irony, by paradox . . .
Ficciones.

A slim and delicate volume that assembles seventeen unusual stories whose erudition mesmerizes, whose complexity amazes, and whose dissimilar faces startle and jolt. For "The South," a dreamlike yarn about one man's delusion regarding primitive gauchos, their duels, and their primal code of valor and prowess, shares its perilous space with "The Secret Miracle," a marvel of mind over matter during the Jewish Holocaust. The mental powers of a sorcerer that allow him to create a man from the incorporeal and elusive substance of dreams (McMurray, 67) in "The Circular Ruins," show a different trait in "Funes, the Memorious," the tragic story of a crippled peon who cannot ever forget any experience of the past. And the inaccessible Book in "The Library of Babel," the Book that is "the formula and perfect compendium of all the rest" (Borges *Labyrinths*, 56), lies idle and undiscovered next to "Death and the Compass," a detective thriller whose metaphysical overtones and ironic slant dramatize "the limits of reason" and "its pitfalls" (McMurray, 16).

However, and regardless of the unusual garments the stories in *Ficciones* may flaunt, the golden thread that embroiders the tapestry of nearly all of these tales is one of the most well-established and time-honored paradigms of Western literature. I am referring to the quest, the quest for knowledge, the quest for the self, the quest for a camouflaged and elusive God.

A constant in Borges's early fiction, this motif first appeared, rather unexpectedly, not in a short story but in an essay. In 1936 he had published a slender book with the improbable title of *Historia de la eternidad*, a volume that contained eight philosophical musings on the most diverse topics. The final item in its table of contents carried the odd and apparently unimaginative subheading, "Dos notas." The first of these "two notes" was a witty and amusing essay on the subtle art of incivility and rudeness; the second was a rather solemn critical review of an Indian novel entitled "El acercamiento a Almotásim" [The Approach to Al-Mu'tasim].[1]

This latter "note" was, however, a bold and unexpected interloper in the world of essayistic writing, for its underlying spirit and essential core were not factual but fictive. A hybrid creature of mixed ancestry, Borges's "The Approach" was thus both fact and fiction, genuine and forged, credible and feigned. Therefore, not being a true essay nor a true story but both, its creator decided in 1944 to house it also in his second home, his alternate world of cosmic wonders, the world of *Ficciones*.[2]

Cross-pollinated by the real and the false, Borges's story begins as a book review by an unidentified and supposedly unbiased literary critic and narrator who may or may not be Borges himself.[3] The book that is the object of the review is a novel written by a lawyer from Bombay City named Mir Bahadur Ali. This novel, a "detective story" with a "mystic undercurrent" (Borges *Ficciones*, 22) had been previously critiqued by Philip Guedalla and, prior to that, by Cecil Roberts, two "almost forgotten" (Christ, 109) writers of the 1930s. Roberts's commentary that Bahadur's book had regrettably fallen under the "double, improbable tutelage" (Borges, 22) of an obscure English novelist and an illustrious twelfth-century Persian poet by the name of Farid uddin Attar, is repeated by Guedalla and duly noted by the narrator in his own review of these critics' reviews. In addition, the narrator sees fit to comment that the two critics had in fact condemned the novel because it was, in their opinion, "a rather uncomfortable combination"

(22) of two dissimilar genres, meaning fiction and allegory, detectory fabrication and the esoteric.

But Borges's own story is also a "rather uncomfortable combination" of two disparate genres—in his case, the editorial piece and fictive prose—thus cloning, in its own peculiar way, the novel it purports to censor and critique. Hence, by basically echoing and mirroring each other, story and novel cast the mold into which the strategy for the remainder of the text will be shaped and set.

The *editio princeps* of *The Approach to Al-Mu'tasim*, the Indian narrative by Bahadur Ali, had appeared toward the end of 1932. Since it had the distinction of being "the first detective novel written by a native of Bombay City" (Borges, 22), it became a modest best-seller and, within a couple of months enjoyed, in the narrator's own words, no less than "four printings of a 1,000 copies each" (22).

In view of the novel's success, a second edition was issued two years later, in 1934. This time the volume carried illustrations and a new title: *The Conversation with the Man Called Al-Mu'tasim*, followed by the subheading *A Game with Shifting Mirrors*. This edition is the one that had just been "reproduced and issued in London by Victor Gollancz, with a prologue by Dorothy L. Sayers" (Borges, 22), and that the narrator/critic has before him and is about to appraise. In fact, he has no choice but to use this version—which he considers to be barely tolerable—because his own quest to find the 1932 edition, a superior work by far, was unsuccessful. James Winchell perceptively points out that the "superiority of the first edition" (203) over the second is "intimated by a metaphysical devaluation revealed in the changed title: where the second promises a 'Conversation' with the 'Man' called Al-Mu'tasim, indicating presence, the first promises only 'the approach' to his *suspected* or intuited presence, implying a passage through a series of stages marked rather by his absence" (203). Thus, the primitive version "approaches the status of sacred text precisely because it is unavailable to the 'infidel' narrator" (Winchell, 202).

At this juncture, the "initial impression of verisimilitude" (Shaw, 19) that was intentionally conveyed by the insertion of real people and real institutions—Guedalla, Roberts, Sayers, the publishing house of Victor Gollancz—begins to unravel when the reader starts to sense that the touted original may not exist. Indeed, not only does the original not exist, but not one of the narrator's bibliographical entries—the two disapproving reviews and the second edition with its parallel version—is either authentic or true.

The hoax has just begun. In Borges's apocryphal document about a novel that somehow replicates a prior text that was read by readers who in turn are read by readers reading a reader, we now learn that its "visible protagonist" (Borges, 23)—implying a hidden and mirroring counterpart—is, like its putative creator, from Bombay City, and like that creator in his youth, a student of the law. A free thinker—but this time like Borges—the young man accidentally becomes involved in a riot between Moslem and Hindu religious factions. He joins the fray, and, with his own hands, "kills (or thinks he kills) a Hindu" (23).

Horrified and frightened, the bloodstained student takes flight, makes for the outer fringes of town, and reaches a garden in disarray that hosts a circular tower in the back. When pursued by "mooncoloured" (Borges, 23) and fiendish hounds, he gains shelter in the tower, a fact that forecasts a parallel success when he finally finds the sanctuary of the elusive Al-Mu'tasim (Wheelock, 150). But first he has to pay his dues: He meets an untouchable, a despoiler of cadavers who makes his living by stealing gold teeth from dead bodies. This man also speaks with rancor and hostility about "certain horse thieves in Guzerat" (Borges, 23), who are, in his own words, "as unclean as the two of us" (23). The student falls asleep and, waking up with the sun, finds that he has been robbed of some silver rupees by his corpse-plundering "opposite and equal" (Winchell, 205). He then decides to "lose himself in the depths of India" (Borges, 24). For he has reached the conclusion that, like the forager he met the night before, he is capable also of "irrational, murderous violence" (Winchell, 204). At this point he realizes as well that, in spite of his incredulity, he was guilty of the sacrificial murder of a Hindu in the name of a faith and a creed he had always rejected and denied (Wheelock, 150). His flight is also prompted by the desire to search for a woman of the robber caste, a "malka-sansi" (Borges, 24), whom the thief cursed and maligned. As Carter Wheelock points out, the student has now concluded that "vilification by such a man is tantamount to praise" (151).

This is then a summary of the narrator's summary of the first two chapters of Bahadur's novel. The rest of the text is condensed in vague statements, glosses, and "place names that trace a geographical, narratological and spiritual circle" (Winchell, 205). In fact, the story that began in Bombay City will end as well in Bombay City, "a few paces away from the garden of the mooncoloured hounds" (Borges, 24). Thus, the protagonist travels the immense geography of Hindustan in a circular orbit of countless leagues and numerous years. During his journey, he comes upon people of the most depraved and sordid class, and takes up their habits of deceit and trickery in "a kind of contest of infamy" (24). Indeed, he conspires, lingers, watches, hesitates, and kills.

But one day, while talking to one of those abhorrent men, he makes a startling discovery: This man, who is evil incarnate, nonetheless harbors an almost imperceptible suggestion of kindness that somehow reduces the iniquity surrounding them. "It was—the narrator adds—as if a more complex interlocutor had joined the dialogue" (Borges, 25). Judging that this tenderness cannot be and is not a part of this man's being, the student concludes that that compassion—fleeting and faint though it may be—is indeed real, and that it is "the reflection of a friend, or of the friend of a friend" (25).

This friend of a friend of a friend must be found. The student tells himself that somewhere in this vast universe a man "from whom this clarity emanates; . . . a man who is this clarity" (Borges, 25) must exist. A pious pilgrim now, he vows to dedicate his life to finding this masked and mysterious source of goodness through the gossamer traces and footprints he may have left in others. Thus, the search for Al-Mu'tasim begins.

The many years he spent living in infamy are now repeated, but as a reversed and diametrically opposed echo. As before, he watches and lingers; now, however, he presages, he questions, he prays, he seeks. As he nears his goal he notes that those who are closer to the absent Al-Mu'tasim show a clearer and greater proportion of holy attributes than other men. However, they are still mere echoes, mere doubles, mere mirrors.

In due time the protagonist reaches a gallery with a beaded curtain behind which a glow, a radiance, dazzles and shimmers. He claps his hands. He asks for Al-Mu'tasim. "A man's voice—the incredible voice of Al-Mu'tasim—urges him to come in" (Borges, 25). And, the novel . . . abruptly . . . ends.

It is hinted that the unnamed student finally found the man who is all clarity; however, the face-to-face encounter between him and Al-Mu'tasim is not disclosed. The beaded curtain protects the answer. Indeed, the truncated climax in Bahadur's novel does not allow for any elaboration on the identity of Al-Mu'tasim; it will be the narrator's task to make manifest and suggest it for us.

Faithful to one of his favorite techniques, Borges, or the narrator/ critic, proceeds to discuss the book and its subsequent versions, thus mirroring and almost cloning his own introduction to his own story. The 1932 version, he states, presents Al-Mu'tasim as a divine being with personal features; the 1934 edition, on the other hand, resorts to allegory. Thus, these parallel renditions can be seen as the different ways in which man has imagined his deity since the beginning of time. The student's pilgrimage—arduous and meandering—is, perhaps, the lay version of the anguished and laborious ascent of the soul to Mount Carmel, as recounted by San Juan de la Cruz (Pérez, 140).

The idea of a unitary God who "accommodates Himself to human diversities" (Borges, 26) and becomes man even to the point of infamy holds no appeal for the narrator. Instead, he favors an incomplete and insufficient God who is in constant movement—another pilgrim like the student/pilgrim—searching for His clone or His better who, in turn, also in constant movement, is lost in His own creation, searching for His own clone or His better, in an endless cycle throughout the endlessness of time. Casually, the narrator reminds us that the name Al-Mu'tasim stands for *The Seeker of Shelter*.

Mention of literary sources for Bahadur's novel closes the main body of Borges's story. Among the various texts cited as hypothetical precursors to the Indian novel, *Colloquy of the Birds* stands out because, like Bahadur's novel, it is summarized and discussed but in a footnote, lengthy and erudite. The poem—which had been mentioned at the beginning of Borges's story—is an allegorical piece by Farid-ud-din Attar, a twelfth-century Persian writer. It tells the odyssey and pilgrimage of a large flock of birds that search for many years and over seven valleys and seven seas for the Simurg, their beloved but faraway king. All they know is that Simurg means "thirty birds" (Borges, 28), and that the Simurg's royal palace "stands on the Kaf, the circular mountain which surrounds the earth" (28). After numerous travails and the death or desertion of most, only thirty pilgrim/birds, "purified by their labors" (28)—like the student/pilgrim before them—reach their own sanctuary, the mountain of the Simurg. When they set foot on it, they realize that "*they* are the Simurg, and that the Simurg is each one of them and all of them" (Borges, 28).

With this poem, "which no longer is an apocryphal creation of Borges" (Alazraki, 22), the narrator interprets and solves the abortive ending of the hypothetical novel: The searcher is the sought, the law student from Bombay is Al-Mu'tasim, and Al-Mu'tasim is not only the student but all men.

But Al-Mu'tasim's face, indeed God's face, is not seen. Perhaps it will never be seen. Perhaps God's face was erased so that God can become every man, so that God can *be* every man. So that God can be the cryptic Al-Mu'tasim, so that God can be the murdered Hindu, so that God can be the despoiler of corpses, so that God can be the student/pilgrim, so that God can be the thirty birds, so that God can be the narrator/critic, so that God can be even Borges himself.

By creating an infinite regression of reciprocal reversions and an unending mimesis of cosmic proportions, Borges can also be the murdered Hindu, and the despoiler of corpses, and the student/pilgrim, and the narrator/critic, and the thirty birds, and the Simurg, and . . .

Echoes echoing echoes . . .
Mirrors mirroring mirrors . . .

NOTES

1. As with everything else in Borges's body of work, even the title of this story is not clear cut. The correct spelling of the name of the being that is the object of the pilgrim's search is unclear, since different editions present it as either "Al-Mu'tasim," "Almotasim," or even "al-Mu'tasim." For consistency's sake, I shall use the first form, "Al-Mu'tasim," for such is the way it appears in the edition that I have consulted for citation in this chapter.

2. The slow and laborious pilgrimage of the actual text of "The Approach" from the realm of the essay (which it never abandoned) to the realm of fiction (where it also resides) is an unexpected and additional echo in the invented saga of the protagonist of this piece. Indeed, in 1941 "The Approach" was reprinted with seven other stories in a collection that was published as *El jardín de senderos que se bifurcan* (*The Garden of Forking Paths*). In 1994, a second group of six stories, under the heading *Artifices*, was added to *The Garden of Forking Paths*, thus giving rise to the first edition of *Ficciones*. The definitive version of *Ficciones*—fourteen stories to which three more ("El fin," "La secta del fénix," and "El Sur") were added, saw the light twelve years later, in 1956.

3. Thomas E. Lyon interprets Borges's first-person narrator as "an entity created and placed between author and reader," and whose role is to set "the tone" and determine "the point of view of a story." Lyon adds that this personal narrator "must not be confused with the author but be understood as a functional invention of his creator" (363).

BIBLIOGRAPHY

Alazraki, Jaime. *Jorge Luis Borges*. New York: Columbia University Press, 1971.

Borges, Jorge Luis. *Ficciones*. With an introduction by John Sturrock. New York: Alfred A. Knopf, 1993.

———. *Labyrinths: Selected Stories & Other Writings*. Edited by Donald A. Yates and James E. Irby. Preface by André Maurois. New York: New Directions, 1964.

Christ, Ronald J. *The Narrow Act: Borges' Art of Allusion*. New York: New York University Press; London: University of London Press, 1969.

Lyon, Thomas E. "Borges and the (Somewhat) Personal Narrator," *Modern Fiction Studies* 19 (Autumn 1973): 363–372.

McMurray, George R. *Jorge Luis Borges*. New York: Frederick Ungar, 1980.

Pérez, Alberto C. *Realidad y Suprarrealidad en los cuentos fantásticos de Jorge Luis Borges*. Miami: Ediciones Universal, 1971.

Shaw, Donald L. *Ficciones*. London: Grant and Cutler, 1976.

Wheelock, Carter. *The Mythmaker: A Study of Motif and Symbol in the Short Stories of Jorge Luis Borges*. Austin: University of Texas Press, 1969.

Winchell, James. "The Oldest Trick in the Book: Borges and the 'Rhetoric of Immediacy,'" *Studies in Twentieth Century Literature* 17 (1993): 197–221.

PART VII

FROM NOVEL TO
SILVER SCREEN

32

Galdós on Film: Doña Perfecta, *a Mexican Melodrama*

Gerard Dapena

Benito Pérez Galdós, universally regarded as Spain's greatest nine-teenth-century novelist, has the peculiar distinction of being the Span-ish writer most frequently adapted to the screen. There are at least a dozen film versions of sundry novels by Galdós, Buñuel's cinemati-zations of *Nazarín* and *Tristana* being the most celebrated.[1] Curiously, two adaptations of Galdós were made in Mexico. *Nazarín* is justly re-garded as one of Buñuel's masterpieces, but the other Mexican refor-mulation of Galdós, Alejandro Galindo's *Doña Perfecta* (1950) starring Dolores del Río, never achieved the same degree of popularity, de-spite the fact that Galindo was one of the most prominent figures of Mexico's Golden Age of Cinema and the director of such classics as *Campeón sin corona, Esquina Bajan*, and *Espaldas mojadas*. His films earned him a reputation for socially conscious subject matter depicted in a realist vein.

Galindo cowrote the screenplay for *Doña Perfecta* following Galdós's story very closely. The town of Orbajosa is renamed Santa Fe, but the action still unfolds in the last quarter of the nineteenth century. How-ever, there are a few noticeable modifications. The most important one, in terms of narrative progression, is the appearance of Doña Remedios early in the film, whereas Galdós introduces her toward the end of the book. In addition, the film does not start with Pepe's arrival at the train station, but with Doña Perfecta's receipt of a letter announcing his impending visit. There are a few minor changes in the characterization of the main protagonists as well. Most notably, Don Inocencio is no longer a priest, but a former seminarian turned lawyer who files claims against the government to recover confiscated ecclesiastical property. Otherwise, he retains the same cunning, scheming nature of the original character. This shift allowed Galindo to maintain Galdós's anticlerical stance without the risk of presenting a clergyman as a villain.

Galindo's other salient transformation involves the character of Doña Perfecta's daughter, Rosario, played by actress Ester Fernández. Although meek and vulnerable as in the book, she is not the frail, unhealthy weakling created by Galdós; instead, she is willful, even a tad disobedient. For instance, in the beginning of the film, when Doña Perfecta refuses to let her see the letter from Pepe's father, Rosario sneaks into her mother's bedroom and reads it in secret. Later, prior to the chapel scene, Galindo's mise-en-scène sets up a furtive rendezvous between Rosario and Pepe in the dining room, while Doña Perfecta awaits in a vestibule in the background. These small details round out Rosario's personality so that Galindo's different ending makes sense.

Nevertheless, in essence the film's plot and characters remain truthful to Galdós's vision, given the numerous analogies between nineteenth-century Spain and Mexico. Political developments resembled those of Galdós's Spain.[2] In addition, the intellectual climate described by Galdós was similar to Mexico's. The 1860s and 1870s witnessed the introduction of positivism into Mexican politics, and liberal politicians and thinkers called for the application of recent scientific discoveries to the fields of economic and social development. At the same time, the government was engaged in an ongoing battle to achieve secularization against a Church in possession of vast wealth and privileges. As a result, the country was torn by the struggle between conservatives and liberals for political and ideological supremacy. Military insubordination, regional rebellions, and increased banditry were rampant. Thus, Galdós's conspiracy of religious fanatics in a forsaken provincial town does not seem entirely foreign to the reality of 1870s Mexico.

Yet beyond these historical references there is little trace of Mexico on screen, even less so than in *Nazarín*. While Buñuel's film opens up to the country's landscapes and displays a colorful array of popular types, Galindo's unfolds mostly in indoor spaces within the confines of an upper bourgeois household. One might ask, then, where is the Mexicanism of Galindo's *Doña Perfecta* to be found? It lies in the text's shift from a "novela de tesis" into a full-blown melodrama, a genre quintessentially associated with the Mexican cinema of the Golden Age.

In 1976 Peter Brooks published his seminal book, *The Melodramatic Imagination*, in which he argued for a reevaluation of melodrama as an alternative to naturalism's depiction of bourgeois society's moral order. He located the origins of melodrama in the aftermath of the French Revolution, when the dissolution of the Ancien Régime and the collapse of the traditional "sacred" created a moral vacuum. Although accepted imperatives of truth and ethics were then challenged, the urge remained to locate and express basic ethical and psychic truths. In Brooks's view, melodrama replaces the loss of a "tragic vision" to become "the principal mode for uncovering, demonstrating, and making operative the essential moral universe in a post-sacred era."[3]

According to Brooks, the ritual of melodrama usually involves the confrontation of good and evil as clearly identified antagonists and the expulsion of one of them. Melodrama seems mostly concerned, then, with "the need to recognize and confront evil, to combat and expel it, to purge the social order."[4] Since the moral occult lies frequently behind the deceptive play of signs, melodrama manifests a fascination with the hidden and a compulsion to know all, to probe into the surface of reality in order to yield its true meaning.

Although Brooks's study concerned itself with nineteenth-century literature, he acknowledged that the cinema has become the prime vehicle in our time for the expression of the melodramatic imagination. Taking a cue from Brooks, a number of film historians have turned to melodrama in an attempt to rehabilitate this most despised of genres as a potential site for a subversive critique of society. Pioneering essays by Thomas Elsaesser and Geoffrey Novell-Smith were followed by groundbreaking works that wed feminism and psychoanalysis to explore the position of women in patriarchy and the specificity of the "woman's film" within the context of Hollywood's classical cinema.[5]

In the 1940s the Mexican cinema underwent unprecedented growth and expansion on a national and international scale. Mexico's films were seen all over Latin America and in Spain, and its film industry managed within the Spanish-speaking sphere to rival Hollywood's grip on the popular imagination. Cantinflas notwithstanding, melodrama, in its various facets, has come to represent Mexico's classical cinema: the nationalistic epics of "Indio" Fernández, the populism exemplified by Ismael Rodriguez's *Nosotros los pobres*, the noirish *cabaretera* film, the cross-generational family drama.[6] Unlike these other models, *Doña Perfecta* typifies a literary and dignified brand of melodrama that sought cultural legitimation among middlebrow audiences through the adaptation of novels by prestigious writers.

In light of Brooks's argument, I wish to examine the various modes in which *Doña Perfecta* functions as melodrama. The novel's generic affiliations have been a point of contention among scholars of Galdós. Some, like Rodolfo Cardona, have advocated its status as tragedy. Others, like Roberto Sánchez, have underscored its melodramatic components. Then there are those, such as Anthony N. Zahareas, who settle for a middle ground, acknowledging the book's *bricolage*, its mixture of tragic, melodramatic, and comic registers. Galdós's barbed irony and nods to classical tragedy, however, are absent from Galindo's *Doña Perfecta*, which ventures recklessly into the rarefied world of melodrama.

If the confrontation of opposing discourses vying for legitimation is a quintessential feature of melodrama, then *Doña Perfecta* clearly qualifies as such. Galdós and Galindo reinforce this through heavy characterization. For instance, the atmosphere of Orbajosa/Santa Fe is depicted as stifling, narrow-minded, and deceitful. Pepe Rey's liberalism is identified with good, while Doña Perfecta's circle, and conservative Spain /Mexico at large, stands for evil. Their clear-cut confrontation is also typical of melodrama's penchant for stark and easily recognizable contrasts. In the film, Galindo resorts to caricature in order to underline this point: Don Inocencio is presented as a slimy, conniving reptile, Doña Remedios as a poisonous magpie, and Jacinto as a leering moron.

Another definition of melodrama conceives it as a journey toward the discovery of evil and the unearthing of a hidden moral truth. Cardona argued that the main theme of Galdós's novel was the unmasking of hypocrisy, and Galindo seems to be of the same opinion.[7] The film is framed between two quotes addressing this issue. At the very beginning, two excerpts from St. Paul's epistle are superimposed over a panorama of the fictional city of Santa Fe: "En lo que condenas a otro, te condenas a ti mismo; haciendo como haces tú, aquellas mismas cosas que condenas," and "Vosotros sois la causa, como dice la escritura, de que sea blasfemado el nombre de Dios." The film, like the novel, ends with the words, "Es cuanto por ahora podemos decir de las personas que parecen buenas y no lo son." This interpretation construes the narrative of *Doña Perfecta* as a rite of passage whereby the young lovers, and by extension the spectator, attain enlightenment upon recognizing the intolerance concealed behind the mask of piety and social civility.

A third approach to melodrama sees it as a discourse striving to legitimate patriarchy, to propagate "the social and sexual identities through which it reproduces its own network of authority."[8] To my mind, such a reading yields the most interesting insights, since, in fact, *Doña Perfecta* appears to uphold the cause of patriarchy, yet ultimately ends up exposing its failure. Pepe Rey arrives in Orbajosa/Santa Fe ostensibly to marry his cousin and assert his property rights. Instead, his intentions of wooing and then eloping with Rosario go awry, and he is beset with endless lawsuits regarding his lands. As the story unfolds, Pepe's patriarchal authority is increasingly challenged and neutralized.

Since father figures (Rosario's, Jacinto's, and even Pepe's father) are notoriously absent from this story, women are left to fend for themselves. Doña Perfecta's husband, we are told, squandered the family fortune gambling and chasing skirts before his early death. Doña Remedios was also left an impoverished widow. The scholarly Cayetano, Doña Perfecta's brother, is a weak and ineffective male, and Pepe's father, stationed in faraway Madrid/Mexico City, is mentioned only in correspondence. Don Inocencio wields some actual power, but he is neutralized by his age and religious vocation. The onus of bearing the phallus falls on the shoulders of Caballuco, a farmhand, yet even he is ultimately manipulated by Doña Remedios and Doña Perfecta.

Excessive maternal passion is the black hole in this scenario. Pepe's undoing has been attributed to Doña Remedios's unrestrained desire for Jacinto's social advancement. In one key scene, she tells Inocencio, "Te olvidas que soy madre. . . . Estoy dispuesta a barrer las calles, a pedir limosna para que mi hijo suba y sea rico." What is often left out of the equation is Doña Perfecta's equally ferocious affection for her daughter. It is specifically this portrayal of two extreme experiences of motherhood that delivers Galindo's film from the realm of the patriarchal family melodrama into the maternal melodrama.

The family melodrama and the maternal melodrama were two extremely popular genres in Hollywood classical cinema of the 1940s and 1950s; they were also preeminent in the Mexican cinema of the Golden Age. As noted, the family melodrama tends to seek the legitimation of the social and sexual identities that are fundamental to patriarchy. Centering on issues of property and patriarchal right, its narrative deals with the survival of the family unit and the process whereby individuals find a place within it.[9]

The maternal melodrama explores mother–son or mother–daughter relations and hinges on the disruption of this intimate connection as the grown-up child eventually turns away from the mother and discovers identity through marriage. The mother–daughter bond is undoubtedly the most subversive because of its representation of intimacy among women and its attempts to map an alternative that supersedes the normal development of the Oedipus complex.[10]

Freud was of the opinion that the discovery of the mother's castration, the crux of the Oedipus complex, unfolded differently for the boy and the girl. While the boy recoils in horror and shifts his identification to his father, the girl remains attached to the mother but resentful of her castration. The daughter thus undergoes a more complex Oedipal process: Her object of narcissistic identification happens to be a castrated, denying subject. Feminist revisions of Freudian psychoanalysis have argued that women have a greater continuity of pre-Oedipal symbolic connections to the mother, who becomes both an object of love and hate. On the one hand, she can be nurturing, and on the other, vengeful and castrated. The daughter is faced with either passive acceptance or rejection of the mother; she feels guilt at achieving independence but resents her dependency.

The maternal melodrama reenacts these alternate scenarios of submission or aggression. Some maternal melodramas retell a mother's journey of self-sacrifice, at the end of which she places her child's needs before her own desires. The grown-up child discovers a new identity through marriage and turns away from the mother. In these instances, the spectator is made to identify with the mother's plight.

But there is another kind of maternal melodrama that depicts a darker image of motherhood, one often tinged with masochism and sadism. These films view a close mother–daughter bonding as unhealthy and a source of neurosis; they depict mothers as monsters who deliberately victimize their children for narcissistic and sadistic ends. Their narratives frequently deal with a daughter's repressed sexual desires, which are thwarted by a domineering mother. The relationship presented is full of ambiguity, oscillating between desire for and hate of the parent. The spectator is here made to identify with the daughter's quest for self-determination.

Doña Perfecta boldly proclaims its allegiance to this tormented kind of melodrama. The film begins with a presentation of the close, affectionate rapport between Doña Perfecta and Rosario in the letter scene. Doña Perfecta is depicted sympathetically at the start as a loving mother sincerely concerned with her daughter's happiness ("No sería cristiano imponer nuestra autoridad de padres"). The change in her attitude toward Pepe is partially determined by Don Inocencio's insidious campaign of misrepresentations. Playing Iago to her Othello, he successfully tarnishes the young man's standing by exploiting Doña Perfecta's prejudices.

Galindo's film, like Galdós's novel, struggles with the ambivalent attraction exerted throughout by Doña Perfecta. She is the true agent in the narrative, exuding the allure of power and authority, not to mention the extra appeal that Dolores del Río's glamorous screen persona adds to the character. Galindo offers a highly energetic portrait of a very decisive and proactive woman. Defined, in war terms, as a weapon at the service of God, she stands at the forefront of the anti-government conspiracy. There is in fact a military-like dimension to her domineering personality, of which she is clearly aware ("¡Qué arrebatada soy!" "¡Ojalá estos impulsos míos un día no me pierdan!"). For example, in one scene absent from the book, Doña Perfecta burns Cayetano's books on Protestants and the Enlightenment: "En esto soy intransigente. Luchar para que en mi casa se viva bajo el temor de Dios." Yet Galindo also draws attention to her behind-the-scenes maneuvers and hypocritical behavior as flagrant contradictions to her alleged rectitude and spiritual purity. He even hints at her violent, murderous disposition ("para cada bicho hay un veneno") in a brilliantly staged garden scene, wherein Doña Perfecta weaves her web of deceit around an impotent Pepe as she sprays pesticides on her flowers.

Tellingly, while Freud appears to theorize passivity and masochism as the assumption of a feminine position, *Doña Perfecta* reverses the traditional assignation of this role. Instead, Pepe Rey is constantly victimized by mysterious enemies and forces, and proves incapable of liberating Rosario from her mother's grasp. Anger leads to frustration and he becomes paranoid, in the feminine way, and repeatedly submits himself to humiliation at the hands of Doña Perfecta and Don Inocencio. This masochistic impulse might almost be interpreted as a sort of patriarchal death wish.

Brooks argued that the melodramatic mode foregrounds what the social order forbids and represses: "The dynamics of repression and the return of the repressed figure the plot of melodrama."[11] Melodrama privileges excess and strives toward moments when repression breaks through. As E. Ann Kaplan has noted, what is mainly repressed in patriarchal society is female desire.[12] Melodramatic narratives often derive their power from the articulation of female sexuality, and their appeal to female audiences is based on their expression of women's deepest unconscious fears and fantasies. It is worthwhile to consider Pepe and Rosario's first encounter on the staircase. In a long shot, we see Pepe approaching a staircase as Rosario descends. Galindo cuts to a close-up of Rosario, then to a close-up of Pepe, then back to Rosario. In accordance with the unwritten rules of melodrama, the usual terms of cinematic scopophilia are reversed: The woman initiates the look; the man becomes the object of erotic contemplation.

Although patriarchal discourse struggles to accommodate the mother's urge for self-expression within its constructs, feminine desire always seems to be in excess of the social system that seeks to contain it. Patriarchy sets limits on a mother's rapport with her child, so that at a certain stage she is expected to yield her to the Law of the Father and allow for her entry into the Symbolic, the complex order of social and psychic identities structured by language. The girl attains her feminine position through marriage and child bearing, the penis substitute, which, according to Freud, permits her to overcome castration anxiety. The disruptive force of unrestrained motherly love threatens to stall this process and derail the child's process of socialization.

Mary Ann Doane turns to Julia Kristeva's theory of the "abject" to shed light on the pervasive cinematic trope of the monstrous mother. Kristeva defines motherhood in relation to the "abject" as that which "disturbs identity, system, order. What does not respect borders, positions, rules." Doane concludes that the mother signifies for the child the realm of the abject against which she must struggle to preserve boundaries; identification with the father serves as a means to hold on to the Symbolic.[13]

Lacking a father, Rosario turns to Pepe (the story repeatedly links and identifies Pepe with the absent patriarch) to accomplish her successful Oedipal drama. Unwilling to concede defeat, to relinquish her phallus and assume her "lack," Doña Perfecta, a truly avenging phallic mother, literally enacts a castration by having Pepe shot dead. At this crucial moment, Galindo's sober visual economy breaks down and the mise-en-scène succumbs to expressionistic convulsions. As Pepe advances at night through the windswept streets of Santa Fe to wrest Rosario away from her mother, highly contrasted hard lighting casts ominous shadows and dramatic music raises the emotional stakes. Fast-paced cutting, extreme close-ups, and eccentric camera angles further destabilize our perception of space, functioning as a visual index to the characters' psychic upheaval. As the film strives for closure, patriarchal order must reassert itself over such extreme disruption and punish Doña Perfecta's transgression through the loss of her daughter's love. Squaring off with her mother, Pepe's dead body at her feet, Rosario arrives at the ultimate truth: "Usted es toda mentira. Dios no puede inspirar tanto egoísmo, tanta maldad." Defiant and empowered, she proclaims her independence: "Me voy, me voy con mi esposo," and walks away behind the soldiers carrying Pepe's corpse. Abandoned by all, Doña Perfecta rushes to the family chapel to pray for forgiveness, as the wind howls through an empty house.

Galdós displaces the mother's unwelcome desire onto the more manageable subject of religious fanaticism and political intolerance. Unlike Galindo's ending, in Galdós the daughter's own desire is short-circuited into a descent into hysteria, madness, and, finally, silence, a scenario common to many novels and women's films.[14] Mary Ann Doane remarks how these repetitive patterns function in the classic Hollywood text as a symptom of the ideological crisis provoked by the need to shift the sexual terms of address of a cinema dependent on masculine structures of seeing.[15]

Mexican culture, and its cinema in particular, has placed great premium on the trappings of patriarchy; naturally, the Mexican melodrama of the 1940s is rife with conflicting discourses that attempt to define the place of the mother–daughter in a rapidly changing society.[16] *Doña Perfecta* conjures a web of filmic intertextual references and reversals. For instance, the image of Dolores del Río cursing her despotic father, who has just murdered her lover at the end of Emilio "Indio" Fernández's *Bugambilia* (1944) reverberates in Ester Fernández's condemnation of her mother. At the same time, Dolores del Río is recast in *Doña Perfecta* from victim into victimizer. Galindo had already touched upon the subject of woman's subjugation in *Una familia de tantas* (1948). This award-winning feature also deals with a daughter's emancipation from an authoritarian parent through the love of an enterprising young man. Unlike *Doña Perfecta*, this film can afford a happy ending: Despite the father's intransigent opposition, the young couple is united and can look forward to a future together. I can only speculate as to what prompted Galindo to revisit this terrain and reverse the terms of the transaction. In the second film, matriarchy sabotages what patriarchy had yielded to, and romantic fulfillment fades into necrophilia, as Rosario leaves with Pepe's corpse.

Film historian and critic Emilio García Riera belittles Galindo's film for its lukewarm political and ideological critique and its cool, restrained manner.[17] Arguably, had Buñuel managed to shoot his version of *Doña Perfecta* we would undoubtedly have a very idiosyncratic film. But I think Riera underestimates Galindo's skillful use of the conventions of melodrama and his method of playing off the ambivalent attraction a female spectator might feel toward Perfecta's power and authority, while proving sympathetic to Rosario's quest for autonomy. Women often find melodramas empowering because they tend to develop and stage scenarios in ways that resist and even subvert dominant ideology. *Doña Perfecta* goes so far in its disruption of the status quo that, despite the final, necessary reinscription, it remains a singularly disturbing yet fascinating rendition of a mother and daughter's "passion and rapture."[18]

NOTES

1. Other film adaptations of Galdós include two versions of *Marianela*, two of *Doña Perfecta*, two of *Fortunata y Jacinta* (one made for TV), two of *El abuelo*, and one of *Tormento*.

2. See Charles A. Hale, *The Transformation of Liberalism in Late 19th Century Mexico* (Princeton, N.J.: Princeton University Press, 1989), esp. ch. 1 and 2.

3. Peter Brooks, *The Melodramatic Imagination: Balzac, Henry James, Melodrama and the Mode of Excess* (New Haven: Yale University Press, 1976), 15.

4. Ibid., 17.

5. Elsaesser and Novell-Smith's essays, along with many other key articles, can be found in Christine Gledhill, ed., *Home Is Where the Heart Is: Studies in Melodrama and the Woman's Film* (London: BFI, 1987). Other useful anthologies on the subject are Jim Cook, Jackie Bratton and Christine Gledhill, eds., *Melodrama: Stage, Picture, Screen* (London: BFI, 1984), and Marcia Landy, ed., *Imitation of Life: A Reader on Film & Television Melodrama* (Detroit: Wayne State University Press, 1991).

6. For a personal, poetic reading of melodrama's influential role in Mexico's cinema, see Carlos Montsivais, "Se sufre, pero se aprende," in *A Través del Espejo: El cine mexicano y su público* (Mexico, D.F.: Ediciones del Milagro, IMCINE, 1994).

7. See Rodolfo Cardona's introduction to the fifth edition of *Doña Perfecta* (Madrid: Cátedra Letras Hispánicas, 1995), 27. Also Roberto Sánchez, *El teatro y la novela: Galdós y Clarín* (Madrid: Insula, 1974), and Anthony Zahareas,

"Galdos' *Doña Perfecta*: Fiction, History, Ideology," *Anales galdosianos* (1976): 29–58.

8. David N. Rodowick, "Madness, Authority and Ideology: Domestic Melodrama of the 1950s," in Gledhill, *Home Is Where the Heart Is*, 270.

9. Geoffrey Novell-Smith, "Minnelli and Melodrama," in Gledhill, *Home Is Where the Heart Is*, 73.

10. Linda Williams has argued for a consideration of the maternal melodrama as a unique expression under patriarchy of "the essential female tragedy of mother–daughter passion, rapture and loss." See Linda Williams, "Something Else Besides a Mother: *Stella Dallas* and Maternal Melodrama," in Gledhill, *Home Is Where the Heart Is*, 318.

11. Brooks, *The Melodramatic Imagination*, 201. Brooks makes note of the melodramatic rituals of psychoanalysis.

12. For a more elaborate exposition of this theme, see E. Ann Kaplan, *Motherhood and Representation: The Mother in Popular Culture and Melodrama* (London: Routledge, 1992).

13. Mary Ann Doane, "The Phallic Mother Paradigm," in Kaplan, *Motherhood and Representation*, 117.

14. Juliet Mitchell has written that "hysteria is the daughter's dis-ease." Juliet Mitchell, *Women: The Longest Revolution* (New York: Pantheon, 1984), 308.

15. Mary Ann Doane, "The 'Woman's Film,' Possession and Address," in Gledhill, *Home Is Where the Heart Is*.

16. See Ana López, "A Cinema of Tears," *IRIS*, Summer 1991, and Joanna Hershfield, *Mexican Cinema/Mexican Women* (Durham, N.C.: Duke University Press, 1996).

17. For a more positive reading of *Doña Perfecta*, see "La elocuencia del odio" in Jorge Ayala Blanco, *La aventura del cine mexicano*.

18. Adrienne Rich, *Of Woman Born* (New York: Bantam Books, 1977), 226. Rich also writes, "The loss of the daughter to the mother, the mother to the daughter, is the essential female tragedy" (240).

BIBLIOGRAPHY

Cardona, Rodolfo. *Introduction to Doña Perfecta*. Madrid: Cátedra, 1995.

Sánchez, Roberto. *El teatro y la novela: Galdós y Clarín*. Madrid: Insula, 1974.

Zahareas, Anthony. "Galdos' *Doña Perfecta*: Fiction, History, Ideology." *Anales galdosianos* (1976): 29–58.

33

Vicente Blasco Ibáñez and the Movie Novel

Rafael T. Corbalán

Vicente Blasco Ibáñez (1868–1928) is mainly known today for works such as *La barraca, Sangre y arena, Los cuatro jinetes del Apocalipsis*, and *Entre naranjos*.[1] He is also known by his nickname, the "Spanish Zola," a description linking him to the naturalistic movement that flourished in Spain in the latter third of the nineteenth century. Little to nothing is known, however, about this author's important contribution to the film industry in the United States or of his efforts to renew early twentieth-century literature with what he called "la novela cinematográfica" ("the movie novel"). In contrast to most of the members of the Generation of '98, who demonstrated scant interest in cinema, Vicente Blasco Ibáñez made an attempt to understand and use the screenplay to communicate better with audiences who read little but who attended movie spectacles en masse in the early years of this century.[2]

In his prologue to *El paraíso de las mujeres* (1921), Blasco Ibáñez explained the reasons that led him to write for films: "Cinematographic expression can provide novels with the universality of a painting, sculpture or symphony. . . . Through the 'seventh art' an author can tell his imagined story to audiences in New York, London and Paris on the same night."[3] This intention of reaching a wide audience was one of the constants of his work. Suffice it to say that his Valencian novels were published in serial format in the Republican newspaper *El Pueblo*, which was bought by the petite bourgeoisie, landless peasants, and the nascent working class of Levante. Recall as well his writings against

General Primo de Rivera and King Alfonso XIII, *Una nación secuestrada* (1924) and *Por España y contra el rey* (1925), which cost him an extended exile in France and a boycott of his work.[4]

The process that brought Blasco Ibáñez to films had two well-defined phases. One began with his early novels and ended in 1908. This period was characterized by many allusions to the cinema within his novels. In fact, an interesting comment in *Entre naranjos* (1900) is one of the first references to film registered in Spanish literature: "That trip, as fast as a scene from a film, left in Rafael a confused jumble of names, buildings, paintings and cities."[5] In addition to its biographical value, this quote also helps to explain the initial impact that films may have had on Blasco Ibáñez, "a confused jumble of names, buildings, paintings and cities," which undoubtedly changed with the passing years.

The second phase began in 1914 after a six-year self-imposed exile in Argentina, where he tried unsuccessfully to found two new towns: Cervantes and Nueva Valencia. After 1914 Blasco Ibáñez firmly declared his intention to produce films and even write expressly for the silver screen. In an interview published in *El Imparcial*, a Madrid newspaper, on February 2, 1916, he said,

It happened one day as I was talking to D'Annunzio that it occurred to me to go into "cinema" as a new road for art. Both of us had been translated into all languages and nearly all dialects, but it is not only words that lose meaning in translation, the very soul of the work does too. . . . Will Cinema always lack psychology? Yes, but it prevails through action. Does it stem from ordinary literature; is it prosaic and excessively accessible? Many an author must have said the same thing with the invention of the printing press, which replaced coddled manuscripts with coarse paper and monotonous characters. I understand all the wariness of the intelligent.[6]

By this time, his novels *La barraca, Entre naranjos*, and *Sangre y arena* had been released in Spain, and in France the first production of *Los cuatro jinetes del Apocalipsis* was being prepared. It was directed by André Heuzé in 1917 and distributed under the title *Debout les morts*. Also during those three years, Blasco Ibáñez tried to establish a film production company in France, which unfortunately vanished in a fire; he directed an adaptation of one of his works for the silver screen, created his first movie plot (a treatment of what would later become the film *Sangre y arena*), and in 1916 wrote a story expressly for the screen: *La vieja del cínema*.

For all this, Vicente Blasco Ibáñez must be ranked as one of the outstanding members of a group of authors who in the early years of the twentieth century began to take interest in movies as a form of artistic expression. In Spain, Jacinto Benavente and the brothers Quintero, inspired by the ideas of the French *Film d'Art*, also adapted their work for movies, founded film production companies, and even wrote directly for the new medium. In Europe, Riccioto Canudo, on whom Blasco Ibáñez wrote a biography, for the first time defined cinema as the "seventh art," and by 1911 writers like Gabriele D'Annunzio were receiving fabulous sums for their scripts. In the United States the new medium quickly gained independence from the influence of theatre, although literary themes continued to be adapted for the movies, albeit with many modifications. David Wark Griffith himself (1875–1948), the creator of such film techniques as close-ups, didn't hesitate to say that literature and film had common narrative elements, and affirmed that parallel action in cinema is the graphical equivalent of the literary "meanwhile."[7]

It was, nonetheless, after World War I that Vicente Blasco Ibáñez came into full contact with the international movie industry and especially Hollywood. His relationship with American studios began with the translation of *Los cuatro jinetes del Apocalipsis* [*The Four Horsemen of the Apocalypse*] into English by Charlotte Brewster and its publishing success in the United States, where within a few days it sold over 100,000 copies.

Emilio Gascó Contell describes in his book, *Genio y figura de Blasco Ibáñez*, the Valencian author's debut on the American literary scene:

One morning he suddenly received a batch of mail much more voluminous than usual: letters, postcards and newspapers, all with postmarks and stamps from the United States. . . . Blasco's first impression was one of mystification and that perhaps one of his friends in the States wanted to play a joke on him. As he continued to wade through the pile, he soon became convinced that all that correspondence was really addressed to him.[8]

The great popularity of *The Four Horsemen of the Apocalypse* in the United States was not due merely to chance, but to the fact that during and after World War I there was a strong demand for literary and cinematic products about the armed conflict. This work, with its depiction of the barbarities of the German military forces under the Kaiser, became a justification to American audiences for their country's entrance into the war. Nevertheless, aside from its espousal of the Allied cause and its defense of democracy and republicanism, two principles for which the author had fought since his youth, the movie stands on its own on many grounds.[9]

As a result of the novel's success in the United States, in 1919 the film production company Metro offered Blasco Ibáñez $200,000 for the movie rights to *The Four Horsemen of the Apocalypse* and bought the rights to some of his other novels for $25,000 each. The Hispanic Society also invited him to give a series of lectures in the United States. During that visit, executives of Metro took him on a tour of their Hollywood studios, where the filming of *The Four Horsemen of the Apocalypse* was underway. T. R. Ybarra, a *New York Times* reporter, accompanied Blasco Ibáñez to the California city and on January 23, 1921, wrote an interesting article about the trip, titled "Blasco Ibáñez, Movie Fan," in which he was quoted as saying, "I'm going to write for the screen. I am not only going to adapt for moving-picture production novels I have written, but I intend to write for the movies direct [*sic*]."[10]

Ybarra's article also explains how the American movie industry functioned in the 1920s and how the marketing of movies influenced the cinematic work of Blasco Ibáñez. At first, it reveals, Blasco Ibáñez wanted to write about the conquest of the Western United States or about the Orient, to which the producers responded that such things were out of fashion. Then he proposed a film on Mexico, which Metro turned down because of the delicate relations between Washington and its southern neighbor. Later he proposed a film based on Spain, and then France, but these ideas were also rejected. Finally, the executives suggested, "Why don't you try something with an American background, American characters, a plot based on modern American life?" They also requested that the script be original, and that it depart from the technical commonplaces to which the movie industry was subject during those years.

That is how *El paraíso de las mujeres* [*The Paradise of Women*] came to be.[11] It was the first novel written by Vicente Blasco Ibáñez expressly for a North American studio. The work, more than 285 pages long, exceeded by far the 70 pages of a typical script. In addition, it displayed a radical change in the author's literary technique, offering a text filled with action and devoid of all "filler." The piece was met with great controversy, to which Blasco Ibáñez himself added by saying in an interview in the United States that American men should treat their women more roughly. It is worth mentioning here that Blasco's scenario was written the same year in which women gained the right to vote in the United States. A kind of *Gulliver's Travels*, it deals with a hypothetical country where the female sex has conducted a revolution against men and now governs very well, but with excessive authority.

El paraíso de las mujeres was never produced, since Metro claimed that filmic techniques of that time did not lend themselves to scenes with giants and midgets or flying apparatus, as proposed by the author. Other reasons not mentioned by the studios, but which surely carried weight in Metro's decision, were its controversial themes: the battle of the sexes and the revolution against the established order at a time when the Soviet Revolution was a very recent event.

In spite of this apparent failure, Vicente Blasco Ibáñez did not lose heart. In a letter written on October 15, 1921, to his friend and biographer Ramón Martínez de la Riva, he says,

Right now I am working a lot, morning, afternoon and night. I am writing movie novels for the biggest and most powerful movie studios of the United States and, naturally, of the whole world: Metro and Famous Play. Until now they have adapted films from my novels; presently I am writing unpublished novels directly for cinema. The world is teeming with screenplay writers, but no one has yet become a worldwide movie novelist.[12]

Through correspondence with Martínez de la Riva, we know today that Blasco Ibáñez sent two completed novels written for the film industry to New York. He also wrote a story of Don Quixote set in modern times, as well as six other pieces that were probably readapted into short-story format and published in *La novela de hoy* in the 1920s.[13]

As for two *escenarios* written by Vicente Blasco Ibáñez that became movies in an American studio, we still preserve the manuscript of *Argentine Love* (1924) in the Motion Picture Academy Library. *Circe the Enchantress*, however, has been lost and is preserved only on film.[14] Although these *escenarios* were simple action tales, with marketable storylines and little psychological observations or descriptive dimensions, Vicente Blasco Ibáñez did create a type of novel, mainly of historical theme, which could be easily adapted to film. This was because many of the contracts he signed with American publishers also included movie rights. His last novels, *La reina Calafia, El Papa del mar*, and *A los pies de Venus*, employ a parallel montage technique, much like that used in movies since Edwin Porter and David Griffith, in which the present and past are interwoven. In another of these works, *En busca del Gran Khan*, which had been acquired by the Hearst group to be published in its newspapers and later adapted to film, the editors returned the manuscript to Blasco Ibáñez so that he could include more love scenes, an element considered indispensable for distribution.

In addition to the novels written with cinematic techniques, many of Ibáñez's works were also adapted to films with extraordinary success. Besides *Los cuatro jinetes del Apocalipsis*, in which Rudolph Valentino became an international star, others of special note include *Blood and Sand* [*Sangre y arena*] (1922), which also featured the Italian actor, and *The Torrent* [*Entre naranjos*] (1926) and *Temptress* [*La tierra de todos*] (1926), both of them starring a young Swedish actress, Greta Lovisa Gustavsson, who was making her American movie debut with the Hispanic-sounding stage name Greta Garbo. The storylines provided by Blasco Ibáñez to American studios served primarily to improve the dissemination of Spain's image internationally and were used to consolidate the so-called star system, which remains to this day. In the case of *The Four Horsemen of the Apocalypse*, a film with very significant political connotations in the 1920s, it was readapted by Metro-Goldwyn-Mayer in 1961 and served as the argument of another political plot, this time based on World War II.

The commercial contact that Vicente Blasco Ibáñez had with the publishing and film industries of the United States put him in territory unknown to his fellow Spanish novelists: that of an author who had to adapt to the wishes of the international modern culture of the masses. This attitude contrasts with avant-garde movements that also emerged in the 1920s and rejected any compromise with the pragmatic debate that continues until today: the debate between commercial popular literature and artistic purity.

NOTES

1. In the bibliography are the titles of Vicente Blasco Ibáñez's novels that have been translated into English and the titles of the movies based on his books.

2. In *I Conversaciones Cinematográficas*, Salamanca 1955, it states, "El cine, que nace con la Generación del 98, no mereció en ella la menor atención." Rafael Utrera in *Modernismo y generación del '98 frente al cine*, is less radical on this account, dividing the Generation of '98 into two groups: *cinematófilos* and *cinematófobos*. Even though the Generation of '98 was the most significant group of authors at the beginning of the twentieth century in Spain, other writers like Benito Pérez Galdós, the Quintero brothers, and Vicente Blasco Ibáñez were well known within the peninsula. (*Conversaciones Cinematográficas* was a gathering of moviemakers and critics organized by Juan Antonio Bardem and held in Salamanca from May 14–19, 1955. Although planned as an annual event, subsequent meetings were curtailed by the Franco government. The statement included here, among others, as well as the major events of the meeting, appeared in the Proceedings of the Conference. The issue bore the numeral I because it was supposed to be the first of a series.)

3. Vicente Blasco Ibáñez, *Obras completas* (Madrid: Aguilar, 1978), (translation mine).

4. Vicente Blasco Ibáñez, *Una nación secuestrada* (Paris: J. Duran, 1924); Vicente Blasco Ibáñez, *Por España y contra el rey* (Paris: Excelsior, 1925). These two works tried to inspire the people to rise up against the monarchical regime. They were clandestinely distributed by airplanes, which entered Spain from France and were paid for by Blasco Ibáñez himself. In an attempt to prevent such action by the author, the government under Primo de Rivera had antiaircraft guns installed on the border and in the surrounding areas of cities like Barcelona.

5. Blasco Ibáñez, *Obras completas*, 579 (translation mine).

6. Mario Aguilar, "Blasco Ibáñez, cinematografista," *El Imparcial*, August 2, 1916 (translation mine).

7. D. W. Griffith (1875–1948), director of the film *The Birth of a Nation* (1915), developed new uses of space and time in film with cinematic techniques such as close-ups, moving camera shots, and fade-ins. Román Gubern, *Historia del cine*, vol. 2 (Barcelona: Lumen, 1979), 119–120.

8. Emilio Gascó Contell, *Genio y figura de Blasco Ibáñez* (Madrid: Afrodisio Aguado, 1967), 195–196 (translation mine).

9. To understand what the German aggression of World War I meant to Blasco Ibáñez, it is indispensable to reread his works of the first phase, especially his book *La catedral* (1903), which expressed his anti-German sentiments. He blamed the kings of Germanic descent, who had ruled Spain in the sixteenth and seventeenth centuries, for the annihilation of the nationalist spirit. Those very principles of brutality and intransigence were for him the origin of the Great War. Writing about Charles V and Philip II, Blasco Ibáñez says in *La catedral*, "It is a Teutonic and Flemish Spain, converted into a colony of Germany, serving as a mercenary under foreign flags, ruining itself in affairs in which it had no interest, hemorrhaging blood and gold in obligation to the so-called Holy Roman-Germanic Empire" (*Obras completas*, 1005; translation mine). Later, Blasco Ibáñez would write, "Religious intolerance, which foreign historians believe spontaneously appeared on Spanish soil, was imported here by the Germanic kaisership" (*Obras completas*, 1006; translation mine). In *The Four Horsemen of the Apocalypse* the author reiterates the idea of Germanic intolerance by writing, "The Germans are crazy with pride, and their madness is dangerous to the world. When those with poisonous ideas of global hegemony disappear, after disgrace refreshes their imaginations and they are content with being a human group—neither superior nor inferior to others—then they shall become a tolerant people, useful . . . and who knows maybe even likable" (329; translation mine).

10. T. R. Ybarra, "Blasco Ibáñez, Movie Fan." *New York Times*, January 23, 1921, sec. 3, p. 16.

11. Vicente Blasco Ibáñez, *El paraíso de las mujeres* (Valencia: Prometeo, 1922).

12. Ramón Martínez de la Riva, *Blasco Ibáñez: su vida, su obra, su muerte, sus mejores páginas* (Madrid: Mundo Latino, 1929), 161 (translation mine).

13. This was a Spanish literary journal founded by Artemio Precioso in 1921. I say "six other pieces that were probably readapted" because Vicente Blasco Ibáñez never mentioned where he had republished these *escenarios*. However, a group of short stories utilizing film techniques and themes, such as *El réprobo* and *La devoradora*, were published in *La novela de hoy* in the 1920s.

14. One copy of *Argentine Love* is preserved today in the Motion Picture Academy Library in California. The text for *La encantadora Circe* [*Circe the Enchantress*] has disappeared or is misplaced in the library. Rafael Ventura Meliá has recently collected most of the *escenarios* written by Vicente Blasco Ibáñez for an exhibition sponsored by Generalitat de Valencia, Spain, which was presented to the public in 1998. Despite an initial report that *La encantadora Circe* was in the Motion Picture Academy Library, neither Rafael Ventura nor I have been able to find this *escenario*.

VICENTE BLASCO IBÁÑEZ'S NOVELS
TRANSLATED INTO ENGLISH

Blasco Ibáñez, Vicente. *The Blood of the Arena*. Translated by Frances Douglas. Chicago: A. C. McClurg, 1911. Trans. *Sangre y arena*, 1908.

———. *The Borgias: Or the Feet of Venus*. Translated by Arthur Livingston. New York: Dutton, 1930. Trans. *A los pies de Venus*, 1926.

———. *The Cabin*. Translated by Francis Haffkine Snow and Beatrice M. Mekota. New York: Knopf, 1917. Trans. *La barraca*, 1901.

———. *The Dead Command*. Translated by Frances Douglas. New York: Duffiel, 1919. Trans. *Los muertos mandan*, 1909.

———. *The Enemies of Woman*. Translated by Irvin Brown. New York: Dutton, 1920. Trans. *Los enemigos de la mujer*, 1919.

———. *The Four Horsemen of the Apocalypse*. Translated by Charlotte Brewster Jordan. New York: Dutton, 1918. Trans. *Los cuatro jinetes del Apocalipsis*, 1916.

———. *The Fruits of the Vine*. Translated by Isaac Goldberg. New York: Dutton, 1919. Trans. *La bodega*, 1905.

———. *The Intruder*. Translated by W.A. Gillespie. New York: Dutton, 1928. Trans. *El Intruso*, 1904.

———. *The Knight of the Virgin*. Translated by Arthur Livingston. New York: Dutton, 1930. Trans. *El caballero de la Virgen*, 1929.

———. *Mare Nostrum*. Translated by Charlotte Brewster Jordan. New York: Dutton, 1919. Trans. *Mare nostrum*, 1918.

———. *The Mayflower: A Tale of the Valencian Seashore*. Translated by Arthur Livingston. New York: Burt, 1929. Trans. *Flor de mayo*, 1895.

———. *The Mob*. Translated by Mariano Joaquin Lorente. New York: Dutton, 1927. Trans. *La horda*, 1905.

———. *The Phantom with Wings of Gold*. Translated by Arthur Livingston. New York: Dutton, 1931. Trans. *El fantasma de las alas de oro*, 1930.

———. *The Pope of the Sea: A Historic Medley*. Translated by Arthur Livingston. New York: Dutton, 1924. Trans. *El Papa del mar*, 1925.

———. *Queen Calafia*. New York: Dutton, 1924. Trans. *La reina Calafia*, 1923.

———. *Reeds and Mud*. Translated by Lester Berberfall. Boston: Humphries, 1966. Trans. *Cañas y barro*, 1902.

———. *Reeds and Mud*. Translated by Isaac Goldberg. New York: Dutton, 1928. Trans. *Cañas y barro*, 1902.

———. *The Shadows of the Cathedral*. Translated by W. A. Gillespie. New York: Dutton, 1909. Trans. *La catedral*, 1903.

———. *Sonnica*. Translated by Frances Douglas. New York: Duffield, 1912. Trans. *Sonnica la cortesana*, n.d.

———. *The Temptress*. Translated by Frances Douglas. New York: Dutton, 1923. Trans. *La tierra de todos*, 1922.

———. *The Three Roses*. Translated by Stuart Edgar Grummon. New York: Dutton, 1932. Trans. *Arroz y tartana*, 1894.

———. *The Torrent*. Translated by Isaac Goldberg and Arthur Livingston. New York: Dutton, 1921. Trans. *Entre naranjos*, 1900.

———. *Unknown Lands: The Story of Columbus.* Translated by Arthur Livingston. New York: Dutton, 1929. Trans. *En busca del Gran Kan*, 1929.
———. *Woman Triumphant.* Translated by Hayward Keniston. New York: Dutton, 1920. Trans. *La maja desnuda*, 1906.

FILMS OF BLASCO IBÁÑEZ'S NOVELS

Argentine Love. Dir. Allan Dwan. Stars Bebe Daniels, Ricardo Cortés, and Mario Majeroni. Paramount, 1924.

La barraca. Dir. Roberto Gabaldón. Stars Domingo Soler, Anita Blanc, Amparo Morillo, and José Barbiera. Interamericana, 1944.

La barraca. Dir. León Klimowski. Stars Alvaro de Luna, Marisa de Leza, Eduardo Fajardo, and Terele Pávez. Radiotelevisión Española, 1979 (television).

Blood and Sand [*Sangre y arena*]. Dir. Fred Niblo. Stars Rodolfo Valentino, Nita Naldi, and George Field. Paramount, 1922.

Blood and Sand [*Sangre y arena*]. Dir. Rouben Mamoulian. Stars Tyrone Power, Linda Darnell, Rita Hayworth, and John Carradine. 20th Century Fox, 1941.

La bodega. Dir. Benito Perojo. Stars Conchita Piquer, Valentín Parera, María Luz Callejo, and Gabriel Gabrio. Julio Cesar, 1929.

Bull and Sand [*Sangre y arena*]. Dir. Mack Sennett. 1924.

Cañas y barro. Dir. Rafael Romero Marchent. Stars José Bódalo, Manuel Tejada, Alfredo Mayo, and Terele Pávez. Radiotelevisión Española, 1977 (television).

Cañas y barro. Dir. Juan de Orduña. Stars María Armendola, Virgilio Teixeira, Aurora Redondo, and José Nieto. Orduña-Pico, 1954.

Circe the Enchantress [*La encantadora Circe*]. Dir. Robert Leonar. Stars Mae Murray and James Kirwood. Metro-Goldwyn-Mayer, 1925.

Debout les morts [*Los cuatro jinetes del Apocalipsis*]. Dir. André Heuzé, 1917.

El tonto de la huerta [*La barraca*]. Dir. José Codina. Film Cuesta, 1914.

Enemies of Women [*Los enemigos de la mujer*]. Dir. Alan Crosland. Stars Alma Rubens, Lionel Barrymore, William Collier, and Gladis Hulett. Cosmopolitan, 1923.

Entre naranjos. Prod. and Dir. Alberto Marro, 1915.

Flor de mayo. Dir. Roberto Gabaldón, 1957.

The Four Horsemen of Apocalypse [*Los cuatro jinetes del Apocalipsis*]. Dir. Rex Ingram. Stars Rudolph Valentino, Alice Terry, Joseph Swickard, and Mabel Von Duren. Metro,1921.

The Four Horsemen of Apocalypse [*Los cuatro jinetes del Apocalipsis*]. Dir. Vicente Minelli. Stars Glenn Ford, Lee Cobb, Ingrid Thulin, and Charles Boyer. Metro-Goldwyn-Mayer, 1961.

Mare Nostrum. Dir. Rafael Gil. Stars María Félix, Fernando Rey, Guillermo Marín, and José Nieto. Suevia Films, 1948.

Mud and Sand {*Sangre y arena*]. Dir. Hal Roach–Stan Laurel, 1922.

Ni sangre ni arena [*Sangre y arena*]. Dir. Alejandro Galindo, 1922.

Sangre y arena. Dir. Ricardo de Baños and Vicente Blasco Ibáñez. Stars P. Alcaide, Matilde Domenech, Mark Andrews, and José Portes. Barcinógrafo, 1917.

The Temptress [*La tierra de todos*]. Dir. Fred Niblo. Stars Greta Garbo, Antonio Moreno, Marc McDermott, and Lionel Barrymore. Metro, 1926.

The Torrent [*Entre naranjos*]. Dir. Monta Bell. Stars Greta Garbo, Ricardo Cortés, Gertrude Olmstead, and Edward Connelly. Metro, 1926.

BIBLIOGRAPHY

Aguilar, Mario. "Blasco Ibáñez, cinematografista." *El Imparcial*, August 2, 1916, p. 1.

Blasco Ibáñez, Vicente. *Argumento de la novela cinematográfica "Sangre y Arena."* Madrid and Valencia: Ramón Soto, n.d.

———. "Bolshevism as a Tyranny." *New York Times*, September 26, 1920, sec. 3, p. 3.

———. "Novelists as Business Men." *New York Times*, January 2, 1921, sec. 3, p. 1.

———. *Obras completas*. 6 vols. Madrid: Aguilar, 1978.

———. *El paraíso de las mujeres*. Valencia: Prometeo, 1922.

Gascó Contell, Emilio. *Genio y figura de Blasco Ibáñez*. Madrid: Afrodisio Aguado, 1967.

Gimferrer, Pere. "Literatura y cine." *Academia* 12 (1995): 35–45.

Gubern, Román. *Historia del cine*. 2 vols. Barcelona: Lumen, 1979.

León Roca, J. L. *Vicente Blasco Ibáñez*. Madrid: Prometeo, 1967.

Lloris, Manuel. "Vicente Blasco Ibáñez o la formación de un escritor de masas." *Insula* 407 (1980): 1, 12.

Martínez de la Riva, Ramón. *Blasco Ibáñez, su vida, su obra, su muerte, sus mejores páginas*. Madrid: Mundo Latino, 1929.

Sarrias, Cristóbal. "Blasco Ibáñez, i Recordarlo o . . . mejor olvidarlo?" *Razón y Fe* 965 (1978): 572–581.

Surís, Andrés. "Técnicas cinematográficas de montaje paralelo en tres obras de Vicente Blasco Ibáñez." *Explicación de Textos Literarios* 5 (1976): 89–94.

———. Técnicas cinematográficas y la obra de Vicente Blasco Ibáñez." Ph.D. diss., University of Minnesota, 1972.

Utrera, Rafael. *Escritores y cinema en España: Un acercamiento histórico*. Madrid: Ediciones JC, 1985.

Ybarra, T. R. "Blasco Ibáñez, Movie Fan." *New York Times*, January 23, 1921, sec. 3, p. 16.

34

García Márquez in Film:
His Image of Women

Donald M. Morales

Gene Bell-Villada has labeled García Márquez a novelist of love who writes about the male–female relationship, its attendant pleasures and frustrations, commitments and ambivalences, private uncertainties and public prejudices, erotic force and everyday suppressions, subjective, complex subtleties and objective, simplifying ritualizations and surprises (177). *Love in the Time of Cholera* (García Márquez, 1988), his first novel after winning the Nobel Prize, places on display most of the qualities Villada outlines. But it is the erotic impulse shaped by machismo that is particularly illustrated in the three Márquez films based on the novel: *Fábula de la Bella Palomera* [*Fable of the Pigeon Fancier*], *Yo soy el que tú buscas* [*I'm the One You're Looking For*], and *Cartas del Parque* [*Letters from the Park*]. His image of Latin women in these films is troubling, for they emerge beyond the contours of magical realism and fall more into the misconstrued patriarchal imagination.

García Márquez has been involved in a number of films associated with his fiction, which is surprising given his displeasure with the screenwriting process: "It bores me," he said recently. "It's a technical task, which I haven't studied well" (Paxman, 55). When asked by Peter Stone in a 1981 *Paris Review* interview about the possibility of transforming *One Hundred Years of Solitude* to film, Márquez replied, "I have no interest in a film, and as long as I can prevent it from happening, it won't. I prefer that it remain a private relationship between the reader and the book" (71). However, the list of Márquez films from 1985 undermines these protestations. In addition to the three based on *Cholera*, Márquez collaborated on *Un señor muy viejo con unas alas enormes* [*Very Old Man with Enormous Wings*], *La increíble y triste historia de la cándida Eréndira y de su abuela desalmada* [*The Incredible and Sad Tale of Innocent Erendira and Her Heartless Grandmother*] from *Collected Stories*, *Milagro en Roma* [*Miracle in Rome*, renamed *The Saint*], and *El verano de la señora Forbes* [*Mrs. Forbes's Summer of Happiness*] in *Strange Pilgrims*. *Edipo Alcalde* (Oedipus Mayor), a transposition of the Oedipus tale into Colombia, is his most recent film venture (Paxman 55).

In truth, Márquez has had a love–hate relationship with film. As a journalist for *El Espectador* (Colombia) during the late 1950s and early 1960s, Márquez was assigned as a film reviewer and during this period studied screenwriting at Rome's Centro Sperimentale. Although he stayed only one year because of the school's technical and directorial emphasis—"it [made] me feel like I [was] in a straight jacket"—he established contacts with directors like Tomás Gutiérrez Alea, who would later collaborate in *Cartas del Parque* (Paxman, 55). In the 1960s of Mexico City he would write screenplays with Carlos Fuentes and independent features, but never felt that the materials produced during that period were palpable examples of cinema. In fact, nothing of that period made it to the screen. By 1966 he was disillusioned with cinema and turned to fiction (Burton, 96). Yet this disappointment never quite extinguished his fire for cinema. Before *Solitude*, everything he wrote was thinly disguised cinema (117). When one views his early stories and novellas with this in mind, there is a certain static quality in the fiction that would arguably fare better as film. He speaks of this ambivalence as a marital tug-of-war: "My relation with it is like that of a couple who can't live separated, but who can't live together either" (Stone, 72).

Since the mid-1980s, he has moved closer not only to film of his fiction but to sponsorship of Latin film festivals and societies. In 1985 he became the founding president of Fundación Nuevo Cine Latinamericano [Foundation for New Latin American Cinema], a Cuban institution that produced Márquez's *Amores Difíciles*, six films for Spanish television. He has supported the School of the Three Worlds (Asia, Africa, and Latin America) in San Antonio de los Baños, Cuba, the XXXI Cartagena Film Festival in Colombia, and Fundovisual Latina in Venezuela (Aufderheide, 70). Today it is ironic that he occasionally teaches screenwriting at the Fundación's International Film & TV School (Paxman, 55).

The three films, *Cartas del parque*, *Fábula de la bella palomera*, and *Yo soy el que tú buscas*, emanate from a few pages of *Love in the Time of Cholera*. *Cartas del Parque* is based on a short period in Florentino Ariza's fifty-one-year, nine-month, and four-day obsessive wait for Fermina

Daza, while in the Arcade of the Scribes he occupies himself writing love notes for unlettered lovers (*Cartas*, 171). He quickly recognizes a letter given to him by a young woman as one he previously wrote for a young man, and begins a feverish correspondence with himself, all the while imagining he is writing to Fermina Daza (172). The three-paragraph fictional episode ends with the nameless couple's marriage and the realization that the scrivener is indeed Florentino. To honor him, the couple names Florentino the godfather of their first child.

Fábula de la bella palomera results from a five-page, nine-paragraph romance with Olimpia Zuleta, an agile girl whom Florentino Ariza encounters chasing her wind-blown parasol (*Fábula*, 214–218). In his carriage he drives her home and learns that she is a mother and is living in the company of an extended family. Several days later, "with the devil in his ear," he passes her home, and after a casual exchange about the homing pigeons she tends, is given one as a thank-you gift (214). Florentino initiates a series of love notes to Olimpia via carrier pigeon, and after three months of failure finds himself to be a man "most avid for love as well as most niggardly . . . who give[s] nothing and want[s] everything . . . run through by the lance of love" (216). Six months after their first meeting the union is consummated, and in a moment of sensual possession Florentino paints in red, "This Pussy is Mine" above her genitals. As Olimpia undresses before her husband that same night with the forgotten message clearly visible, the spouse slashes her throat. With remarkable distance, Florentino reads of the incident and eventual arrest of the husband several days later, but his concern is more over the signed love notes and Fermina Daza's learning of his infidelity than the tragic death of Olimpia.

Yo soy el que tú buscas derives from the shortest *Cholera* segment of all, Leona Cassiani's one-line rejoinder rejecting the advances of Florentino: "Behave yourself. I realized a long time ago that you are not the man I am looking for" (*Yo soy*, 258). Although the reference is short, Leona's presence is pervasive throughout the novel, as she becomes the true woman in Florentino's life. His initial misperception of her as an "emboldened black, young, pretty . . . whore beyond the shadow of a doubt" quickly changes as she rises in seven years to the general secretaryship of Uncle Leo XII's River Company of the Caribbean, one step below Florentino. Despite her "feminine charms . . . and ardent African body," no proposition is made until the tenth year of their relationship. By then it is too late. "I would feel," she says, "as if I were going to bed with the son I never had," despite Florentino's being twenty years her senior. Her ensuing story of an earlier rape becomes the central issue of the film.

Márquez's imagination is more at play in these *Cholera* films than in the ones based on short stories, although sufficient liberties are taken with *Milagro en Roma* and *El verano de la Señora Forbes*. *Cartas del Parque* is on the surface the least objectionable to Latin feminine verisimilitude. The young couple, now called María and Juan, become fully developed characters in the film. Florentino is transformed into the gentlemanly Pedro, who instructs Juan on the intricacies of floral grammar: "I will love you eternally" is symbolized by a daisy leaf with a bud. He also instructs María on the language of handkerchiefs: "If you knot it in your hands, it means I am yours until death. And, of course, if you clench it tight . . . very tight in your right hand, the meaning is clear. . . . I am immensely happy" (*Cartas*, English subtitles). *Cartas* concludes with María declaring her love for the scrivener through these motions of the kerchief.

Susana Conde in "Readerly and Writerly *Letters from the Park*," doesn't see the film in such a benign fashion, however. The scrivener is more an aging poet recapturing the power of the word through the young couple (106). Although Pedro mocks himself by equating his trade with that of his whore companion, Milagros, he is one of three males who are complicit in the acquisition of the female: two within the economy of letter writing and the third within the objective order of the law (postal worker) (111). By being complicit in this masquerade, María has emptied herself of her own voice in order to contain the male's (110). Conde sees the women in the film—María, Milagros, and Matilde (María's godmother who is raising her)—as falling into the machista perception of madre/mujer, with the Virgin Maria and the whore Milagros framing the surrogate Matilde (112). Even Milagros's marriage is seen by Conde as "her capture in another prison, since her affections rest clearly with Pedro" (112).

María Valdés places the lowly position of women in Latin America squarely on the shoulders of religious teaching, "from the injunction to obey the father and husband to the view of women's bodies as the instruments of Satan for the perdition of men. Those basic ideas, [are] repeated endlessly from pulpit to confessional" (48). It is not coincidental, then, that Conde finds religious significance in the women of *Cartas*: María as the Virgin Mary; Matilde, the German and Italian names of saints; and Milagros, the Spanish word for miracles (118). This association further locks the women into predictable masculine perceptions that are authorized by religion.

In *Fábula de la bella palomera*, set in Brazil, Florentino is now Orestes, a foppish libertine who has affairs with his friends' wives while seeking the woman of his mother's imagination. The meeting with Olimpia, Fulvia García in the film, essentially follows the form of *Cholera* through the exchange of notes. There is the additional presence of his fawning mother (Tránsito in *Cholera*), who reveals through dreams what will happen to Orestes: "An old love will offer you a new love" (*Fábula*,

English subtitles). This is actualized when the wife of Orestes's dying friend, his first paramour, ends his torment over Fulvia by somehow giving her over to Florentino.

In a stunning rain-swept scene, Orestes is driven to near insanity over desire. He cries out, "What I can't explain is how a man like me can be driven to this madness." Fulvia too reveals her sensuality in a pulsing monologue:

I felt a wild desire to remain enslaved all my life, but only for you. . . . I felt an emptiness in my heart as if I were your widow. . . . At first, when the pigeons flew [overhead carrying messages], I felt as if I had gone with them in body and soul from my house to yours and from your house to mine. . . . Imagine, a married woman saying these things to another man. . . . True suffering is when you are unable to love. (*Fábula*, English subtitles)

The film ends with Orestes, an aged man, looking at Fulvia's grave and listening to the voice of his mother: "Orestes, do you see now, Orestes? Dreams are always right. True suffering is when you are unable to love" (*Fábula*, English subtitles). A jet passes over.

Yo soy el que tú buscas turns into a psychosexual thriller as Leona Cassiani is reinvented into the married and vivacious model Natalia. After a commercial shoot, a leather-jacketed motorcyclist, having watched Natalia change clothes in her own car, follows and rapes her. Yet the wantonness of the act is lessened because Natalia's words to the rapist after her release imply an unconscious complicity: "Why did you rape me? . . . Couldn't you have tried another way?" (*Yo soy*, English subtitles). Márquez cleverly turns what could be a lugubrious tale into theater of the absurd, for the rest of the film is a bizarre quest to reconnect with the rapist, much in the manner that Leona Cassiani fantasizes over her rape. The Leona of *Love in the Time of Cholera* remembers how the rapist "made instantaneous and frenetic love to her. Lying there on the rocks, her body covered with cuts and bruises, she had wanted that man to stay forever so that she could die of love in his arms . . . but she was sure she would have known him in a crowd of a thousand men because of his shape and size and his way of making love" (García Márquez 1988, 258). The film, in the name of the magical real, finds the rapist's image omnipresent: his smell indelibly fixed on her body, his image engraved in her mirror.

Natalia's quest leads her to a desolate cemetery where she is now gang raped. But again Márquez deflects our emotional rage with the intervention of Salamander, a cross-dressing, fire-eating cabaret performer who comforts her after her night of terror. The next day she is scolded by her other guardian angel, Matilde, who questions, "Is that what you are looking for?" The search, however, continues as the three travel to a colony for recovering rapists, where Natalia runs into an old friend, Carolina, an actress who works as a therapist. After she offers Natalia a lead about a former zoo employee who fits the description of her rapist, Natalia meets him, realizes that he is not the one, and seduces him. By now she is out of her mind with desire for the original rapist. Incredibly, none of the other sexual abuses bothers her, for she would get raped a thousand times to find him. "I'd know him in the dark" (*Yo soy*, English subtitles). She is seen at Enrique's bar responding to the advances of low-life men, and watches a woman sitting at a table singing the lyrics to a song playing in the background:

When this love was born
Out of worry and hate
Death was lurking in the doorway.
Your body surrendered itself
Against your will. (*Yo soy*, English subtitles)

The lyrics underline Márquez's theme in all of the *Amores difíciles* films: namely, the close proximity of love and death. This theme is played out in the whirlwind finish of *Yo soy*. Natalia meets and embraces her rapist at a masquerade party, but the lover is knifed to death by Salamander, who himself bursts into flame from his own love for Natalia. Returning home to confess to her husband, Natalia is mortified to find that her husband's touch seems cold, for his passion can never equal that of her rapist's.

The license Márquez takes with these films confirms stereotypes of women. One should not be surprised, because Márquez is reflecting a concept of machismo that Octavio Paz spells out brilliantly in *Labyrinth of Solitude*. Paz, voicing the Mexican concept of womanliness, writes,

The Mexican considers woman to be a dark, secret and passive being. . . . The Mexican woman quite simply has no will of her own. Her body is asleep and only comes really alive when someone awakens her. She is an answer rather than a question, a vibrant and easily worked material that is shaped by the imagination and sensuality of the male. . . . Women are imprisoned in the image masculine society has imposed on them. (37, 198)

In the *Cholera* films, Márquez has manipulated his women to fall neatly into these precepts of machismo. The lives of María, Fulvia, and Natalia rest upon their slavish need for men despite differences in their own social standing or economic independence. María is the lovely, protected aristocrat who becomes the pawn of both Pedro and Juan; Fulvia, the most brilliant pupil the schoolteacher ever had, is Orestes's most prized conquest; Natalia is a successful model and actress who turns into her rapist's slave.

Colombian anthropologist Ximena Pachón points out, "At the turn of the century, a Colombian woman had three choices: get married at 16, enter a convent, or become an old maid" (Brooke, A6). One could argue that because the time frame of *Carta* and *Fábula* is the early 1900s, the image of the women in these films is appropriate. However, *Yo soy* is very contemporary, and still it presents the most slavish of women. Why does Márquez insist on this posture? How close is it to present reality?

Today women outnumber men at Colombian universities by 52 to 48 percent. The average birthrate for Colombian women decreased from 7.4 in the 1960s to 2.7 in the 1990s. Leonor Montoya Alvarez, president of Banco de Colombia, the country's largest bank, notes, "I no longer run into girls who say they want to marry well and never work. Having economic independence is part of a Colombian woman's self-esteem" (Brooke, A6). These numbers and observations represent a precipitous change in the mindset of Latin women over a considerable number of years.

At the 1990 Seminar on Feminism and Culture in Latin America, mention was made of the first generation (1910–1950) of

> women intellectuals who rose in Buenos Aires, Sao Paulo, Rio de Janeiro, Santiago de Chile, Montevideo, Mexico City and Havana. Alfonsina Storni, Victoria Ocampo (Argentina), Gabriela Mistral (Chile) and other women activists of the post-revolutionary period saw through the hypocrisies of revolutionary edicts and began a history of political involvement seeking legal, social and economic justice. The Sáenz-Pena Law of 1912, for example, granted universal suffrage in Argentina, but excluded women; the Mexican Constitution of 1917 did not include women in its concept of citizenship; neither did the Cuban Family Code. (Bergmann et al., 4)

One quickly learns that there were women of importance other than the iconographic Sor Juana Inés de la Cruz, but very little of the reality of Colombian women is reflected in Márquez's films. Paz argues in *Labyrinth of Solitude* that Latin women can be themselves only by destroying the image in which the world has imprisoned them (198).

Despite Márquez's comment that "there's not a single line in all my work that does not have a basis in reality" (Stone, 54), the women in Márquez's films fall incredibly into stereotype and fail to rise above the strictures of machismo, a cultural reality to which Márquez is wedded.

REFERENCES

Aufderheide, Patricia. "Latin American Cinema and the Rhetoric of Cultural Nationalism: Controversies at Havana in 1987 and 1989." *Quarterly Review of Film and Video* 12, 4 (1991): 61–76.

Bell-Villada, Gene H. *García Márquez: The Man and His Work*. Chapel Hill: University of North Carolina Press, 1990.

Bergmann, Emilie, Janet Greenberg, Gwen Kirkpatrick, et al., eds. *Women, Culture, and Politics in Latin America: Seminar on Feminism and Culture in Latin America*. Berkeley and Los Angeles: University of California Press, 1990.

Brooke, James. "Women in Colombia Move to Job Forefront." *New York Times*, July 15, 1994, p. A6.

Burton, Julianne. "Learning to Write at the Movies: Film and the Fiction Writer in Latin America." *Texas Quarterly* 18 (Spring 1975): 92–102.

Cartas del parque. Dir. Tomas Gutiérrez Alea. Screenplay, Eliseo Alberto Diego, Tomás Gutiérrez Alea, and Gabriel García Márquez. Televisión Española S.A. International Network Group, 1988.

Conde, Susana. "Readerly and Writerly *Letters from the Park*." *Journal of Film and Video* 44, 3–4 (1992–1993): 105–118.

Fábula de la bella palomera. Dir. Ruy Guerra. Screenplay, Ruy Guerra and Gabriel García Márquez. Televisión Española S.A. International Network Group, 1988.

García Márquez, Gabriel. *Love in the Time of Cholera*. New York: Penguin, 1988.

Paxman, Andrew. "On the Lot with García Márquez." *Variety*, March 26–31, 1996, p. 55.

Paz, Octavio. *The Labyrinth of Solitude and Other Writings*. New York: Grove Weidenfeld, 1985.

Stone, Peter H. "The Art of Fiction LXIX: Gabriel García Márquez." *Paris Review*, Winter 1981, pp. 45–73.

Valdés, María Elena de. "*One Hundred Years of Solitude* in Women's Studies Courses." In *Approaches to Teaching García Márquez's "One Hundred Years of Solitude*," eds. María Elena de Valdés and Mario J. Valdés. New York: MLA, 1990.

Yo soy el que tú buscas. Dir. Jaime Chavarri. Screenplay, Juan Tebar, Jaime Chavarri, and Gabriel García Márquez. Televisión Española S.A. International Network Group, 1988.

PART VIII

TEXTS INTERTWINED

35

Play It Again, Sam:
The Reappearance of Spanish Plays
in Género Chico Parodies

Patricia Bentivegna

The parody, of course, is not the special province of the nineteenth century, since it can be traced back at least to classical Greek and Roman literature. A particularly Spanish form is found in the *género chico* [small genre], consisting of one-act theatrical pieces that flourished in Spain during the final decades of the nineteenth century. They used both spoken and sung dialogue to parody works of many kinds: plays from Spain and other countries, operas and operettas, the *zarzuela grande* (usually with three or four acts), and the *zarzuela* of the *género chico* itself. This presentation will examine the parody technique as seen in representative Spanish plays premièred from 1844 to 1911.

The techniques of the *género chico* parodist begins with the choice of a title that is usually a pun. They go on to include the lowering of the social scale of the characters, the comical deformation of names, colorful language that often combines colloquialisms with mock-heroic style, stepping out of character, and spoken or musical quotations from other works. Essential to the humorous effect is the familiarity of the theater audience with the original work, and for this reason most parodies were presented with very little delay. The popularity of the lyric theater of the time ensured that the musical quotations would also be quite familiar, and they are used repeatedly to embellish certain stock situations. Three of the most frequently used works—*Marina, La Gran Vía*, and *La verbena de la Paloma*—are still in the repertoire today.

The first parody to be considered is one that appeared over forty years after the original play. Here lapse of time did not pose a problem, since the Romantic version of the Don Juan theme—the *Don Juan Tenorio* (1844) of José Zorrilla—is a special case in the theatrical history of both Spain and the Spanish-speaking Americas. Because it was traditionally presented every year around All Souls' Day, audiences learned it practically by heart and quotations from it abound, often appearing when least expected. The inevitable doctoral dissertation just on parodies of this most famous and beloved of all Romantic plays will be written, and it would not be surprising if others were to follow. The verse of the *Tenorio* itself is a kind of music and really does not require any other melody; therefore, most imitations limit themselves to changing words and phrases for a comical effect. This is the situation in much of the 1886 *zarzuela, Juanito Tenorio*, a sort of quixotic parody in that the title personage has taken into his head to imitate his namesake. Zorrilla's hero enumerates the days required by his seduction technique (translations are mine).

Don Juan Tenorio (1844)

Uno para enamorarlas,	One day to court them,
otro para conseguirlas,	another to seduce them,
otro para abandonarlas,	another to abandon them,
dos para sustituirlas,	two to replace them,
y una hora para olvidarlas. (45)	and an hour to forget them.

Juanito's version requires the same length of time and ends with a colloquial expression that provides the comic effect:

Juanito Tenorio (1886)

Tardo un día en conseguirlas,	It takes me a day to seduce them,
las adoro dos o tres	I adore them for two or three,
y a los tres o cuatro días	and three or four days later,
si te he visto no hay de qué. (11)	sorry, I don't remember you.

Don Juan is very democratic in his amorous pursuits, as he declares:

Don Juan Tenorio

Desde una princesa real	From a royal princess
a la hija de un pescador	to a fisherman's daughter,
¡oh! ha recorrido mi amor	oh! my love goes up and down
toda la escala social. (44)	the entire social scale.

Juanito echoes his final lines exactly and adds a humorous reference to the theater of the time. The affluent patron of the arts would have a season ticket to the opera at the Real (royal) Theater, and, of course, Zorrilla's princess is a royal personage:

Juanito Tenorio

Desde la abonada al Real	From the patron of the Royal Theater
a la artista de obrador,	to the working girl
ha recorrido mi amor	my love goes up and down
toda la escala social. (13)	the entire social scale.

Six months earlier than *Juanito Tenorio* was the première of *La Gran Vía*, one of the most popular of all *zarzuelas* and one that is still frequently performed. It is in the form of a musical review that satirizes the municipal project of the construction of a great avenue in Madrid, a project that would necessitate the destruction of many smaller streets and plazas, which are personified by members of the cast. One of these is the Caballero de Gracia, who is usually portrayed as an elderly dandy. Attesting to the ongoing popularity of this work is the fact that it was presented with English dialogue and Spanish musical numbers at the Jarvis Conservatory in Napa, California, in July 1996. This version featured a rather youthful Caballero de Gracia:

La Gran Vía (1886): Vals del Caballero de Gracia

Caballero de Gracia me llaman	They call me the Caballero de Gracia
y efectivamente soy así,	and indeed that's the way I am,
por mis amoríos todo Madrid	for it's well known that all of Madrid
pues sabido es a mí me conoce.	knows about my conquests.
Es verdad que estoy un poco antiguo,	It's true that I'm a bit out of date,
pero que en poniéndome mi frac	but when I'm all dressed up in tails
soy un tipo gentil	I'm a genteel type
de carácter jovial	of jovial character
a quien mima la sociedad.	and spoiled by just everyone.
Chorus: De este silbante la abuela murió.	This dude's grandma must be dead.
Caballero: Yo soy el caballero que con más finura	I'm the gentleman who with most elegance
baila en los salones comilfó.	dances in the salons *comme il faut*.
Chorus: Siendo tan cursi querer presumir.	He has to do his own bragging.
Caballero: Y las niñas se dislocan por	And the girls really put themselves out
quererme hacer tilín. (109)	to impress me.

This number from *La Gran Vía* is used to introduce the character who portrays Juanito Tenorio's friend, the doctor bearing the name of the original Don Juan Tenorio's nemesis, don Gonzalo de Ulloa:

Juanito Tenorio
Don Gonzalo de Ulloa me llamo   I'm called Don Gonzalo de Ulloa,
y efectivamente ése soy. (18)   and indeed that's who I am.

In his 1878 drama *Consuelo*, the post-Romantic playwright Adelardo
López de Ayala relates the story of a woman who chooses wealth and
position over love and finds that she has made a decision that ruins
her life. The title of the parody version is *Consuelo . . . de tontos* (1878), a
reference to the proverb that begins with the phrase "Mal de muchos."
The corresponding expression would probably be "Misery loves company." The heroine is now named Desconsolación, a transformation of
the original name that reverses its meaning of "consolation" and removes the religious connotation. The parodist soon turns to the lyric
theater so familiar to the audience of the time.

Marina was first presented as a *zarzuela* in 1855 and was changed to
an opera in 1871 by the elimination of the spoken dialogue and the
elaboration of the musical numbers. It is the story of two young people
in love who must endure a series of rather unlikely misunderstandings until everything is straightened out. The opening *romanza* of the
hero, the sea captain Jorge, is rather taxing for a tenor, who does not
have a chance to warm up his voice before hitting the high notes. He
sings of his joy in returning to the coast of Spain after a voyage to the
Americas:

Marina (1855/1871): **Llegada de Jorge**
Costa la de Levante   Mediterranean coast,
playa la de Lloret,   beach of Lloret,
dichosos los ojos   how happy I am
que os vuelven a ver.   to see you again.
(*zarzuela* 21; opera 59)

This fragment became a standard allusion to the return from a voyage.
Fernando, the rejected suitor of Consuelo, becomes the fireman
Francho, who appears at her door singing his version of the arrival of
Marina's sweetheart:

Consuelo . . . de tontos (1878)
Tapias las de esta casa   Walls of this house
que cuesta un duro al mes,   that cost five pesetas a month,
dichosos los ojos   how happy I am
que os vuelven a ver. (5)   to see you again.

The successful suitor, the wealthy Ricardo, is the parody counter-
feiter Bernardo, who makes pesetas that are "casi / tan buenas como
las buenas" [almost as good as the good ones] (10). Ricardo leaves

Consuelo for the Italian singer Adela; Bernardo abandons Desconsolación for a flamenco singer. The final line of Consuelo as the curtain falls is "¡Qué espantosa soledad!" [What horrible solitude!] (711). Her parody counterpart changes it to "¡Qué espantosa soleá!" (35), a pretext for a flamenco number in which she is joined by the chorus.

Benito Pérez Galdós, best known for the vast range of his novels, is also the author of several works for the theater. His *La de San Quintín* [The Duchess of San Quintín] (1894) portrays the Buendía family during a time of social change. The octogenarian José Manuel de Buendía has prospered as a result of hard work and thrift and is now revered as the family patriarch. (It must be remembered that at the time of this play concern for the welfare of one's family was not considered to be a reason for opprobrium.) His ne'er-do-well son, César, a middle-aged widower, has put his energy into the pursuit of the fair sex. The title refers to the delightful and resourceful Rosario, the impoverished duchess of San Quintín, a distant niece who decides to share her future with the avowed socialist Víctor, who was for a time erroneously believed to be the illegitimate son of César.

The parodies of this play were not long in coming; indeed, two of them appeared within a month. The first, *La del capotín o Con las manos en la masa*, transfers the action to that popular *género chico* setting, the *barrios bajos* [popular neighborhoods] of Madrid. The title requires a rather elaborate explanation.

The first part of this typical nineteenth-century double title, found also, for example, in the English novel, is based on the former occupation of the parody's heroine. She has been transformed from a duchess into a former stage performer whose greatest role was in the *zarzuela, La canción de la Lola* [The Song of Lola] (1880), known then as "Fanny." That work is best known for the song beginning "Con el capotín tin tin" [With a little cape], a catchy tune that would later appear even in such odd places as filmed versions of the adventures of O'Henry's Cisco Kid. It has been recorded in a folk version by the Basque folk group Los Bocheros.

La canción de la Lola (1880): Chorus

Con el capotín tin tin tin tin tin tin,	With a little cape,
que esta noche va a llover,	for tonight it's going to rain,
con el capotín tin tin tin tin tin,	with a little cape,
a eso del amanecer. (44)	just around dawn.

Fanny is thus "la del capotín" [the girl with the cape].

Since Galdós's duchess shows her democratic leanings by helping with the baking of rolls in the family kitchen, she is literally "con las manos en la masa" [with her hands in the dough], the Spanish equivalent of being "caught with her hands in the cookie jar," usually a satirical reference to political corruption. Names are changed, not to "protect the innocent" in this case, but to amuse the audience. Don José becomes "Noé" [Noah], known as "el Patriarca" [the Patriarch] because he resembles the "gachó del arca" [the guy who built the ark]. His son is now called Malanoche [bad night], a reversal of the family surname Buendía [good day].

This parody contains several other quotations from the musical theater. The following rhythmic excerpt is from the song of a sailor in *Marina*:

Marina: Tango (or Habanera) of Roque

Dichoso aquel que tiene	Happy the man whose home
la casa a flote, la casa a flote,	floats on the ocean wave;
a quien el mar mece	the sea gently rocks
su camarote, su camarote,	his cabin, his cabin,
y oliendo a brea, y oliendo a brea	back and forth it sways
al arrullo del agua se balancea,	as the tar perfumes the breeze,
y oliendo a brea, y oliendo a brea	back and forth it sways
al arrullo del agua se balancea.	as the tar perfumes the breeze.
(*zarzuela* 60; opera 209–211)	

The parodist connects the concept to the Biblical ark, adding an insult:

La del capotín o Con las manos en la masa (1894): Chorus

Dichoso aquel que tiene	Happy the man whose home
la casa a flote,	floats on the ocean wave,
y que además es tonto	and who is also
de capirote. (13)	a real lame brain.

Also included is the famous drinking song from *Marina*, which is the opening choral number in *La del capotín*. Here is the original:

Marina: Brindis

A beber, a beber, a ahogar	Let's drink, let's drown out
el grito del dolor,	the sound of our sorrow,
que el vino hará olvidar	for wine will make us forget
las penas del amor,	the pangs of love.
(*zarzuela* 40; opera 176–177)	

And this is its parody:

La del capotín o Con las manos en la masa: Chorus

A beber, a beber, a apurar	Let's drink, down the hatch
el rico peleón,	with this cheap booze,

que hoy cumple ochenta años	because this fine gentleman
este buen señor. (7)	is eighty years old today.

This parody includes several other references. It was soon followed by *La de Vámonos* [The Girl from Let's Go], using many of the same techniques—musical numbers and the ubiquitous *Tenorio*. Besides referring to *La Gran Vía*, it also quotes the most famous *zarzuela* of the *género chico, La verbena de la Paloma* [The Feast of Our Lady of the Dove], which had premièred earlier the same month.

A later play of Galdós, *Mariucha* (1903), inspired the parody *Feúcha* [The Ugly Girl], in which the allusions include the *Tenorio, La Gran Vía, La canción de la Lola*, the 1897 *zarzuela, La revoltosa* [The Troublemaker], and even Calderón's seventeenth-century *La vida es sueño* [Life Is a Dream].

Other authors who did not escape the parodists include Joaquín Dicenta, whose tragic drama *Juan José* (1895) inspired parodies that quote *La Gran Vía, La verbena de la Paloma, La canción de la Lola*, and, of course, the *Tenorio*. More famous outside of Spain is Jacinto Benavente, whose *La losa de los sueños* [The Sepulcher of Dreams] (1911) became *La lata de los celos* [Jealousy Is Such a Nuisance] (1911), with references to *La verbena de la Paloma* and Calderón's *La vida es sueño*. Benavente's winning of the Nobel Prize in 1922 made his name internationally famous. He is probably best known for his *Los intereses creados* [Vested Interests] (1907), an interesting interpretation of the Italian commedia dell'arte.

As might be supposed, the parodies themselves have not been recorded. Several of the musical fragments they include originate in works that are rarely performed nowadays, but that can be heard in recordings. There are frequent opportunities to attend performances of *Marina, La Gran Vía*, and *La verbena de la Paloma*.

One does feel rather envious of the theater audiences who could decipher for themselves the several layers of meaning contained in the parodies of the time. They are admittedly minor literary forms, but their exaggerations and distortions can provide interesting insights into the original works, as well as enjoyment of the humor displayed.

BIBLIOGRAPHY

Arrieta y Corera, Emilio. *Marina*. Libretto by Francisco Camprodón y Lafont and Miguel Ramos Carrión. 3 acts, Teatro Real, March 16, 1871. Madrid: Unión Musical Española, 1946.

Barraycoa, Francisco, and Romea, Alberto. *La lata de los celos*. 1 act, Lara, December 28, 1911. Madrid: R. Velasco, 1912.

Benavente Martínez, Jacinto. *La losa de los sueños*. In *Obras completas*, 5th ed. Vol. 3. Madrid: Aguilar, 1940.

Camprodón y Lafont, Francisco. *Marina*. Music by Emilio Arrieta y Corera. 2 acts, Circo, September 21, 1855. Mexico: Imprenta Calle Avenida de la Penitenciaria, 1889.

Casero y Barranco, Antonio, and Larrubiera, Alejandro. *Feúcha*. 1 act, Eslava, December 11, 1903. Madrid: R. Velasco, 1903.

Chueca Robres, Federico, and Valverde, Joaquín (padre). *La Gran Vía*. Libretto by Felipe Pérez y González. 1 act, Felipe, July 2, 1886. Madrid: Unión Musical Española, n.d.

Dicenta y Benedicto, Joaquín. *Juan José*. 3 acts, Comedia, October 29, 1895. Barcelona: Maucci, n.d.

Granés y Román, Salvador María. *Consuelo . . . de tontos*. 1 act, Apolo, June 15, 1878. Madrid: J. C. Conde, 1878.

———. *Juanito Tenorio*, 2d ed. Music by Manuel Nieto y Matáñ. 1 act, Martín, November 27, 1886. Madrid: R. Velasco, 1891.

López de Ayala y Herrera, Adelardo. *Consuelo* (1878). In *Nineteenth Century Spanish Plays*, ed. Lewis E. Brett. New York: Appleton-Century-Crofts, 1935.

López Silva, José, and Shaw, Carlos Fernández. *La Revoltosa*. Music by Ruperto Chapí y Lorente. 1 act, Apolo, November 25, 1897. Barcelona: Cisne, n.d.

Lucio y López, Celso, and Palomero, Antonio. *Pepito*. 1 act, Comedia, November 21, 1895. Madrid: R. Velasco, 1895.

Merino y Pichilo, Gabriel. *La del capotín o Con las manos en la masa*. Music by Luis Arnedo y Muñoz. 1 act, Romea, February 17, 1894. Madrid: R. Velasco, 1894.

Pérez Galdós, Benito. *La de San Quintín* (1894). In *Nineteenth Century Spanish Plays*, ed. Lewis E. Brett. New York: Appleton-Century-Crofts, 1935.

———. *Mariucha* (1903). In *Obras completas*. 4th ed. Vol. 6. Madrid: Aguilar, 1961.

Pérez y González, Felipe. *La de vámonos*. Music by Joaquín Valverde y San Juan. 1 act, Apolo, February 26, 1894. Madrid: R. Velasco, 1894.

———. *La Gran Vía*. Music by Federico Chueca Robres y Joaquín Valverde (padre). 1 act, Felipe, July 2, 1886. In *El género chico (Antología de textos completos)*, ed. Antonio Valencia. Madrid: Taurus, 1962.

Saltiveri Vidal, Antón, and Asmarats, Joseph. *Quan mo's té*. 1 act, Principal, February 18, 1897. Barcelona: Establiment Tipográfich, 1897.

Valencia, Antonio, ed. *El género chico (Antología de textos completos)*. Madrid: Taurus, 1962.

Vega y Oreiro, Ricardo de la. *La canción de la Lola*. Music by Federico Chueca Robres and Joaquín Valverde (padre). 1 act, Alhambra, May 25, 1880. In *El género chico (Antología de textos completos)*, ed. Antonio Valencia. Madrid: Taurus, 1962.

———. *La verbena de la Paloma o El boticario y las chulapas y celos mal reprimidos*. Music by Tomás Bretón y Hernández. 1 act, Apolo, February 17, 1894. In *El género chico (Antología de textos completos)*, ed. Antonio Valencia. Madrid: Taurus, 1962.

Zorrilla y Moral, José. *Don Juan Tenorio* (1844). In *Representative Spanish Authors*, 3d ed. Vol. 2, ed. Walter T. Pattison and Donald W. Bleznick. New York: Oxford University Press, 1971.

ORIGINAL PLAYS

1844 *Don Juan Tenorio*   José Zorrilla y Moral

1878 *Consuelo*   Adelardo López de Ayala y Herrera

1894 *La de San Quintín*   Benito Pérez Galdós

1895 *Juan José*   Joaquín Dicenta y Benedicto

1903 *Mariucha*   Benito Pérez Galdós

1911 *La losa de los sueños*   Jacinto Benavente y Martínez

PARODIES

1886 *Juanito Tenorio*   Salvador María Granés y Román (libretto); Manuel Nieto y Matáñ (music)

1878 *Consuelo . . . de tontos* Salvador María Granés y Román

1894 *La del capotín o Con las manos en la masa*   Gabriel Merino y Pichilo (libretto); Joaquín Valverde y San Juan (music)

1894 *La de Vámonos*   Felipe Pérez y González (libretto); Joaquín Valverde y San Juan (music)

1895 *Pepito*   Celso Lucio y López and Antonio Palomero

1897 *Quan no's té*   Antón Saliveri Vidal and Joseph Asmarats

1903 *Feúcha*   Antonio Casero y Barranco and Alejandro Larrubiera

1911 *La lata de los celos*   Francisco Barraycoa and Alberto Romea

MUSICAL WORKS QUOTED

1855/1871 *Marina*   Francisco Camprodón y Lafont (libretto); Emilio Arrieta y Corera (music)

1880 *La canción de la Lola*   Ricardo de la Vega y Oreiro (libretto); Federico Chueca Robres and Joaquín Valverde (padre) (music)

1886 *La Gran Vía*   Felipe Pérez y González (libretto); Federico Chueca Robres and Joaquín Valverde (padre) (music)

1894 *La verbena de la Paloma* Ricardo de la Vega y Oreiro (libretto); Tomás Bretón y Hernández (music)

1897 *La revoltosa*   José López Silva and Carlos Fernández Shaw (libretto); Ruperto Chapí y Lorente (music)

Against the Grain: A Revisionist View of Golden Age Icons in Fuentes's Terra Nostra

Jane C. Simon

In his essay, *Cervantes o la crítica de la lectura*, Carlos Fuentes describes the relationship of Don Quixote and Sancho Panza as the fusion of past and present: the illusions of chivalry and ideals of justice, abundance, and liberty of Don Quixote and the practical realism of Sancho and his very real-world daily struggle for existence. More important, says Fuentes, this fusion is accomplished "con palabras y sólo con palabras . . . único sitio de encuentro de los mundos" (Fuentes, *Cervantes*, 1976, 32).[1] Thus, the parody of chivalric tales and the portrayal and critique of Spanish Renaissance society are superseded by the central reality of the novel, which is "la crítica de la creación dentro de las páginas de su propia creación, *Don Quijote*. Y esta crítica de la creación es una crítica del acto mismo de la lectura" (33).[2]

Fuentes further states that the origin of this essay lies in the work he had been doing for the previous six years on his sixth novel, *Terra Nostra*, a novel that deals in large part with the period of Spanish history in which Cervantes was writing and in which the Americas were colonized. The aim of my study is to look at the relationships between Fuentes's essay, his novel, *Terra Nostra*, and some of the literary and artistic works that inhabit it, the most important of which is Cervantes's *El Ingenioso hidalgo Don Quijote de la Mancha*. I intend to focus, in particular, on Fuentes's use of the critical and self-evaluative aspects of writing and reading that were first practiced by Cervantes.

Fuentes also quotes Octavio Paz, who called *Don Quijote* "la épica de una sociedad en lucha consigo misma" (16).[3] He is describing the period of the Counter-Reformation, when the Spanish monarchy had closed ranks with the Catholic Church to suppress both free thought and ethnic diversity. Jews and Moors were expelled or forced to convert (as Cervantes clearly showed, particularly in the episode on Ricote the Moor), and any privileging of their contribution to the Spanish cultural heritage was severely repressed. In Fuentes's words, "La triple herencia de España optó por la clandestinidad y el disimulo. Pero el lenguaje, la sensibilidad y las tensiones del arte y la literatura españolas serían marcados para siempre por el pluralismo de su auténtica herencia cultural" (Fuentes, *Cervantes*, 1976, 65).[4] For him, this aspect of the background of *Don Quijote* is crucial in the development of his own country, Mexico, as the repressive social system of Spain was exported with the *conquistadores* to America and imposed on the New World, with enduring results.

Terra Nostra deals ostensibly and primarily with sixteenth-century Spain. Although it begins and ends in twentieth-century France and its center section is an oneiric vision of Mexico on the eve of the conquest, it concentrates, for the most part, on the court of Felipe II. In addition, however, twentieth-century Mexico hovers like a spectral presence throughout the book, finally appearing in a short and frightening chapter toward the end. It is the modern world and its heritage of monolithic repression with which Fuentes is principally preoccupied.

The reverberations of *Don Quijote* can be found both in the historical preoccupation and in the form, themes, and characters of Fuentes's book. *Terra Nostra*, like *Don Quijote*, is divided into multiple short chapters. The style is narrative and the games of illusion and reality, of truth and fiction, invented by the genius of Cervantes are apparent not only in those themes and characters, but in images or leitmotifs that appear and reappear throughout the book: mirrors, maps, bottles filled with manuscripts, collage-like masks (symbols of self-realization through literature and art or of illusion), and the recurring presence of both Don Quixote and Cervantes as characters. Fuentes is clearly patterning his work on the process Spadaccini and Talens describe in speaking of Cervantes's novel: a text that is not only a mirror, but a kaleidoscope, a shattered mirror that disseminates "a multiplicity of images . . . mobile, fragmentary and contradictory . . . that no longer reflect but re-*produce* reality," a text that challenges us to participate in the process of creation, to gather and rearrange the fragments and to re-*produce*, with the author, our own version of the story (Spadaccini and Talens, xv–xvi).

Thus, characteristically, the authorship of *Terra Nostra*, like that of *Don Quijote*, is questioned and blurred. The court painter, Fray Julian, who is the confessor and confidant of the king and court, narrates parts of the book. There are episodes similar to Cervantes's intercalated tales that are narrated by other characters or found on manuscripts in bottles thrown into the sea by one hand and retrieved by another. There is a point at which Fray Julian leaves for the New World and passes his job as narrator on to "the Chronicler," an otherwise unnamed figure whose adventures, including the loss of a hand at the Battle of Lepanto and a period of captivity among the Moors, suggest his identity. But there are also segments of the story with no clear narrator, and moments when the origin of a story and the identity of a speaker are a mystery. A chapter begins, "¿Empiezas a entender, mujer? Valdréme de Ludovico" (Fuentes 1975b, 538), and the unknown narrator-behind-the-narrator continues, speaking in the voice of Ludovico, one of the central characters. (One cannot help but think here of Cervantes's Cide Hamete Benengeli and of the narrator behind him who continually interrupts the story with tales of lost and rediscovered bits of manuscript.)[5]

There are regular changes in the narrative from third to first to second person. The game of mirrors, so aptly played by Cervantes, is also being played here, for the same reasons and with some of the same material (including Cervantes himself). Fuentes makes clear in his essay that this aspect of Cervantes's writing is of capital importance to him:

Esta es la última pregunta de Cervantes: ¿quién escribe los libros y quién los lee? . . . las palabras son la primera y natural instancia de la propiedad común. Entonces, Miguel de Cervantes o James Joyce sólo pueden ser dueños de las palabras en la medida en que no son Cervantes y Joyce, sino todos: son el poeta. El poeta nace después de su acto: el poema. El Poema crea a sus autores, como crea a sus lectores. (Fuentes, *Cervantes*, 1976, 95, 110)[6]

The work of art, once it has left the hand of the artist, is common property, and an author who recognizes this and makes his work a participatory exercise—as do Cervantes and Fuentes—shares whatever authority he has with those who read and with those who are read. The work and the characters in it take on lives of their own, as both Cervantes and Fuentes make abundantly clear.

Fuentes further questions reality and illusion through the use of multiple versions of each story: of the story of Don Quixote, of the stories of Don Juan and of Celestina (also characters in *Terra Nostra*), of the stories of Christ, of the heretics of Flanders, of the "comuneros de Castilla," and of the encounter of Europeans with the Americas. Uniting and echoing them all are the stories of the half-brothers and possible heirs of Felipe II, at once triplets and a single individual whose life will last only as long as his two brothers continue to sleep and dream his existence. They are identified with the Flemish heretics, with

Don Juan, with Don Quixote (who may also have been Don Juan, in his youth), with Agrippa Postumus, the half-brother of the Roman Emperor Tiberius, with Quetzelcoatl and his dark double, the god of blood and death, and with a crippled Parisian orphan named Polo Febo. Ludovico explains the multiple versions to Felipe, saying that each reader will create his or her own version of the story that will have as much validity as any other version, since it belongs to each of them as much as to its creator. The versions found within the covers of the book are only a beginning.

Many of the characters in the book are literary personae that Fuentes has borrowed from a multitude of sources. Felipe and his family are the principal historical characters, but even they are not unequivocally historical; Fuentes skews the facts for the purpose of his story. Among other things, Felipe II is presented as the son of Felipe I, whereas he was in reality his grandson; here he is married to Elizabeth I of England, when in reality he was married to her half-sister, Mary Tudor; he is represented as having no heirs, whereas the succession of the real Felipe II continued for another hundred years.[7] These historical liberties are taken in part on behalf of artistic license, but they are also a part of Fuentes's aesthetic credo: Each author creates his own reality (as does each reader) and Fuentes's reality is meant to be ambivalent and shifting. Fray Julian speaks for his author when he advises the Chronicler to cultivate loose ends.

Each of the more protean characters, in addition to having multiple life stories, has multiple, or at least dual, sides to his or her personality. Fuentes's Don Quixote is still an idealist, but he confesses that he was, in his youth, a libertine who used the services of an old procuress, made love to Dulcinea, killed her father, fled, and changed his name. When he later returned to challenge the statue of her father, it only laughed at him and told him that he would live to see his readings and imaginings become reality, but a reality that no one else would see, thus turning him into an object of ridicule: "te matará el ridículo, pues nadie sino tú verá a esos gigantes, magos, y princesas, tú verás la verdad, pero sólo tú, los demás verán carneros y molinos" (Fuentes, *Terra*, 1975b, 582).[8]

In this deliberate confusion of the identities of two diametrically opposed literary figures, Fuentes suggests that extremes of personality are always found with their doubles. Not only do Don Quixote and Don Juan share a life experience, but it has been given an additional twist that adds several wrinkles to each of their fictional existences.[9] Furthermore, with his reversal of truth and illusion in the story of Don Quixote he takes the game a step farther, forcing us to reflect again on Cervantes's sleight of hand.

Celestina too has a dual personality: She is both a beautiful and alluring young woman and an aged, vulgar procuress. In his essay on

Cervantes, Fuentes calls the literary character "sibila secreta, protectora celosa de las verdades que los hombres persiguen y prohiben porque temen lo que el espejo de la hechizera refleja: la imagen del origen, la visión mítica, fundadora, del alba de la historia" (Fuentes, *Cervantes*, 1976, 50–51).[10]

Celestina's re-creation in *Terra Nostra* portrays her not only as she was in Fernando de Rojas's drama, but as she might have been in her youth: The young seductress is the embodiment of men's dreams; the aging hag is their greatest fear. Both have magical powers, like the duo in Fuentes's *Aura*: the ability to grant every wish. But as the young woman grants them, the aged crone exacts the price. Fuentes's young Celestina is capable of giving identity to one who has none, of restoring memories that were lost, and of renewing a dying race, but as she ages she passes her secrets on to a younger incarnation, so that her character is constantly renewed and recreated and she becomes the Celestina of Rojas who forgets her magic youth and lives only for the day and its limited reality.

Central to the action of the book are the three half-brothers of Felipe. They are identical in looks (all three bear a cross imprinted on their backs and, curiously, six toes on each foot, an imperfection that both echoes the superstitious fear of differences and simbolizes their mixed blood). They embody multiplicity. Their number can perhaps be identified with the Holy Trinity. As one of them tells Ludovico, "La cifra de la dispersión. . . . Jesús vino a dispersar: el poder de la tierra era de uno; él se lo entregó a todos" (Fuentes, *Terra*, 1975b, 573).[11] But it is also undoubtedly the expression of the triple heritage of Spain: Jewish, Moorish, and Christian. Another character who is put to death by Felipe—a young man who is variously called Miguel, Michah, and Mihail ben Sama (Michael of Life)—has the same triple heritage, is identified with the brothers, and is also a double of Cervantes (the Chronicler), aptly representing the loss of life and talent that resulted from the repressive Hapsburg policies.

The brothers are raised by Ludovico, Felipe's lover in his youth and his opposite, a wanderer and a teacher, who makes the three orphans into spiritual brothers. He converts them into something they would not otherwise have been, through love. Where Felipe rejects and kills, Ludovico protects and preserves. He is also a translator, one who through knowledge and understanding is able to bridge the gap between languages, cultures, and peoples. He studies for a time in the synagogue in Toledo, where the old Rabbi tells him,

Lee; traduce; . . . las distintas fes se alimentan de una común sabiduría. No sé cuál sea la tuya, ni te interrogo al respecto. Hijos del libro somos todos, judíos, moros y cristianos, y sólo si aceptamos esta verdad viviremos en paz unos con otros. (Fuentes, *Terra*, 1975b, 526)[12]

Ludovico represents those who read and write, communicate and unite—"sons of the book"—the salt of the Earth and the hope of the future.

In contrast to this proliferation of life and reincarnations of other characters and ideas, there is a progressive narrowing of the persona of Felipe II, the defender of the Catholic faith and of the monolithic and pervasive Hapsburg monarchical system in Spain. His story, from his youth through his campaigns in Flanders to the building of the Escorial and finally to his death, is baroque, but it becomes gradually impoverished as he ages. His pathological rigidity is evident in his fascination with the polymorphous and frightening disorder of Fray Julian's painting, a painting whose description closely resembles one of Hieronymus Bosch's nightmarish visions, and is thus the complementary opposite and shattered mirror of Felipe's own unforgiving order. For Felipe, all the loose ends—Fray Julian's "cabos sueltos" (Fuentes, *Terra*, 1975b, 660)—are tied up, and what remains is simply an endless repetition of the despair, nostalgia, anguish, and disillusionment of Felipe's existence.

While Felipe has in his youth the possibility of more than one destiny—he can follow the selfish and restrictive policies of his ancestors or he can remain youthful, venture forth, and look for new worlds (represented by the sea)—he turns his back on change. It is only through his double, Ludovico (the companion, lover, and conscience of his youth), that he maintains, for a time, any contact with or understanding of what might have been. Ludovico tries to convince him that he has a second chance to change the course of events, but the inertia of Felipe's heritage, his surroundings, and his own past are too powerful; his future is already written. His decision to turn away from the world and its multiplicity—the decision that will ultimately impoverish both Spain and its colonies—is in keeping with his desire to be the end of his line, to have no heirs of his own and to suppress the three usurpers. In fact, his wish—that Spain continue, even after his death, in the absolute rigidity that he has imposed upon it—is a seeming impossibility that is realized. When he does return, in a vision, to Castile in the twentieth century, he finds the Valle de los Caídos (Fuentes, *Terra*, 1975b, 763).[13]

It is through Guzmán, Felipe's secretary and lieutenant, that the future that Felipe imagines is realized. A member of the minor aristocracy, dispossessed by the growing power of the urban bourgeoisie and the rising demands of the working class, he is a threat both to those classes he considers to be beneath him and to those above, the ruling family that has allowed these changes to occur: "secreto enemigo . . . de quienes todo y de quienes nada tienen" (Fuentes, *Terra*, 1975b, 231).[14] As Ludovico counsels and Felipe debates, Guzmán foments and then suppresses a rebellion, just as Felipe had done in his youth, to impress his father and show himself worthy of power. The description of the rebellion, interspersed with segments of a letter from the Junta of Avila, identifies it with the defeat of the "comuneros de Castilla" in 1521, of which Fuentes speaks in his essay on Cervantes. Contrary to the opinion of more conservative historians, he maintains that it was not the last gasp of the feudal nobility against the centralizing impulse of the monarchy, but a bid for rights on the part of the urban bourgeoisie, whose defeat crushed the pluralistic and democratic tendencies of medieval Spain in its transition toward modernity (Fuentes, *Cervantes*, 1976, 53–57). Guzmán has patiently undermined the authority of Felipe and is responsible for the act itself, but it is Felipe's example and inaction that makes it possible.

It is not surprising that following the rebellion Guzmán asks to be allowed to lead an expedition to the New World to seek his fortune, and that he subsequently writes to Felipe, describing with relish the horrors of the Conquest. The signature he adopts, "el Muy Magnífico Señor don Hernando de Guzmán" (Fuentes, *Terra*, 1975b, 710), makes amply clear that he is identified with Cortés, Columbus, and the other early exploiters and despoilers of the Americas.[15]

None of the characters in the book, finally, is a developed personality, a real person. All are figures, alternatives, consciousnesses that represent the various possibilities of life, the various forms and destinies that human existence can take. A recurring theme is precisely that of recurrence, return, and reincarnation. Ludovico, the teacher and perennial student, often expresses this theme:

—Viajo del espíritu a la materia. Regreso de la materia al espíritu. No hay fronteras. Nada me es vedado. Pienso que soy varias personas mentalmente. Luego soy varias personas físicamente. . . .

—Una vida no basta. Se necesitan múltiples existencias para integrar una personalidad. (Fuentes, *Terra*, 1975b, 539)[16]

It is a theme that not only is expressed many times and incorporated into the recurring images and characters in the story, but is also parodied in the last chapter, where the twentieth-century media is shown to gobble up and grind out even the most iconoclastic philosophies. Population control is being practiced through ritualistic slaughter, and radio and television, maintaining that those sacrificed will have the opportunity to continue their development in some other existence, ironically participate in the propaganda necessary for this effort.

In an essay on *Terra Nostra*, Lois Parkinson Zamora emphasizes the influence on Fuentes of the ideas of Giambattista Vico, who rejected the scientific positivism of his century and proclaimed that history is not an absolute, but a "science of humanity." Fuentes, she says, who has often remarked that history is written by novelists, affirmed in an interview that Vico was "probably the first philosopher who says *we* create history" (Parkinson Zamora, 250). It is in the writing of history that the meaning of the events it relates comes together and makes sense in relation to those who read it. Parkinson Zamora continues (speaking of Fuentes's essay, *Cervantes o la crítica de la lectura*),

Fuentes develops what he has presented novelistically, a theory of the *communal and multivocal* text based on a radically historical view of language. For Fuentes as for Vico, the future of language and culture is contained in and dependent upon the recuperation of the language of the past, language which provides a mythic infusion into contemporary forms. (252, emphasis added)

It is clear that for Fuentes anything is possible and everything is meaningful through language, that the past—whether literary or historical—can be remade, and that life itself will be affected by this process. The ubiquitous green bottles filled with manuscripts that continually turn up throughout the book—found with or given to or left behind by the three step-brothers, thrown into the sea by Tiberius's scribe, Theodorus, and by the Chronicler at the Battle of Lepanto, thrown by Celestina into the Seine to Polo Febo (in the first chapter), and found in his apartment in Paris (in the final chapter)—all contain words, language, communications that are the source and the basis of palpable reincarnation. Not only do characters return in *Terra Nostra*, but ideas as well. In the Synagogue of Toledo, Ludovico is told by the ancient Rabbi, "Las ideas, sabes, nunca se realizan por completo. A veces se retraen, inviernan como algunas bestias, esperan el momento oportuno para reaparecer: el pensamiento mide su tiempo" (Fuentes, *Terra*, 1975, 545).[17]

It is through words and only through words—the only possible place, as Fuentes says, where worlds can meet—that time, history, and its injustices are defeated. At the end of the first chapter of the book, Celestina sees Polo Febo fall into the Seine in Paris on July 14, 1999. Subsequently, both are central to the action of the book, and in the final chapter, they meet again in Paris on December 31, 1999. "¿No estás cansado?" she asks him. "Peregrino, has viajado tanto desde que caíste del puente aquella tarde" (Fuentes, *Terra*, 1975b, 778).[18] He protests that he has been in his room reading manuscripts since that time, that she is talking of a novel he has read and that she must have read as well. But she answers,

—¿Por qué no piensas lo contrario? . . . ¿por qué no piensas que los dos hemos vivido lo mismo, y que esos papeles escritos por fray Julián y el Cronista dan fe de nuestras vidas?

—¿Cuándo? ¿Cuándo?

—Durante los seis meses y medio que pasaron entre tu caída al río y nuestro encuentro aquí, esta noche. (Fuentes, *Terra*, 1975b, 778)[19]

It is in the words and the reality they create that Celestina believes, and that she would have Polo and us believe; as we read, *we* live them as well and participate in their creative process. No matter the logic of historical time, of bodies, or of space, the important time and place— those that will endure—are within the words and pages of the book. It is through the transformations that are accomplished in such books and in their readers—the sons of the book—that life learns the patterns of art and the path to a more rational and humane future.

NOTES

1. "With words and words alone . . . the only possible place where worlds *can* meet" (Fuentes, *Don Quixote*, 1976, 21). Fuentes translated his original essay into two other essays ("Cervantes, or the Critique of Reading" in *Myself with Others* [1990], and *Don Quixote or the Critique of Reading* [1976]), each slightly different from the other and from the original Spanish version. The translation that I have used is *Don Quixote or the Critique of Reading*, which is closer to the Spanish.

2. "The critique of creation within the pages of his own creation, *Don Quixote*. And this critique of creation is, as we shall see, a critique of the very act of reading" (Fuentes, *Don Quixote*, 1976, 21).

3. "The epic of a society struggling against itself" (Fuentes, *Don Quixote*, 1976, 12).

4. "The triple heritage of Spanish culture, indeed, went underground. Yet the fact remained that the language, the sensibility and the tensions of Spanish art and literature were forever marked by the plurality of its true cultural inheritance" (Fuentes, *Don Quixote*, 1976, 33).

5. "Do you begin to understand, woman? I shall make use of Ludovico" (Fuentes, *Terra*, 1993, 531).

6. "This is Cervantes's last question: Who writes books and who reads them? . . . Language is the first and most natural instance of common property. If this is so, then Miguel de Cervantes is only the owner of his words in the same measure that he is not Miguel de Cervantes, but all men: like Joyce's Dedalus, he is the poet, singing the uncreated conscience of his race, mankind. The poet is born after his act, the poem. The poem creates its author, much as it creates its readers" (Fuentes, *Don Quixote*, 1976, 49–51).

7. It is supposedly the libertine behavior of Felipe I (el Bello) against which Felipe II reacts; the defeat of the Armada by the navy of Elizabeth I is represented as a fitting end to the hostile union of Felipe and his wife; the succession of Felipe II continued with the same sterility with which he ruled; and the second Escorial obviously represents the repressive regime that Spain exported to Mexico.

8. "Ridicule will kill you, for no one but you shall see those giants and magicians and princesses, you will see the truth, but only you; others will see sheep and windmills" (Fuentes 1993, 576).

9. James A. Parr draws a similar psychological parallel in "The Body in Context: Don Quixote and Don Juan."

10. "Secret sybil, the keeper of the deeper truths that men outlaw because they fear what is mirrored in them: the image of origin, the mythic, founding vision of the dawn of history" (Fuentes, *Cervantes*, 1976, 29).

11. "It is the cipher of dispersion. . . . Jesus came to disperse: the power of the earth belonged to One; Jesus distributed it among all men" (Fuentes 1993, 566).

12. "Read; translate; . . . all faiths are nourished from a common wisdom. I do not know your faith, nor shall I question you in that respect. We are all sons of the Book, Jews, Moors, and Christians, and only if we accept this truth shall we live in peace one with another" (Fuentes 1993, 519).

13. His view was perhaps bleaker than it would be today, as *Terra Nostra* was written and published before the death of Franco; on the other hand, it might be even more bleak today, given the hemogenization of our multinational world.

14. "Secret enemy both of those who have everything and of those who have nothing" (Fuentes 1993, 225).

15. "The Most Magnificent Señor don Hernando de Guzmán" (Fuentes 1993, 705).

16. "I travel from spirit to matter. I return from matter to spirit. There are no frontiers. Nothing is forbidden me. I believe I am several persons mentally. Then I am several persons physically. . . . One lifetime is not sufficient. Many existences are needed to fulfill one personality" (Fuentes 1993, 531–532).

17. "Ideas, you know, are never completely realized. At times they recede, they hibernate as some beasts do, and await the opportune moment to reappear: thought bides its time" (Fuentes, *Terra*, 1993, 538).

18. "Aren't you tired, Pilgrim? You have traveled far since you fell from the bridge that afternoon" (Fuentes, *Terra*, 1993, 774).

19. "Why not believe the opposite? . . . Why not believe that we two have lived the same things, and that the papers written by Brother Julian and the Chronicler give testimony to our lives?

"When? When?

"During the six and a half months that passed between your fall into the river and our meeting here, tonight" (Fuentes, *Terra*, 1993, 774).

BIBLIOGRAPHY

Cervantes Saavedra, Miguel de. *El ingenioso hidalgo Don Quijote de la Mancha.* Barcelona: Editorial Ramón Sopena, S.A., 1962.

Fuentes, Carlos. *Aura.* New York: Farrar, Straus, and Giroux, 1975.

———. *Cervantes o la crítica de la lectura.* Mexico, D.F.: Cuadernos de Joaquín Mortiz, 1976.

———. "Cervantes, or the Critique of Reading." In *Myself with Others.* New York: Noonday Press, 1990.

————. *Don Quixote or the Critique of Reading*. Austin: Institute of Latin American Studies, University of Texas at Austin, 1976.

————. *Terra Nostra*. Mexico: Editorial Joaquín Mortiz, S.A., 1975.

————. *Terra Nostra*, trans. Margaret Sayers Peden. New York: Farrar, Straus, and Giroux, 1993.

González Echevarría, Roberto. "*Terra Nostra*: Teoría y práctica." *Revista Iberoamericana* 47 (1981): 289–298.

Parkinson Zamora, Lois. "Magic Realism and Fantastic History: Carlos Fuentes's *Terra Nostra* and Giambattista Vico's *The New Science*." *Review of Contemporary Fiction* 8 (1988): 249–256.

Parr, James A. "The Body in Context: Don Quixote and Don Juan." *Bodies and Biases, Hispanic Issues* 13 (1996): 115–136.

Spadaccini, Nicholas, and Talens, Jenaro. *Through the Shattering Glass: Cervantes and the Self-Made World*. Minneapolis: University of Minnesota Press, 1993.

37

Integrating Multiple Texts in Pablo Iglesias, *an Original Play with Music by Lauro Olmo*

Donald R. Kuderer

The première in 1984 of Lauro Olmo's 1982–1983 play, *Pablo Iglesias*, was met with critical acclaim for its human dimension, its honest and vivid representation of a moment in the life of Spain, and its innovative staging techniques.[1] The play was accorded the 1984 "Dorín" Theatre Award for the best production of that year. However, this major post-Franco play has received very little scholarly attention, a surprising fact given the richness of its diverse aspects: the social commentary that permeates the work, the integration of multiple texts in the reliving of key moments in the life and times of Pablo Iglesias, its unique theatrical devices, and its present-day political implications.

The writing of *Pablo Iglesias* and its première coincided with the re-emergence of the Spanish Socialist Workers Party as the ruling political party in democratic elections held in 1982. Olmo's play ends with the news of Pablo Iglesias's election in 1910 as the Spanish Socialist Workers Party's first elected representative to the Spanish Parliament. It attempts not only to rescue Iglesias from oblivion, but to rescue that whole momentous period by recreating and reliving the life and times of Iglesias. To achieve this, Olmo blends no fewer than forty different texts to coincide with important moments in the experience of Iglesias.[2] The texts are very diverse and clearly illustrate the breadth of Olmo's own research and his enormous skill in creating the play.

Olmo admitted that he was attracted by Iglesias's personality and saw a need to tell his life story. As he writes in the introduction to the play,

The general ignorance about his life is surprising, because it is a life that, given its consequences, constitutes an essential element in measuring the exemplarity and kindness of an extraordinary human existence. . . . A living Pablo Iglesias exists within the heart of the people. When a man transcends the limits of whatever form of militancy and becomes through his commitment a prime example of human behavior, this example becomes everyone's heritage." (9–10)[3]

In one sense Olmo aspires to the portrayal of Iglesias as a saint, whose good works, integrity, dedication, and moral values are direly needed in contemporary Spain. Various sources refer to Pablo Iglesias using the labels "saint," "apostle," "teacher," "educator," and "hero." But Olmo also humanizes Iglesias, portraying him as a figure of flesh and blood. He is a human being who happens to represent a model of human behavior, a good person, but not exempt from human frailties.

In a note preceding Part I, Olmo states that the play is "not meant to be anything less than a single voice springing forth from a synthesis" (9). This synthesis is derived from many fundamental contributions, chief among which are a real-life interview as well as three essential biographies of Iglesias. The interview with Iglesias, conducted in 1914 by the reporter Enrique González Fiol, serves as the main structural device of the play, as Olmo draws specific questions posed by González Fiol and incorporates material from Iglesias's responses. In his play, however, Olmo sets the interview by González Fiol to coincide with the 1910 elections rather than 1914.

The action of the play begins during the initial moments of awaiting the results of the 1910 parliamentary elections and ends later that same day with the news of Iglesias's victory. Iglesias, now sixty years of age, is being interviewed in his office by the reporter, González Fiol. Within this structural device of the interview, Pablo's recollections evoke memories that are subsequently relived on stage via flashbacks, without his reverting to any other than his present-day character. His words, actions, and inflections of the voice, the voices offstage and voice-overs, the entrance of other characters, the changes in music and lighting, and the use of stage props signify the change of scenes from one recollection to the next.

Together, the interview and biographies provide essential material in Olmo's portrayal of the life, formation, and human dimension of Iglesias. Many passages in Olmo's play are taken verbatim from the biographies. Other passages are reworked by Olmo to suit the play. A blend of what Pablo is known to have stated—historical reports, his own writings, and the real-life interview—is combined with the voice created by Olmo, which adds the author's personalized perception of Pablo Iglesias. Upon recreating the events and people, Olmo reads historical reality by blending representative fictional characters and dramatic effects that might have corresponded to the life and times of his protagonist.

Numerous examples from the play illustrate Olmo's skill and astuteness in creating a work so rich in content and meaning. The first appears at the very beginning of Part I. Olmo indicates in the stage directions that "we hear the rhythmic vibrations of a printing press that will dominate the scene whenever indicated" (13). The vibrations become louder at times to accentuate the moment and the message being conveyed. The sounds of the printing presses also reiterate the influence of Pablo's first jobs in several printing shops, the site of his early struggles against social and economic abuses and the source of his development as the leading spokesman of the working classes.

The somber Galician musical score, "*Negra sombra,*" also serves to create the "atmosphere," as Olmo indicates in the stage directions (19). The music is a prelude to tender and moving moments that are relived on stage between Pablo and his mother. In the first of these moments, Pablo tells González Fiol about the powerful force his mother was in his life. In this scene she is on her hands and knees, scrubbing clothes in a wash basin. The scene contrasts with "the happy vignettes of boisterous girls that those one-act farces tend to show us" (24). Olmo uses this scene to criticize the lighthearted approach to life portrayed by writers of comic one-act pieces or short farces popularized in Spain at the end of the nineteenth century, a time when many Spaniards were struggling to survive.

The intensity of the poverty and illiteracy is conveyed in a subsequent scene. Stage directions indicate that sheets of propaganda begin to fall from the ceiling. Multiple characters depicting the Spanish poor and hungry enter the stage, a procession of the unfortunate hobbling and shuffling along. They surround Pablo. Among them are his mother and brother, conveying a sense of abandonment. Beneath it all some measures of *Negra sombra* are again heard. This scene also depicts Pablo's younger brother, Manuelín, dying in his mother's arms. As she clutches her son, the music of *Negra sombra* becomes more noticeable. Mother and son Manuelín disappear offstage as Pablo remains, contemplating the poor who are gathered around him. Among them, the Simpleton of Coria, who exemplifies the illiteracy of the population, attempts to read the sheets of propaganda. Finally, he carries one in his mouth, intending to eat it. Pablo grabs it from him and before the Simpleton's amazed look, begins to read it. Among the important messages we hear are,

Let us now stop considering that humility and poverty are a virtue. The Spain of misery, which has come parading her wounds and her nudity to the doors of temples and palaces, has lasted such a long time that the effects have disappeared. There are those who have inspired the repugnance of work and have reveled in the indescribable enjoyments and the spiritual riches of well-being. With their exalted and fanatical yearnings, the rich taught Spaniards to disdain earthly goods. (38)

The character, the Simpleton of Coria, is derived from a canvas by the great Spanish court painter, Diego Velázquez (1599–1660).[4] The portrait depicts Juan de Calabazas, a servant to Fernando de Austria and later to King Philip IV. Olmo's reference to such Spanish painters as Velázquez and Goya recalls some of their paintings, which depicted the lower classes and the suffering, injustices, and oppression experienced by many Spaniards.

In another scene not nearly as intense as the one just discussed, Olmo integrates the last lines of Scene 2 and all of Scene 3 from Ricardo de la Vega's lyrical *zarzuela, La verbena de la Paloma o El boticario y las chulapas y celos mal reprimidos*. Written in 1894, this night festival by de la Vega, with music by Tomás Bretón y Hernández, is described by Richard Herr as a "joyous and witty tale of the old quarter of Madrid" (133). The one-act prose work is developed around a conflict of love and the case of a jealous lover. Other than a few changes in the stage directions from de la Vega's work, Olmo remains faithful to the original. What becomes unique is the transition from de la Vega's operetta back to Olmo's play. Stage directions indicate that a Neighbor Lady enters and approaches Pablo, who remains lost in thought. (Pablo calls the Neighbor Lady "Missus Rita," a popular character from *La verbena*.) Now two guards from *La verbena* also appear, and as they blend with the world of Pablo, two works of fiction merge into one.[5]

Pablo quickly awakens from his reverie when he hears the news of his mother's death. Shortly, the lifeless body of Juana Posse advances toward stage center, and the music of the *Negra sombra* is heard once again. The somber tone and pervasive grief of the moment are broken by children's laughter and the reliving of a trip made in 1860 by Juana, Pablo, and Manuelín from El Ferrol in Galicia to Madrid, where they hoped to locate an uncle in the employ of the Count of Altamira. Soon after arriving in Madrid, Juana finds out that the uncle is dead.

The children's laughter and adventures on the trip are abruptly contrasted with Juana Posse's sadness at leaving Galicia. Stage directions indicate the following: "Touchingly, with a background of earthy sadness underscored by several bars of the '*Negra sombra*,' a heartfelt, intimate voice is heard reciting, bringing to mind Rosalía" (73). The voice offstage recites in Galician the following lines from Rosalía de Castro's poem, "Adiós ríos, adiós fontes":

Adiós, ríos, adiós fontes;
adiós, regatos pequenos;
adiós, vista dos meus ollos:

non sei cando nos veremos. (73)
Farewell, rivers, farewell springs;
farewell little pools;
farewell, sight of my eyes:
I know not when we will see one another again.[6]

A scene in which a street vendor of harlequin romances now appears on stage and calls out various titles provides further evidence of
Olmo's underlying commentary on the events of the period under
study. One of these titles, *El judío errante* [*The Wandering Jew*], takes on
great significance in view of the 1845 French work by Eugène Sue, *Le
Juif errant*. Richard D. Sonn, in a study of anarchism and cultural politics in *fin de siècle* France, notes that the French anarchist, François-
Claudius Ravachol, was supposedly turned toward anarchism by a
reading of Sue's work.[7] In Olmo's play the stage directions indicate,
"From afar comes the following song with an air of revolutionary chorus. A neighbor lady sings it" (119). Her voice offstage sings, "Dansons
la Ravachole, / vive le son, vive le son; / dansons la ravachole, / vive
le son de l'explosion" (45). The Neighbor Lady then enters, and when
Pablo inquires about the origin of the revolutionary song, she explains
that Felisa, a cigar vendor, sings it. Felisa reportedly goes out with a
"beanpole of a Frenchman" who makes bombs. The Neighbor Lady
goes on to recount an episode at the Tobacco Factory when Felisa tells
other workers about dynamite and making a bomb and planting it "next
to a bunch of those rich parasites that live off the sweat of others. . . . The
result is the most marvelous and comforting thing" (46).

It is important to note that the reference to *The Wandering Jew* and to
Ravachole are not included in the real-life interview nor in the biographies. They represent a clear example of Olmo's drawing from diverse
texts in order to develop a crucial moment in the play. It is well-documented that the Spanish government attempted to quell potential anarchist and socialist movements in Spain precisely because of the
terrorism that had occurred in Paris. Paul Lafargue, for example, fled
the Paris Commune and arrived in Spain in 1871, seeking converts to
the workers' cause. Lafargue is a character in Olmo's play. His appearance coincides with "La Marseillaise," the French national anthem.
Stage directions indicate that he carries *The Communist Manifesto* in his
hands, opens it, and with a voice both sufficient and adequate to the
solemnity of the moment, reads an excerpt from the document as the
sounds of the anthem grow silent (53).

Returning to his Spanish heritage, Olmo also incorporates three passages drawn from Chapter 42 of Miguel de Cervantes's *Don Quijote*.
As Pablo assumes Quixotic postures, a childlike voice offstage exclaims
in rebuttal to the cruel owner of the print shop where the young Pablo
was so mistreated,

Oh, you, whoever you are, big boss, who dares to touch the weapons of the most valiant knight errant who ever took up a sword, heed what you do and do not touch them if you do not want to sacrifice your life in payment for your boldness. (27)

Suddenly Pablo regains his normal appearance and again addresses the audience. Reciting some lines from *Don Quijote* that he had set for an edition being prepared in the print shop where he was working, he tells how they made him meditate: "Let the tears of the poor find more compassion within you but no more justice than the testimonials of the rich," and "Seek to discover the truth amidst the promises and gifts of the rich as among the sobs and misfortunes of the poor" (27).

In yet another scene, a Blind Balladeer and Lazarillo, his guide, appear downstage. Olmo indicates in his directions that the blind man "looks like a sketch by Castelao" (53), an artist called "the apostle of Galician nationalism."[8] Of paramount importance here is the Galician influence. Like thousands of Galicians, Castelao, Iglesias, and Olmo himself left Galicia at an early age. Castelao's sketches depict the emigrant experience, as well as the characteristic suffering of his people. The Galician past would forever remain a strong part of Olmo's and Iglesias's personas.

At last, the election results bring the play to fruition. Pablo's adopted son, Juan Almela Meliá, announces, "Father! You're the first Spanish socialist member of Parliament! Hundreds of organ grinders have come out into the streets of Madrid to proclaim it!" (102). The stage directions go on, "The jubilant streets of Madrid are filling up with the music of the organ grinders . . . the shouts and the organ grinder music intensify" (102). The swelling of the organ grinder music coincides with the appearance of Iglesias seated on a bench of the Spanish Parliament. The music and the shouts cease, and the voice of the President of the Congress is heard proclaiming, "Your lordship, Don Pablo Iglesias has the floor!" (102). Stage directions call for the vibrating and rattling of printing presses, as though symbolizing Iglesias's words. The rhythmic rattling is raised to the maximum.

The action over, the play concludes with an "Epilogue in the Style of Antonio Machado," a poetic, celebratory tribute to Iglesias's struggle on behalf of the Spanish people. Machado's lifetime (1875–1939) coincided with many of the historical events and figures depicted in Olmo's play, so Olmo's poem celebrates the life of Iglesias in a lyrical fashion, just as Machado did in honor of the educational reformist, Giner de los Ríos. Iglesias, like Giner, dreamed of a reflourishing of Spain, and it is this spirit that was in need of revival in the Spain of the 1980s. The following verses from the poem convey Olmo's passionate eulogy:

You came from poverty
and in poverty you dwelled: . . .
Adversity was your guide. . . .
If anyone called for the future,
it was you, worker of dawn, . . .
Henceforth, Pablo-People,
to name you is to name
"The cause";
the truth, comrade,
of a working Spain. (203)

Through this play Olmo adds his name to the list of those who have paid homage to the figure of Pablo Iglesias. His dramatic text clearly shows great depth and enormous skill at integrating multiple texts within a diverse composite of artistic techniques and genres.

NOTES

1. Lauro Olmo was born in 1921 in Barco de Valdeorras (Orense), in Galicia. His father emigrated to Argentina when Lauro was a young boy. When Lauro was eight years old his mother moved to Madrid in search of a better life. Lauro and his younger brothers were temporarily placed in an orphanage because their mother was unable to provide for them. Lauro spent most of the Spanish Civil War years in Alicante, having been relocated there because of the bombings in Madrid. He returned to Madrid, where he remained until his death in 1994. Olmo, a member of the Spanish Social Realist generation of playwrights, is best known for his first major play, *La camisa* (1961). Other plays that followed include *La pechuga de la sardina*, *El cuarto poder*, *English Spoken*, and *El cuerpo*. He also wrote novels, short stories, and poetry. Olmo's works prior to *Pablo Iglesias* have been given considerable attention through valuable critical studies by Angel Berenguer, José Monleón, Phyllis Zatlin, Martha Halsey, and Patricia O'Connor, among other significant theatre specialists and literary critics.

2. In addition to the interview and the three biographies, Olmo incorporates excerpts from the poetry of Antonio Machado and Rosalía de Castro, passages from *Don Quijote de la Mancha*, a fragment of the first workers' manifesto, as well as many newspaper headlines and a litany of historical events of the period, announced by town criers and newspaper vendors. There are also many musical texts and fragments of music: a somber Galician composition, the French national anthem, the Spanish national anthem, a processional march, music of organ grinders, a contemporary waltz, a doggerel, the clatter of printing presses, a revolutionary chorus, a children's ditty, references to *La Traviata*, the clashing of hammer and anvil, scenes from a Spanish operetta, and numerous other effects.

3. All translations from Spanish, French, and Galician texts are mine, unless indicated otherwise. This and subsequent page numbers correspond to the original texts.

4. The "Bobo de Coria" [Simpleton of Coria] alludes to Juan de Calabazas. The painting, *El bufón Calabacillas*, is erroneously called *El bobo de Coria*.

5. Olmo appears to convey here Pablo's love for the theatre, a sense confirmed by Meliá's biography, which indicates that Pablo himself had wanted to be an actor. Meliá adds, "Surely, the last *zarzuelas* and lyrical *sainetes* known by him were *La verbena de la Paloma, Gigantes y cabezudos* and *La viejecita*" (122).

6. A romantic writer of Galician origin, Rosalía de Castro (1837–1885), like Olmo and Iglesias, lived most of her life in Madrid. She is best known for her lyrical poetry, which expresses a longing for her native Galicia, vividly depicted in the passage and music Olmo has included in his play. Her writings also convey a social concern, a condemnation of the poverty in Galicia.

7. Ravachol, who terrorized Paris with a series of bombings, was executed in 1892 at the age of thirty-three, becoming a cult figure in the process. Sonn writes, "Ravachol's name was applied to an updated version of the French Revolutionary air, '*Carmagnole*,' whose old refrain '*Vive le son de l'explosion*' seemed newly relevant in the era of dynamite, and emphasized the explosive's auditory effect. '*Ravacholiser*' also enjoyed some success as a verb meaning 'to blow up'" (121).

8. Alfonso Rodríguez Castelao (1886–1950) was a medical doctor, sketch artist, painter, politician, ethnographer, narrator, and playwright. His greatest calling was being a caricaturist and cartoonist. He was also active in the Galician nationalist movement, particularly after 1936. Gilmour describes Castelao as the "'apostle' of Galician nationalism" (256), and Carr indicates that Castelao was a "Galician artist and journalist, whose *Sempre en Galiza* (1944) is the bible of Galician nationalism" (70).

BIBLIOGRAPHY

Carr, Raymond. *Modern Spain 1875–1980*. Oxford: Oxford University Press, 1980.

Castelao, Alfonso. *Cousas da vida-1*. Edited by Francisco Campos. Madrid: Akal Editor, 1981.

Gilmore, David. *The Transformation of Spain: From Franco to the Constitutional Monarchy*. London: Quartet Books, 1985.

González Fiol, Enrique. *Domadores del éxito. Confesiones de su vida y de su obra*. Madrid: Sociedad Editorial de España, 1915 (pp. 211–241 comprise González Fiol's interview with Pablo Iglesias).

Herr, Richard. *An Historical Essay on Modern Spain*. Berkeley and Los Angeles: University of California Press, 1971.

Kulp-Hill, Kathleen. *Rosalía de Castro*. Boston: Twayne, 1977.

Meliá, Juan A. *Pablo Iglesias. Rasgos de su vida íntima contados por J. A. Meliá*. Madrid: Morata, 1926.

Olmo, Lauro. *Pablo Iglesias*. Coruña: Ediciós Do Castro, 1984.

Riquer, Martín de, ed. *Don Quijote de la Mancha*. By Miguel de Cervantes. 2 Vols. Barcelona: Editorial Juventud, S.A., 1971.

Sonn, Richard D. *Anarchism and Cultural Politics in Fin de Siècle France*. Lincoln: University of Nebraska Press, 1989.

Vega, Ricardo de la. *La verbena de la Paloma*. Madrid: Sociedad de Autores Españoles, 1907.

Velázquez. Madrid: Ministerio de Cultura, 1990 (a publication prepared by the Spanish Ministry of Culture for the Diego Velázquez art exhibit at the Prado Museum in Madrid, January–March 1990).

Zugazagoitia, Julián. *Pablo Iglesias: una vida heroica. Correspondencia inédita con Enrique de Francisco*. Madrid: Akal Editor, 1976.

38

Parallel Worlds in
The House of Bernarda Alba *and*
Like Water for Chocolate

Cecilia Townsend

Federico García Lorca's *La casa de Bernarda Alba* [*The House of Bernarda Alba*] and Laura Esquivel's *Como agua para chocolate* [*Like Water for Chocolate: A Novel in Monthly Installments, with Recipes, Romances, and Home Remedies*] offer us a comprehensive picture of the transcultural elements that unite two matriarchal figures. The thematic interconnection, the social context, and the parallel characters demonstrate how such matriarchies develop and function despite the differences of geography and time in their literary incarnations.

As we enter the reality of both texts, we are presented with the same family structures. Both homes subsist in an extreme situation of tyranny and conflict induced by the protagonists' similar qualities and perspectives. Indeed, Esquivel's Doña Elena de la Garza and Lorca's Bernarda Alba are "birds of a feather." Both are matriarchs who come upon this circumstance when their husbands die. Both are consumed with the same basic motivation: to exact obedience and conformity from the daughters who inhabit their homes. And both of them exhibit a faithful adherence to tradition and community opinion, maintaining their family honor unilaterally through constant vigilance and repression. The verbal affect of both mothers is comparable, and their mandates frame and delineate the extent of their daughters' choices. In short, within the familial context the matriarchs dominate, control, and ultimately subjugate the will of their female offspring.

When Doña Elena announces to her daughter Tita that she cannot marry Pedro since tradition demands that the youngest take care of the parent until death, Tita tries to protest. But Doña Elena responds, "You don't have an opinion, and that's all I want to hear about it. For generations, not a single person in my family has ever questioned this tradition, and no daughter of mine is going to be the one to start" (Esquivel, 11). In like fashion, Bernarda decrees the parameters of her matriarchal power when she dictates to her daughters the conditions of mourning for their father in the first act of Lorca's play: "For the eight years of mourning, not a breath of air will get in this house from the street. We'll act as if we'd sealed up the doors and windows with bricks. That is what happened in my father's house—and in my grandfather's house" (Lorca, 157).

Both mothers make themselves known from the start as domineering women whose commands must be obeyed or severe punishment will ensue. This essential trait, which pervades the two characters, is the underlying force behind the transfiguration of the daughters into victims without volition and without voice. Bernarda leaves no room for doubting her will when she denies Magdalena the right to go out into the fields, escaping for a moment the cloister of their mourning: "In this house you'll do what I order. You can't run with the story to your father any more. Needle and thread for women. Whiplash and mules for men" (Lorca, 158). Doña Elena speaks in the same tones when she punishes Tita for pretending to have a headache in order to avoid the engagement party of Pedro, the man she loves, and her sister Rosaura:

"I won't stand for disobedience," Mama Elena told her, "nor am I going to allow you to ruin your sister's wedding, with you acting like a victim. You're in charge of all the preparations starting now, and don't ever let me catch you with a single tear or even a long face, do you hear?" (Esquivel, 27)

To both women, even a loveless marriage is preferable to flouting convention. The marriages of Rosaura and Pedro and of Angustias and Pepe el Romano receive the blessings of the mothers simply because they perpetuate the social system. Both unions respect tradition and "proper etiquette," whether or not the marriage is emotionally sound. As Lorca's Magdalena frankly states,

If he [Pepe] were coming because of Angustias's looks, for Angustias as a woman, I'd be glad too, but he's coming for her money. Even though Angustias is our sister, we're her family here and we know that she's old and sickly, and always has been the least attractive one of us! (Lorca, 164)

The story repeats itself in the Mexican home when Pedro Muzquiz and his father arrive to ask Doña Elena for Tita's hand in marriage.

She explains that it is impossible for Pedro to marry Tita, and then politely counters that if he really wants to get married, she would suggest her daughter Rosaura, who is only two years older than Tita.

How do such matriarchies come into being? Actually, as an extension of the male-centered patriarchy endemic to both Christianity and Islam and ingrained in the Hispanic psyche for hundreds of years. In the case of the Mexican it is important to note the influence of the sexually repressive patriarchal Aztec culture as well. In short, it is from the perpetuation of the father figure that the power of these dominating women flows.

For Bernarda and Doña Elena, blind obedience to tradition is the key to their authority. Bernarda can proclaim that they shall all be secluded behind closed doors and windows, simply because that is what was done in the house of her father and of his father before. Doña Elena, a continent away, reiterates to Tita, "For generations, not a single person in my family has ever questioned this tradition, and no daughter of mine is going to be the one to start" (Esquivel, 11).

For centuries this generational obedience served as bedrock for the Spanish family, and by extension for the Hispano-American family as well. It is not an historical coincidence that the Spaniards who conquered the New World came from a tradition imprinted with an 800-year-old Arab presence. The Arab harem and the Christian convent had much in common. The homes provided an area set aside for physical containment, where the daughters were kept under their mothers' vigilance. In the suffocating air of the Spanish home, just as in its Mexican counterpart, it was imperative to limit women to a sexually repressed world of constant supervision. So it was there that passions were unleashed, causing eruptions that could end in death or insanity.

In Lorca, Angustias feels relief because by marrying she will be able to "leave this hell" (Lorca, 169), unlike her sisters, who are condemned to continue living inside the maternal prison. In Esquivel, when Tita finds herself outside that maternal home she realizes for the first time,

At her mother's, what she had to do with her hands was strictly determined, no questions asked. She had to get up, get dressed, get the fire going in the stove, fix breakfast, feed the animals, wash the dishes, iron the clothes, fix dinner, wash the dishes, day after day, year after year. (Esquivel, 109)

This automation that "normalizes terror" (Morgan, 307) is produced by a daily violence that limits the free will of the daughters in both homes. The result is an "alienation from the inner self" (330). Tita is converted into an automaton who mechanically performs her daily chores. The same apathy is evident in Bernarda Alba's home when Amelia asks Martirio if she has taken her medicine and she replies, "I do things without any faith, but like clockwork" (Lorca, 135). As María Dolores Costa points out in her article, "Under One Roof: The Alba Family Meets the Chen Family" (107), this mechanization of the affective self is the result not only of alienation from the external world, but also of the emotional distancing that the women undergo within their family contours.

The physical socializing space that encloses the women must not be disturbed by the presence of a male. Paul Vieille affirms in *Family Alliance and Sexual Politics* that the Muslim woman is forbidden to place herself in a situation where she can awaken male sexual desires. This is the crucial concern that unites both Bernarda and Doña Elena. Bernarda's daughters cannot look even furtively at a man. Omnipotent and omnipresent, she asks Angustias, "For what—and at whom were you looking?" Angustias replies, "Nobody," to which Bernarda angrily retorts, "Answer me. Whom were you looking at?" Hearing her denials, Bernarda descends upon her and beats her, shouting, "You mealy-mouthed hypocrite!" (Lorca, 159).

Doña Elena too must always be on the watch to contain the repressed emotions of Pedro and Tita. She happens upon an intimate moment between them, a moment when Tita feels that "she could have stayed in his arms forever, but a look from her mother made her pull away in a hurry" (Esquivel, 38). When Doña Elena asks her what Pedro told her and Tita denies that he said anything, her mother responds, "Don't play the innocent with me. You'll be sorry if I ever catch you around Pedro again" (38).

It is this Christian identification of sex with sin that portrays the female as an immanent source of danger. It coincides with the Muslim view that a woman must be kept apart from the male presence from infancy on, not to protect her, but rather to protect men from her uncontrolled sexuality. As Vieille tells us, the Muslim woman is believed to possess a sexuality nine times greater than a man's. Given this assumption, it is easy to understand the need to confine and limit her physical and emotional environs. Both Lorca's and Esquivel's texts are saturated with language that disparages womanhood. The daughters of both matriarchs are judged guilty on the sole count of their femininity. Their problem is that they belong to the female sex.

Lorca's female characters themselves broach this issue when Bernarda alludes to the footprints that the women have left at the site of her husband's burial, "as though a herd of goats had passed through" (Lorca, 157). She repeats the slur when talking with her maid La Poncia about the quarrel that Angustias caused by daring to look at and listen to the men who had come to pay their respects. Referring to Angustias, she says, "That one takes after her aunts. . . . Oh, what one has to go through and put up with so that people will be decent and not get out of line!" (Lorca, 160). Literally, Bernarda's expression is "run back to the wilds." Bernarda is referring to the old Spanish proverb, "The goat will always run back to the brush," which equates loosely to "A leopard will never change its spots." This comparison of the woman to the goat, symbol of unbridled impulses, converts her sexual drive into an irresistible force that, if unchecked, will follow the dictates of her lustful desires.

From this it can be inferred that if women are permitted to be aware of their sexual desires, the results will be disastrous—which is borne out in the case of Gertrudis in *Like Water for Chocolate*. Gertrudis experiences her first throes of sexuality thanks to a highly delectable dish of "Quail in Rose Petal Sauce" (Esquivel, 51), prepared by Tita. So great is its physical combustion that it sends a flow of vapor coursing through all of her pores. Gertrudis goes out to the patio looking for refreshing water to quell her ardor. When she sees a Federal soldier on horseback approaching her, it is clear that passion leaps from every pore of her being. This sexual awakening is not normal, it is lustful; like a capital crime, it is sinful. So it is no mere coincidence that Gertrudis ends up in a brothel. There is no room in the New World for a woman of Gertrudis's ilk, just as there is none for any of the ancestral characters of Lorca's world. The woman who dares to defy cultural dictates and explore her sexuality must pay a high price: She will be marginalized.

In both works it is this constant sexual vulnerability, this repressive social code, that accounts for the self-loathing so well expressed by Amelia, another of Bernarda's daughters: "To be born a woman is the worst possible punishment" (Lorca, 176). Similarly, Chencha, the maid in the Mexican household, after being raped by the Federal soldiers laments her own depreciation: "You know how men are. They all say they won't eat off a plate that isn't clean" (Esquivel, 134). Both these women have suffered, but instead of reacting overtly, they internalize their victimization.

If we analyze closely the young protagonists of each work, Esquivel's Tita and Lorca's Adela, we find similar cultural situations. Dispossessed of their innate right to sexual exploration and castrated by maternal domination, they are forced to accept the yoke of virginity as a paragon of virtue. But Adela and Tita rebel. Both experience sexual ecstasy behind the backs of their mothers, all the while feeling guilty for having enjoyed the forbidden pleasures. When Tita eagerly touches Pedro's pulsating member, she withdraws her hand, "frightened not by what she has discovered, but by a cry from Mama Elena" (Esquivel, 98), who wants to know where she is. Frightened, Tita goes to her bed, where she spends "a tortured night, enduring her desire to urinate along with another urge" (98). When at last the love between Pedro and Tita is consummated, the disapproving maternal power is stronger even than death. Thus, the ghost of Doña Elena lets Tita know, "You have blackened the name of my entire family, from my ancestors to this cursed child you carry in your belly!" (173).

The same disapproval surfaces in Lorca's drama when Adela and Pepe el Romano consummate their desire at the end of Act II. Adela confides to Martirio that she felt as if "dragged by a rope" (Lorca, 185) to surrender to her lover, and her sister recoils with envy, rage, and revulsion. Bernarda, alerted by Martirio's violent reaction, is suddenly distracted by a mob that is about to lynch a young woman who has killed her illicit infant. Bernarda lustily approves the savage retribution, as Adela, filled with terror, grasps her own belly and cries, "No, don't kill her, no!" (175). Bernarda mercilessly goes on, "Finish her before the guards come! Put hot coals in the place where she sinned! . . . Kill her! Kill her!" (186). There is no forgiveness for the daughter who defies maternal authority and vigilance. It is this same force that motivates Doña Elena, the Mexican tyrant, to condemn her daughter from beyond the grave.

Having lost the battle of wills, Bernarda demonstrates a monstrous egocentricity when dealing with the death of Adela, who has chosen to hang herself rather than live without Pepe el Romano. Compassionless, obsessed only with her own public image, she exclaims, "My daughter died a virgin! Take her to her room and dress her as though she were a virgin. No one will say anything about this! She died a virgin. Tell them, so that at dawn, the bells will ring twice" (Lorca, 201).

Tita's end in *Like Water for Chocolate* at first seems to contrast happily with Adela's destiny in her Spanish village. After waiting for twenty-two years, she will finally achieve a normal life with Pedro. But the death of Pedro in her arms signals the end of the novel. In Tita's passionate metaphor, her nuptial bed has turned into a flaming pyre. If we take a moment to look beyond the magical veil that elevates Tita and Pedro's union to a metaphysical plane, we realize that she suffers the same fate as Adela. Metaphorically, death crowns the freedom of sexual exploration.

Quite clearly, Doña Elena and Bernarda Alba spring from the same cultural seed. On their backs rests the heavy weight of shaping, controlling, and socializing the future generations of their sex. Patriarchy depends in great measure on how far the maternal authority is extended within the family setting. In *The House of Bernarda Alba* and *Like Water for Chocolate* both mothers recognize the source of their power. They are not men, but they realize that theirs is the responsibility to symbolize the masculine presence in their homes. When Prudencia, Bernarda's neighbor, notices that she has "to fight like a man" (Lorca,

188), Bernarda admits it willingly. The same masculine traits are found in Doña Elena. Alone, she confronts the revolutionary army, instilling in the soldiers a "childlike fear of maternal authority" (Esquivel, 90). Afterward, she proceeds to let her pistol do the talking, arousing the captain's admiration for her valor.

It is a high price that both women pay to retain their authority. Both must denounce their own sex, then find themselves on a different ambiguous ground; they belong to neither gender. They lose their feminine attributes when they assume masculine traits to control their daughters. At the same time, both take pride in their acquired masculine authority. Bernarda does not need her husband to guarantee her daughters' obedience. She is more than sufficient to keep order, as the maid points out when she warns of the war of emotions that has been unleashed among her single daughters. Bernarda tells her, "Fortunately, my daughters respect me and have never gone against my will" (Lorca, 183). When Poncia insists that without continual vigilance her daughters will "fly up to the rooftops," Bernarda never doubts that she has the ability to bring them down. Confidently she replies, "I've always enjoyed a good fight" (183). The ability to govern her home with an iron hand, without a masculine presence, is also a point of pride to Doña Elena de la Garza: "I have never needed for anything; all by myself, I've done all right with my ranch and my daughters. Men aren't that important in this life" (Esquivel, 80).

In conclusion, the dominant Christian–Muslim heritage of Spain, with its definition of femininity, was perpetuated there and in the New World not only by the system of the patriarch. It was perpetuated as well by women such as our two protagonists, who promoted the status quo and in so doing extended their own authority. Bernarda Alba and Doña Elena de la Garza are part of a culturally socializing bridge that effectively spanned Spain and the New World, acquiring archetypal dimensions through the power bestowed on them by patriarchal tradition and socioreligious structures. In their fictional representations, they reveal the modus operandi by which women of both continents have been forced into subjugation and conformity. But their importance acquires a stature that reaches beyond the limits of fiction. The socializing force that they unleash still resonates in the ears and subconscious of today's generation and of generations to come.

BIBLIOGRAPHY

Britt, Linda. "Translation, Criticism or Subversion? The Case of *Like Water for Chocolate*." *Translation Review* (1995): 48–49.

Costa, Maria Dolores. "Under One Roof: The Alba Family Meets the Chen Family." *Confluencia* 10 (1994): 107–117.

Esquivel, Laura. *Like Water for Chocolate: A Novel in Monthly Installments, with Recipes, Romances, and Home Remedies*. Translated by Carol Christensen and Thomas Christensen. New York: Doubleday, 1992.

Galerstein, Carolyn. "The Political Power of Bernarda Alba." *Themes in Drama* 7 (1985): 183–190.

García Lorca, Federico. *Three Tragedies: Blood Wedding, Yerma, The House of Bernarda Alba*. Translated by James Graham Luján and Richard L. O'Connell. Great Britain: Western Printing Services, 1941.

González Stephan, Beatriz. "Para comerte mejor: cultura canibalesca y formas literarias alternativas." *Nuevo Texto Crítico* 5 (1992): 201–215.

Morgan, Robin. *The Demon Lover: On the Sexuality of Terrorism*. New York: W. W. Norton, 1989.

Ozimek-Maier, Janis. "Power Plays in *La Casa de Bernarda Alba*." In *Speech Acts in Hispanic Drama*, ed. Elias L. Rivers. Proceedings of the Stony Brook Seminar, summer 1984. Newark, N.J.: Juan de la Cuesta, 1986.

Robertson, Sandra. "¡Quiero salir!" la articulación del deseo en el teatro de Lorca." *Teoría y práctica del teatro* 2 (1994): 76–83.

Rude, Roberta N., and Turner, Harriet S. "The Circles and Mirrors of Women's Lives in *The House of Bernarda Alba*." *Literature in Performance* 3 (1982): 75–82.

Taylor, Diana. "Interiority and Exteriority in García Lorca's *La Casa de Bernarda Alba*." *Estreno* 15 (1989): 19–22.

Vieille, Paul. *Family Alliance and Sexual Politics*. Edited by Lois Beck and Nikkie Keddie. Cambridge: Harvard University Press, 1944.

Part IX

WORD PICTURES AND STROKE OF BRUSH

39

Speaking in White Cloth: Painting on Writing, Writing on Painting

(A Presentation in Dialogue Form)

L. Beatriz Arnillas and Adrián Pérez Melgosa

APM: In her studies on Incan cosmology, Constance Classen notes how in their first encounters with Western writing the Incas referred to it as "speaking on white cloth" (127). They thought the paper talked directly to the reader in a voice no one else was able to hear. Ricardo Palma portrays a particular instance of this belief in his story, "The Letter Sings" (Palma, 147–148). The protagonists of this story are two Inca servants who carry ten melons and a letter to the city dwelling of their Spanish master. Hiding the letter under a rock so that it couldn't "see" and therefore not "speak" of their actions, they sat down on the way and ate two melons. When they arrived in Lima, the lord read the letter and asked the servants about the missing fruit. Astonished by the ability of the letter to report on what had happened, one of the servants told the other that the letter certainly had "sung."

This is a perfect allegory to describe the works of Beatriz Arnillas, for hers are paintings that speak to us through writing, images, and color, springing from the white cloth of the canvas, blurring the frontiers between text and image. But unlike the writing in Palma's story, these white cloths speak to every viewer, to today's "masters" as well as "servants." She juxtaposes borrowed and original symbols, providing them with new significations that link the cultural and the personal. In her painting the mixture of old and new becomes a strategy to trace her private genealogy within the framework of gender and racial oppression in Latin America.

Like the servants of Palma's story, we can say that these canvases "sing" through pictorial and textual signs, making visible the numerous connotations they have acquired throughout history. They explore the meanings of the terms "Creole," "mestizo," and "hybrid" in a performative way.[1] A crossbreeding of genres, techniques, and media, these paintings are mongrel compositions in which quotes from the hagiographies of Saint Rose of Lima or Saint Martín de Porres mix with anecdotes from Ricardo Palma's *Peruvian Traditions*, verses by Alfonsina Storni, and ideas from the critical essays of Nelly Richards or Pablo Macera. Calligraphic fragments blend into human portraits, animals, landscapes, still lifes, and icons of American and European virgins. Within the limited space of the canvas's frame, these eclectic elements attempt to blur the limits between "high art" and popular culture, present and past, history and legend.[2] Mimicking the dynamics of Latin American ethnic, economic, and gender groups, letters and images struggle to find a window of visibility to "speak" to the viewer, to reach out with their messages, even if, as a result, they end up silencing other elements of the composition. Arnillas's genealogical exploration of oppression in Latin America unveils the inherent heterogeneous nature of any human identity. As literature becomes painting in these canvases, we also perceive how painting itself is a writing that selects, categorizes, and identifies the elements of the universe.

LBA: I came to the United States in 1986. After five years in this country, I realized that I had a new identity that combined both my Latina U.S. and my Spanish Peruvian experiences. I understood better how I felt after reading Alfred MacAdam's essay on syncretism and exile: "Exiles belong nowhere, only retaining the character they had before leaving their homeland. And this identity, like the notion of mestizaje, derives from negation: mestizos and exiles define themselves as much by what they are not as by what they are" (9).

The text and images in my works comment on my own hybrid condition. Doris Sommer observes that there is an old tradition in Latin American literature and art that aims to portray the cultural fictions by which we live (73). I use texts that create bridges with my culture of origin while addressing contemporary issues for the Latino peoples in the United States. These texts help me reconstruct my identity. Before coming here I was a Peruvian, but in the United States I obtained a mixed identity, one so complex that it is always in the process of becoming, never being fully defined.

My paintings are simultaneously murals and "retablos." In his essay on the mural art of Cuzco, Pablo Macera talks about the abbreviated character of mestizo art (68). I perceive Latin hybridization in the United States as a parallel phenomenon to the aesthetic syncretism of the colonial mural art in Peru that Macera describes. I collage his text with images, weaving what the writer said about the syncretic art of

Cuzco artists into my hybrid expressions. I merge the public nature of the murals with a popular form of domestic art in Latin America: the "retablo." Retablos are portable narrative shrines used for worship within the family unit. Macera explains that Peruvian retablos evidence the influence of the Catholic inside the Andean space (6). In terms of their form, my images exist within a compounded space that is both abstract and figural, representing miscegenation between the private and shared spaces, between the pagan and Christian practices of the retablo (Figure 39.1).

Figure 39.1
La Magia de los Nombres: Martín. **1996, Acrylic on wood, 48 × 36**

APM: Several historic pasts and presents blend into this painting. Condensed in it we also find all the different creative strategies used by Beatriz Arnillas in this group of works: selective quotations from literary works and from other paintings, reappropriation, translation from literature to painting, and symbolic allusion.

A ghostly knight wielding a sword crosses on his galloping horse the threshold of a colonial limestone building, while a ribbon captions the scene with the words, "La Magia de los Nombres: Martín" [Martín and the Magical Power of Names]. The ghostly figure alludes to Santiago Matamoros, "Saint James the Moorslayer," fighting the "infidel" on his horse, a frequent motif among the imagery of most Catholic churches in Latin America. But against the colonial backdrop of the painting, far away from the religious wars of medieval Spain, the "infidel" acquires a different meaning. It becomes the native populations of Latin America. War and religion, conquest and mission, the Creole interpretations of Spanish Catholicism and chivalry are the referents for these figures.

Painted over the left side of the building, almost as graffiti, we find the final letters of an inscription that starts on a dark background occupying the upper left corner. The impersonal, capital letters read,

(FAMOSO ANTIGUO
HIBRIDO)
RESULTADO DE UN
UNIVERSO HETEROGENEO DE
ABEVIATURAS
RESUMENES Y
RESIDUOS

The artist's words (in parentheses) precede Pablo Macera's description of Cuzco's mural painting (1983, 68), turning Macera's observation about the eclectic and synthetic essence of popular art into a depiction of the nature of Fray Martín de Porres, patron of social justice.[3] The monk embodied the meaning of the "heterogeneous universe of abbreviations, summaries, and residues." His person was the meeting point of two races and three cultures. The words "famous, ancient, and hybrid" also refer to current art and literary debates on postmodernity in Latin America within the framework of postindustrial capitalism. Nestor García Canclini explains,

More than a new paradigm, postmodernism is a peculiar type of construction on the ruins of modernity, raiding its vocabulary and adding premodern or non-modern ingredients. . . . In Latin America we have a similar process in as much as we live in an age of traditions that have not vanished, a modernity that never quite arrives, and a postmodern questioning of the evolutionary projects that enjoyed hegemony during this century. (46)

By placing the word "hybrid" together with "ancient," this painting questions the novelty of the condition of hybridity, showing how it was already present in the colonial identity of Fray Martín.

The lower half of the painting recasts elements from the other two sections. It shows a black and white goose with a yellow head that reflects the light of the colonial building. The goose represents Martín de Porres. His black and white feathers point as much to the colors of the Dominican habit as to Martin's mestizo origins. The black, white, and yellow of the head convey the European, the indigenous, and the African identities that converged in his body. Each element of this painting represents one of the cultural conventions employed throughout history to represent Latin American reality: Creolization (the dominance of the American-born Spanish), mestizaje (the conflicted role of people of mixed blood), and hybridity (the resulting syncretic cultural production).

What can the life of Martín de Porres, as interpreted by this painting, teach us about postmodernism and hybridization? For 400 years the figure of Fray Martín de Porres captured the popular imagination of Peru. This might be explained by his emblematic position regarding racial oppression in Latin America and the particular interpretation of his character made by his biographers in the stories that inspired this painting. His double racial origin is of central concern to all the stories about Martín. Historian Rubén Vargas Ugarte says of Martín, "On the second of June of 1603 Brother Martín de Porras, mestizo, son of Juan de Porras from Burgos, and Ana Velásquez, free black, offered himself to this convent for all the days of his life."[4] Ricardo Palma records similar information, but in it the individuality of the mother has disappeared, as has her status of freeperson: "This holy man was born in Lima on December 9th, 1579, and was the natural son of the Spaniard Juan de Porres, knight of Alcántara, and of a Panamanian slave."[5]

The struggle to reconcile his double origin seems to be the engine that provides the energy for most of his miracles. In the miracles recorded by Ricardo Palma we find a first group in which Martín brings together members of competing species. Perhaps the most famous is the story of the cat, mouse, and dog whom he convinced to eat together from the same dish.[6] A second group of miracles shows him transforming "imperfect objects" into "perfect" ones. When Martín brought dark bread into the convent, his superior requested him to change it into white bread, which Martín did forthwith (264–265). Although the miracles of Martín have the power to alter the natural violent instincts of animals, he is unable to effectively counter social hierarchies of race. In this painting, where Martín embodies an allegory of hybrid, mestizo, and Creole identities, the miracle portrayed is that of giving names to the objects of the universe: the ability of words to create and perpetuate differences by assigning specific meanings to them. In the world of Martín, giving a name is not an act of representation but of creation.

LBA: My painting *Lima, Dicen, Es Su Boca* (Figure 39.2) uses ideas and derivations from "El mito de la escuela" [The Myth of Schooling], a story recorded by Alejandro Ortiz de Rascaniere from an interview he conducted with Don Isidoro Huamani, an Inca elder, in 1971 (238–243). This myth explains the alienating experience of the mestizo. The

Figure 39.2
Lima, Dicen, Es Su Boca. **1997, Acrylic on canvas, 48 × 36**

image in my painting is a broken representation of José Olaya, a Peruvian national hero, taken from the painting by José Gil de Castro (1827). Both painter and model were mestizos. Olaya holds in his hands the letters that will become proof of his commitment to the independence of the Creoles (Peruvian-born Spanish people) from Spain, and the cause of his martyrdom. Olaya's head has been replaced by a broken and mixed-up indigenous pattern, symbolizing the mestizo's historical cultural alienation. I have changed the name of the addressee from Bernardo Tagle to "padrecito Viracocha." Bernardo was a Peruvian Creole independence leader. Viracocha is the maker of the world in Incan mythology, a bearded trickster who tests people's integrity through games and jokes.

When the Incas saw the Spaniards disembarking from their ships with their bearded faces, they mistook them for Viracocha. This is also the name that the old man uses when addressing Rascaniere in "El mito de la escuela." Surrounding the portrait of Olaya we find parts of the political map of Peru. This is a visual description of the land for Creoles and mestizos only, for the modern political map of Peru means little to people of indigenous blood. Incan peoples and other indigenous nations had no participation in the process of creating the political nation as we know it today, and are poorly represented in our democratic processes. The text on the top section quotes a fragment of an Incan description of the same territory, drawn in a mythical way: "There are nations that have come out of her eyes (the Mother Earth's) . . . those nations see far away in time."[7] In the lower left corner the text paraphrases Don Isidoro again: "Lima they say, is her mouth (Mother Earth's), and Cuzco, her beating heart" (Ortiz de Rascaniere, 238). These texts and images are emblematic of the rhetorical linguistic powers of the Creole culture in contrast with the mythical oral and visual energy of the indigenous Andean culture.

APM: The paintings representing Olaya and Martin are a performative study of miscegenation. The blending of the Spanish writing and indigenous images is a metaphoric rendition of the mixture of two cultures within the mestizo body. These paintings study "mestizaje" as a category created within cultural conventions, not biological ones. If these works expose race as a culturally created category, functional only within the "magical power of names," the other art works in this collection apply the same conceptual frame to the study of gender as a created category.

LBA: The categories "mestizo" and "indigenous" have one important thing in common with women: They are at the margins of the neocolonial structure in Latin America, they remain unempowered, and their identity is defined by their role in relation to the categories of "white" and "male." Mestizos, Andeans, and women are all outsiders in the neocolonial mentality. For the purpose of my paintings, it was Alfonsina Storni, an Argentinian poet, who expressed it most clearly. Her poems inspired the canvases *Dolor de Siglos* (Figure 39.3) and *Nuestra Señora de las Angustias* (Figure 39.4).

Dolor de Siglos quotes a fragment of Storni's poem "Peso Ancestral":

one of your tears fell into my mouth
and I knew the pain of
centuries upon tasting it; my soul cannot bear all this
weight.[8]

In Storni's text I sensed the act of handing down the culture of victimhood from mother to daughter. By layering a grid with sections of a landscape over the verses of Storni and a background representing a garden, I formed an abstracted space where dissimilar realities coalesce simultaneously. There is a stylized shape of a shell next to Storni's text. This shell is a borrowed image from colonial murals, and

Figure 39.3
Dolor de Siglos. **1996, Acrylic on canvas, 42 × 42**

Figure 39.4
Nuestra Señora de las Angustias. 1996, Acrylic on canvas, 36 × 36

it is a popular symbol of femininity and of pilgrimage. In the lower left corner of the painting, a withering rose alludes to another of Storni's poems, *La Inquietud del Rosal*. The rose represents "purity" and suffering, and is also a symbol of femininity. The shell and the rose that circulate throughout my works become recurring symbols that affirm or question feminine roles. Through repetition, they build a self-referential language, reminding us that each painting needs to be viewed within the larger context of the collection.

The title of *Nuestra Señora de las Angustias* came out of Ricardo Palma's "El divorcio de la condesita" (60). The story portrays another example of the oppressive feminine heritage. In it a woman forces her thirteen-year-old orphan niece to marry a sixty-year-old man. Presiding over this scene, Palma describes a figure of "Our Mother of Sorrows," which, Palma assures us, was an integral part of the typical living room decoration in the Lima of the eighteenth century. After many years of struggle, our heroine manages to survive her marriage, still young and virgin. Palma's stories seem to say, "This is how things are." His stories do not condemn or defend. They merely reflect Peruvian idiosyncrasies (Bryce Echenique, xvii–xix). My painting mixes this story with Storni's poem and with icons from my own family. The garden of the previous painting has turned into trees with red branches, which are also veins and arteries connecting the image of fruit and productivity to kinship and reproduction. Superimposed are the face of my great-grandmother and a hand symbolizing Alfonsina's images of the handed down feminine culture of victimhood.

I interpret Rosa de Lima, a very popular icon of feminine sanctity, as a good example of the way gender oppression works within Peruvian identity (Figure 39.5). The hagiographies explain in great detail the self-inflicted martyrdom that led this virgin to her holy state. Rosa was one of those contradictory icons given to young women as role models. She provided a mythology of the connections between body and soul and a formula for becoming worthy of love through suffering. My image repeats the form of the shell as a giant feminine presence that invades the space like a tidal wave. Its energy comes in destroying all the oppressive structures as well as any goodness within them. This symbol of femininity then becomes the power of destruc-

Figure 39.5
Rosa de Lima. 1996, Acrylic on canvas, 90 × 101

tion, even self-destruction. Rosa played the role of redeemer amid the many sins of the abusive colonial Lima. She had conversations with God, predicted events, and negotiated divine and earthly favors.

I painted Rosa's face as I imagined her when I visited her home as a young child in 1965: her body hanging by the hair from a nail on the wall. In the lower right corner, the small rose from *Dolor de Siglos* reappears here dying, like a discarded fragment of identity. This same rose surfaces again in another painting about identity, inspired by a narration of Pablo Neruda. In this story the Chilean poet explains how he found one of the female statues of his collection. As he goes to pick up this *Guillermina* in a suburb of Lima, my painting quotes his thoughts: "it could be a ship's figurehead, it could be a saint" (40). It is interesting that Neruda thought only of those two choices. He added with wit, "I was drawn by her beauty, by her boldness, and then, when I saw her shining nakedness, I called to my friends on the corner. Well, at least she is no saint!"[9]

For the native painter, the earth was and is seen as the mother, or *pacha mama*: mother earth and mother of human kind. This female association with land survived the process of transculturation, so for the mestizo culture the American continent is also female. My Amazon women in *Cinnamon in the Air* represent this mythical representation of the continent as woman (Figure 39.6). The scene derives from the narration of the chronicler Friar Gaspar Carvajal. These women warriors were encountered several times during the sixteenth century, but their existence was not corroborated by later more "scientific" excursions. Their absence, like the legend of El Dorado, leaves an open thread in the weft of our history. My Amazons represent that which was not conquered and remains alive among Latin Americans; in other words, cultural resistance.

APM: Saints, poets, masochistic mystics, mourning virgins, patriotic martyrs, these characters who populate Beatriz Arnillas paintings affected their society through their lives, the stories written about them, and their representations in popular paintings. Their memories and representations preside over the flow of everyday life in colonial and postcolonial Latin America. Beatriz Arnillas focuses on the sorrow, pity, self-deprecation, hopelessness, and victimization of women and nonwhite racial groups. Even when enjoying small triumphs, like the one of the "condesita" or that of Martín with the animals, the characters that inspire these paintings can perform only passive and secret acts of resistance. Nevertheless, while depicting these characters as cherishing their victim roles, her paintings also recast them as heroes and heroines. We can see this especially by comparing Ricardo Palma's tales about St. Rosa de Lima with the painting *The Self-Inflicted Martyrdom of St. Rosa de Lima*. The hagiographies of St. Rosa tell numerous

Figure 39.6
Cinnamon in the Air. 1996, Acrylic on canvas, 49 × 61

stories about how she strove to inflict upon herself the same amount of physical pain and suffering as Christ had endured throughout his life. This self-punishment is certainly an example of internalized oppression, but it is something more. Palma tells the story of how Rosa negotiated truces with the mosquitoes that crowded the orchard where she prayed, allowing them to sting her except when she thought it was disrupting her concentration (200–201). I see this as emblematic of how she used her self-discipline and chastisement: Rosa was trying to gain control over the sources of her own pain. Most of the characters who inspired these paintings walk a dangerous line where social oppression turns into self-oppression. At that conflictive point when the self regains control of its destiny by imitating the oppression that others are imposing upon it, the characters in these stories pay perhaps too high a price.

NOTES

1. This term refers to the way Arnillas's paintings enact the message they try to communicate. While the subject of the paintings is the blurring of ethnic and cultural boundaries in Latin America, the form of the paintings is in itself

a sample of that condition. By enacting their message through its form, these paintings are performative.

2. George Yúdice (552) explains the historical dichotomy between "art" and "artisanry" in Latin America. Here we use terms "high art" and "popular culture" to include also nonvisual art forms. Art and artisanry, Yúdice says, are presented in different levels of valuation that reflect how visual cultures in Latin America see them: Art has a "higher mission," than that of salvaging memory. Art appeals to the spirit, artisanry to the material.

3. The name of Fray Martín appears with two different spellings in various sources, Thus, Ricardo Palma spells his name Martín de Porres, while Rubén Vargas Ugarte prefers to call him Martín de Porras.

4. This fragment is my translation of the records of Martín's ordination kept at the Convento Nuestra Señora del Rosario. The original reads, "En 2 de Junio de 1603 hizo donacion de sí a este convento para todos los días de su vida el Hermano Martín de Porras, mulato, hijo de Juan de Porras, natural de Burgos y de Ana Velázquez, negra libre" (Vargas Ugarte, 38).

5. My translation from Ricardo Palma. In the Spanish original the text reads, "Nació este santo varón en Lima el 9 de diciembre de 1579, y fue hijo natural del español don Juan de Porres, caballero de Alcántara, y de una esclava panameña" (264).

6. Ricardo Palma referred to this miracle in the couplet, "y comieron en un plato, perro, pericote y gato" (264).

7. The original text in Spanish reads, "hay pueblos que han salido de sus (Pachamama's) ojos . . . esos pueblos ven lejos en el tiempo" (Ortiz de Rascaniere, 238).

8. My translation of Storni's original verses:

te salió una lágrima y me cayó en la boca, . . .
(. . .)
dolor de siglos conocí al beberla,
el alma mía soportar no puede todo su peso. (141–142)

9. Excerpt from "Isla Negra." Translation by Alastair Reid (Neruda).

BIBLIOGRAPHY

Bryce Echenique, Alfredo. "Para volver a Palma." In *Tradiciones Peruanas*, ed. J. Ortega. Madrid: Ministerio de Cultura, 1992.

Classen, Constance. *Inca Chronology and the Human Body*. Salt Lake City: University of Utah Press, 1993.

Damian, Carol. *The Virgin of the Andes*. Miami Beach, Fla.: Grass Field Press, 1995.

de Carvajal, Fray Gaspar. *Relación del nuevo descubrimiento del Río Grande de las Amazonas*. Quito: Biblioteca Ecuatoriana Amazónica, 1992.

García Canclini, Néstor. "Modernity after Postmodernity." In *Beyond the Fantastic: Contemporary Art Criticism from Latin America*, ed. Gerardo Mosquera. Cambridge: MIT Press, 1996.

Gheerbrant, Alan. *The Amazon, Past, Present and Future*. New York: Harry Abrams, 1988.

Glave, L. Miguel. *De Rosa y Espinas*. Lima: IEP ediciones, 1993.

MacAdam, Alfred. "Syncretism and Exile." In *Review: Latin American Litera-ture and Arts.* New York: The Americas Society, Spring 1997.

Macera, Pablo. "El arte mural cuzqueño." In *Revista de Ciencias Sociales.* Lima: Universidad del Pacífico 4, 1983.

———. "Del arte popular peruano." Separata del *Boletín de Lima* 19. Lima: Editorial Los Pinos, 1982.

Marechal, Leopoldo. *Vida de Santa Rosa de Lima.* Buenos Aires: Emecé Editores, 1943.

Neruda, Pablo. *Pablo Neruda, Absence and Presence.* Translated by Alastair Reid. New York: W. W. Norton, 1990.

Ortiz de Rascaniere, Alejandro. "El Mito de la Escuela." In *Ideología mesiánica del mundo andino.* Lima: J. Ossio, 1993.

Palma, Ricardo. *Tradiciones peruanas.* Madrid: Aguilar, 1961.

Richard, Nelly. "Chile, Women and Dissidence." In *Beyond the Fantastic: Con-temporary Art Criticism from Latin America,* ed. Gerardo Mosquera. Cam-bridge: MIT Press, 1996.

Sommer, Doris. "Irresistible Romance: The Foundational Fictions of Latin America." In *Nation and Narration,* ed. Hommi K. Bhabha. New York: Routledge, 1990.

Storni, Alfonsina. *Obras Completas: Poesías.* Buenos Aires: Sociedad Editora Latinoamericana, 1976.

Vargas Ugarte S. J., Rubén. *El Beato Martín de Porras.* Lima: Tercera Edición, 1948.

Yúdice, George. "Postmodernism in the Periphery." *South Atlantic Quarterly* (Summer 1993): 543–555.

40

Painting the Poetic Image: Lessons James Wright Learned from Hispanic Poets and Painters

Sarah Wyman

In the 1950s the poet James Wright and his friend Robert Bly introduced Hispanic poets' names and notions to North American readers. They published numerous translations and various critical essays in the influential journal Bly edited, titled *The Fifties*, then *The Sixties*, and finally, *The Seventies*. In this way the art of Juan Ramón Jiménez, Antonio Machado, Miguel Hernández, César Vallejo, Jorge Guillén, Pedro Salinas, and Pablo Neruda hit the enormously energized and experimental art scene in the United States. Along with international developments in painting and the legacy of Anglo-American Imagism, innovations by Spanish-speaking poets helped bring forth the intense "deep image" in North American poetry. James Wright's watershed volume, *The Branch Will Not Break* (1963), decisively demonstrates the inspirational force of Hispanic writers on one poet's work.

Several specific poems illustrate the main points of this development. First, Machado's "Noche de verano" provides an example of the use of light and dark imagery as a structuring device. Second, Jiménez's "Rosa del mar," a poem Wright translated, asserts itself as an artistic reality constructed of simple yet enigmatic images. Through the use of repetition the poem creates an illusion of movement that corresponds to the fragmentary nature of human perception. Finally, Jiménez's "Conciencia Plena" prefigures Wright's "The Jewel." Both poets use similar exotic images to paint vivid poems expressing consciousness. I will also briefly examine Wright's debt to the political and philosophical engagement of these Hispanic poets. Visual works by Hispanic artists will serve to illustrate various poetic ideas that know no bounds of medium.

By the turn of the century, poets in the Americas and Europe were abandoning standard verse forms in favor of experiments in free verse. Simultaneously, Pablo Picasso, Juan Gris, and others rejected traditional modes of pictorial illusion in favor of their own radical inventions. Parallels between modes of signification in early twentieth-century poetry and painting suggest a shared road in innovation. Many Hispanic poets and artists, including Vicente Huidobro, Diego Rivera, and Carlos Mérida, spent considerable amounts of time working together alongside Picasso, Gris, and their entourage in Paris, where Cubism began in 1907 or 1908. As members of common intellectual circles, poets and painters forged artistic movements. Picasso illustrates this phenomenon in his famous work, *The Three Musicians* (1921), a synthetic Cubist portrait of the painter and two poets, Guillaume Apollinaire and Max Jacob. Creative ideas blossomed as well between artists who never met.

The Spanish poet Antonio Machado, for example, taught Wright the technique of creating poetic spaces in terms of light and dark imagery. In Machado's poem "Noche de Verano," an ephemeral picture of a summer night in a village square, the poet appears like a ghostly witness:

Es una hermosa noche de verano.
Tienen las altas casas
abiertos los balcones
del viejo pueblo a la anchurosa plaza.
En el amplio rectángulo desierto,
bancos de piedra, envonimos y acacias
simétricos dibujan
sus negras sombras en la arena blanca.
En el cenit, la luna, y en la torre,
la esfera del reloj iluminada.
Yo en este viejo pueblo paseando
solo, como un fantasma. (*Campos de Castilla*, 1907–1917)

Images of whiteness, openness, and light—the acacias, the white sand, moon, and glowing clock—contrast with dark shadows and a night setting. The space in the first quatrain, due to the short length of the second and third lines, visually emphasizes the openness of the initial night image, the "anchurosa plaza." Wright's poem "Beginning," with its light and dark patterning, spacial considerations, and otherworldly speaker, offers striking similarities to the poem by Machado.

The moon drops one or two feathers into the field.
The dark wheat listens.
Be still.
Now.
There they are, the moon's young, trying
Their wings.
Between trees, a slender woman lifts up the lovely shadow
Of her face, and now she steps into the air, now she is gone
Wholly, into the air.
I stand alone by an elder tree, I do not dare breathe
Or move.
I listen.
The wheat leans back toward its own darkness,
And I lean toward mine. (*The Branch Will Not Break*, 1963)

Robert Bly identifies the woman of Wright's poem, the "slender woman [who] lifts up the lovely shadow of her face," as the "Mysterious Hidden Woman," an unsentimental figure of tenderness and calm who "began to rise from the earth in the USA in the 1950's." Bly traces her origins to the Hispanic world, saying, "She appeared strongly and sweetly in Spain from 1890 or so to 1937" (29). He then cites her passage through the work of Machado, Jiménez, and Federico García Lorca. We might also find her in paintings of such artists as Picasso, Gris, Carlos Mérida, Diego River, and José Clemente Orozco. She may not be in the woman's form as we expect her, but in the very paint strokes, or hidden in the spaces around a form. Bly continues: She inspires a trust in the natural world and signals the presence of aesthetic qualities in a language of transcendence (29). Language during the time of her appearance, the turn of the century, was no longer considered a tool of representation of reality, but rather a means of suggesting or inferring new realities.

In Wright's "Beginning," the light of the moon, its feathers, and the white flowers of the elder tree contrast with the dark images of wheat, shadow, and the dim, phantomlike poet. One could transform the written poem into a graphic design by shading dark images and circling light ones. The poet carefully controls the directionality of action: leaves fall, a face, then a body rises, the speaker and wheat retreat. Such attention has been paid to the disposition of lines upon the page that the poem, folded horizontally in the middle, exhibits an almost perfect symmetry of line lengths. Wright, like Machado, treats the page as a canvas, writing an arguably concrete poem in terms of visual imagery.

In fact, the chiaroscuro effect of this particular Machado poem informs Wright's work as a whole. The word "dark" in its various forms occurs over forty times in *The Branch Will Not Break*. Wright admits in an interview, "Most of the things that I've written about so far do have a certain darkness to them, an emotional darkness" (McElrath, 141). The depths of this darkness suggest a wonder at mystery more often than a descent into despair. In his review of Pablo Neruda's *The Heights of Macchu Picchu*, Wright says, "Great poetry folds personal death and general love into one dark blossom" ("I Come," 191). The evocation of darkness intensifies the visual act of discerning the poetic image.

Wright's darkness also owes a debt to Juan Ramón Jiménez's predilection for ambiguous meanings and to his notion of transcendence. The poet and scholar Michael Graves points out Wright's link to Jiménez in his attention to "the delicate presence of the vividly vanishing." Graves explains that Wright's translations of Jiménez "advocate an imaginative transcendence of reality and provide a confirming model of a key concern of Wright's work . . . the need to confront the quick vanishing of the vividly sacred in a world where absence seems like the only enduring presence" (7, 4). Think again of the falling feathers of Wright's "Beginning," and of the woman who disappears "wholly." Where do they go?

Such ambiguity of meaning is a keynote of early twentieth-century painting. Elements of a visual artwork may make sense only in the context of the visual or verbal work itself. Each painting, drawing, or poem constitutes its own reality and leaves interpretation up to the "reader." For example, the central blue patch in Carlos Mérida's *Paisaje* (1915) may denote shadow, house, or body of water. In Federico García Lorca's *Perspectiva Urbana con Autorretrato* (1932), an ellipse denoting "eye" in one part is read as "face" in relation to other parts of a space, and as "leaf" in the context of the parts of a plant to the left (Figures 40.1 and 40.2). In a more elaborate example, Pablo Picasso's *Le Poète* (1912) (Figure 40.3), certain curves signify earlobe, cheek, and mustache, according to their relation with each other. Outside the frame of the picture any of these curves would be meaningless. Wright and the Hispanic poets create artistic worlds where odd floating women and passing phantom poets make perfect sense.

Juan Ramón Jiménez, for example, called himself a painter before he called himself a poet. At the age of fourteen or fifteen he painted a canvas in oil entitled *Crucifixión*. The intensity of this work prefigures his later passion for poetry as a religion in itself. As he matured he traded brush for pen, but never abandoned an orientation toward the visual image. Treating the poem as an art object, Jiménez carefully considers the visual aspects of the work. In his most "painterly" poems he eliminates traditional narrative content and maintains an intense focus on the image. True to our human perception, he studies discrete phenomena, fragmenting external reality into a multiplicity of sense data. Aubrey Bell borrowed the art-history term "impressionist" to describe Jiménez in 1925: "He is the impressionist painter rather than

Figure 40.1
Carlos Mérida, *Paisaje*, ca. 1915. Oil on Canvas, 39 × 46.5 cm

CARLOS-MÉRIDA·AL·DR.ERNESTO·MOLINA·

Collection of Rolando Keller. Photo: Angela Caparroso

the sculptor, and his poetry is in fact an ever-flowing transparent stream" (Bell, 210). While Bell's attention to the visual nature of Jiménez's work proves fruitful, he may well have likened these poems to other contemporary experiments in expression, especially Cubism.

James Wright translated Jiménez's poem "Rosa del Mar," and included it in his own *Collected Poems* of 1971. Wright has described Jiménez's work in terms of a "plainness" that can "pierce the familiar certainty" and "place a new soul into whatever is real" (Molesworth, 223). Wright made an abrupt shift from traditional verse in his volume *Saint Judas* to a more colloquial free-verse style in *The Branch Will Not Break*. For both poets, establishing a calm, reflective tone and mood became a key component in the creation of a poem. Jiménez writes,

La luna blanca quita al mar
el mar, y le da el mar. Con su belleza,
en un tranquilo y puro vencimiento,
hace que la verdad ya no lo sea,

Figure 40.2
Federico García Lorca, *Perspectiva urbana con autorretrato / Self-Portrait in New York*, 1929–1932

y que sea verdad eterna y sola
lo que no lo era.
Sí.
¡Sencillez divina,
que derrotas lo cierto y pones alma
nueva a lo verdadero!
¡Rosa no presentida, que quitara
a la rosa la rosa, que le diera
a la rosa la rosa!

Figure 40.3
Pablo Picasso, *Le Poète*, 1912. Oil on Canvas, 60 × 48 cm

Courtesy of Oeffentliche Kunstsammlung Basel, Kunstmuseum. Photo: Oeffentliche Kunstsammlung Basel, Martin Bühler

In the manner of the Cubist painter, Jiménez has limited his palette, simplified his subject matter, and developed a concept (compare with Picasso's *Girl with Mandolin*, 1910). He has acknowledged the fragmentary nature of human perception by viewing his conceptual objects—the moon, the sea, and the rose—from a multiplicity of perspectives.

The poem spins spatially on the pivotal "Sí." The repetition of the word "mar," like that of "rosa," creates an overall commonality of sense that exists through time as the reader combines word with word with word. Through the syntagmatic or linear act of reading, the reader takes in the unfolding contexture of the poem, then combines parts into a whole. According to a parallel dynamic of perception, we puzzle through Picasso's *Poète* as well.

Works by the Frenchman Marcel Duchamp and the Mexican José Clemente Orozco illustrate experiments in using repetition to bring movement to the canvas. Duchamp's proto-futurist *Nude Descending a Staircase, No. 2* (1912) owes a debt to the discovery of time-lapse photography. In *Zapatistas* (1931), Orozco uses his stylized guerrillas to express the anonymous masses and the force of their literal and figurative movement to the left. In these two paintings the artist creates a dynamic illusion, but in most Cubist works, and in this Jiménez poem, the aspect of movement corresponds to that of the viewer or speaker, who perceives data and then synthesizes. Imagine the experience of entering a room. The eyes focus on sections of the scene, and the mind formulates an image composed of whatever it finds: furniture, walls, books, and so on. This process corresponds to the act of reading discussed earlier.

Even the most enigmatic images, the most obscure artistic languages, communicate on some level. In *The Branch Will Not Break* Wright takes three unfamiliar figures and arranges them according to the "organic pattern of parallelism," which he relates to Chinese and Hispanic poetry (Kalaidjian, 105). Like Ezra Pound, Hispanic poets of the first twenty years of the century used juxtaposition to imply comparison between images. Think of Jiménez's implicit comparison of the moon and the rose. Wright adopts these ideas of "parallelism of image" as a structuring device in his own work.

Spring Images
Two athletes
Are dancing in the cathedral
Of the wind.
A butterfly lights on the branch
Of your green voice.
Small antelopes
Fall asleep in the ashes of the moon.

The resonance between these three images depends on a common relationship of delicacy, quiet tone, and diminishing activity. Each line, or even each word, finds its unique significance in context, in relationship to all the other words in the poem. In the same way, a blue smudge stands for sky in one painting, or a certain rhombus reads "eye" in a Cubist painting.

This poem compares best to certain passages in the work of Pablo Neruda. Rejecting the term Surrealism, Wright calls such mysterious images "Baroque figures of speech." In 1968 Wright and Bly published a joint translation of Neruda's poetry. Bly offers this introduction: "[Neruda's] imagination sees the hidden connections between conscious and unconscious substances with such assurance that he hardly bothers with metaphors—he links them by tying their hidden tails. He is a new kind of creature moving about under the surface of everything" (Janssens, 119). The integrity of Wright's "Spring Images" depends on such risk taking, on constructing Baroque figures that seem well-grounded. The Spanish critic José Ortega y Gasset warns against trying to make sense of modern art in terms of the external world. He begs readers and viewers to view these art works as autonomous, artistic realities.

Ortega employs the metaphor of a window overlooking a flower garden to describe the dynamic of early twentieth-century painting. The content or reality-based aspect of the work he likens to the garden itself, seen through the window. However, if the viewer arrests his or her focal depth at the window pane (or the aesthetic essence), the garden appears as blurry patches of color pasted on the pane itself. Ortega explains, "la mayoría de la gente es incapaz de acomodar su atención al vidrio y trasparencia que es la obra de arte; en vez de esto, pasa al través de ella sin fijarse y va a revolcarse apasionadamente en la realidad humana que en la obra está aludida" (23). Elitism aside, Ortega urges us to look at the modern work as an artistic expression in its own right rather than as a reproduction of or commentary on external reality.

In "Spring Images" Wright uses syntactic variation as a verse form in itself. Here, parallelism functions on the level of grammar as well. Each sentence stanza employs a loose structure: subject, verb, complement, including a dependent "of" phrase that relates to the connective "de" in Spanish. The assonance of long e's in "athletes" and "cathedral" and of short i's in "in" and its echoing "wind" exemplify the "parallelism of sound" that Wright also offered as one of his defining poetic techniques. Jimenez uses long "i's" as an aural structuring device in "Rosa del mar," contrasting "quita . . . tranquilo y . . . vencimiento" in the first three lines with the predominant open vowel sounds, and balancing them in the second half of the poem, "Sencillez divina . . . presentida . . . quitara . . . diera." When Wright writes, "the branch of your green voice," he has given a visual quality (green branch) to a sound element.

Wright learned from the Hispanic poets the technique of defamiliarizing external reality through poetic expression. Wright's mysterious poem "The Jewel" imagistically echoes Jiménez's "Conciencia Plena" so closely that one wonders whether Wright intended such a connection. Jiménez writes,

Tú me llevas, conciencia plena, deseante dios,
por todo el mundo.
En este mar tercero,
casi oigo tu voz; tu voz del viento
ocupante total del movimiento;
de los colores, de las luces
eternos y marinos.
Tu voz de fuego blanco
en la totalidad del agua, el barco, el cielo,
lineando las rutas con delicia,
grabándome confúljido mi órbita segura
de cuerpo negro
con el diamante lúcido en su dentro.

Here is Wright's poem, "The Jewel":

There is this cave
In the air behind my body
That nobody is going to touch:
A cloister, a silence
Closing around a blossom of fire.
When I stand upright in the wind,
My bones turn to dark emeralds.

Wright, too, speaks of consciousness, and his images remind us of Jiménez's. Wright acknowledges the intense sensuality of poems such as this one: "At the center of that book [*The Branch Will Not Break*] is my rediscovery of the abounding delight of the body I had forgotten about" (Kalaidjian, 106). Wright's poem expresses his message less explicitly, but Jiménez's work is no less abstract. In both poems, visionary bodies undergo transformation. Transcendence is indicated by the voids left behind, the voice almost heard and the mysterious "black body" in Jiménez, the enveloping silence in Wright. The poets spill a pile of common images—body, fire, wind, jewel—for the reader to piece together. The space after "silence" must be read as a rhythmic pause, an almost positive, signifying space within language.

James Wright also found a precedent for his politically and philosophically engaged poetry in the work of Hispanic poets. Latin American poets have a long history of political unrest, from ancient wars to present-day instability. Many Spanish writers of the 1930s had to choose between fighting in the Spanish Civil War and going into exile. Wright writes a eulogy for Miguel Hernández, who died shortly after being released from a prisoner of war camp during the Spanish Civil War. "In Memory of a Spanish Poet" begins with the subject's own (translated) words: "Take leave of the sun, and of the wheat, for me," which reminds one of Wright's poem "Beginning," in which the wheat "leans back toward its own darkness."

On a local level, Wright protested the exploitation of coal miners in his native Ohio and West Virginia. On a global level, he decried the Vietnam War and wrote such poems as "Eisenhower's Visit to Franco, 1959." For an epigraph, he chooses words from the Spanish philosopher Unamuno: "We die of cold, and not of darkness." In the poem itself, an image of Machado sums up the Spanish poet in terms of light shining in darkness: "Antonio Machado follows the moon, / Down a road of white dust."

James Wright learned many innovations and new freedoms from Hispanic poets. In these last poems he creates a sort of multimedia assembly, reminiscent of Cubist collage or papier collé (see *Still Life with Chair Caning* [1912] by Pablo Picasso). In *The Branch Will Not Break*, he incorporates historical events, news of the day, images of famous people, their words in quotes, and characteristic motifs from their canvases. The intensity of Wright's "deep image," almost concrete on the page, contrasts with the shimmering instability of the poetic expression as a whole. At times Wright reaches a level of abstraction that may risk clarity, yet never fails to communicate.

BIBLIOGRAPHY

Bell, Aubrey F. G. *Contemporary Spanish Literature*. New York: Alfred A. Knopf, 1925.

Bly, Robert. "James Wright and the Slender Woman." *American Poetry Review* 17, 3 (1988): 29–33.

Crunk (pseudonym of Robert Bly). "The Work of James Wright." *The Sixties* 8 (1966): 52–78.

Gleizes, Albert, and Metzinger, Jean. *Cubism*. London: Adelphi Terrace, 1913.

Gombrich, E. H. *Art and Illusion*. Princeton, N.J.: Princeton University Press, 1969.

Graves, Michael. "Crisis in the Career of James Wright." *The Hollins Critic* 22, 5 (1985): 1–9.

Henricksen, Bruce. "Poetry Must Think: An Interview with James Wright." *New Orleans Review* 6 (1979): 201–207.

Jannsens, G.A.M. "The Present State of American Poetry: Robert Bly and James Wright." *English Studies* 51 (1970): 112–137.

Jiménez, Juan Ramón. *Diario de un poeta recién casado*. Madrid: Calleja, 1917.

Kalaidjian, Walter. "Many of Our Waters: The Poetry of James Wright." *Boundary 2* 9, 2 (1981): 101–121.

Machado, Antonio. *Campos de Castilla*. In *Poesías completas* (1907–1917). Madrid: Renacimiento, 1917.

McElrath, Joseph R., Jr. "Something to Be Said for the Light: A Conversation with James Wright." *Southern Humanities Review* 6 (1972): 134–153.

Molesworth, Charles. "James Wright and the Dissolving Self." *Salmagundi* 22–23 (1973): 222–233.

Ortega y Gasset, José. *La deshumanización del arte e Ideas sobre la novela*. Madrid: Revista de Occidente S.A., 1925.

Shklovsky, Victor. "Art as Technique." In *Russian Formalist Criticism: Four Essays*, eds. Lee T. Lemon and Marion J. Reis. Lincoln: University of Nebraska Press, 1965.

Smith, Dave. *The Pure Clear Word: Essays on the Poetry of James Wright*. Urbana: University of Illinois Press, 1982.

Stein, Kevin. *James Wright: The Poetry of a Grown Man*. Athens: Ohio University Press, 1989.

Wright, James. *Above the River: The Complete Poems*. New York: Noonday Press and Hanover, N.H.: University Press of New England, 1992.

———. *The Branch Will Not Break*. Middletown, Conn.: Wesleyan University Press, 1963.

———. *Collected Poems*. Middletown, Conn.: Wesleyan University Press, 1963.

———. "The Art of Poetry XIX." *Paris Review* 62 (1975): 34–61.

———. "I Come to Speak for Your Dead Mouths." *Poetry* 112, 3 (1968): 91–194.

———. "The Music of Poetry." *American Poetry Review* 15, 2 (1986): 43–47.

PART X

THE POINTED
PEN AT LARGE

41

The Literary Relationship between Derek Walcott and Gabriel García Márquez

H. Wendell Howard

Derek Walcott, 1992 recipient of the Nobel Prize for Literature, is a poet and playwright formed by a West Indian heritage of African and European traditions. He openly and frequently admits his poetic indebtedness to English-language poets, particularly W. H. Auden, but he demonstrates the African influences in the colorful dialect of St. Lucia, his West Indian home, that permeates many of his poems and much of his dramatic dialogue. These divided loyalties have prompted him to characterize his childhood as "schizophrenic." In "A Far Cry from Africa," he says that the blood running in his veins is poisoned by the conflict between the English language that he loves and the African heritage that is essential to his existence. He asks if he is to betray them both, or if somehow he can return that which they have both given him. He doesn't know which way to turn (*Collected Poems*, 18).

In "Another Life," also an autobiographical poem, he discovers the answer to his dilemma when he realizes the unique atmosphere and excellence of the Caribbean despite its Third World status. This poem emphasizes that uniqueness in lines which depict a pact between Walcott, the poet, and his friend, a painter. The two of them swore that they would not leave their island home until they had recreated in pictures and poems its foliage-clogged terrain, its unrecognized, self-indulgent shoreline, and its unrefined dialect (*Collected Poems*, 194).

This commitment to root his work in the common life, legends, and language of Caribbean culture, in conjunction with his openness to

and appreciation of major voices of that same atmosphere, quite naturally drew Walcott to the work of Gabriel García Márquez. *The Autumn of
the Patriarch* Walcott judged—after reading it for the third time—to be
"the most powerful Caribbean novel that I've read, even though it comes
out of South America" (Baer, 51). Then, in an interview with Ned Thomas
in 1980, Walcott confessed that his poem, "The Star-Apple Kingdom,"
was closely modeled on *The Autumn of the Patriarch* (Baer, 66).

Before examining the specific relationships between Márquez's novel
and Walcott's poem, we must understand the common cultural–linguistic and thus literary milieu behind the two works. In talking with
Sharon Ciccarelli in 1997, Walcott noted that he lives in a part of the
world where a dominant cultural influence is Spanish, or at least Spanish-sourced, so that he feels a greater affinity with Spanish-American
writers than with persons writing in England or the United States.
The Spanish-sourced writer and the West Indian poet

have a similar historical origin, similar problems of self-resolution, and I can
recognize a sensibility as being very close to mine. So not only is there a possibility of real cultural and creative exchange. . . . So that if I understand Spanish, if I can read Márquez in his language, then I understand him through my
immediate inquiry: what do we have in common? Whereas I know that (and I
say this without any desire to give offense) I have a way of thinking that may
be totally alien to the African. I probably am a total stranger to the African,
whereas I am not a stranger to Márquez. (Baer, 46–47)

Later in that same conversation he argued that Márquez has an in-
stinctive way of handling the natural and the legendary in close proximity. Walcott understands this ability to create "more than a replica
of what happened during the day, more than a record of who said
what," because he himself creates a literature that is much more compelling than "the stilted naturalism of much metropolitan literature";
he comes from the same cultural–linguistic background.

Talking of a like linguistic background is not saying that Walcott's
and Márquez's languages are the same. Walcott's background is the
French–English of St. Lucia. Márquez's is the Spanish of Colombia.
The truth of our point lies in the two writers' keen-sightedness, quality of ear, and capacity to animate the things they set eye on. Joseph
Brodsky, 1987 winner of the Nobel Prize for Literature, says that
Walcott's lines are resonant and stereoscopic because language for him
is an epic device. "Everything this poet touches," he says, "reverberates like magnetic waves whose acoustics are psychological and whose
implications echo" (Brodsky, 270). Later in that same essay on Walcott
in *The New York Review of Books*, Brodsky goes on, "He acts out of the
belief that language is greater than its masters or its servants, that poetry, being its supreme version, is therefore an instrument of self-bet-

terment for both; i.e., that it is a way to gain an identity superior to the confines of class, race, and ego." These words, particularly from Walcott's point of view, are equally applicable to Gabriel García Márquez, for whom, Walcott says, Spanish literature is not an inheritance. It is new, very new, because the language is something that is brought to him fresh. He then adds, "The sound of Márquez is like a lot of leaves in a tree" (Baer, 185). So is the sound of Walcott.

No small part of this sound is Márquez's fecundity of phrase. He makes us see things differently from the way we have ever seen them before because his language is studded with charming bits: a woman with "passionate health," a man with "mentholated voice," the succulent sea that only needed a flame underneath it "to cook the great clam chowder of the universe," the Patriarch who was "a worse jinx than gold," a darkness "disturbed only by the patient digestion of the cows," the "senile backwater of the hammock," a town where "the goats committed suicide from desolation," the long hours of "the dead doldrums of power," the mother who was not even shown "the inside of [her son's] sighs," and on and on in a steady stream of idiomatic wizardry.

Walcott's language is also verbal magic: women "rise like letters" then "resettle in swastikas," another woman has eyes of "frayed denim," someone is as "calm as a kitchen clock without hands," the bows in a young girl's braids are "white satin moths," Caribbean ibises are "practicing for postage stamps," "sharks with well-pressed fins/ ripping [us] small fry off with razor grins," "the grey-iron harbour/ opens on a sea-gull's rusty hinge." All these examples and hundreds more demonstrate how superbly he captures observed details in a fixity of language.

These linguistic witnesses to the genius of both writers are only a part of the totality that dazzles the reader, and in the case of Gabriel Garcia Márquez are part of the "blend of fantasy and hyperbole, exhibited in a context of reality that is known as magic realism" (Epstein, 62). In *The Autumn of the Patriarch* the dictator lives for more than 200 years in mythical time, perpetuating his unearned power over his unloving subjects by devastating them with squalor, rot, and bestiality. Reality is also damaged because truth has been controlled to the point that no one knows what the truth is. For example, the Patriarch had found Patricio Aragones, a perfect double with a doglike loyalty, to become the official imposter. No one knew who the real Patriarch was, not even the concubines they shared. Neither of the men nor any of the women themselves ever knew whose child was whose or by whom. He also ordered that the clock in the tower should strike two times, not twelve, at twelve o'clock so that life would seem longer. In fact, time is not just changed in *The Autumn of the Patriarch*; it is stopped. The novel opens at the end of life:

Over the weekend the vultures got into the presidential palace by pecking through the screens on the balcony windows and the flapping of their wings stirred up the stagnant time inside, and at dawn on Monday the city awoke out of its lethargy of centuries with the warm, soft breeze of a great man dead and rotting grandeur. (Márquez, 1)

Then the story moves forward and backward in a nonlinear form and with a shifting of points of view in mid-unpunctuated sentences that convey endless stasis. The one truth in all of this is that the people are being lied to all the time. The narration is largely in the mind of the General of the Universe, but Márquez often enters other minds to speak in the collective voice of all the people in the blasted nation. As William Kennedy writes, "Through relentless immersion of the reader in these exquisitely detailed perspectives, [Márquez] illuminates the monster internally and externally and delivers him whole" (16), just as the colossally overblown Patriarch serves up whole one of his rivals as the main course at a banquet. Perhaps the most unforgettable visual hyperbole in *The Autumn of the Patriarch* is the Americans forcing the dictator—an amalgam of Latin American dictators: Trujillo, Batista, Perón, Hernández Martínez, and Duvalier—to give them the sea as payment for his debts:

So they took away the Caribbean in April, Ambassador Ewing's nautical engineers carried it off in numbered pieces to plant it far from the hurricanes in the blood-red dawns of Arizona, they took it away with everything it had inside general sir. (Márquez, 245)

No matter how many details we present, we cannot recapitulate the novel. At every turn fireworks of various kinds explode, so the whole is far greater than the sum of its parts. In the details, however, we can initially see the novel's influence on Walcott. For example, Walcott imitates Márquez's unforgettable visual hyperbole that we just cited. In *The Star-Apple Kingdom*, he changes Márquez's numbered pieces of the Caribbean into bolts of cloth—lace-trimmed aquamarine, azure-colored satin, green silk, and so on—that represent the Caribbean that is sold by seven prime ministers to the conglomerate at a markup, rather than the Ambassador's engineers carrying it off to Arizona as they do in *Autumn of the Patriarch* (*Collected Poems*, 390).

Again, Márquez's presentation of the idea of solitude—what greater isolation exists than that of the unloved dictator perpetuating his undeserved power for an unending length of time?—is echoed in Walcott, particularly in terms of his "Robinson Crusoe" figures—images of the castaway, the hermit, the artist—that emphasize separation and the failure of community. Shabine in the opening section of *The Star-Apple Kingdom*, titled "Schooner Flight," experiences the solitude of the scapegoat, of the poet, of the native weeping for his island. Shabine's being made the scapegoat for the corrupt minister for whom he smuggled scotch—when that minister investigates himself—also parallels Márquez's indictment of the leader who betrays his people to line his own pockets and to play games of power. The section titled "Koenig of the River" is also a poem of solitude. Koenig, the sole survivor of a shipload of missionaries, finds a river that he resolves to dominate. In a kind of madness he rages within himself, steers his small vessel into the dense river mist, and is lost. The title piece, "The Star-Apple King-dom," has a Jamaican narrator who experiences the solitude that comes from feeling divorced from his heritage and his island home. As he rises in estate, he still feels a kind of solitude because he never quite fits into the new order. In the dream into which the narrator sinks the new exploiters and powerbrokers corrupt the possibilities inherent in independence by parcelling and marketing the islands "in ads for the Caribbean Economic Community," a continuation of cutting up the sea and selling it to conglomerates.

Finally, at least for our purposes here, Márquez uses surrealism to present the "public corruptions and private anguishes" of his corner of the world that, in Salmon Rushdie's words, "are more garish and extreme than they ever get in the so-called 'North'" (Rushdie, 3). Walcott also employs surrealism to present his dauntless Third World that is epic in its abundant political and social reality. We must hasten to note, however, that Walcott is naturalistic, expressionistic, imagis-tic, hermetic, and confessional, as well as surrealistic.

The connection between the two authors that Walcott characterizes as modeling on Márquez is certainly more than the mere influence of one work on another. In Walcott's Nobel lecture (1992), *The Antilles, Fragments of Epic Memory*, he notes the "elegaic pathos" with which "outsiders" view the Caribbean. He says that he can understand the mood because the melancholy of the Caribbean is contagious. The ways, however, in which English, French, and some exiled writers describe that sadness are incorrect, for their failure to comprehend the "light" of the Caribbean as well as the people on whom it falls. Márquez and Walcott have a like understanding of that light and of the people.

When we spoke of *The Autumn of the Patriarch's* moving in a nonlin-ear fashion, we emphasized the stasis that such a structural device conveys. Quite correctly we implied the negativity of a stasis that is the consequence of the evil dictator. Another dimension of that stasis, however, exists in the lives of the Antillean people that "outsiders," particularly tourists, fail to realize, or will not let themselves under-stand. The culture of Márquez's and Walcott's world is not evolving; it is already shaped. It is not an idyll to its natives; it is the source of their working strength. What the tourist or exile sees as lethargy in the people on whom the light falls is actually the patience that is the width of Antillean life. Failing to understand this fact, the outsider asks the wrong thing of it, demands of it an ambition it has no interest in. Consequently, when tourists claim that they "love the Caribbean," meaning, as Walcott says, that someday they plan to return for a visit but could never live there, they are repeating a common "civilized" insult. Walcott further notes that a traveler is incapable of love because the two concepts are contradictory: A traveler is in motion; love is a condition of statis. If a person returns to that which he or she loved in a country and remains there in statis, the lover of that part of the world ceases to be a traveler and becomes a native. This stasis is positive.

John Sturrock has said that García Márquez is committed to showing "that our first freedom—and one which all too many Latin American countries have lost—is of the full resources of our language" (Sturrock, 451). Rebekah Presson makes a similar point about Derek Walcott by titling her interview with the Caribbean poet, "The Man Who Keeps the English Language Alive" (Baer, 189). Walcott, talking about a writer's working within a language to generate excitement in a reader, says that every time he re-reads Ishmael Reed, "His work is fresh to me, and as exhilarating and as funny as it was at the first reading. There is a delight in it. . . . Reed's is a most fertile kind of writing" (46). Then the *New York Times* concludes that Ishmael Reed is as close as we are likely to get in English to Gabriel García Márquez. We have come full circle to the sound that is like a lot of leaves in a tree.

Gabriel García Márquez's work in its totality is epic, for as in Walcott's works of epic character, one recognizes the need to itemize the universe in which the author finds himself, a universe, in spite of all else, in which human values are perennial. Thus, if *The Star-Apple Kingdom* is modeled on *The Autumn of the Patriarch*, and we have shown that it is, the much larger conception of the relationship of Derek Walcott and Gabriel García Márquez is that both writers, through the humanistic and universalizing elements of myth, imagination, and aesthetic perception, impart a highly original vision of human beings and their world.

REFERENCES

Baer, William, ed. *Conversations with Derek Walcott.* Jackson: University Press of Mississippi, 1996.

Brodsky, Joseph. "On Derek Walcott." *The New York Review of Books,* November 10, 1983, pp. 39–44.

Epstein, Joseph. "How Good Is Gabriel Garcia Márquez?" *Commentary,* May 1983, pp. 59–65.

Kennedy, William. "The Autumn of the Patriarch." *The New York Times Book Review,* October 31, 1976, pp. 1, 16.

Márquez, Gabriel Garcia. *The Autumn of the Patriarch*. Translated by Gregory Rabassa. New York: HarperCollins, 1991.

Sturrock, John. "The Unreality Principle." *The Times Literary Supplement*, April 15, 1977, p. 451.

Rushdie, Salman. "Angel Gabriel." *London Review of Books*, September 16–October 6, 1982, pp. 3–4.

Walcott, Derek. *The Antilles, Fragments of Epic Memory*. New York: Farrar, Straus, and Giroux, 1992.

———. *Collected Poems 1948–1984*. New York: Farrar, Straus, and Giroux, 1986.

42

Metaphors of Progress: The Transmigration of The Kiss of the Spider Woman

Adrián Pérez Melgosa

The novel *The Kiss of the Spider Woman* contains a set of independent narrative fragments relating to each other like the different elements in a set of Chinese boxes. Each narrative "box" attempts to contain and redefine the meaning of all the other narrative fragments it frames. In turn, each is reframed and redefined by others. One of the main themes of this intertextual game is the tension between the reality of the characters and that represented in the products of the culture industry.[1] The novel aligns these products, especially movies, with a simplified version of reality intentionally tailored to support a single and uncontested point of view. The novel also challenges its readers to imitate the creative process of its protagonists. Valentín and Molina, prisoners in Buenos Aires during the military dictatorship of the 1970s, tell each other their favorite movies as they wait for a resolution of their cases. While retelling the movie stories, they creatively reshape their meaning. Now that *The Kiss* has become a theater play, a Hollywood film, and a Broadway musical, we can say that the novel's version of the culture industry has turned out to be a prophecy. Each of these entertainment genres has chosen to reduce the nebula of meanings in the book to a simple and unified message. It is up to us, the public, to fulfill the second part of the prediction by retelling the story of *The Kiss* in a way that opens up new social and individual significations.

Among the critics there has generally been a very positive evaluation of these transformations of the novel into new cultural products.[2] Puig himself declares in an interview with Bárbara Mújica,

Cuando vi el guión y las primeras versiones de la película, me puse más que furioso. . . . Pero después me sorprendí al ver que el público recibía el mensaje que yo había querido comunicar con la novela, aunque a través de una vía diferente. Francamente, yo no esperaba que el público reaccionara tan favorablemente. (5)

When I saw the script and the early versions of the movie, I got very angry. Afterwards, I was surprised to see that the public was receiving the very message I had wanted to communicate in the novel, albeit through a different path. Frankly, I did not expect the public to react so favorably.

But the complex irony arising from the transformation of *The Kiss* into a movie has not escaped a sector of the critics. Leonard Cheever observes that when Puig uses films in his novels, they always show the pernicious effects of the "Hollywood version" of reality on the characters (13–14). Jonathan Tittler reads the desire of Puig's characters to flee into the comfort of cinema as symptomatic of a deep alienation (109–110). *The Kiss* portrays not only the alienation of movie going. It also wrestles to devise a creative way through which the characters can step out of those fictions in order to reestablish a meaningful connection among themselves.

In the course of the novel Valentín and Molina redefine the standardized narratives of personal and social progress they encounter in the movies they have consumed. Within its internal play of textual fragments, the word "progress" emerges as a problematic arena that acquires different meanings according to the specific media and cultural contexts in which it is uttered.[3] By contrast, the theater play, the movie, and each of the musical adaptations aligns itself with a single version of progress, recreating the alienation without giving the spectators any guidance about possible ways to counter it.

Since the end of World War II there have been three major theories of progress: modernization, dependency, and hybridity. Hirschman first formulated the modernization theory in the early 1960s, and it became the model for the economic backbone of President Kennedy's Alliance for Progress.[4] Modernization contends that in order to improve their economic and social conditions, the nations of Latin America must imitate the economic structures and way of life of the developed nations. In the 1970s André Gunder Frank challenged the modernization theory. Describing the economic situation in Latin America as one of dependency, he posed a cause–effect relationship between the hyperdevelopment of Western Europe and the United States and the underdevelopment of Latin America. The implication of the dependency model is that modernization would only perpetuate underdevelopment in the Latin American region. Progress would come only by breaking up with the modernity model of the West. In 1981 Arthur Morris published his theory of economic hybridity or regional differentiation. It describes the economy of Latin America, and by extension the social groups participating in it, as a hybrid system in which dependence and isolation from the world market are simultaneously operative, each progressing according to the internal logic of its needs.

Three of the six movie stories included in *The Kiss of the Spider Woman* provide symbolic renderings of these theories of "progress." The movies draw a connection between the social environment that the theories analyze and the personal relationship between Valentín and Molina. Through these movie stories the protagonists learn how to "progress" in their personal relationship and bridge the gap between the stereotypical notions they have of each other. Valentín, a committed guerrilla who is trying to subvert the state, gains a deeper understanding of the revolutionary implications of his cellmate's homosexuality. Molina understands the need to struggle for political change. The first of the movie stories presenting narratives of progress relates to Val Lewton's film, *I Walked with a Zombie* (1943). The other two movies containing representations of theories of progress are Puig's own inventions: *A Guerrilla at Le Mans* and *The Story of Hedy Lamarr*.[5]

According to Leslie Halliwell, the plot of *I Walked with a Zombie* was "mirthfully borrowed from Jane Eyre" (500), a connection that gives an extra turn of the screw to *The Kiss of the Spider Woman*'s ironic play of genre migrations. The action takes place in a Caribbean island during 1943. The island appears as a primitive environment immersed in a culture of magic, superstition, and tyranny. A plantation owner from the United States vows to help the witch doctor become the absolute ruler of the island in exchange for help in recruiting a zombie labor force. In Molina's words, the foreign capitalist "came to the island to get himself rich and started off by treating the peons like dirt" (Puig 1991, 185). A nurse who arrives from New York in a modern boat brings change to this stagnant situation. She has been hired by the capitalist to help with the care of his demented wife. The witch doctor is no match for the nurse's training in modern medicine. She uncovers the agreement between the two men and frees the local population from their zombie curse. In the narrative model of the movie the society had been bound to an underdeveloped past until the plantation owner came and imposed a colonial system. The nurse brought with her the medicine of modernization to rid the population of their past curses. The movie presents a society approaching progress through the gradual transition from primitive to colonial to modern, or in terms of the story, from superstition to slavery and on to freedom. This definition of progress coincides with that of the modernization theory.

The second movie, *A Guerrilla at Le Mans*, represents Latin America as a dependent society. The protagonist of this story is a young man living in an unnamed tropical country during the 1960s. His father owns a plantation that he controls like the lord of a feudal state, treating his workers as serfs. The cheap labor that the workers provide allows the plantation owner to have a second life in the French Riviera, and his son to enjoy the cosmopolitan life of a Formula One racing pilot. In the end a violent revolution kills the protagonist and his family, leaving the country in the hands of guerrilla forces. The movie establishes a connection between the development of industrialized economies and the underdevelopment of Latin America. Since this movie shows how underdevelopment is necessary for the existence of the developed world, change in this movie does not come through the gradual adoption of modernity, but through a violent revolution.

The Story of Hedy Lamarr is the last of three stories in *The Kiss* that take place in Latin American locales. It also offers a different perspective on how to attain social and personal progress. In this case a metonymical relationship exists between Latin America and the female protagonist, a beautiful and successful Mexican bolero singer. After a powerful tycoon convinces her to marry him, she becomes a prisoner in his mansion on a small Mexican island. A reporter who is researching her husband's scurrilous business dealings for a story manages to get close to her and they fall in love. After the singer and the journalist escape together, the tycoon uses his connections to make sure they do not find a way to earn a living. The newspaperman becomes a fisherman, the only activity that escapes the control of the tycoon. Soon he falls sick, and the singer is forced to become a prostitute to pay for his medical care. In this story the millionaire tycoon, who possesses an international business and a cosmopolitan lifestyle, coexists side by side with the small fishermen whose economy, although dependent on the international markets, is totally removed from the influences of modernization. It is a portrait of a hybrid economy, one in which modernity and tradition remain adjacent to each other. The journalist, the singer, and her husband live in an economy produced by the intentional exchange of goods. The fishermen, living side by side with the technologies of progress, can survive without the products and services introduced by the tycoon of modernity.

The production sites of these three narratives can be established very clearly in Puig's text. *I Walked with a Zombie* is pure Hollywood, *A Guerrilla at Le Mans* is fashioned in the style of French car-racing movies of the 1960s, and *The Story of Hedy Lamarr* is a composite of Mexican melodramas from the 1950s. By identifying each narrative with a determinate national film industry, the novel relates each theory to a determinate national culture with a history of power relations within and toward Latin America. Thus, the modernization theory becomes a Hollywood version of Latin America. Dependence would represent a European point of view, while *The Story of Hedy Lamarr* offers a Mexican, and by extension, Latin American theory concerning its own economic situation. While scholars of economics and political science present these theories as the logical interpretation of carefully compiled data, the movies present "modernization," "dependence," and "hybridization" as practices. They set the living environment from which the characters carve out their lives. *The Kiss* portrays these theories as fictional clichés through which the world sees Latin America and its inhabitants. Through the dialogs between Valentín and Molina about the films, the novel reappropriates the clichés to provide a new definition of "progress," one that not only exposes the inadequacy of each of the three economic models, but transcends their stereotypes and contradictions.

In one of the final dialogs between the two inmates, Valentín makes a subdued declaration of independence, breaking with the stereotypes present in the movies and in his ideology. He redefines isolation as the possibility for a clean start toward progress. By establishing a relationship of mutual respect with Molina, he also implies a new kind of politics. During this epiphany Valentín ponders,

In a sense we're perfectly free to behave however we choose with respect to one another, am I making myself clear? It's as if we were on some desert island. An island on which we may have to remain alone together for years. Because, well, outside of this cell we may have our oppressors, yes, but not inside. Here no one oppresses the other. (Puig 1991, 202)

Throughout the novel Molina has a duplicitous relationship with Valentín. While getting emotionally closer to his cellmate, Molina has also been negotiating with the warden for a possible parole if he gets any useful information about Valentín's comrades. In exchange for his collaboration, he even convinces the warden to supply him with healthy food and medicine. The warden's providing Molina with exactly the items that a mother would normally bring him reinterprets creatively the relationship of dependence between the prisoner and his keeper. From a parasite who is advancing his career at the expense of Molina, the warden becomes transformed into a nurturing agent. Ultimately, hybridization is recast into an affective and sexual relationship between the prisoners, a vehicle through which each one can acquire the positive traits of the other. By the end of the novel, the prisoners have redefined the modernization, dependence, and hybridization models of progress in a creative and nonconfrontational way. They recast each of the three in terms of mutual collaboration, nurturance, and freedom, rather than competition.

After being an extremely successful novel, *The Kiss of the Spider Woman* reappeared in public transformed into a theater play by Manuel Puig himself. The stage incarnation of the narrative is a synthesized version of the novel. Only one of the six movie stories in the novel, *The Cat People*, is present in the play. The relationship between Valentín and Molina develops much faster in the play, and their sexual encounters are reduced to just one. The mise-en-scène of the play acts as a narrator. It communicates the emotional and psychological transformations of the characters through changes in the design of the scene, lights, and sound. Some of the textual threads that were completely separated in the novel (the footnotes, Molina's visits to the warden after his release, and the police report) appear in the play interwoven as part of the dialog between Valentín and Molina.[6] The compartmentalization of the bureaucratic, scientific, and colloquial discourses was central to the novel. It conveyed a sense of competition and disagreement among disciplines about individual, sexual, and social identities. By synthesizing the complex intertextuality of the novel, the play also eliminates the implied critique of the dominant theories of progress that were so patent in the novel.

We can see this especially in the major change in the "focalizer" of the story and the play.[7] While the narrator of the novel always follows Molina's movements, making him and his homosexuality the center of the action, the play gets its continuity from Valentín's constant presence on stage, thus highlighting his political struggle as the main theme. Becky Boling studies the change from novel to play in Puig's narrative and reaches a similar conclusion by noting the play's hierarchical arrangement of signs. She concludes,

The play stands out as being much more political, because physically the images of hierarchy, the privilege of dark and light, and the setting within the cell strongly suggest the situation of an oppressive system and that of political/social victim. On stage power becomes substantial, physical reality. (85)

These material symbols of power are a projection of Valentín's thought processes. He replicates in his thinking the same mechanisms that have created the system he rebels against. These structures that understand the "other" in terms of an enemy are the same that rule the narratives of *The Cat People* and of the dependency theory. By choosing a Hollywood production as the only movie that Molina retells in the theater version, Puig produces yet another effect. He concentrates on the United States as the site of production for theories that establish economic or cultural dependence. The theater within the theater present in Molina's reenactment of the film conveys the possibility of a resistance to the theory of progress through modernization.

The film version provides a further stage in the evolution of *The Kiss of the Spider Woman*. In 1986 Hector Babenco directed the film version, based on Leonard Schrader's adaptation of Manuel Puig's novel. Puig's participation in the script was minimal and only during its early stages of production. This distance between the novelist and the film is doubly ironic, given Puig's lifelong connection to the world of movies as a frustrated director and as script writer for a number of productions. The movie also reduces the six movie stories to a single one. The chosen movie this time was *Her Real Glory*, the romantic story of Leni, a French cabaret singer, and Weiner, an officer of the German occupation army in France during World War II. This change intensifies a trend that had already started in the play. The three movies representing three theories of progress—as applied by the multinational entertainment industry to Latin America—have disappeared. Without them the film breaks the symbolic link that the novel establishes between the imprisonment of Valentín and Molina and the social, economic, and political theories imported into Latin America from Europe and the United States.

While the novel used the three movies analyzed here to represent Latin America as the locus of contending social narratives, the movie introduces Doctor Americo, a character that represents America as a whole, as if joined in a common destiny. As a leader of the democratic resistance to the government, he becomes a metaphor of modernization, the theory of progress defended in the film. Doctor Americo is an old, weak, benevolent looking man with a long gray beard. Overall, he bears a close resemblance to Walt Whitman in his old age. To introduce this character, the film changes Valentín's identity significantly. A political science major in the novel, Valentín becomes a journalist in the movie. His revolutionary ideals do not come from a thoughtful consideration of society as a whole, but from daily exposure to information documenting the brutality of the government. While Valentín is an active guerrilla leader in the novel, his only illegal action in the film is to "trickle information about the government's brutality outside the country." The crime for which he is now incarcerated was giving his passport to Doctor Americo, who needed it to escape from the country. The whole symbolic spectrum of the novel, in which sexual liberation is joined to social liberation, becomes in the film a struggle between a dictatorial and a democratic vision of society.

If in the three movies that Molina recounts about Latin America it was always the role of female characters to symbolize the continent's backwardness, dependence, and state of exploitation, the movie chooses Doctor Americo to represent a very different view of the continent. He is an enlightened male who fights to lead Latin America in the path of progress. When Valentín gives his passport to Americo at a modern train station, he is also giving up his identity to vicariously catch the train of progress.

In the summer of 1992 *The Kiss of the Spider Woman, the Musical* opened in Toronto under the direction of Harold Prince. This show presented the most dramatic transformation of the novel, and perhaps the one that required the largest leap between genres. It is also the one in which Manuel Puig had the least input. Sheridan Morley, the drama critic for the *Spectator* and the *Herald Tribune*, recounts how in 1986, on starting the project,

Harold Prince brought Manuel Puig to New York City to meet with Kander and Ebb [composers of the music and the lyrics, respectively]. Although Puig's insight and ideas were very useful, as a novelist he was not up to the unique demands of providing a book for a stage musical.

Finally, it was Terrance McNally who wrote the book for the musical. After opening in Toronto, the new adaptation of *The Kiss of the Spider Woman* traveled to London, and from there to New York City. In these new venues Puig's story became an international product, attuned to the economic concerns of an extremely expensive form of entertainment and to the social debates current among its prospective audiences.

The most visible changes in this version concern the technology involved in the production and the new elements of the script. Jerome Sirlin prepared an extremely complex set and lighting that emphasized the sense of entrapment and isolation of the protagonists. The two main components of the sets were multiple layers of steel jail bars together with computer-generated projections of monumental spider webs. The musical's book also changed the novel substantially. The spectator hears all the official information about Molina and Valentín in the musical number that serves as a prologue for the show. In this presentation, Valentín's character has mutated once more. He becomes a young terrorist who blames the state for the poverty and misery of his childhood. Like all the versions after the novel, the musical cut down dramatically the number of movies within the text, here to just two. Both of them were specially created for the musical. The first one, entitled *Amazon Love*, is a romantic love story set in a South American jungle. It has lost the political confrontations and the class struggle that were central to *A Guerrilla at LeMans*. A second movie, *Flame of St. Petersburg*, takes the action of *Her Real Glory* away from Nazi Germany and into Russia at the time of the Revolution. Tatyana, the protagonist caught between two loves and two social systems, dies to save her

Bolshevik boyfriend. Another important change is the creation of Aurora, a character who embodies the "Spider Woman" and acts as an emblem of glamour, romantic love, and death simultaneously. Aurora appears only at the thresholds marking the different stages in the development of Valentín and Molina's relationship. She functions as a framing device filtering all the scenes of the musical through her allegorical renderings of love and death.

Each of these changes seems to be calculated to appeal to a particular section of the prospective audiences. In a very interesting analysis of the musical, David Román and Alberto Sandoval interpreted some of the elements of the mise-en-scène as symbols of an AIDS subtext. To support their conclusion they mention the cage at the center of the stage, the quilts, and the popular protests put together by the other inmates, the tragic deaths, and visibility of blood. The fact that in 1993 the American Foundation for AIDS Research adopted "The Day After That," one of the show's songs, as its official anthem corroborates their argument (568). When the box-office receipts of the musical started to decline, Garth Drabinsky, the producer, changed the actress interpreting Aurora in order to appeal to different constituencies of the audience. When María Conchita Alonso took over the title role from Vanessa Williams, the producer hoped that she would "draw a Hispanic audience as steadily as Williams drew African Americans" (Toobin, 30). The physical location of *The Kiss of the Spider Woman, the Musical* was moved into a cosmopolitan setting. The constraints deriving from its need to be economically viable as a musical, the technological fireworks, and the changes added to the narrative caused the abandonment of the open version of progress given at the end of the novel and the adoption of a single model based on hybridity. In all, the musical reduces and refocuses the complex meanings in the novel in order to speak to particular social constituencies who might fill the theater.

With each adaptation of *The Kiss of the Spider Woman* to a new genre, with wider circulation and higher production costs, its message gradually lost the ambiguity and symbolic richness of Puig's novel. The play, the movie, and the musical reconstitute a unified vision of "progress" in agreement with the economic and social constraints of each genre. These three adaptations ignore the critique of the dominant versions of "progress" performed by the novel. By including the modernization, dependence, and hybridity theories in the movie stories Molina and Valentín share, the novel casts a prophecy about the workings of the culture industry. It predicts that industrially produced narratives can include in their representations only a single and stereotypical version of progress. As creative interpreters of the film, the play and the novel, it is we who must now derive from them our own personal definitions of progress.

NOTES

1. For a definition of the term "culture industry," see "The Culture Industry: Enlightenment as Mass Deception" by Max Horkheimer and Theodor Adorno (1988), and "Culture Industry Reconsidered" by Theodor Adorno.

2. Michael Boccia, perhaps one the most enthusiastic critics says, "Rarely has a narrative been converted from film to novel to film and perhaps just as rarely translated so well" (418).

3. Raymond Williams's definition of "progress" highlights only the impact of technology on social values: "Progress, in particular, is the history of those inventions, which 'created the modern world.' The effects of the technologies, whether direct or indirect, foreseen or unforeseen, are as it were the rest of history. The steam engine, the automobile, television, the atomic bomb, have *made* modern man and the modern condition" (Williams, 1990, 12). This definition seems to have generated most of the accounts of progress present in encyclopedias and technocratic political discourses. I would focus instead on another side of "progress," on how novels, films, and economic theory account for that "rest of history" to which Williams refers.

4. Albert Hirschman, the economist who generated this theory, proposed the diffusion of "modernity" as the solution for regional development. He argued that the improvement of the economy in Latin America depended upon "'trickle down' processes through which modern technology was diffused to all parts by the gradual elimination of barriers to mobility of information and capital. 'Trickle down' effects would lead to the interregional convergence of income levels" (Morris, 1981, 21).

John F. Kennedy's project for an Alliance for Progress with Latin America is an early political offspring of this economic teaching. On August 5, 1961, President Kennedy and Secretary of the Treasury Douglas Dillon presented the "Alliance for Progress, a Program for the Peoples of the Americas" to the Inter-American Economic and Social Council. In their respective addresses, Dillon and Kennedy conveyed the two fundamental principles on which the Alliance was to be founded: Dillon emphasized the need for a break with a past, which he depicted as rooted in poverty, injustice, and primitive political and economic practices. Kennedy, by contrast, stressed the fact that this Alliance fostered traditional links and that its agenda was not as new as it might seem. In a manner almost telegraphic, Dillon conveyed the gist of Hirschman's modernization theory: a chain reaction in which the development of urban centers, their industrialization, and the dissemination of modern medicine would "trickle down" to the farmers in the interior, enabling them to own the land they worked. It would eventually result in the democratization of the state's institutions.

5. The titles of the movies Molina recounts are absent from the text of *The Kiss*. Most of them, however, can be traced back to existing films. There are different opinions about which of the stories Molina tells are based on real movies and which are invented. Stephanie Merrim, for example, gives the titles of three movies that underlie Molina's stories: *The Cat People, The Enchanted Cottage*, and *I Walked with a Zombie*. Merrim identifies the second movie story with the title *Destino*, and describes it as "the Nazi propaganda film"

(303). Sloan de Villo connects two of the stories to three Hollywood titles: the Val Lewton films *The Cat People* (1943) and *I Walked With A Zombie* (1943), and Victor Halperin's *The White Zombie* (1932). Laura Rice-Sayre identifies the following movies: "Jacques Tourneur's horror film *The Cat People*" (250), "the Nazi propaganda film *Her Real Glory*" (251), "*The Enchanted Cottage*" (253) and "*I Walked With A Zombie*" (254).

6. Molina's dialogue, for example, integrates part of the information that the reader of the novel gets through the footnotes. He introduces a vulgarized version of Freud's theory of Oedipus's complex when complaining that people always tell him "that I was pampered too much when I was a kid, and that's how I got this way, That I'm too tied to my mother's apron strings but it's never too late to change and all I need is a good woman because there's nothing better than a good woman" (Puig, 1991, 26).

7. For a description of the semiological importance of the term "focalizer," see Mieke Bal's *Narratology: Introduction to the Theory of Narrative*, especially pp. 102–106.

REFERENCES

Adorno, Theodor. "Culture Industry Reconsidered." *New German Critique* 1, 6 (1975): 12–19.

Bal, Mieke. *Narratology: Introduction to the Theory of Narrative*. Translated by Christine van Boheemen. Toronto: University of Toronto Press, 1988.

Boccia, Michael. "Versions (Con-, In-, and Per-) in Manuel Puig's and Hector Babenco's *Kiss of the Spider Woman*, Novel and Film." *Modern Fiction Studies* 32 (1986): 417–426.

Boling, Becky. "From *Beso to Beso*: Puig's Experiments with Genre." *Symposium: A Quarterly Journal in Modern Foreign Literatures* 44, 2 (1990): 75–87.

The Cat People. Dir. Jacques Tourneur. With Simone Simon and Kent Smith. RKO, 1942.

Cheever, Leonard A. "Puig's *Kiss of the Spider Woman*: What the Movie Version Couldn't Show." *Publications of the Arkansas Philological Association* 13, 2 (Fall 1987): 13–27.

de Villo, Sloan. "Manuel Puig's *Kiss of the Spider Woman* as Post-Literature." *International Fiction Review* 14 (1987): 23–26.

Dillon, Douglas. "Statement by Secretary Dillon." *Department of State Bulletin*, August 28, 1961, 356–360.

Frank, André Gunder. *Dependent Accumulation and Underdevelopment*. New York: Monthly Review Press, 1979.

Halliwell, Leslie. *Halliwell's Film Guide*. 7th ed. New York: Harper and Row, 1989.

Hirschman, Albert O. "Ideologies of Economic Development in Latin America." In *Latin American Issues, Essays and Comments*, ed. Albert O. Hirschman. New York: Twentieth Century Fund, 1961.

———. *Journeys Toward Progress*. New York: Twentieth Century Fund, 1963.

Horkheimer, Max, and Adorno, Theodor. "The Culture Industry: Enlightenment as Mass Deception." In *Dialectic of Enlightenment*. New York: Continuum, 1988.

I Walked with a Zombie. Dir. Jacques Tourneur. With Frances Dee and James Ellison. RKO, 1943.

Kennedy, John Fitzgerald. "Alliance for Progress, a Program for the Peoples of the Americas." *Department of State Bulletin*, August 28, 1961, 355–356.

The Kiss of the Spider Woman. Dir. Hector Babenco. Screenplay Leonard Schrader. With William Hurt, and Raul Julia. MGM, 1985.

The Kiss of the Spider Woman, the Musical. Dir. Harold Prince. Book Terrance McNally. Music John Kander. Lyrics Fred Ebb. With Chita Rivera, Brent Carver, and Anthony Crivello. Live Entertainment Corporation of Canada, 1992.

Merrim, Stephanie. "Through the Film Darkly; Grade 'B' Movies and Dreamwork in *Tres Tristes Tigres* and *El Beso de la Mujer Araña.*" *Modern Languages Studies* 14 (1985): 300–312.

Morley, Sheridan. "A Stunning and Courageous Hit." In *Kiss of the Spider Woman CD Booklet.* New York: RCA Victor, 1992.

Morris, Arthur. *Latin America: Economic Development and Regional Differentiation.* Totowa, N.J.: Barnes and Noble Books, 1981.

Mújica, Bárbara. "El mundo imaginario de Manuel Puig." *Américas* [Spanish ed.] 38, 3 (1986): 2–7.

Puig, Manuel. *El Beso de la Mujer Araña.* Barcelona: Seix Barral, 1976.

———. *The Kiss of the Spider Woman.* Translated by Thomas Colchie. New York: Random House, 1991.

Rice-Sayre, Laura. "A Feminist–Materialist Reading of Manuel Puig's *The Kiss of the Spider Woman.*" In *Textual Analysis: Some Readers Reading,* ed. Mary Ann Caws. New York: MLA, 1986.

Román, David, and Sandoval, Alberto. "Caught in the Web: Latinidad, AIDS, and Allegory in *The Kiss of The Spider Woman, the Musical.*" *American Literature* 67 (1995): 553–585.

Tittler, Jonathan. *Manuel Puig.* New York: Twayne, 1993.

Toobin, Jeffrey. "A New Spider Woman." *The New Yorker,* January 16, 1995, p. 30.

Williams, Raymond. *Keywords.* New York: Oxford University Press, 1990.

43

Children's "Subversive Literature": Heriberto Frías, Antonio Skármeta, and Ana María Shua

Howard M. Fraser

Ariel Dorfman has commented on the thralldom of children's literature and the power it exerts upon young people. In his essay, "Inocencia y neocolonialismo": Un caso de dominio ideológico en la literatura infantil," Dorfman discusses how children's literature functions as a force of socialization that teaches children to conform to society's dominant values and can neutralize children's rebellious nature. Recent critical studies, however, suggest another direction for children's literature. Rather than reflecting adult values and muffling rebellion, children's literature can serve as a force of subversion that calls into question young readers' blind acceptance of society's dominant values. Alison Lurie, Pulitzer Prize–winning novelist and author of *Don't Tell the Grown-Ups: Subversive Children's Literature*, presents classic tales of children's literature that she claims encourage children to defy authority and rebel against it. When children behave subversively, they become more flexible and mature and shatter the rigidity of social conventions or the "rules of life" as espoused by adults. The three writers chosen for this essay will furnish different examples of subversive children's literature: Heriberto Frías retells Mexican history in order to provide a populist antidote to violent authoritarianism in Porfirian Mexico, Ana María Shua projects a feminist agenda incarnated in a young girl who swims the frozen waters of the South Atlantic, and Antonio Skármeta's young soccer player outwits Pinochet's plan of family betrayal.

Subversive children's literature in Latin America seems to arise during periods of social and political upheaval, and the genesis of subversiveness in literature for young people occurs at the end of the nineteenth century during modernism, when the future of the continent, if not of all humanity, is the focus of the general "crisis in beliefs" that characterizes the apocalyptical atmosphere of the *fin de siècle*. Seen from our perspective one century later, modernist literature for children and adults is clearly politically incorrect. It maintains a subversive questioning of bourgeois life and ideas and rubs against the grain of materialism by trying to undercut the materialistic values of the times. Modernism offers an idealistic alternative to society's self-satisfied interest in preserving the status quo.

A case in point of children's literature that reflects this crisis of beliefs and subversively questions adult values in the interest of political and social change is José Martí's collection of history, poetry, and fiction for children, *La Edad de Oro* (1889). Martí's children's magazine has been interpreted as an organ of change because of the presence of its author's radical ideology and coherent vision of a liberated Cuban nation.

Similarly, Martí's contemporary, Heriberto Frías, offers several literary interpretations of Mexican history with a politically liberal agenda, most appropriate for the questioning of the authoritarian regime of the Mexican dictator Porfirio Díaz. Heriberto Frías was a muckraking Mexican journalist whose best-known novel, *Tomochic* (1894), is a scathing condemnation of the Mexican army's massacre of a small town in Sonora. Frías's presence at the demolition of an entire village and the annihilation of all its inhabitants left upon him an indelible impression of the abuse of government power under the *Porfiriato*. The novel has been compared to Stephen Crane's *The Red Badge of Courage* for its depiction of unleashed violence and blood lust, and has also been called a forerunner of the novel of the *Revolución Mexicana* for its exposé of corruption and the misuse of power during Díaz's authoritarian regime.

Less well known is Frías's collection of indigenous legends and historical sketches published in his *Biblioteca del Niño Mexicano* (1902), a series of vignettes written for children, that provide a graphic depiction of violence from pre-Columbian times through the nineteenth century. Given Frías's opposition to Díaz's authoritarianism, it is to be expected that the author's subversive spirit can be felt in a publication for Mexican children. His *Biblioteca* consists of eighty-five pamphlets, similar to the dime novels of that era, that cover the sweep of Mexican history. Its importance derives as much from its subject matter, a panorama of violent chapters in Mexican history down through the ages, as from its graphic portrayal of human mutilation and mayhem published in both color and black-and-white drawings. Not previously recognized for his illustrations of children's literature is the artist who rendered these shocking scenes, Mexico's master caricaturist and mentor of Diego Rivera, José Guadalupe Posada.

A sample of the *Biblioteca's* vignettes that are accompanied by Posada's violent illustrations provides entrée into Frías's protest of Mexican authoritarianism. From the onset of Hispanic–indigenous contacts, for example, Frías sees the mirror image of Díaz's militarism and crimes against humanity reflected in Spanish and Aztec responses to the other. In the second number of his *Biblioteca*, "El combate de Ocelotzin y Prado Alto" (Figure 43.1), Frías projects his dual critique of Hispanic and indigenous violence and will to annihiliate as the authoritarian responses to patriotism. For their bloody tradition of slavery and murder, Moctezuma and the *aztecas* are viewed as enemies of freedom who deserve defeat. But Frías also takes the Spaniards to task for their myopic glorification of violence against their indigenous adversaries. Frías inserts Bernal Díaz among the Spanish forces to provide a thoughtful antidote to the Spaniards' *fanfarronada*. When a puffed-up Spaniard capitán boasts somewhat apocalyptically, "Ahora, no nos queda más que vencer ó morir. . . . Lucharemos hasta hacer de este país una inmensa y gloriosa tumba española" (Frías 1987, 6), Bernal Díaz's magnanimous voice of moderation responds, "¡O azteca! . . . Dios dirá" (7).

This episode serves as a prologue to the bloody scenes of Mexico's most infamous massacre, Cortés's siege of Cholula, whose carnage resembles the siege of Tomochic that so horrified Frías. The first paragraph of number 3 of the *Biblioteca*, "La matanza de Cholula o A sangre y fuego, fuego y sangre" (Figure 43.2), seems to be as much a warning to the youthful reader as a preview of slaughter: "Lo que vais a leer es tremendo, es atroz y sangriento. . . . ¡Es, amigos lectores, el cuadro de una matanza sin igual, en que parece que se han vuelto locos los hombres para asesinar, para verter sangre en arroyos que inunda la sagrada ciudad de Anáhuac!" (Frías 1987, 3).

To judge from Frías's sweep of history and his comprehensive vision of violence, the first episode of the *Biblioteca* that deals with Mexico's modern period of independence (number 69), "La victoria de Tampico y el mártir de Cuilapa" (Figure 43.3), for example, decries the bloodshed that has stained the pages of Mexican history: "¡Cuánta sangre se va a derramar aún antes de que llegue el progreso y a la prosperidad que le ha dado la paz bajo la dirección de un gran gobernante!" Frías suggests here that the ideological struggle for progress still continues despite the official proclamations of achieving status of a modern nation.

Considering the ideological direction of the more than four-score episodes in the *Biblioteca del Niño Mexicano*, there are probably addi-

Figure 43.1

Figure 43.2

Figure 43.3

tional reasons why Frías claimed to be the Cervantine compiler of Mexican myths and legends. Throughout the *Biblioteca* Frías espouses a liberal and antiauthoritarian ideology, which complements his radical politics in opposition to Porfirio Díaz. The *Biblioteca del Niño Mexicano* contains many references to Frías's liberalism and opposition to authoritarian and imperialist rule, be it indigenous, Spanish, or Mexican. In this way Frías can be said to have created a subversive ideology for Mexican children at the turn of the twentieth century.

Almost one century later, two distinct variations of Frías's subversive children's literature emerge in Shua's "Mis aventuras en el Polo Sur" and Skármeta's "La composición." Despite their differences, we can sense similarities to support the notion of subversion that lies at the heart of literature for young people during a period of crisis. What we have in both these modern writers is a sense of youthful independence from the adult world and even rebelliousness against some aspects of oppression. Whereas Shua's "Mis aventuras en el Polo Sur" is a rather tame fantasy about a young girl's flouting her wanderlust in the face of personal danger, Skármeta's story depicts Pinochet's reign of terror within an apparently innocuous frame of a young boy's competition in a school composition contest as he protects his family from repression and torture. In both cases, children act alone, without regard for their personal safety, to solve problems in their daily lives. In a sense, the subversion they pose challenges their readers to be independent thinkers and critics of their societies.

Shua's "Mis aventuras en el Polo Sur" (1988) is a delightful excursion into the freewheeling world of children's fantasy. Like Sendak's *Where the Wild Things Are*, her dreamlike escapism contains a spark of antiadult subversion. The young narrator sets a subversive, confrontational tone in the opening paragraphs. Recalling her own youth when people used ice boxes stocked with real blocks of ice, the narrator challenges her readers to accept this story at face value: "y si no me creés, preguntale a tu mamá" (Shua, 12). Her defiant tone becomes a leitmotif of her foolhardy independence as she reasserts her own authority later in the story to those young readers who may some day profit from a similar experience: "y si no me creés, probá un día a meterte en la boca de una ballena viva y vas a ver qué cómodo que estás" (22). At the end of the story, the narrator once again defiantly affirms the truth of this tall tale as she describes how the whales salute her with synchronized vapor spouts: "y si no me creés preguntale a mi hermana Alisú que estaba parada en la baranda de la costanera y la salpicaron toda" (31).

Having established herself as the purveyor of truth in her whale of a tale, Shua's young narrator develops an elaborate scheme to earn money for her longed-for Amazonian expedition by transporting icebergs from the South Pole and selling them to deliverymen in Argentina. To effect this capitalistic plan she swims nonstop to the South Pole, fortified only by purloined chocolate bars for sustenance. The little girl's plan, however, requires utmost secrecy, and herein lies her subversive intent. She dresses in street clothes "para disimular" (14) and waits at the *costanera* until dark. Although she informs her parents about her plan, she fundamentally distrusts grownups ("las personas grandes son buenas pero tontas" [15–16]), as she considers herself quite self-sufficient to select materials for her adventure.

She swims eight hours in the open sea, sleeps on her back, and dreams of the great iceberg as though it were Italian ice glistening across the spectrum of crystalline flavors. But she is awakened to a harsher reality. The water temperature falls and she is chilled by frigid waters. A great white shark swims toward a young whale seemingly abandoned by its mother, thus providing a mirror image of the lone girl swimming in the ocean. But she is equal to this Herculean task. She heroically saves herself and protects the baby when she kicks the shark in the head to run it off. The baby whale's mother, grateful for the calf's rescue, keeps the narrator warm in her cavernous mouth (Figure 43.4). This episode is also subversive to an extent, because of the girl's unflinching eagerness to expose herself to danger: "Me acosté en su blandísima lengua, donde me hundí como en un colchón de agua, y me tapé con un pliegue de la piel" (Shua, 20).

They arrive at the region of naturally forming icebergs, the whales' native waters. Fifty whales surround and greet them (Shua, 26), and only now does the impracticality of the narrator's plan become clear. Inevitably, the cold waters yield to warmer temperatures as they move north toward Argentina. To reduce the loss of ice through melting, the narrator urges the whales to increase their speed, but to no avail. All that's left of the bergs are fifty large bars of ice that the little girl hastens to hawk to the crowd of curiosity seekers on shore as they enter the port. Undaunted by the meager success of her epic journey, she returns home, drinks her milk, and ponders a new way to organize "mi gran expedición a la selva del Amazonas" (32) (Figure 43.5).

Skármeta's great achievement in "La composición" (1978) is his ability to conceal the child's subversive behavior beneath the mask of innocence, seeming indifference, and play. This is all the more admirable when we realize that "La composición" takes place amidst the state-sponsored kidnaping, torture, and murder of ordinary citizens in Pinochet's Chile, a violent world to which Pedro, the young protagonist, seems oblivious. In a sense his indifference is to be expected because the young boy, a nine-year-old, has just celebrated his birthday and yearns for a real leather soccer ball. Skármeta captures the counterpoint between Pedro's playful passes, dribbles, and shots on goal, side by side with neighbors taken prisoner by Pinochet's army and his

Figure 43.4

mos llegado a la zona donde los témpanos se desprenden de la costa helada y empiezan a derivar por el océano. Y en segundo lugar, mi amiga Malena se había encontrado con sus amigos y familiares: una manada de cincuenta ballenas retozaba a nuestro alrededor.

Figure 43.5

Después me fui a casa a tomar la leche mientras pensaba alguna otra manera de conseguir el dinero que necesitaba para organizar mi gran expedición a la selva del Amazonas.

parents huddling near the radio avid for news of the latest atrocities in far-off Santiago.

From the very outset of the story, Pedro seems to be ill-equipped to take on Pinochet's Wehrmacht. The innocent little boy is quizzical about why his folks listen to the radio, and sees in their rapt attention nothing more than idle curiosity: "ponían las orejas contra el receptor como si les fueran a repartir dulces por sus agujeros" (Skármeta, 10). Pedro's own puerile appetites are echoed in his response to the arrest of Daniel, the owner of the candy store. As he sees the soldiers take Daniel away, he considers himself eligible to receive free treats from the *dueño*'s son, the store's new manager and Pedro's best friend (Figure 43.6).

Pedro's immaturity seems to forebode a disastrous denouement soon thereafter when a military officer enters his classroom and announces a contest for all schoolchildren (Figure 43.7). The youngsters are invited to write a theme, "Lo que hace mi familia por las noches" (Skármeta, 11), in which, like Nazi youth a generation earlier, they are expected to unwittingly betray their parents to the military government. When Pedro confesses to his classmates his pursuit of the *premio gordo*, a gold medal and ribbon with the colors of the Chilean flag, the reader suspects a sorry repetition of disappearance, torture, and death for Pedro's own parents.

Figure 43.6

Figure 43.7

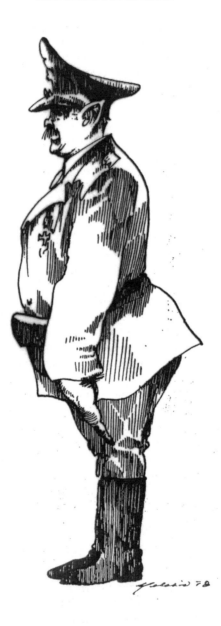

But Skármeta rescues Pedro's family from this potentially cata-
strophic turn of events through a deft combination of subterfuge,
gamesmanship, and the wiles of the sly Pedro, whose declaration early
in the story, "Soy chico, pero inteligente y rápido" (10), becomes a self-
fulfilling prophesy of his victory over Chile's fascists. The reader can
see how the boy's competitiveness and will to win in the face of over-

whelming opposition provides a subtext and pretext for his outwitting the nefarious military espionage contained in the writing assignment of "La composición." Life is a game for Pedro from the opening moments of the story. His feints, dribbles, and imaginary scores against more powerful opponents in football underline his positive sense of self and feed his euphoria of victory.

Now we more fully understand his self-congratulatory claim, "Soy chico, pero inteligente y rápido," in several contexts. What began as a statement of a runt's will to succeed against unfavorable odds in sports embodies Pedro's tacit awareness of the political strife raging about him and his desire to participate in a battle his parents do not want him to enter. For example, as Pedro witnesses the evidence of arrests and overhears talk of political subversion on the radio, he asks his parents about their politics and ponders his own allegiances:

—Papi!—exclamó entonces—, ¿Yo también soy antifascista?

El padre miró a su esposa como si la respuesta a esa pregunta estuviera escrita en los ojos de ella y la madre se rascó el pómulo con una cara divertida hasta que dijo:

—No se puede decir.

—¿Por qué no?

—Los niños no son antinada. Los niños son simplemente niños. Los niños de tu edad tienen que ir a la escuela, estudiar mucho, jugar harto y ser cariñosos con sus padres. (Skármeta, 11)

Pedro's subversion, his sabotage of the military's operation, constitutes the remainder of the story. His composition's only stir of conflict appears in the fictitious chess game he has his folks play while he does the chores. Pedro's astounding coup in this essay is his mastery of the game of fiction and the narrator's power to seduce readers to believe an imaginary reality. By entering the competition, Pedro realizes that his and his family's salvation consists of manipulating images and symbols to produce an illusion, one of innocuous if not insipid family activity. Pedro's father realizes his son's wisdom and subversive spirit upon reading the composition as he closes the story with the following: "Bueno—dijo—. Habrá que comprar un ajedrez, por si las moscas" (Skármeta, 12).

In conclusion, what young people read and what overt and covert messages appear in children's literature to either overturn or reinforce their society's values are sobering for adults. These messages are especially important when we consider the irony of Ariel Dorfman's critique of children's literature at the opening of this chapter. Dorfman cautions us all to regard children with respect because they may be the revolutionaries of tomorrow. Dorfman reflects upon the function of literature for children who inevitably stand at a crossroads of life. They either take the roles their parents prescribe for them or overturn tradition. Children's literature comes alive for us when we see how young people wrestle with these challenges, as we have seen in the works of Heriberto Frías, Ana María Shua, and Antonio Skármeta. Children's literature makes us aware of the subversive power to change the world that resides in all children, as they sleep beside us in the darkness.

REFERENCES

Dorfman, Ariel. "Inocencia y neocolonialismo: Un caso de dominio ideológico en la literatura infantil." In *Ideología y medios de comunicación*. Santiago: Amorrortu Editores, 1973.

Frías, Heriberto. *Biblioteca del Niño Mexicano*. Mexico, D.F.: Porrúa, 1987.

———. *Tomochic*. 3d ed. Prologue and notes by James W. Brown. Mexico, D.F.: Porrúa, 1976.

Lurie, Alison. *Don't Tell the Grown-Ups: Subversive Children's Literature*. Boston: Little, Brown, 1990. Lurie's introduction has been translated into Spanish and appears under the title "Literatura infantil: Defensa de la subversión." In *Quimera: Revista de Literatura* [a Spanish magazine of children's literature], 11 (July 1992): 8–11.

Martí, José. *La edad de oro*. Havana: Editorial Gente Nueva, 1889. (Originally published in New York.)

Shua, Ana María. *Expedición al Amazonas*. Buenos Aires: Colección Pan Flauta, 1988.

Skármeta, Antonio. "La composición." *La Semana de Bellas Artes* [México] 35 (1978): 10–12.

Name Index

Title Index

About the Editor and Contributors

LILIANA BEATRIZ ARNILLAS grew up in Lima, Peru, where she first began her studies of art, and then lived for two years in the pre-Incan village of Catacaos, south of the city of Piura. Having received her master's degree in fine arts at the University of Kentucky, she taught at Seton Hill College in Greensburg, Pennsylvania, and is presently at Texas A & M. She has had numerous exhibits throughout the United States.

FERNANDO BARROSO, born in Havana, Cuba, enjoys doctorates of law and of philosophy and is professor emeritus of Spanish at James Madison University. His published works include books on the Spanish naturalist novelist Emilia Pardo Bazán and on Hispanic civilization, as well as an annotated edition of Jenaro Prieto's *El socio*. He has participated in numerous scholarly conferences and has authored articles on Alarcón, the conquest of America, and questions of theology.

ANNA BARTOS has sung on the operatic and concert stages of the United States, Canada, Mexico, the Caribbean, and Russia, and is considered one of the foremost interpreters of Spanish and Latin American song literature. A recording artist who has also toured with her one-woman show, *Maja*, she presently conducts master classes and teaches voice at New York University. She is codirector of the Enchanted Forest Opera, which presents musical plays for children, and is an artist-in-residence for the New York Foundation for the Arts. Her paper on "The Golden Age Revisited in 20th Century Art Songs" was presented as a lecture-recital at our Hispanic Connection Conference.

PATRICIA BENTIVEGNA, professor emerita of Spanish at St. Francis College in Pennsylvania, has for many years been one of the luminaries of our teaching organizations. A devotee of theater and of *zarzuela*, she has made more than fifty presentations at conferences throughout the United States and abroad, and her articles have been much solicited and well received. Her recent retirement now provides her the opportunity to turn her love of *zarzuela* into a full-time vocation.

DAVID G. BURTON is an associate professor of Spanish at Ohio University in Athens. He is the author of a book on the legend of Bernardo del Carpio and many articles on Spanish literature of the Renaissance and early Baroque, namely on Garcilaso, Juan de la Cueva, and *La gran sultana* of Cervantes. He is a devout aficionado and connoisseur of grand opera.

CONSUELO CARREDANO, pianist, musicologist, librettist, and author of many articles and books on Mexican music, is presently a researcher for the Carlos Chávez National Center for Musical Investigation, Documentation, and Information. A contributor to the *Dictionary of Spanish and Spanish American Music*, she is awaiting the forthcoming release of her book on Adolfo Salazar. Dr. Carredano is the wife of composer Mario Lavista.

RAFAEL T. CORBALÁN, associate professor of Spanish at the City University of New York, completed his studies for the baccalaureate and master's degrees in his native Spain and his doctorate in New York. His book, *Vicente Blasco Ibáñez y la nueva novela cinematográfica*, has also been published in an abridged bilingual version in France. Dr. Corbalán, who was a successful journalist before entering the teaching profession, is director and editor of the literary and arts publication *Cuadernos de Aldeeú*.

GERARD DAPENA, who did his undergraduate work in art history in Madrid, earned a master's degree in cinema studies from New York University and completed his doctorate at CUNY in twentieth-century painting and sculpture. His related minor is film, in which he has had considerable professional experience as administrator for the Joseph Papp Public Theater in New York. He teaches at the Parson School of Design.

ZENIA SACKS DASILVA, initiator and codirector of the Hispanic Connection Conference and editor of this volume, is a professor of Spanish at Hofstra University. She is the author of many textbooks, among them, on the university level, the *Concept Approach* series, the cultural history *Márgenes: Historia íntima del pueblo hispano*, the *Experiencias* program, and two literary collections. Her secondary school texts include *Usted y yo, Nuestro mundo, Vuelo*, and the *Persona a persona* series. A specialist in peninsular literature, she is now completing an anthology of humor and charm in Hispanic literature.

JOHN LOUIS DIGAETANI, professor of English and theater at Hofstra University, has published extensively on both literature and opera. His books include *Opera and the Golden West, Puccini the Thinker, An Invitation to the Opera: Facts on File, Richard Wagner and the Modern British Novel*, and *Penetrating Wagner's Ring: An Anthology*.

JOHN DOWLING, distinguished professor emeritus of romance languages and dean emeritus of the Graduate School of the University of Georgia, has authored four books, seven editions of literary texts, and more than one hundred and fifty articles. His areas of investigation include Cervantes, Spanish drama from the Golden Age to the present, nineteenth- and twentieth-century literature, *zarzuela*, and grand opera.

The late HOWARD M. FRASER was a professor of modern languages and literatures at the College of William and Mary and a scholar of exceptional distinction. Director and associate editor for many years of the prestigious *Chasqui, Revista de Literatura Latinoamericana*, associate editor of *Hispania*, and review editor of the *Latin American Literary Review*, he was the author of the books *Magazines and Masks: Caras y Caretas as a Reflection of Buenos Aires* and *In the Presence of Mystery: Modernist Fiction and the Occult*, as well as of a language text, chapters in six anthologies, and a plethora of articles and reviews. His participation in the Hispanic Connection Conference will long be recalled.

DONALD E. FRITZ, associate professor in the Department of English at the University of Texas-Pan American has authored a number of professional articles and a book called *Anatomy and the Last Picture Show: A Matter of Definition*. He is a recognized authority on the subject of Mexican and Peruvian masks.

JEANNE FUCHS, formerly associate dean of the College of Liberal Arts of Hofstra University, is a professor emerita of comparative literature and languages, with a specialization in French. She has published a book entitled *The Pursuit of Virtue: A Study of Order in "La Nouvelle Héloise*," has coedited the proceedings of a conference called *The World of George Sand*, and has written articles on Rousseau, Marivaux, Musset, and Sand.

MARIO HAMLET-METZ received his doctorate from the University of Virginia and is currently a professor of French and comparative literature at James Madison University. He has published more than thirty articles on nineteenth-century French literature and on opera, and is the American correspondent for the Italian magazine *L'Opera*. He has lectured throughout the United States and Europe, including at the Kennedy Center in Washington, D.C., at La Scala in Milan, and in Paris.

BEN A. HELLER, formerly of Hofstra University, is currently associate professor of Spanish at Notre Dame. A specialist in Latin American literature, he is coauthor of an anthology entitled *Huellas de las literaturas hispanoamericanas* and has published a book on the poetry of the Cuban José Lezama Lima. Although his primary focus is the nineteenth and twentieth century, his articles and lectures range into the Colonial period as well.

H. WENDELL HOWARD is a professor of English recently retired from St. John Fisher College in Rochester, New York. A musician as well as a scholar, he has a degree in voice from the Juilliard School of Music and has published more than ninety articles in professional and literary journals. His book, *The Fiction of Louis Auchincloss*, has been accepted for publication, as are at least five more articles. His collection of poetry entitled *In Praise of Women* has been submitted.

JACK B. JELINSKI is an associate professor of Spanish at Montana State University in Bozeman, Montana. An educator of extraordinary dedication, he has engaged in numerous professional activities, as well as publishing some twenty scholarly articles, primarily on twentieth-century Hispanic writers, and another twenty book reviews.

JAMES J. KOLB, professor of drama at Hofstra University, is a gifted director and scholar who has published more than twenty-five articles on theater from classical to Renaissance to contemporary. He is coeditor of a two-volume compendium entitled *Art, Glitter, and Glitz: The Theatre of the 1920's Celebrates American Diversity*, and has lectured widely on diverse aspects of the dramatic and musical stage. He is an extraordinary connoisseur and devotee of grand opera.

JOANN KRIEG, professor of English and American studies at Hofstra University, has published widely in both fields. Her book, *A Whitman Chronology*, and her editorship of *Walt Whitman: Here and Now* are recognized as major contributions to that expertise. Dr. Krieg has directed several conferences at Hofstra and has edited the volumes of their selected proceedings.

DONALD R. KUDERER, professor of Spanish at the University of Wisconsin–La Crosse, received his doctorate from the University of Missouri–Columbia in 1996. He has worked intensively on contemporary Spanish and Spanish American theater and has presented papers on Alfonso Sastre, Rodolfo Usigli, and Lauro Olmo.

KEVIN S. LARSEN is a professor of Romance languages and literatures at the University of Wyoming. His published books include *"La ciencia aplicada": Gabriel Miró y la tradición científica* and a critical edition of Miró's *Dentro del cercado*. He has also been extraordinarily prolific in the publication of some fifty articles, primarily on nineteenth-century Peninsular literature and the Generation of '98, another thirty reviews and abstracts, and translations from Portuguese and French.

MARIO LAVISTA is one of the most prominent Mexican composers of today and his work is well known throughout Latin America. Deviating from the linear time of Western tradition, his music displays the circular conception of time found in indigenous cultures and synthesizes Mexico's Indian and European antecedents through a unique musical "magic realism."

ALICE LEVINE is associate professor of English at Hofstra University. She coedited, with Jerome McGann, the first four volumes of Byron manuscripts in the series *Manuscripts of the Younger Romantics* (Garland Publishing, 1985–1988), and is currently working on a Norton critical edition of Byron's selected poetry and letters. Since 1994 she has served as book review editor of the *Keats–Shelley Journal*.

DAVID H. MACBRIDE holds a master's degree in music from Columbia University and a B.M. from the Hartt College of Music in West Hartford, Connecticut, where he presently serves as associate professor of composition and theory. The recipient of many awards, grants, and commissions, he has seen his works performed not only throughout the United States, but in such foreign venues as Germany, Austria, and Egypt.

NORA DE MARVAL-MCNAIR, professor of Spanish at Hofstra University, earned her doctorate in laws in her native Argentina and another in Hispanic literature from New York University. Author of many articles and lectures on the short fiction of Borges, she is now preparing a full-length book on his works. Her other publications include studies of Cervantes's *Retablo de Maese Pedro*, the *sainetes* of Florencio Sánchez, and the novels of Beatriz Guido, as well as a collection of Spanish and Latin American short stories.

ADRIÁN PÉREZ MELGOSA wrote his doctoral dissertation on "Imagining the Present of the Americas: Three Readings of *The Kiss of the Spider Woman* and *The Mambo Kings Play Songs of Love*." Formerly assistant professor of Spanish at Seton Hall College, he now teaches comparative literature and film at the Stony Brook campus of the State University of New York. He has lectured and published extensively, primarily on contemporary literature. He has also done translations, film and book reviews, and has delivered many papers at literary conferences.

BARBARA D. MILLER received her Ph.D. in 1996 from the State University of New York at Buffalo in Spanish language and literature, with a secondary specialization in comparative literature. Currently an assistant professor of Spanish at Buffalo State College, she has also taught at the University of Richmond, SUNY Buffalo, the University of Richmond, and the Universidad de Salamanca, and has published articles on literary subjects ranging from Golden Age pastoral heroines, to García Lorca, to the contemporary Latin American novel.

DONALD M. MORALES, who received his doctorate in English with a dissertation on African-American folk elements in contemporary black American drama, has published ten articles and has made some thirty presentations in that and related fields. His expertise includes the current theater of Africa. A professor at Mercy College in New York, he is a musician as well, having performed for many years as a saxophonist with the Jazzmobile Workshop.

ROSEANNA MUELLER is professor of Spanish and humanities, supervisor of foreign languages, and coordinator of humanities at Columbia College in Chicago. Her publications include *Montemayor's "Diana": A Translation and Introduction* and "Two Unofficial Captive Narratives: Gonzalo de Guerrero's *Memorias* and Cabeza de Vaca's *Naufragios*," plus translations of poetry and a variety of professional articles.

RHODA NATHAN is professor emerita at Hofstra University and current president of the George Bernard Shaw Society of America. She has been a Fulbright Scholar in New Zealand, an appointment that generated two books about the writer Katherine Mansfield. In her major field, American literature, she has written a cultural history, *The American Vision*, as well as many articles. She has published extensively on Anglo-Irish drama and is now completing a book on Shaw's influence worldwide.

ELIEZER OYOLA, born in Humacao, Puerto Rico, is professor of Spanish at Evangel College in Springield, Missouri, and the author of *Los pecados capitales en la literatura medieval española*. His articles include

"Simbología animal y moralidad en Juan Ruiz y Ramón Llull," "Poeta en Nueva York: Lorca y la experiencia de la ciudad moderna," "Aspects of Theatrical Language in Tirso's *Burlador*," and "Crucifixión y vanguardia: imágenes sacroprofanas en un texto de García Lorca." He is currently preparing three language textbooks in Spanish in addition to a work on the "problem of evil" in Juan Ruiz.

PINA PALMA pursued her literary studies both in her native Italy and in the United States, where she received her doctorate from Yale University. Currently associate professor of Italian at Southern Connecticut University, she has published such essays as "Marino's *Adone* and the Birth of Poetry," "The Education of a Courtesan: Nanna's Teachings in Aretino's *Dialoghi*," and "Between Heroes and Peasants: Levi and the Political Consciousness of the Abyssinian War in "Cristo si é fermato a Eboli.'" She is a contributor to *Dante's Encyclopedia* (2000).

SALVADOR ANTON PUJOL has taught at the University of California–Los Angeles, the University of Kansas, and Wake Forest University. His primary fields of research are eighteenth- to twentieth-century Spanish literature and contemporary Catalan literature. He has made presentations at several conferences and has published an article entitled "Galdós: tres finales metaficticios."

LUIS R. QUIROZ is professor emeritus at St. Michael's College of Colchester, Vermont. Born in Bolivia, he has enjoyed a long and successful teaching career in the United States, where he has helped organize Latin American festivals and theatrical performances and participated in the formation and editing of several bilingual publications. He now resides in California.

RODERICK S. QUIROZ is a scientist, a musicologist, and a literary scholar. Having completed a distinguished career as a meteorologist with the National Oceanographic and Atmospheric Administration and published some seventy articles in scientific journals, he turned his interest to the study and teaching of Spanish language and literature, most recently at Georgetown University. His literary contributions include articles on Antonio Machado and Gil Vicente and on musical versions of Golden Age poetry from Boscán through Lope de Vega. Coauthor in 1996 of a *catalogue raisonné* of the lithographs of Prentiss Taylor, he has since published a series of articles focusing on print exhibitions, particularly on aspects of the work and correspondence of the great Spanish painter Francisco Goya.

JANE C. SIMON has taught Spanish and French on both the secondary and college levels for many years. She is presently completing her doctorate in Spanish, French, and Portuguese at the University of Minnesota in Minneapolis, where she is a teaching associate.

PILAR DEL CARMEN TIRADO, whose doctoral work at Brown University focused principally on sixteenth- and seventeenth-century Spanish literature, was an assistant professor of Spanish at the State University of New York at Plattsburgh. Now teaching at the University of Southern Maine, she has published articles on parody in *Lazarillo de Tormes*, and is an avid student of early Spanish and Sephardic music.

CECILIA TOWNSEND, who wrote her master's thesis on the poetics of César Vallejo, has taught at Washington State University and the University of Florida in Gainesville. She has presented various papers at literary conferences, including "Diálogo posmodernista intertextual: *Naufragios* y Cabeza de Vaca."

SARA VÉLEZ, second in command at the New York Public Library for the Performing Arts, has had extensive training in music history, theory, piano, violin, and voice at several of the world's finest conservatories, and dance at the Metropolitan Opera School of Ballet and the Ballet Russe School of Monte Carlo. She has lectured widely on García Lorca.

JEANNINE WAGAR, formerly assistant professor of music at Hofstra University, has conducted in both Mexico and the United States. Having directed the famed Prism Orchestra of New York and the North Jersey Philarharmonic, she was named music director of the Arkansas Philharmonic Orchestra. Her book, *Conductors in Conversation: Contemporary Conductors Discuss Their Profession*, has been critically acclaimed, as have her many recordings.

DALE WASSERMAN, creator and book writer of the Broadway musical *Man of La Mancha*, has also authored the renowned *One Flew Over the Cuckoo's Nest*. His more than eighty theatrical works, screenplays, and television movies have brought him such recognition as the Tony Award of the American Theater Wing, the New York Critics Award, the Molière Prize in France, several distinguished awards in Spain, and the Japan Musical Award. He is currently preparing three musicals, two straight plays, and a new film.

SARAH WYMAN, who received her doctorate in English from the University of North Carolina, temporarily detoured her academic career to live in Konstanz, Germany, with her husband and young children and teach English there. She still pursues her abiding interest in American and Spanish poetry and the visual arts, and is now embarking on a teaching career on the college level in the United States.

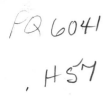